Women Philosophers in the Long Nineteenth Century

Women Philosophers in the Long Nineteenth Century

The German Tradition

Edited by
DALIA NASSAR AND KRISTIN GJESDAL

Translated from German by
ANNA C. EZEKIEL

OXFORD
UNIVERSITY PRESS

OXFORD
UNIVERSITY PRESS

Oxford University Press is a department of the University of Oxford. It furthers the University's objective of excellence in research, scholarship, and education by publishing worldwide. Oxford is a registered trade mark of Oxford University Press in the UK and certain other countries.

Published in the United States of America by Oxford University Press
198 Madison Avenue, New York, NY 10016, United States of America.

Library of Congress Cataloging-in-Publication Data
Names: Nassar, Dalia, editor. | Gjesdal, Kristin, editor.
Title: Women philosophers in the long nineteenth century :
the German tradition / edited by Dalia Nassar and Kristin Gjesdal.
Description: New York, NY, United States of America :
Oxford University Press, [2021] | Includes bibliographical references and index.
Identifiers: LCCN 2021012796 (print) | LCCN 2021012797 (ebook) |
ISBN 9780190868031 (hb) | ISBN 9780190868048 (paperback) |
ISBN 9780190868062 (epub)
Subjects: LCSH: Women philosophers—Germany. |
Philosophy, German—19th century.
Classification: LCC B2743 .W66 2021 (print) | LCC B2743 (ebook) |
DDC 193—dc23
LC record available at https://lccn.loc.gov/2021012796
LC ebook record available at https://lccn.loc.gov/2021012797

DOI: 10.1093/oso/9780190868031.001.0001

Contents

Editors' Introduction   1
    The Period and Its Questions   2
    Scope of the Volume   7
    An International Enterprise   8
    The Status of Women (Philosophers)   9
    Questioning the Canon   12
    Challenging the Boundaries of Philosophical Discourse   14
    Constellations and Solidarity   17
    Concluding Thoughts   19

Translation, Acknowledgments, Sources   20

1. Germaine de Staël (1766–1817)   23
    Introduction   23
    On Women Writers   30
    Kant   38
    On the Influence of the New Philosophy on the Sciences   51

2. Karoline von Günderrode (1780–1806)   62
    Introduction   62
    On Fichte's *The Vocation of Humankind*   70
    Philosophy of Nature   75
    The Idea of Nature   81
    The Idea of the Earth   82

3. Bettina Brentano von Arnim (1785–1859)   85
    Introduction   85
    Selections from *Günderode*   92

4. Hedwig Dohm (1831–1919)   122
    Introduction   122
    Nietzsche and Women   128
    The New Mother   139
    The Old Woman   145
    On the Agitators of Anti-feminism   150

5. Clara Zetkin (1857–1933)   154
    Introduction   154
    For the Liberation of Women!   162

Women's Suffrage   167
Save the Scottsboro Boys!   174

6. Lou Salomé (1861–1937)   177
    Introduction   177
    Selections from *The Erotic*   184

7. Rosa Luxemburg (1871–1919)   206
    Introduction   206
    Wage Labor, selections from *Introduction to Political Economy*   214

8. Edith Stein (1891–1942)   241
    Introduction   241
    Selections from *On Empathy*   248

9. Gerda Walther (1897–1977)   273
    Introduction   273
    Selections from *A Contribution to the Ontology of Social Communities*   281

Bibliography   311
    Cited in Editors' Introductions   311
    Cited in Translated Texts   319
Index   323

Editors' Introduction

The long nineteenth century—the period beginning with the French Revolution and ending with World War I—was a transformative period for women philosophers in German-speaking countries and contexts.[1] Philosophically speaking, this period spans romanticism and idealism, socialism, Nietzscheanism, and phenomenology. Contributing to these movements, women philosophers explored a wide range of philosophical topics and styles, helped shape philosophy's agenda, and translated their thoughts into activism and practice. This last point is significant: being excluded from formal academic education and positions, many women philosophers developed a way of philosophizing that was more activist in spirit and geared toward communicating with ordinary people rather than university colleagues and students. In and through their practice of philosophy, women philosophers gained an increasing sense of agency, challenged existing doctrines, built networks across cultures and language barriers, and drew upon and developed connections between various philosophical traditions. Thus, the works produced by women philosophers often offer a different angle on the history of philosophy; these works help us to rethink both the intellectual history of the nineteenth century and the systematic questions that motivated and underpinned its philosophical developments. Moreover, they reveal to us the ways in which philosophy was once practiced—and how philosophy can and indeed should be pursued: in dialogue with, rather than in abstraction from, our daily lives. In essence, the

[1] In an article from 2005, Eileen O'Neill argues that the nineteenth century was not a particularly friendly century for women philosophers, in part because of what she describes as the "purification" of philosophy—i.e., philosophy taking on a very specific, and narrow, conception of what constitutes a philosophical work. O'Neill's focus, on French and British philosophy, may have led her to overlook the thriving intellectual cultures in German-speaking countries, in which women were increasingly significant contributors. Furthermore, as we will also argue below (in section 4), the best-known figures in German philosophy of the nineteenth century (including the Schlegel brothers, Hegel, Kierkegaard, and Nietzsche) sought to make progress by challenging established models of philosophy. As such, it would be a mistake to claim, without further qualifications, that the nineteenth century was an era of philosophical "purification." Instead we see an increasing will to institutionalize philosophy and turn it into a modern, academic discipline. For O'Neill's point, see her "Early Modern Women Philosophers and the History of Philosophy," *Hypatia* 20, no. 3 (2005): 185–197.

Women Philosophers in the Long Nineteenth Century. Dalia Nassar and Kristin Gjesdal, Oxford University Press.
© Oxford University Press 2021. DOI: 10.1093/oso/9780190868031.003.0001

contributions of nineteenth-century women in the German tradition demonstrate that philosophy has the potential to transform lives and also to be transformed by our lived experiences and practices.

The Period and Its Questions

To better understand the development of nineteenth-century philosophy—and women's contributions to it in particular—a quick historical detour is in order. In nineteenth-century Germany, women had few options for education outside the home. Before 1820, there were a total of twenty-two secondary state schools for girls, most of which only offered the most minimal form of education. While this number increased over the century, reaching a high of seventy-one in the years between 1873 and 1880, by the end of the century, there were, again, a total of twenty-two secondary state schools for girls.[2] Private schools were also an option—one that was increasingly popular by the middle of the century. However, these schools were only available to the upper and middle classes, and as with the public schools, their level of education did not come close to the education in boys' schools. For instance, while languages were offered at girls' high schools—including English, French, and Italian—ancient Greek and Latin were never offered. These subjects, however, were required for university entry in Germany throughout the nineteenth century.[3]

Within philosophy, however, education—including the education of women—was becoming an increasingly important topic. By the end of the eighteenth century, the ideas of humanity and universal human rights were at the heart of philosophical discussions, and in German-language intellectual life and culture, in the circles around Immanuel Kant and in post-Kantian philosophy, there was an interest in education that was sparked by Jean-Jacques Rousseau's *Émile* (1762).[4] While Rousseau was far from progressive in his thoughts on women and education, his arguments for the value of education for the development of personality, agency, and citizenship were widely discussed. In a Rousseauian spirit, families of means began

---

[2] James C. Albisetti, *Schooling German Girls and Women* (Princeton, NJ: Princeton University Press, 1988), 37, table 1.

[3] Albisetti, *Schooling German Girls*, 48.

[4] For a helpful study, see Mary Seidman Trouille, *Sexual Politics in the Enlightenment: Women Writers Read Rousseau* (Albany: SUNY Press, 1997).

to educate their daughters through tutors and, in some instances, drew on informal family connections to gain permission for their daughters to attend university lectures. There was, in this period, an increasing recognition of women as potential audiences for and producers of philosophy. The romantic salons in Berlin and Jena gave women an arena in which they were exposed to and sometimes participated in systematic, philosophical debates, and journal editors began to seek out women's writings. A journal such as Friedrich Schiller's *Die Horen* published work not only by Johann Wolfgang von Goethe, Johann Gottlieb Fichte, Johann Gottfried Herder, August Wilhelm Schlegel, and Alexander von Humboldt but also by Louise Brachmann, Friederike Brun, Amalie von Imhoff, Sophie Mereau, Elisa von der Recke, and Caroline von Wolzogen.[5] Henriette Herz and Rahel Varnhagen, the latter a formidable letter writer and the subject of an early study by Hannah Arendt,[6] were well-known intellectuals and conveners of two prominent Berlin salons.[7] While it is an open question to what extent they were able to intellectually participate in (rather than simply facilitate) the salons,[8] Herz and her salon clearly influenced Friedrich Schleiermacher's ethical notion of social life.[9] Dorothea Schlegel and Caroline Schlegel-Schelling played a significant role in the development of the romantic salon in Jena and in the emergence of romanticism as a philosophical-literary

[5] See Janet Besserer Holmgren, *The Women Writers in Schiller's* Horen: *Patrons, Petticoats, and the Promotion of Weimar Classicism* (Newark: University of Delaware Press, 2007); and Katherine R. Goodman and Edith Waldstein, *In the Shadow of Olympus: German Women Writers around 1800* (Albany: SUNY Press, 1992).

[6] Hannah Arendt, *Rahel Varnhagen: The Life of a Jewess*, ed. Liliane Weissberg, trans. Richard Winston and Clara Winston (Baltimore: Johns Hopkins University Press, 1997).

[7] There are a number of illuminating essays on the romantic salon in Hartwig Schultz, ed., *Salons der Romantik. Beiträge eines Wiepersdorfer Kolloquiums zu Theorie und Geschichte des Salons* (Berlin: De Gruyter, 1997). For an account of the connection between salon culture and letter writing, see Konrad Feilchenfeldt, "'Berliner Salon' und Briefkultur um 1800," *Der Deutschunterricht. Beiträge zu seiner Praxis und wissenschaftlichen Grundlegung* 36 (1984): 77–99; Liliane Weissberg, "Turns of Emancipation: On Rahel Varnhagen's Letters," *Cultural Critique* 21 (Spring 1992): 219–238; Liliane Weissberg, "Schreiben als Selbstentwurf. Zu den Schriften Rahel Varnhagens und Dorothea Schlegels," *Zeitschrift für Religions- und Geistesgeschichte* 47 (1995): 231–253.

[8] For this point, see Hannah Lotte Lund, "Emanzipation in Halböffentlichkeit? Geschlechterverhältnisse und politische Partizipation im literarischen Salon um 1800: Eine Annäherung," in *Revolution und Emanzipation. Geschlechterordnungen in Europa um 1800*, ed. Katharina Rennhak and Virginia Richter (Cologne: Böhlau Verlag, 2004), 33–47; and Barbara Becker-Cantarino, *Schriftstellerinnen der Romantik. Epoche—Werke—Wirkung* (Munich: C. H. Beck, 2000), 190–198.

[9] See Friedrich Schleiermacher, *Essay on a Theory of Sociable Behavior*, ed. and trans. Peter Foley (Lewiston, NY: Edwin Mellen, 2006). See also Becker-Cantarino, *Schriftstellerinnen*, 189–190. Another helpful source is Jane Kneller, "Feminism," in *The Oxford Handbook of German Philosophy in the Nineteenth Century*, ed. Michael N. Forster and Kristin Gjesdal (Oxford: Oxford University Press, 2015), 534–555.

movement. Karoline von Günderrode and Bettina Brentano von Arnim also contributed to the development of philosophical romanticism. The very concept of romanticism was, in fact, given philosophical resonance through the work of Germaine de Staël, the erudite French intellectual whose feuds with Napoleon had thrown her into years of exile and whose study of German art and thought, originally published in no fewer than ten thousand copies, was destroyed on Napoleon's order.

In the second half of the century, women's rights activists established institutes for the education of women, with the aim of preparing them for the vocations open to them (usually as schoolteachers) and helping them to achieve wage equality with men.[10] This marked an important moment for women who wished to pursue education beyond high school. Although these institutes were often practical in their orientations, they provided women with an intellectual milieu in the form of lectures, journals, and meetings. They were, furthermore, extremely popular. In Prussia, for instance, the number of women educators went from 1,752 in 1861 to 8,380 in 1891.[11]

While German women's participation in the workforce remained around 30 percent throughout the nineteenth century (a figure that accords with other European countries, such as France and Norway), by the second half of the century, women were becoming increasingly active in social justice movements, spearheading debates about the social and political implications of Marxism and Nietzscheanism, and marching for women's suffrage.[12] Thus, we find Hedwig Dohm and Clara Zetkin, among others, challenging well-known philosophers on their views of women and arguing for women's suffrage, gender equality, and social justice. Sadly, only a few of these early feminists lived to witness the enfranchisement of German women in November 1918. Nonetheless, women's enfranchisement was something to celebrate. When German women went to the polls for the first time, on

---

[10] Jean H. Quataert, *Reluctant Feminists in German Social Democracy, 1885–1917* (Princeton, NJ: Princeton University Press, 1979; repr. 2015).

[11] Albisetti, *Schooling German Girls*, 83.

[12] In 1816, 29.6 percent of women were employed; in 1907, 25.6 percent were employed. See Ulla Knapp, "Frauenarbeit in Deutschland zwischen 1850 und 1933, Teil I," *Historical Social Research/ Historische Sozialforschung* 28 (1983): 42–62, here 62, table 3. In comparison, in the United States, only 11 percent of women were employed in 1882. See W. Stieda, "Frauenarbeit," *Jahrbücher für Nationalökonomie und Statistik/Journal of Economics and Statistics*, 3rd ed., Vol. 2, 57, no. 2 (1891): 189–208, here 193, 195. The majority of German women (60 percent) worked in agriculture, although married women working full-time in manufacturing rose by 200 percent between 1882 and 1907. Robyn Dasey, "Women's Work and the Family: Women Garment Workers in Berlin and Hamburg before the First World War," in *The German Family*, ed. Richard Evans and W. R. Lee (London: Routledge, 1981), 221–255, here 249–250n4.

January 19, 1919, the artist Käthe Kollwitz made a record of this momentous day in her diary: "Sunday. Election day. Voted for the first time. . . . I'd been looking forward to this day so much."[13]

In 1866, the University of Zurich was the first European university to formally admit women students, and in 1867, it became the first institution to award a PhD to a woman. In Switzerland, few women had access to secondary schools, and the majority of women who came to study philosophy at the University of Zurich came from elsewhere. Rosa Luxemburg came from Poland, Lou Andreas-Salomé from Russia, to mention only two examples. After earning a PhD in economics, Luxemburg dedicated herself to writing on economic and social justice and to activism. Salomé went on to write independent studies of Friedrich Nietzsche and Sigmund Freud and developed an account of embodiment and what she calls the erotic (sensuous) sphere alongside a set of original contributions to psychoanalysis, including a theory of bisexuality.

By the early twentieth century, a number of German universities followed the example of Zurich.[14] Women were thus able to play an active role in the development of both the neo-Kantian and phenomenological movements.[15] What is more, women's contributions were also being gradually recognized from within academia. There was not only Edith Stein, whose work remains well known today. There was also Hedwig Conrad-Martius, whose essay on positivism won the prize for best original work in philosophy awarded by the University of Göttingen in 1912,[16] and Gerda Walther, who gave the keynote address at the Freiburg Society of Phenomenology in 1918.

---

[13] Käthe Kollwitz, *Die Tagebücher* (Berlin: Akademie Verlag, 1989), 400.

[14] For an overview of the admission of women to German universities, see Patricia M. Mazón, *Gender and the Modern Research University: The Admission of Women to German Higher Education, 1865–1914* (Stanford, CA: Stanford University Press, 2003).

[15] In terms of neo-Kantians, the works of Marie Boeuf, Grete Hermann, Hedwig Bender, Else Wentscher, and Gertrud Simmel (publishing under the name of Marie Luise Enckendorff) should be mentioned. We thus disagree with Sebastian Luft's claim, in the introduction to his 2015 neo-Kantianism reader, that "there are no women represented in this entire movement." See "Editor's Introduction," in *The Neo-Kantian Reader*, ed. Sebastian Luft (London: Routledge, 2015), xxvii. In the phenomenology camp, we find Edith Stein, Else Voigtländer, Gerda Walther, Hedwig Conrad-Martius, among others. Edith Landmann-Kalischer draws on and contributes to both movements. For a discussion of her work, see Samantha Matherne, "Edith Landmann-Kalischer on Aesthetic Demarcation and Normativity," *The British Journal of Aesthetics* 60, no. 3 (July 2020): 315–334, https://doi.org/10.1093/aesthj/ayaa007 and "Edith Landmann-Kalischer's Moderate Objectivism about Aesthetic Value" (forthcoming).

[16] The names of the competitors were sealed, and to the astonishment of the prize judges, a woman had won. Two hundred essays were entered for the prize.

These are just some of the women who helped further German-language philosophy through their pioneering work. Research on their contributions has shed important new light on nineteenth-century philosophy, disclosing unexpected points of continuity between what scholars often regard as un-related intellectual movements—the late Enlightenment, romanticism, ide-alism, socialism, Nietzscheanism, and phenomenology. For instance, while Brentano von Arnim was a key figure in romanticism, in the 1840s, her Berlin-based salon became increasingly political and her writings more fo-cused on questions of social and economic justice.[17] Similarly, Walther's turn to phenomenology followed her Marxist upbringing, and her interest in social community betrays her political background.

Spanning the arc from enlightenment and romanticism to phenome-nology, each of the women included in this volume was interested in the real-world implications and outcomes of her theorizing. Excluded from pursuing traditional careers in the university, they did not write for an academic elite or respond to narrow theoretical questions. Women philosophers simulta-neously explored and expanded the range of philosophical topics addressed and the ways in which philosophy is done—building on but also going be-yond existing philosophical forms. The questions these women investigated include, but are not limited to, the following:

- What are the boundaries of philosophical discourse?
- What is the relationship between philosophy and art?
- What is the relationship between philosophical theorizing and practice?
- What ought to be the relation between philosophy, academia, and the world beyond the university?
- How might philosophy enable a deeper understanding and the realiza-tion of self-determination?
- How can philosophy become more engaged with life (social, biological, and emotional)? What advantages might philosophy gain in this way?
- How can we use philosophical tools to better understand and improve the conditions of disenfranchised and marginalized groups (victims of slavery and colonialization, economically and otherwise oppressed groups)?

[17] See Ingeborg Drewitz, *Bettine von Arnim. Romantik—Revolution—Utopie* (Dusseldorf: Diederichs, 1969).

- How have philosophers erred in their understanding of gender, and how might we employ philosophy to demonstrate their failings?
- To what extent is the history of philosophy gendered and based on illegitimate criteria of inclusion and exclusion?

Scope of the Volume

In contemporary anglophone academia, the study of nineteenth-century philosophy is well established. Though this was an important period for women philosophers, little attention has been paid to their works. The present volume makes available—as an invitation to further reading and scholarship—a selection of newly translated texts by nine nineteenth-century women philosophers: Germaine de Staël, Karoline von Günderrode, Bettina Brentano von Arnim, Hedwig Dohm, Clara Zetkin, Lou Andreas-Salomé, Rosa Luxemburg, Edith Stein, and Gerda Walther. It seeks to cover many of the central subfields that make this such a vibrant period in the history of philosophy: philosophy of nature (Günderrode, Stein), philosophy of consciousness and embodiment (Günderrode, Salomé, Stein, Walther), philosophy of history (Staël, Brentano von Arnim), ethics (Günderrode), social and political philosophy (Staël, Günderrode, Dohm, Zetkin, Luxemburg, Walther), aesthetics (Staël, Brentano von Arnim, Salomé), epistemology broadly construed (Günderrode, Dohm, Stein, Walther), women's experiences (Staël, Günderrode, Dohm, Zetkin), and philosophy of economics (Zetkin, Luxemburg).

German philosophers are well represented in standard nineteenth-century syllabi. Introductions to nineteenth-century philosophy typically include the German romantics and idealists, Arthur Schopenhauer, Karl Marx, and Nietzsche. Søren Kierkegaard is often presented in light of his response to romantic philosophy and Hegelianism. The present volume is oriented toward contributions that define a philosophical lineage from romanticism to phenomenology. The point, to be sure, is not to prioritize the German tradition along the lines of language areas or nations (at the beginning of the century, Germany was not yet politically unified). We have sought, rather, to demarcate a constellation of texts that relate to each other and also to communicate with and critique the philosophers whose works are typically read and studied in the context of nineteenth-century philosophy. We hope that our efforts to highlight works by these philosophers will inspire further research into the authors included in this volume and also into German-language and German-culture philosophers beyond our selections. Moreover, as scholars of nineteenth-century philosophy, we hope that this initiative will help bolster research on women philosophers in other traditions, language areas, and lineages of thought.[18] Thus, we regard this volume as part of a larger effort to offer a critical genealogy that can help us scrutinize standard narratives in the history of philosophy.

An International Enterprise

The women we have concentrated on in this collection both drew on and inspired philosophers across national borders and cultural boundaries. One example of this is the work of Swiss-French Staël, in particular her *Germany* (1810/1813). Staël, at the time, was widely known across Europe as the author of the bestselling novels *Delphine* (1802) and *Corinne* (1807). Her work was swiftly translated into English (the English translation of *Germany* appeared in the same year as the original French) and served as a source of inspiration for Ralph Waldo Emerson and other Boston transcendentalists, including Margaret Fuller and the American abolitionist and philosopher Lydia Maria Child.[19] Child not only produced important work arguing for equal rights across gender and race, but she also wrote a popular biography of Staël.[20] Fuller, a formidable force for gender equality (and a self-styled Yankee Corinne!), partially translated Brentano von Arnim's 1840 *Günderode* into English in the same year it was published. Two years later, she composed an essay for Emerson's journal, *The Dial*, extolling the work as a paragon of Platonic friendship. In England, Mary Wollstonecraft honed her arguments through a critical discussion of Staël's reading of Rousseau.[21]

---

[18] Important work has already been done in this vein. An example of this is Dorothy G. Rogers, *America's First Women Philosophers: Transplanting Hegel, 1860–1925* (New York: Continuum, 2005). For an overview of women philosophers in the Western tradition, see Mary Ellen Waithe, ed., *A History of Women Philosophers*, 4 vols. (Dordrecht: Kluwer, 1995).

[19] For this point, see Lydia Moland, *Never the Same Again: The Radical Conscience of Lydia Maria Child* (Chicago: University of Chicago Press, forthcoming) and Lydia Moland, "Lydia Maria Child on German Philosophy and American Slavery," *British Journal for the History of Philosophy* (2020), doi: 10.1080/09608788.2020.1763911.

[20] For an account of Staël's influence on Child, see Lydia Moland, "Is She Not an Unusual Woman? Say More: Germaine de Staël and Lydia Maria Child on Progress, Art, and Abolition." In *Women and Philosophy in Eighteenth-Century Germany*, ed. Corey Dyck (Oxford: Oxford University Press, 2021).

[21] See Mary Wollstonecraft, "Art. XLIX," *Analytical Review* 4 (August 1789). See also Trouille, *Sexual Politics*, 221–235.

While living in Paris (1882–1889), Zetkin became an important member of the city's émigré circles and established herself as a key figure among the German social democrats. Salomé, in turn, was Russian by birth and retained an interest in Russian philosophy and literature throughout her life. The debate about Nietzsche's work—to which both Dohm and Salomé contributed—was transnational, involving not only German intellectuals but also Russian and Scandinavian women writing in the nineteenth century. Luxemburg worked to develop socialism in Germany, while also maintaining a notable political and philosophical voice in her native Poland. Luxemburg's analysis of imperialism in her 1913 book *The Accumulation of Capital* was the first attempt to understand imperialism from within a socialist framework and remains crucial in the context of European philosophy and in discussions of decolonialization in Africa and Latin America. Moreover, several women philosophers in German-speaking areas drew on the works of Harriet Taylor, John Stuart Mill, and Wollstonecraft. Wollstonecraft's *A Vindication of the Rights of Woman* was translated into German in 1793/1794 (albeit with occasional footnotes explaining to the German readership the purported absurdities of the more radical arguments articulated in the work).[22] Overall, the period and philosophies in question are marked by a distinctly transnational orientation and the forging of international networks.

The Status of Women (Philosophers)

In the long nineteenth century, it was not only women philosophers who were discussing the status of women and women's life more generally. Men—philosophers, politicians, and activists—were also thinking about these questions. Some of these men supported women's education and their social and political rights and facilitated women's writing and their access to education. Others were reactionary and even hostile. An important representative of the progressive camp was the prominent jurist and mayor Theodor

---

[22] For this point, see Birgit Mikus, *The Political Woman in Print: German Women's Writing 1845-1919* (Oxford: Peter Lang, 2014), 24–26; and Ulrike Weckel, "Gleichheit auf dem Prüfstand: Zur zeitgenössischen Rezeption der Streitschriften von Theodor Gottlieb von Hippel und Mary Wollstonecraft in Deutschland," in *Tugend, Vernunft und Gefühl. Geschlechterdiskurse der Aufklärung und weibliche Lebenswelten*, ed. Claudia Opiz, Ulrike Weckel, and Elke Kleinan (Münster: Waxmann, 2000), 209–249. By contrast, Olympe de Gouges's 1791 *Déclaration des droits de la femme et de la citoyenne*, for which the author had to pay with her life, had little immediate effect in Germany.

von Hippel (1741–1796). Hippel was a friend of Kant's and a staple of the Königsberg intellectual circles. In his anonymously published 1792 treatise, *On Improving the Status of Women*, Hippel argued for the education and full participation of women in citizenship.[23] In that vein, he reminds readers who are likely to respond that women need to stay at home with their children that parenthood is a shared responsibility. He supports his argument for women's education and political representation by a wealth of examples, taken from history (queen regents) but also philosophy and neighboring academic fields.[24]

The view defended in Hippel's work, which was initially read as a satire, became the object of Fichte's scorn in his 1797 *Foundations of Natural Right*.[25] In this work, Fichte maintains that once a woman is married to a man, "the husband is the administrator of all her rights; she wills her rights to be asserted and exercised only insofar as *he* wills them to be. He is her natural representative in the state and in society as a whole."[26] Furthermore, following a path already pursued by Kant, then contested by Hippel, Fichte denies that women can contribute to science, philosophy, and universal arguments and claims that women's writings should be limited to special women's literature.[27] Men's voices, by contrast, are by default considered scientific and universal. Along the same lines, we read in G. W. F. Hegel's *Philosophy of Right* (1821) that "women may well be educated, but they are not made for the higher sciences, for philosophy and certain artistic productions, which require a universal element."[28]

---

[23] Hippel had also written a text on marriage, simply titled *On Marriage*. This work was initially published in two editions (1774 and 1775), but the 1792 edition, published the same year as *On Improving the Status of Women*, was significantly more radical in its scope and claims. For Hippel's works in English, see Theodor Gottlieb von Hippel, *The Status of Women: Collected Writings*, ed. and trans. Timothy F. Sellner (Bloomington, IN: Xlibris, 2009). See also Carol Strauss Sotiropoulos, *Early Feminists and the Educational Debates: England, France, Germany 1760–1810* (Madison, NJ: Fairleigh Dickinson University Press, 2007), 172–189.

[24] Hippel's examples include Queen Kristina of Sweden (1626–1689), Anne Tanneguy-Lefèvre Dacier (1654–1720), Mary Astell (1666–1731), Catherine Macaulay (1731–1791), Ernestine Christine Reiske (1735–1798), Sophie von La Roche (1730–1807), and Friedrika Baldinger (1739–1786).

[25] See J. G. Fichte, *Foundations of Natural Right according to the Principles of the Wissenschaftslehre*, ed. Frederick Neuhouser, trans. Michael Baur (Cambridge: Cambridge University Press, 2000), e.g., 266–270, 298–307. In a different mode, Amalia Holst thanks Hippel for his support of women in her 1802 *Über die Bestimmung des Weibes zur höheren Geistesbildung*, ed. Berta Rahm (Zurich: Ala Verlag, 1984), 16. Importantly, Holst is not willing to go as far as Hippel when it comes to granting women full access not only to education but also to public offices and politics. See Weckel, "Gleichheit auf dem Prüfstand," 222–223.

[26] Fichte, *Foundations of Natural Right*, 299.

[27] Fichte, *Foundations of Natural Right*, 304–305.

[28] Hegel's reflections continue: "The difference between man and woman is the difference between animal and plant: the animal is closer in character to man, the plant to woman, for the latter is a more

Both Fichte and Hegel had socialized with women writers and philosophers in the salons. Fichte had even met with Staël, who allegedly compared his idealist system, founded on the fundamental principle of a self-positing consciousness, to a fantastical tale of the kind we find in the stories about Münchhausen's marvelous feats.[29] Moreover, within the milieu and the salon circles of which Fichte and Hegel were part, a number of individuals had defended more inclusive attitudes toward women (examples include Hippel but also Schleiermacher and the Schlegel brothers).[30] Indeed, such attitudes may have been a reason Fichte and Hegel felt the need to insist on their reactionary views. Although the works of Hippel and Wollstonecraft were largely met with disbelief in Germany, they also received fair and respectful reviews.[31] In other words, we cannot simply excuse Kant, Fichte, and Hegel as products of their time. Among the roster of views available, they consciously chose reactionary positions, and we need to hold them accountable for that. Furthermore, as we rethink the philosophical canon, we should not ignore the role that Hegel played in its establishment. His enormous success has had a significant impact on our understanding of the history of philosophy and our general ignorance about the role that women played in its development—as well as the role played by male philosophers who, like some Enlightenment and early romantic thinkers (Hippel, the Schlegels, Schleiermacher), regarded philosophy as an open, collaborative enterprise, of which women should be part.[32]

peaceful [process of] unfolding whose principle is the more indeterminate unity of feeling. When women are in charge of government, the state is in danger, for their actions are based not on the demands of universality but on contingent inclination and opinion." G. W. F. Hegel, *Elements of the Philosophy of Right*, ed. Allen Wood, trans. H. B. Nisbet (Cambridge: Cambridge University Press, 1991), 207. For a broader discussion, see also Alison Stone, "Hegel on Law, Women and Contract," in *Feminist Encounters with Legal Philosophy*, ed. Maria Drakopolou (London: Routledge, 2013), 104–122.

[29] J. Christopher Herold, *Mistress to an Age: A Life of Madame de Staël* (Indianapolis: Bobbs-Merrill, 1958), 270. Staël would later write to Jacobi that she much preferred a Kantian combination of realism and idealism. The source of this anecdote seems to be the American traveler and scholar, George Ticknor. See Roger Paulin, *The Life of August Wilhelm Schlegel: Cosmopolitan of Art and Poetry* (London: Open Book, 2016), 234.

[30] In his essay "On Philosophy: To Dorothea," Friedrich Schlegel strongly encourages his interlocutor (and women in general) to study philosophy. This invitation is also realized in the essay's style, which seeks to mirror the intimate dialogue that takes place at a salon. Friedrich Schlegel, Über die Philosophie: An Dorothea [On Philosophy: To Dorothea]," in *Kritische Friedrich-Schlegel-Ausgabe*, Vol. 8, ed. Ernst Behler, Jean Jacques Anstett, and Hans Eichner (Munich: Schöningh, 1958–), 41–62.

[31] See, again, Weckel, "Gleichheit auf dem Prüfstand," esp. 234.

[32] Kneller argues that the idea of *symphilosophy* necessarily involves relative openness toward women's philosophizing in the period. She points out, though, that this ideal was often not realized in practice. See Kneller, "Feminism." In her 2017 *New York Times* piece on the canonization of philosophy, Christia Mercer points to Hegel as one of the key figures in the emergence of a historical understanding

By the end of the century, things had, however, begun to change. More male authors were following Hippel's example and argued for the equality of women. Socialists made these arguments most forcefully, in particular August Bebel and Friedrich Engels. At the 1875 meeting of the German socialists in Gotha, Bebel agitated for universal suffrage, and in his 1879 book, *Woman and Socialism*, he argued that "there can be no emancipation of humanity without the social independence and equality of the sexes."[33] Similarly, Engels wrote in his 1884 *The Origins of the Family, Private Property and the State* that "the first condition for the liberation of the wife is to bring the whole female sex back into public industry."[34] Bebel and Engels influenced, among many others, Zetkin, who developed her own emancipatory socialist philosophy. By the end of the century, more women (such as Dohm) were willing to take reactionary views to task. In doing so, they also challenged widespread presuppositions about what counts as philosophy and what does not.

Questioning the Canon

Once we stray beyond the best-known philosophers and their works, we have fewer critical editions and collected works to draw on. Texts are often outdated, editions diverge, translations are incomplete or nonexistent, and critical interpretations are few and far between. Scholars of early modern philosophy have made important headway in this respect. Through meticulous research and efforts to distribute the works of women philosophers, they have enriched their area of study both historically and systematically.[35]

of philosophy that excludes women. "Descartes Is Not Our Father," *New York Times*, September 25, 2017, https://www.nytimes.com/2017/09/25/opinion/descartes-is-not-our-father.html.

[33] August Bebel, *Woman under Socialism*, trans. Daniel De Leon (New York: Schocken, 1904; repr. 1971), 5–6.

[34] Friedrich Engels, *Origin of the Family, Private Property and the State: In Light of the Researches of Lewis H. Morgan*, ed. Eleanor Burke Leacock, trans. Alec West (New York: International Publishers, 1972), 138.

[35] English-language monographs and volumes include Jacqueline Broad, ed., *Women Philosophers of the Seventeenth Century: Selected Correspondence* (Cambridge: Cambridge University Press, 2002); and Karen Green, *A History of Women's Political Thought in Europe, 1700–1800* (Cambridge: Cambridge University Press, 2014). See also Project Vox from Duke University, http://projectvox.org/about-the-project; the SSHRC project Extending New Narratives in the History of Philosophy, www.newnarrativesinphilosophy.net; and a project on the history of women philosophers and scientists (which extends into the twentieth century), coordinated by Ruth Hagengruber of Paderborn University, https://historyofwomenphilosophers.org. Book publications,

Not only is their work a source of inspiration for scholars studying earlier and later periods, but it has also triggered systematic discussions concerning canon formation, historical inclusion criteria, and processes of exclusion.[36] Furthermore, these discussions have raised challenging meta-philosophical questions about nonstandard philosophical genres (letters, notes, drama, etc.) explored by women philosophers in the early modern period.[37] This work has inspired the present volume.[38]

In the nineteenth century, philosophers challenged traditional ways of writing philosophy. Indeed, it would be no gross exaggeration to propose that many of the best-known nineteenth-century philosophers—the Schlegel brothers, Hegel, Kierkegaard, and Nietzsche—sought to make philosophical progress by questioning established models of philosophizing. In the early part of the century, philosophers returned to the genres of the fragment and the essay, argued for the significance of the arts in expanding and deepening knowledge, and developed dialectical-historical approaches to philosophy. Scholars such as Dieter Henrich, Manfred Frank, Frederick Beiser, Jane Kneller, and Elizabeth Millán have shown how a challenge to traditional philosophical form goes hand in hand with profound systematic commitments in this period.[39] Similar concerns re-emerge in the latter part of the nineteenth

including a large volume with newly commissioned articles on early modern women philosophers edited by Karen Detlefsen and Lisa Shapiro (for Routledge), are forthcoming.

[36] Eileen O'Neill, "Disappearing Ink: Early Modern Women Philosophers and Their Fate in History," in *Philosophy in a Feminist Voice: Critiques and Reconstructions*, ed. Janet A. Kourany (Princeton, NJ: Princeton University Press, 1997), 17–62.

[37] On the difficulties of incorporating early modern women philosophers into the canon (and the opposition toward such incorporation), see O'Neill, "Early Modern Women Philosophers." On how philosophical canons have shaped what we regard as core questions—and how, in turn, rethinking these core questions might result in an entirely different canon (in the early modern period)—see Lisa Shapiro, "Revisiting the Early Modern Philosophical Canon," *Journal of the American Philosophical Association* 2, no. 3 (2016): 365–383.

[38] We also want to mention the forthcoming *Oxford Handbook of Nineteenth-Century Women Philosophers in the German Tradition*, ed. Kristin Gjesdal and Dalia Nassar (New York: Oxford University Press) and *The Oxford Handbook of British and American Women Philosophers in the Nineteenth Century*, ed. Lydia Moland and Alison Stone (New York: Oxford University Press).

[39] See, for instance, Dieter Henrich, *Konstellationen. Probleme und Debatten am Ursprung der idealistischen Philosophie (1789–1795)* (Stuttgart: Klett-Cotta, 1991); Manfred Frank, *"Unendliche Annäherung." Die Anfänge der philosophischen Frühromantik* (Frankfurt: Suhrkamp, 1997), a partial English translation of which can be found in Manfred Frank, *The Philosophical Foundations of Early German Romanticism*, trans. Elizabeth Millán-Zaibert (Albany: SUNY Press, 2004); Frederick C. Beiser, *German Idealism: The Struggle against Subjectivism 1781–1801* (Cambridge, MA: Harvard University Press, 2002); Frederick C. Beiser, *The Romantic Imperative: The Concept of Early German Romanticism* (Cambridge, MA: Harvard University Press, 2003); Elizabeth Millán-Zaibert, *Friedrich Schlegel and the Emergence of Romantic Philosophy* (Albany: SUNY Press, 2008); Jane Kneller, *Kant and the Power of Imagination* (Cambridge: Cambridge University Press, 2007). Furthermore, in his more recent work, Beiser makes note of two forgotten women philosophers who were important in the development of pessimism: Agnes Taubert (1844–1877), the wife of Eduard von Hartmann, and

century, when philosophers increasingly turned their attention to meta-philosophical questions dealing with both the history (and historicity) of philosophy and the philosophy of history. (It is not for nothing that we speak of an awakening of a historical consciousness in the nineteenth century.) It is easy to forget that it was not long ago that a number of the nineteenth-century philosophers whose contribution we now take for granted were themselves excluded from the standard anglophone canon in philosophy (e.g., Fichte, Friedrich Schelling, Schopenhauer, and Nietzsche, to mention a few)—not in the sense that their works were not read (they certainly were) but in the sense that their works, often due to their philosophical form, were not seen as essentially contributing to philosophy as an academic discipline.

Today we have come a long way with critical editions, translations, and nineteenth-century scholarship that are philologically sound and systematic. In this sense, scholars who are looking to include works by women philosophers from this period in their syllabi and scholarship face a kind of challenge that they are already familiar with. The efforts to broaden the reception of German-language philosophy to include figures such as Johann Georg Hamann, Herder, Goethe, Friedrich Heinrich Jacobi, Fichte, Schelling, Novalis, the Schlegel brothers, Friedrich Hölderlin, Schleiermacher, Alexander and Wilhelm von Humboldt, Hartmann, and many others give grounds for optimism and offer, methodologically and systematically, examples to follow. Canons are evolving, and the field of nineteenth-century philosophy is expanding. Moreover, the philosophers represented in this volume themselves facilitate interesting discussions of canons and canon formation. We see this in Staël's ambitious attempts to retrieve the formation of German philosophy in the early nineteenth century and again in the writings of Brentan von Arnim and of Stein and Walther in the early twentieth century.

Challenging the Boundaries of Philosophical Discourse

Where scholarship in nineteenth-century philosophy has lagged, other disciplines have pushed forward. For some decades now, history, political science, German studies, and literary studies have been investigating the contributions of nineteenth-century women thinkers to their disciplines.

Olga Plümacher (1839–1895). See Frederick C. Beiser, *After Hegel: German Philosophy 1840–1900* (Princeton, NJ: Princeton University Press, 2014); and Frederick C. Beiser, *Weltschmerz: Pessimism in German Philosophy, 1860–1900* (Oxford: Oxford University Press, 2016).

As such, they have furnished us with important resources for understanding and integrating the works of women into the canon. After all, the nineteenth century predates a later honing of disciplinary boundaries and the formation of philosophy as a professional discipline.

Across gender divisions, writers in this period explored their ideas in what today is regarded as nonstandard philosophical forms (poetry, drama, essays, fragments, etc.). Especially in the first half of the century, many of the women philosophers whose work we have included in this volume also wrote novels, drama, and popular essays. These were indeed forms that could express a sense of urgency and inspire action. Furthermore, given that women (philosophical) writers were often stigmatized as unwomanly and ostracized both socially and in terms of their work, writing in non-discursive and non-academic genres may have seemed like an option that came with a lesser personal cost, as well as a better chance at successful distribution and readership. However, while we acknowledge that philosophical insights are not indexed to an academic form, we have sought, mostly for pragmatic reasons, to focus on texts that engage the philosophical writing practices of the time and thus left out, for now, important works composed in genres such as poetry and novels. It is our hope, though, that renewed interest in the work of the women philosophers included in this volume will generate an interest in the full varieties of forms through which they expressed themselves.

Research on women philosophers has gone hand in hand with an even more comprehensive effort to critically assess and systematically expand the boundaries of philosophical discourse to encompass works beyond the standard European and anglophone cultures. One example of this is the Oxford University Press series New Histories in Philosophy (edited by Christia Mercer). Works by some of the women included in this collection testify to an inclusive notion of philosophy—not just stylistically (letters, fragments, novels, etc.) or in terms of topics (education, poverty, women's rights) but also in terms of openness toward non-European cultures and engagement with questions of global injustice. Examples worth mentioning include Günderrode's play *Muhammad: The Prophet of Mecca* (1804), Staël's novella *Mirza* (1786), and Salomé's sustained interest in Russian culture.

Some of the philosophers whose work is presented in this collection explicitly thematize their status as women writers and thinkers (e.g., Staël, Günderrode, Dohm, and Zetkin). Some directly contribute to feminism, engaging with questions concerning gender and sexuality in ways that remain relevant today (e.g., Staël, Dohm, and Zetkin). However, not all women supported the women's movement or the call for women's suffrage. In the same way that twenty-first-century women philosophers can defend more or less progressive views, so it is the case with women philosophers of earlier periods. Some women were sensitive to and reflective about their privileges, whether education, class, or belonging to the intelligentsia of the time. Others held positions that were heavily influenced by their class and social-economic privileges, took their privileges for granted, and expressed little or no concern for those who were in more precarious situations.[40] This, too, is part of the legacy of women philosophers. Just as it is the case with Kant, Fichte, Hegel, and Nietzsche, any attempt to take the contributions of these philosophers seriously will have to try to identify the promising *and* less promising aspects of their works. Furthermore, the budding phenomenological movement gave rise both to politically bold resistance *and* to problematic figures such as Else Voigtländer (1882–1946). In 1937, Voigtländer sought membership in the National Socialist Party. She was excluded from pursuing an academic career by the Prussian law against women's right to obtain a habilitation (the degree required for an academic career in Germany), and she worked as the director of a women's prison throughout the period of National Socialism.[41]

Women philosophers in the nineteenth century often discussed and critiqued the works of their colleagues. More often than not, these were male figures who held academic positions and worked with prominent publishing houses. As discussed above, some of these male philosophers facilitated works by their women friends and companions and acknowledged them as equals in the field. Others went some way in supporting women philosophers but stopped short when it came to endorsing these women's right to pursue their

[40] While addressing the situation of women, both Staël and Dohm were, at times, blind to their privileges, whether intellectual or financial. Similarly, some of the later interest in Nietzsche's work was driven by a celebration of the "exceptional" woman. We find this in the work of Salomé and, even before Nietzsche, in Staël. Furthermore, Nietzsche's work was adopted by women who pursued a more conservative agenda (Laura Mohr, writing as Laura Marholm, 1854–1928) and women who pursued a radical one (the anarchist Emma Goldman, 1869–1940). For this point, see Kneller, "Feminism"; for a book-length study, see Carol Diethe, *Nietzsche's Women: Beyond the Whip* (Berlin: De Gruyter, 1996). Dohm argues against the anti-feminist appropriation of Nietzsche's work in *Die Antifeministen. Ein Buch der Verteidigung* (Berlin: Holzinger, 2015 [originally published in 1902]), part of which is included in this volume.

[41] See George Heffernan, "Phenomenology, Psychology, and Ideology: A New Look at the Life and Work of Else Voigtländer," *Phenomenological Investigations* 1 (2021): 1–49. Drawing on early phenomenology as well as Nietzsche's work, Voigtländer's 1909 dissertation, "Über die Typen des Selbstgefühls," published as *Vom Selbstgefühl. Ein Beitrag zur Förderung psychologischen Denkens* (Leipzig: R. Voigtländer, 1910), discusses the phenomenology and psychology of self-feeling. See Íngrid Vendrell Ferran, *Die Emotionen. Gefühle in der realistischen Phänomenologie* (Berlin: De Gruyter, 2008); and Íngrid Vendrell Ferran, "The Emotions in Early Phenomenology," *Studia Phaenomenologica* 15 (2015): 349–374. For a discussion of the link between Nietzscheanism and National Socialism among conservative women philosophers, see Diethe, *Nietzsche's Women*, esp. chap. 5.

habilitations in order to qualify for academic positions.[42] Finally, as we have seen, some made explicitly derogatory remarks about women's intellects. Nonetheless, the works of some of these (male) philosophers inspired and delivered important premises to women philosophers. In the twentieth century, the best-known example may be Simone de Beauvoir's adaptations of Hegel's analysis of the dialectics of recognition.[43] Among the thinkers represented in our collection, Staël draws on and critiques the works of Rousseau. In Dohm's work, we find an acute critique of Nietzsche's misogyny alongside a deep interest in his critical-methodological tools and his understanding of the self as fundamentally creative.

This way of doing philosophy—through a critical discussion of the history of philosophy and engagement with one's contemporaries—is a cornerstone of the European tradition. By grappling with the arguments of past philosophers, later thinkers were able to hone their thoughts and press philosophy toward bold and new hypotheses and conclusions. At stake is an awareness that history provides a bounty of arguments and positions and that overlooking the arguments developed in the past would border on historical, systematic, and sometimes also ideological blindness. From this point of view, we hope that the texts presented in this volume will be read in tandem with the works of philosophers traditionally studied in nineteenth-century classes; only thus can the full originality of these works be appreciated. The works of the women philosophers in this period are not mere appendices to the tradition—they are a crucial part of it.

Constellations and Solidarity

Whether in a spirit of neglect or admiration, it may be tempting to think of women philosophers as one school of thought. While we have found overlaps and explicit points of dialogue between the philosophers included in this volume, we resist sharp classifications of this kind. Instead, we recommend the approach facilitated by Dieter Henrich's notion of intellectual constellations: we see nineteenth-century women philosophers as a flexible group whose works display family resemblances but are still sufficiently different to create productive tensions and disagreements.

---

[42] In contrast to Husserl, who did not support Stein's desire to write a habilitation, Karl Jaspers supported Walther. See our introductions to chapters 8 and 9.

[43] For a discussion of this point, see Nancy Bauer, *Simone de Beauvoir, Philosophy, and Feminism* (New York: Columbia University Press, 2001).

Much nineteenth-century philosophy challenges the notion that systematic philosophy must be anchored in universal principles from which further principles follow with deductive necessity. For the women philosophers in this volume, this challenge takes two forms. First, they seek to develop forms of philosophizing that engage with the reader's emotions, imagination, and experience. Second, they often pursue a descriptive approach that aspires to be concrete, historical, empirical, and bottom-up (rather than deductive and top-down).

For the women philosophers represented in this volume, exploration of a wider spectrum of philosophical forms goes hand in hand with practical engagement. In light of their critique of philosophical abstractions, the romantics were wedded to the view that philosophical theory cannot be divorced from practice—in both senses of the term, i.e., the practice of philosophy itself and the living out of one's ideas in practice. Günderrode, for one, regarded philosophy as a tool through which we can posit a (morally) better world, one in which women are recognized as self-determining subjects. She was not, however, convinced that philosophy carried out in a merely abstract manner can achieve this goal and regarded the imagination as essential for helping us grasp and realize the good life. Brentano von Arnim's publications are largely based on or inspired by actual correspondences, and their philosophical content is influenced by the lived experiences of their respective authors, including experiences of poverty and social injustice. Staël, in turn, published on one of the most pressing social issues of her time: abolitionism. In her discussions of the status of women writers, Staël sought to carve out a space for women intellectuals. Furthermore, she herself was nothing short of a formidable political force, who not only wrote works on the French Revolution but also played a key political role both during and after the Napoleonic years in Europe.[44] Later in the century, with the rise of socialism, philosophy and practice came together in an even more direct manner. By directly engaging the life of the working poor, Zetkin carried out socialist ideals further than either Marx or Engels. A similar attitude was later taken up by Stein and Walther, both of whom saw in phenomenology a significant potential to grapple with and change people's lives. In the nineteenth century, philosophy increasingly shaped the public sphere, and this new public role, in turn, also transformed philosophy.

One ought to remember, though, that women philosophers, even in the early twentieth century, were barred from pursuing an academic career. That

---

[44] See Glenda Sluga, "Madame de Staël and the Transformation of European Politics, 1812–17," *International History Review* 37, no. 1 (2015): 142–166.

is, if women philosophers turned to the practical sphere, it was often because they were deprived of a choice—if they were to pursue their philosophical orientations, it would have to be outside of the ivory towers of academia. Yet this position of relative marginality translated into a commitment to a broader, practical idea of philosophy. Thus, even for Stein, Walther, and the first generation of women philosophers who could obtain a PhD (a dissertation but not yet a habilitation), phenomenology furnished resources for thinking systematically about social, biological, and emotional life. In one way or another, for the thinkers whose works are included in this volume, philosophical practice must be understood in terms of its real-life commitments.

Furthermore, while these women were largely excluded from the practice of academic philosophy, many of them were not only publishing their work but also gaining a large readership. Yet their works have been systematically underrepresented in the philosophical canon. Though the exclusion of women philosophers from the academy (first as students and then as teachers) and from the canon was fundamentally unjust, many of the women in this volume found creative ways to use, expand, and engage with philosophical ideas and methods. Hence, including women in the philosophical canon does not only add a few new names. It expands our understanding of philosophy itself.

Concluding Thoughts

In our research into women's contributions to the philosophical development of the nineteenth century, we have been surprised by the light these contributions shed on this period and the extent to which they challenge our current understanding of its various movements and their relations (e.g., romanticism and socialism, socialism and phenomenology). Despite their differences, these philosophers were united in their commitment to lived experience, in their interest in the ways in which philosophy can transform (or fail to transform) everyday lives, and can be transformed by these lived experiences. While we are still in the early days of critical scholarship on the philosophical contributions of nineteenth-century women philosophers, the original works by these women speak to us in terms that command systematic philosophical attention and force us to reflect on how philosophy, as a discipline, has developed. They challenge us to think differently—and carefully—about the history of philosophy and about philosophy's potential both within and outside of the academy: that is, about what philosophy can and ought to achieve.

Translation, Acknowledgments, Sources

The texts in the volume have been translated by Anna C. Ezekiel, and the references in the translations are Ezekiel's, with the exception of Staël's writings, which were translated from the French by Stephen Gaukroger and Dalia Nassar, with references by Nassar. In several instances, the texts appear in English for the first time. In our selections, we have tried to focus on central yet accessible works by each author. Each chapter opens with an introduction to the thinker, her historical-intellectual context, and her work.

The selected texts contribute to a diverse set of philosophical traditions, including German idealism, German romanticism and *Naturphilosophie*, socialism, Marxism, phenomenology, as well as the fields of psychology and sociology. Each of these disciplines has its own technical language and its own tradition of English translations for German terms. In general, the translations strive to respect these traditions and, as much as possible, follow common practice in word choice. We have only attempted to impose terminological consistency across the volume where this did not conflict with an established practice or result in anachronistic use of language within a particular field.

One of the most important goals of these translations was to be accessible to new readers in philosophy. In accordance with this aim, the translations try to avoid language that may create barriers for some readers. Inclusive and gender-neutral language is used wherever possible, including the gender-neutral singular *they*. While mindful of historical writing styles, modernized forms of speech have at times been used in order to facilitate readability.

Having completed her translations, Anna Ezekiel wishes to thank Dr. Katerina Mihaylova at the Martin-Luther-Universität Halle-Wittenberg for her nuanced and inventive advice on many difficult points of translation. Dalia Nassar and Kristin Gjesdal wish to thank Jennifer Milam and the Sydney Intellectual History Network at the University of Sydney; the Department of Philosophy at the University of Sydney; the Nineteenth-Century Study Group at the University of Sydney; Matthew Sussman of the English Department at the University of Sydney; the Department of Philosophy at Temple University; the Greater Philadelphia Philosophy Consortium; and Colby College. We would also like to thank the excellent

Women Philosophers in the Long Nineteenth Century. Dalia Nassar and Kristin Gjesdal, Oxford University Press.
© Oxford University Press 2021. DOI: 10.1093/oso/9780190868031.003.0002

librarians, without whose assistance this project would not have been possible: Temple University's Fred Rowland, the librarians at the University of Tübingen, and those at the Universitätsbibliothek Johann Christian Senckenberg, University of Frankfurt, especially Raschida Mansour. We also wish to thank the participants at the University of Sydney, Colby College, and Temple University's Women in Philosophy workshop (Philadelphia, fall 2018). We are grateful for discussions with and comments from Karen Detlefsen, Colin Chamberlain, Moira Gatens, Stephen Gaukroger, Katherina Kinzel, Cat Moir, Anne Pollok, and, last but not least, Lydia Moland. We thank Jacinta Shrimpton (University of Sydney) and Meryl Lumba and Raciel Cuevas (Temple University) for competent research assistantship. Thanks also to the honors students at Temple who have served as active readers of translations and introductions in progress. We acknowledge the Faculty Collaborative Research Scheme (2016–2018) and the University of Sydney Faculty of Arts and Social Sciences for supporting the project "Theories and Conceptions of Life from the Nineteenth Century to the Present." Finally, we are grateful for the unfailing competence and enthusiasm of Anna Ezekiel and for her patience and embrace of this project from the very beginning.

The texts are translated from the following sources:

Arnim, Bettina von. *Die Günderode*. Grünberg: W. Levysohn, 1840.

Dohm, Hedwig. "Nietzsche und die Frauen." *Die Zukunft* 25 (1898): 534–543.

Dohm, Hedwig. "Die neue Mutter." *Die Zukunft* 31 (1900): 513–519.

Dohm, Hedwig. "Die alte Frau." *Die Zukunft* 14 (January 3, 1903): 22–30.

Dohm, Hedwig. "Von den Scharfmachern des Antifeminismus." "Aus der Frauenwelt." *Vossische Zeitung*, September 29, 1912.

Günderrode, Karoline von. From the *Nachlass*. Used with permission from the Universitätsbibliothek Johann Christian Senckenberg, University of Frankfurt. Ms. 207r–215v; 132–135; 139–140; 143–168; 187–a89; 192–197; 55r–56v; 282r–284r.

Luxemburg, Rosa. *Einführung in die Nationalökonomie*. Edited by Paul Levi. Berlin: E. Lau'sche Verlagbuchhandlung, 1925.

Salomé, Lou Andreas-. *Die Erotik*. Frankfurt am Main: Rütten & Loening, 1910.

Staël-Holstein, Mme. la Baronne de. Chapter 4, "Des Femmes qui cultivent les Lettres." In *De la littérature considerée dans ses rapports avec les institutions sociales*, 305–315. 2nd ed. Paris: Charpentier, 1800.

Staël-Holstein, Mme. la Baronne de. Chapter 4, "Kant." In *De l'Allemagne*, Vol. 3, 67–95. 2nd ed. Paris: H. Nicolle, 1813; reprinted from London: John Murray, 1813.

Staël-Holstein, Mme. la Baronne de. Chapter 10, "Influence de la nouvelle Philosophie sur les sciences." In *De l'Allemagne*, Vol. 3, 143–164. 2nd ed. Paris: H. Nicolle, 1813; reprinted from London: John Murray, 1813.

Stein, Edith. *Zum Problem der Einfühlung*. Halle: Buchdruckerei des Waisenhauses, 1917.

Walther, Gerda. *Ein Beitrag zur Ontologie der sozialen Gemeinschaften*. Halle: Max Niemeyer, 1922.

Zetkin, Clara. "Für die Befreiung der Frau!" *Protokoll des Internationalen Arbeiter-Congresses zu Paris*, July 14–20, 1889, 80–85. Foreword by Wilhelm Liebknecht. Nürnberg: Wörlein, 1890.

Zetkin, Clara. "Das Frauenstimmenrecht." *Der Internationale Sozialisten-Kongreß zu Stuttgart 18–24 August 1907*, 40–47. Berlin: Vorwärts, 1907.

Zetkin, Clara. "Rettet die Scottsboro-Negerknaben!" *MOPR, Zeitschrift für Kampf und Arbeit der Internationalen Roten Hilfe*, no. 4 (1932): 1–3.

We have also consulted:

Dohm, Hedwig. *Ausgewählte Texte*. Edited by Nikola Müller and Isabel Rohner. Berlin: Trafo, 2006.

Günderrode, Karoline von. *Sämtliche Werke und ausgewählte Studien. Historisch-Kritische Ausgabe*, 3 vols. Edited by Walter Morgenthaler. Frankfurt: Stroemfeld/ Roter Stern, 1990–1991.

Zetkin, Clara. *Ausgewählte Reden und Schriften*. Vol. 1. *Auswahl aus den Jahren 1889 bis 1917*. Vol. 3. *Auswahl aus den Jahren 1923 bis 1933*. Berlin: Dietz, 1957.

1

Germaine de Staël (1766–1817)

Introduction

Political theorist, historian, and novelist Anne Louise Germaine de Staël-Holstein (née Necker, 1766–1817), also known as Madame de Staël, has been characterized in many ways. Staël, as she is referred to in present-day scholarship, was a formidable political strategist and thinker. She was a key player in redrawing the political map of Europe after the Napoleonic Wars. Napoleon saw her as his sworn enemy and had her exiled from Paris—repeatedly and with varying distance, depending on his temper and level of aggression. Her novels *Delphine* (1802) and *Corinne, or Italy* (1807) were international bestsellers. At that point, however, she was already known as a philosopher. Her early work includes the 1796 *A Treatise on the Influence of the Passions upon the Happiness of Individuals and of Nations*. She had also published her magisterial survey of European literature and its social importance, *The Influence of Literature on Society* (1800). When *Germany* was published in 1813, Staël's philosophical spirit was loudly celebrated across Europe. In the influential *Edinburgh Review*, James Mackintosh put it as follows: "An account of metaphysical systems by a woman is a novelty in the history of the human mind. Whatever must be thought of its success in some of its parts, it must be regarded on the whole as the boldest effort of the female intellect."[1] Staël's work—along with the very idea of a woman philosopher in the nineteenth century—was indeed a novelty.

Among the philosophers presented here, Staël is the only one who wrote in French. She was born into a Swiss family but grew up in Paris. Her father, Jacques Necker, was the director general of finance to King Louis XVI, which made him one of the most powerful men in France. Her mother, Suzanne Curchod, was a well-known socialite, whose Friday gatherings were frequented by Denis Diderot, Georges-Louis Leclerc (Comte de Buffon), Edward Gibbon, David Hume, Paul-Henri Thiry (Baron) d'Holbach, and Jean-Baptiste le Rond d'Alembert.

---

[1] James Mackintosh, "*De l'Allemagne*, par Madame la Baronne de Staël-Holstein, 3 vols. London 1813," *Edinburgh Review* xxii (October 1813): 198–239.

In 1786, at age twenty, Staël was married to Baron Erik Magnus Staël von Holstein, the Swedish envoy to France and much her senior. As a married woman, Staël remained financially independent and established her own intellectual circles. The marriage, which was formally dissolved in 1797, gave her the title of baroness and afforded her diplomatic status. In 1793, Staël left Paris for England. In England, she lived with Louis de Narbonne, a former minister under Louis XVI, until the end of the Reign of Terror (1794). Her return from England marked the beginning of her fourteen-year long relationship with the political activist, philosopher, and writer Benjamin Constant, who was allegedly the father of one of her five children (only three of whom survived). Another important friend and travel companion was philosopher August Wilhelm Schlegel. Schlegel worked as a tutor for Staël's children and was also a conversation partner and friend from 1804 onward.

Staël traveled widely in Europe and Russia. After she was exiled from Paris in 1803, she established her own circles—a virtual who's who of early-nineteenth-century European culture—at the family property Château de Coppet near Geneva.[2] She describes this period in the posthumously published *Ten Years' Exile* (1821). In 1811, six years before her death, Staël married a Swiss officer, John Rocca. She returned to England two years later and, along the lines of her previous work, collected material for a study under the preliminary title *On England*.

Staël's life as a public intellectual started when, at age twenty-two, she published *Letters on the Works and the Character of J. J. Rousseau*. The work was published anonymously, but the identity of the author was widely known. Staël treats Rousseau as a sensitive, poetic soul who is subject to constant misunderstandings. She discusses the philosophical affinities between Rousseau and David Hume and elaborates central philosophical concepts such as sentiment and enthusiasm. But Staël's early work also contains reflections on what it is like to read Rousseau as a young woman. While she maintains a traditionalist position on women in the public domain, she lauds the life of the mind and, by way of example (a young woman publishing a book on a philosopher), counters Rousseau's conservative take on women readers and writers. Three years before her death, she furnished the book with a new preface, while also making some modifications to it. In the meantime, this early work had appeared in a new edition as well as an English

---

[2] Ernst Behler, "La doctrine de Coppet d'une perfectibilité infinie et la Révolution française," in *Le Groupe de Coppet et la Révolution française. Actes du quatrième Colloque de Coppet, 20–23 juillet 1988*, ed. Etienne Hofmann and Anne–Lise Delacrétaz (Lausanne: Institut B. Constant, 1990), 255–274.

translation and had been (critically) discussed by, among others, Mary Wollstonecraft.[3]

Staël's philosophically most productive period began in the mid-1790s. She published a number of political, philosophical, and literary essays, including *A Treatise on the Influence of the Passions*. With its emphasis on self-perfection and its celebration of nature, the work, along with *Germany*, contributed to the development of romantic philosophy across Europe.

Like Johann Gottfried Herder, Wollstonecraft, and Alexander von Humboldt, Staël was engaged in abolitionism. In 1793, Olympe de Gouges—another French thinker, critic of colonialism, and author of *Declaration of the Rights of Woman and the Female Citizen* (1791)—had been executed for her criticism of the revolutionary government. A few years later, Staël published *Mirza* (1795, but written, on Staël's account, nine years earlier), which portrays a well-educated woman from West Africa. There is no shortage of Eurocentric tropes and attitudes in Staël's novella. Yet, with its reflections on the wrongs of slavery and the myopic European sense of superiority, *Mirza* challenged common stereotypes about race and gender.[4] Staël's abolitionist work continued through the 1810s.[5] In a letter to Thomas Jefferson, she makes it clear that if Americans "succeed in doing away with slavery in the South, there would be at least one government in the world as perfect as human reason can conceive of it."[6]

Staël's work is often said to draw on Immanuel Kant, especially his 1790 *Critique of the Power of Judgment*. Staël had probably discussed Kant with Wilhelm von Humboldt (who resided in Paris between 1797 and 1801), Charles de Villers (the French translator of Kant's work), and Henry Crabb Robinson (a student of Friedrich Schelling's, who stayed at Coppet in 1804).

---

[3] See Trouille, *Sexual Politics*, chap. 5. Later, Mary Wollstonecraft Shelley, Wollstonecraft's daughter and the author of *Frankenstein*, includes a biography of Staël in *Lives of the Most Eminent French Writers*, Vol. 2 (Philadelphia: Lea and Blanchard, 1840), 298–343. Another biography was published by Lydia Maria Child: *The Biography of Madame de Staël and Madame Roland* (Boston: Carter and Hendee, 1832).

[4] For discussions of this part of Staël's production, see Karen de Bruin, "Romantic Aesthetics and Abolitionist Activism: African Beauty in Germaine de Staël's *Mirza ou Lettre d'un voyageur*," *Symposium: A Quarterly Journal in Modern Literatures* 67, no. 3 (2013): 135–147; and Françoise Massardier-Kenney, "Staël, Translation, and Race," in *Translating Slavery: Gender and Race in French Women's Writings, 1783–1823*, ed. Doris Y. Kadish and Françoise Massardier–Kenney (Kent, OH: Kent State University Press, 1994), 135–145.

[5] In 1814, she published "Préface pour la traduction d'un ouvrage de M. Wilberforce" and "Appel aux Souverains."

[6] "Letter to Jefferson," in *Madame de Staël: Selected Correspondence*, ed. Georges Solovieff and Kathleen Jameson-Cemper, trans. Kathleen Jameson-Cemper (Dordrecht: Springer, 2000), 368. See also Richmond Laurin Hawkins, *Madame de Staël and the United States* (Cambridge, MA: Harvard University Press, 1930), 5; and Biancamaria Fontana, *Germaine de Staël: A Political Portrait* (Princeton, NJ: Princeton University Press, 2016).

However, in earlier works such as *The Influence of Literature on Society*, Staël mentions Kant and deliberately establishes an alternative to the Kantian idea of aesthetic autonomy by arguing that literature must be situated within a larger social context. Furthermore, Staël regards literary achievements, at their best, as stimulating tolerance and political advancement within a given culture.

Germany was based on Staël's close study of German-language literature and philosophy before, during, and after her five trips to the German lands in the period between 1789 and 1808. Along the lines of Voltaire's *Letters on the English* (1733), Staël seeks to understand German-language culture and, by the same token, expand the horizons of her fellow French by exposing them to a culture they often regard condescendingly. Defying the call for French nationalism during Napoleon's occupation of German-speaking territories, she critiques French prejudice and national pride and also addresses the phenomenon of cultural prejudices and bias at large. It is telling that in 1810, the first printed batch of the book, allegedly published in an astonishing ten thousand copies, was destroyed by Napoleon's forces. As a consequence, Staël's work only reached a general audience three years later, when it was published (in French) in England. The work became enormously popular and played a crucial role in the increased interest in German culture around the world. It inspired, for instance, the first group of Americans to go to Germany to undertake PhDs there.[7] In turn, Margaret Fuller, the American women's rights activist, took on the identity of a self-styled Yankee Corinne.

In her final years, Staël worked on her study of the French Revolution, *Considerations on the Principal Events of the French Revolution*.[8] The book was published the year after her death, and Staël had only reviewed two of the three parts of her manuscript. An English translation was published the following year. By this point, she had become a well-known political thinker. But already in 1797, the year she first met Napoleon, she had completed *On the Current Circumstances Which Can End the Revolution* (published two years later).[9]

---

[7] Kurt Mueller-Vollmer mentions Edward Everett, George Ticknor, and George Bancroft. Ticknor's own letter to Jefferson betrays how he relied on Staël's cultural guidance during his stay in Germany. See Kurt Mueller-Vollmer, "Staël's *Germany* and the Beginnings of an American National Literature," in *Germaine de Staël: Crossing the Borders*, ed. Madelyn Gutwirth, Avriel Goldberger, and Karyna Szmurlo (New Brunswick, NJ: Rutgers University Press, 1991), 147–148.

[8] For a discussion of Staël's notion of liberty, see Chinatsu Takeda, *Mme de Staël and Political Liberalism in France* (Singapore: Palgrave Macmillan, 2018).

[9] For a revision of the 1818 English translation, see Germaine de Staël, *Considerations on the Principal Events of the French Revolution*, ed. Aurelian Craiutu (Indianapolis: Liberty Fund, 2008).

For this volume, we have chosen a chapter from *The Influence of Literature on Society* ("On Women Writers") and two key chapters from *Germany* ("Kant" and "On the Influence of the New Philosophy on the Sciences").

The chapter from *The Influence of Literature on Society* addresses the general situation of women through the lens of women writers. With works such as *Letters on Rousseau* and *The Influences of the Passions* behind her, Staël was already a celebrity. Her chapter details the difficulties of being a woman writer but also discusses the importance of cultivating and listening to women's voices and addresses the education of women writers and readers. She thus anticipates her reflections on women's social situation and cultural status in the famous "Corinne's Letter" that punctuates her 1807 novel. In her view, the situation of women is bleak even in the so-called enlightened circles in France. Women are subject to social sanctions and cannot fully flourish as human beings. While a knack for amusement is easily forgiven, intellectual ambitions are not: "Women are forgiven if they sacrifice their household occupations for the sake of worldly amusements, but if they take their study seriously, they are accused of pedantry." Staël assumes that there is a deep-seated human need for recognition.

Thus far, she follows Rousseau. However, she goes beyond Rousseau's agenda when she argues that while the public is willing to foster a woman's need for social approval, it is quick to deny it to her if she strays from traditional gender expectations. However, in Staël's view, women writers are not only held back by negative social sanctions. In addition, positive encouragement of non-intellectual pastimes will curb a woman's development: "the pleasantries that are leveled against them from all directions, these pleasantries manage to discourage talent, to dry up the very source of confidence and exaltation." Arguing historically, Staël points out that this has not always been the case: Sparta and Rome exemplify societies that allowed women some degree of intellectual self-realization. In France, by contrast, women are not treated as full human beings. If a presumably enlightened society fails on this front, then, Staël argues, more enlightenment is needed. And as far as the project of enlightenment goes, there are significant gains for a society that educates women writers and readers, which include the development of genuine conversation partners and educators. As Staël puts it, "The key to achieving reasonable goals, to developing social and political relations based on enduring foundations, is the enlightenment, instruction, and perfection of women and men, nations and individuals."

Germany dedicates a separate section to the study of philosophy. In this context, only two chapters are named after philosophers. The first is named after Kant (included here), the second after Friedrich Heinrich Jacobi (whom Staël had met and corresponded with in the years between 1800 and 1804). Jacobi is taken to have posed the greatest challenge to Kantian philosophy, a challenge that forced post-Kantian philosophers to move beyond the confines of Kant's three *Critiques*. This challenge (in part) had to do with Kant's notion of the thing-in-itself, the idea of an object that is independent of the forms of human understanding and therefore inaccessible to human knowers. Jacobi, further, had insisted that philosophy should not only involve analysis of concepts and conditions of normativity but also a philosophy of existence. Staël takes up Jacobi's challenge.

For Staël, Kant's philosophy presents an answer to questions she had been discussing in her early work, including that of the unity of the human mind. Kantian philosophy offered her a way to conceptualize the interdependence of the intellectual faculties and feeling. In her reading, it is Kant's achievement to have connected the "evidence of the heart with that of the understanding." He had made the mind a single focus where "all our faculties harmonize." Moreover, Kant had pointed out the independence of the mind over against the domain of a causally determined nature. She views Kant as an anti-materialist but also emphasizes his early work in science and his aversion to traditional metaphysics.

Staël is interested in Kant's conception of the limitations of knowledge (and points out, in this respect, an affinity with Jacobi). "No one knows what life is," Staël writes. She has little patience with philosophers who set about to reason about life. Arguing along the lines that Bettina Brentano von Arnim would take up some years later, Staël claims that anyone attempting to analyze life would, in the end, come to the conclusion that "they do not live at all." As she elaborates, "It is the same with God, conscience, and free will. You must believe in them because you feel them: no argument will change this fact." For Staël, what we believe in, when we believe, is the co-belonging of the human mind with the universe as such. Staël describes this as enthusiasm or a feeling of being uplifted by life.

With her emphasis on feeling, Staël's interpretation of Kant alleviates some of the worries with which Herder, Schiller, Schelling, and Schleiermacher had approached his work. Moreover, Staël is interested in how the insights of German idealism have been applied beyond philosophy, narrowly conceived. This is clear in "On the Influences of the New Philosophy on the Sciences." Here Staël takes on a perspective that is similar to, yet also goes beyond, the one we find in the second part of Kant's *Critique of the Power of Judgment*. In order fully to comprehend nature, she contends, we need to see it as an organized whole. Such a holistic point of view, in turn, can only be obtained through the synthesizing work of imagination (Staël uses the term "divination," familiar from the work of Herder, Schleiermacher, and others).

In her discussion, Staël situates romantic philosophy of nature in its historical, scientific, and philosophical contexts. She also argues for the superiority of the new German approach over earlier forms of rationalism and empiricism. In Staël's view, this new philosophy of nature has the advantage of uniting experimentation and speculation. As Staël puts it, we should not "renounce the experimental method, which is so necessary in the sciences. But why not develop—as a supreme guide for this method—a more encompassing philosophy, one that would embrace the universe in its totality, and which would not scorn *the nocturnal side of nature*, expecting instead to illuminate it?"

Staël's philosophy of nature is among the most original parts of her work.[10] Other original contributions include her political philosophy, philosophy of history, philosophy of literature, philosophy of feeling and passions, and philosophy of religion. Some scholars have argued that when turning to German philosophy, Staël already had a worked-out independent position, especially with respect to religion and history.[11] Yet, precisely because Staël had worked out her position, she could actively and critically engage the views of the German philosophers. In addition to Kant and Jacobi, she found the works of Herder, Goethe, Schiller, and Schleiermacher to be of particular importance.

During her lifetime, Staël's work was widely disseminated in Europe and the United States. In Germany, Staël's early essay on literature, *Essay on Fiction* (1795), was translated by none other than Goethe (initially for Schiller's *Die Horen*). In the United States, three different translations of *Corinne* were initiated within a year of its publication in France. *Germany* appeared in the United States in 1814. Staël's work influenced, among others, Friedrich Schiller, Lord Byron, Bettina Brentano von Arnim, Dorothea von Schlegel, George Sand, Margaret Fuller, Lydia Maria Child, Kate Chopin, Henry James, Ralph Waldo Emerson, Giacomo Leopardi, Alexander Pushkin, and Georg Brandes.

In political history and political theory, Staël is recognized as a key strategist and a champion of liberty. In a famous anecdote, she, along with Russia and England (!), was characterized as a third political superpower. Her work in philosophy, however, makes it clear that she also deserves a prominent place in this field.

---

[10] Mueller-Vollmer discusses this point in "Staël's *Germany*."
[11] See John Claiborne Isbell, *The Birth of European Romanticism: Truth and Propaganda in Staël's "De l'Allemagne"* (Cambridge: Cambridge University Press, 1994), 114.

On Women Writers

"Unhappiness is like the black mountain of Bember, on the extremes
of the sizzling Kingdom of Lahore. While you are climbing it, you
don't see anything before you but barren rocks; but once you are at
the top, the sky is above your head and at your feet is the Kingdom
of Kashmir."

—Bernardin, *La chaumière indienne*[12]

The position of women in society is once again uncertain from a number of
perspectives. The desire to please excites women's spirit [*esprit*], while reason
counsels them to remain unknown. And everything is as arbitrary in their
success as it is in their failures.

I believe that there will come a time in which the philosophical legislators
will pay serious attention to the education of women, to the civil laws that
should protect them, to the duties that must be imposed upon them, and
to the happiness that can be guaranteed to them. However, in the current
context, women are, for the most part, neither part of the order of nature
nor of the order of society. Those who succeed in some things lose out in
others. Those qualities which may at times harm them may, at other times,
serve them. In one moment, they are everything—and then suddenly they
are nothing. From one angle the destiny of women resembles that of a freed
person living in a monarchy: if they seek to achieve a higher status—one
which the laws have not granted them—they are regarded as criminals; if
they remain slaves, they are oppressed.

While it is generally agreed that it is best if women devoted themselves
to domestic activities, men unaccountably pardon women who pay no attention to their domestic affairs but harshly judge those who demonstrate a
particular talent. In women men tolerate the degeneration of the heart more
than they do the mediocrity of the spirit, while the most perfect honesty can
hardly achieve true superiority.

I will consider the different causes of this peculiarity. I will begin by examining the cultivated woman within a monarchy and contrast her to the cultivated woman in a republic. My aim will be to outline the principal differences
of these two political contexts and show how these differences affect the

---

[12] [Staël quotes from the 1790 novel, *La chaumière indienne*, by Jacques-Henri Bernardin de
Saint-Pierre.]

destiny of women who aspire to achieve literary renown [*gloire*]. I will then consider, in a general manner, the sort of happiness that women who seek such renown can expect.

Within monarchies, women have to fear ridicule; within republics, they have to fear hatred.

It is the nature of things that in a monarchy, where proprieties are so subtly held onto, any extraordinary action, any attempt to move beyond one's place, must at first appear ridiculous. Whatever you have to do because of your social standing, because of your position in life, is always met with approval. But when you seek to do something for yourself, beyond the obligations of your position, you are immediately judged with severity. The natural jealousy which all humans have can only be appeased if you find a way to excuse your success—if I may put it this way—by portraying it as something that you had to do on account of your social standing or situation in life. But if you chose not to hide your success in this way, if people come to believe that your only motive is to distinguish yourself, you will annoy those who have the same ambitions and seek the same path.

Men can always hide their *amour-propre* [self-esteem] and their desire to be lauded under the appearance, or reality, of the strongest and most noble passions. But when women write, one always assumes that it is in order to display their abilities. Thus the public grants them approval only very reluctantly. It is precisely because the public thinks that women cannot do without its approval that approval is withheld. This holds in life more generally: it is almost always the case that as soon as someone thinks that you have a strong need for a person, that person will cool toward you. When a woman publishes a book, she makes herself entirely dependent on public opinion, and those who dispense this opinion make her profoundly aware of this dependence.

In addition to these general causes, which are equally present in all nations, there are distinctive circumstances that are specific to the French monarchy. The spirit of chivalry has been in some instances a hindrance to women's cultivation. This same spirit also inspires a greater distancing within women who cultivate their writing, turning them away from their primary interest, namely the sentiments of the heart. In men, an honorable delicacy could inspire repugnance for having to submit to public critique. This gives them even stronger reason to be displeased when they see those whom they are charged to protect—their wives, their sisters, their daughters—running the risk of being judged by the public, or giving the public the right to make them a topic of conversation.

A great talent triumphs above these considerations. Nonetheless, it is difficult for a woman to carry nobly the reputation of an author, to reconcile it with the independence of an elevated rank, and lose nothing in the process: her reputation, her dignity, her grace, the ease and the naturalness that should characterize her habitual manner and conduct.

Women are forgiven if they sacrifice their household occupations for the sake of worldly amusements, but if they take their study seriously, they are accused of pedantry. And if they do not immediately rise above the pleasantries that are leveled against them from all directions, these pleasantries manage to discourage talent, to dry up the very source of confidence and exaltation.

Some of these disadvantages cannot be found in republics, especially in a republic that seeks to advance enlightenment. Perhaps it would be natural in such a state that true literature would be the occupation of women, and that men would concern themselves solely with the heights of philosophy.

In all free nations, the education of women has been guided by the spirit of the constitution upon which they are founded. In Sparta, women were accustomed to the exercise of war; in Rome, they were expected to be austere and patriotic. If one agrees that the fundamental principles of the French republic are enlightenment and philosophy, it would be very reasonable to encourage women to cultivate their intellect [esprit] so that men could discuss with them those ideas that interest them.

Nevertheless, since the Revolution, men have decided that it is politically and morally useful to reduce women to the most absurd mediocrity. Men address women only in the most miserable language devoid of any delicacy or sense. For this reason, women no longer have any inducement to develop their reason. This has not, however, resulted in an improvement of morality. By inhibiting the expansion of ideas, we have not returned to the simplicity of an earlier time. Rather, the result of this inhibition is nothing other than a decrease in sense, a decrease in delicacy, a decrease in understanding public opinion, and a decrease in the means for dealing with solitude.

What holds for the various current dispositions of the understanding has come to pass in this instance: one always assumes that it is enlightenment that is the cause of our problems, and to repair this, reason is demoted. The problems of enlightenment can, however, only be addressed through greater enlightenment. After all, it is either the case that morality is a false idea, or that the more enlightened we are, the more we are attached to this idea.

If the French could give their women all the virtues of the English—their modest morals, their taste for solitude—they would do very well to prefer these qualities to those of a shining spirit. But what they would then find would be women who never read, who know nothing, who are not able to have a conversation with an interesting idea, with a felicitous expression, or with an elevated language. Furthermore, this happy ignorance would hardly lead them to focus on their homes. In fact, their children would become less dear to them, since they would no longer be capable of guiding their education. The world would at once become more necessary and more dangerous to them. Thus one would only be able to speak to them of love, but this love would not possess the delicacy which could have replaced morality.

Numerous advantages of great importance to the morality and happiness of a nation would be lost if women were rendered insipid or frivolous. Women would have far fewer means for calming the furious passions of men. They would no longer (as previously) maintain a command in matters of opinion. For women are the ones who animate everything that possesses humanity, generosity, and delicacy. Only those beings who are outside of politics and ambition, and who possess noble sentiments, can exhibit contempt toward base actions, recognize ingratitude, and know how to honor misfortunes. If, in France, women whose judgments matter and whose manners inspire true respect no longer existed, then the opinions of society would have no power over the actions of men.

I firmly believe that in the Ancien Régime, where opinion exercised a salutary authority, this authority was the work of women distinguished by their sense and character. We often refer to their eloquence—when they were inspired by a generous intention, when they pleaded against a cause of misfortune, or when they expressed a sentiment that required courage and displeased authority.

During the course of the Revolution, it was these same women who once again gave the greatest proof of their devotion and energy.

In France men can never become sufficiently republican to accept completely the independence and natural pride of women. There is no doubt that women had too much influence on public affairs during the Ancien Régime. But women are equally dangerous if they are unenlightened and lacking in reason. Their ascent would, in such a context, result in an increased taste for excessive wealth, an increase in undiscerning choices, [and] in choices lacking in delicacy. In this way they would debase, rather than exalt, those whom they like. Would the state gain anything from such an outcome? Should the very rare danger of meeting a woman whose superiority is in disproportion to the destiny of her sex deprive the French republic of the renown it enjoys in the art of pleasing and living in society? For, without women, society can be neither agreeable, nor interesting. Is it not the case that women who are deprived of sense or deprived of the capacity for conversation—which depends on the most distinguished education—harm society rather than embellish it? They introduce a kind of silliness and group gossip, an insipid gaiety, which will alienate all truly superior men and reduce the brilliant assemblies of Paris to nothing but young people who have nothing to do and young women who have nothing to say.

One can find these problems in all human affairs. They can undoubtedly be found in women's sense of superiority to men, in the *amour propre* of capable people, in the ambition of heroes, in the imprudence of great souls, in the irritability of independent characters, in the impetuousness of courage, etc. Mustn't we then do our best to resist these natural tendencies and ensure that all of our institutions are working against the corruption of our faculties?! It is hardly self-evident that this corruption would benefit either the dominion of the family or that of governments. Women without a sense for conversation or for literature are very good at finding a way out of their duties. And nations lacking in enlightenment do not know what they want, and thus change their leaders quite often.

The key to achieving reasonable goals, to developing social and political relations based on enduring foundations, is the enlightenment, instruction, and perfection of women and men, nations and individuals.

One could have fears for the spirit of women only on account of a delicate concern for their happiness. It is of course possible that by developing their reason, women would become aware of the hardships that are often part of their destiny. But this same reasoning would have to be applied to enlightenment more generally and its effect on the happiness of all of humanity—and this question appears to me to have already been decided.

If the situation of women within civil society is very imperfect, then we must work on improving—rather than stunting—the development of their spirit. It is valuable for both the enlightenment and the well-being of a society that women carefully develop their spirit and reason. Only one circumstance could lead to real unhappiness on account of a cultivated education: when a woman, who has achieved intellectual distinction, feels the need for renown.

But this risk should not prejudice society, since it would only seriously affect a small number of women, whom nature subjects to an unfortunate desire for superiority.

If a woman seduced by renown [*célébrité de l'esprit*] were to exist, and she wanted to achieve renown, how easy it would be to dissuade her from it, if we were to get to her in time! We would demonstrate to her the horrible destiny that would await her. Look at the social order, we would tell her, and you will soon see that it is deeply opposed to a woman who seeks to raise herself to the same level of renown as that of men.

As soon as a woman is identified as a distinguished person, the public becomes generally prejudiced against her. Those lacking in taste only judge according to certain common laws, to which they adhere without too much difficulty. At first, everything that lies outside of the ordinary displeases those who regard the course of life as nothing more than the preservation of mediocrity. A superior man already frightens them. But a superior woman, having herself opened up a new path, will astound and therefore disturb them even more. Nonetheless the talents of a distinguished man—who is almost always destined to a career—could become useful to those same people who ascribe the least significance to the charms of thought. A man of genius can become a powerful man, and from this perspective, the envious and the foolish will pay heed to him. A cultivated woman [*femme spirituelle*], however, is only called upon to speak to them about those things which interest them the least: novel ideas or elevated sentiments. Her fame is thus nothing but a tiring noise to them.

Celebrity [*la gloire*] can be condemned in a woman because it stands in stark contrast to her natural destiny. Austere virtue condemns celebrity even in that which is good in and of itself, insofar as renown is a deviation from perfect modesty. Cultivated men [*hommes d'esprit*], surprised to encounter rivals among women, do not know how to judge them—whether with the generosity of an adversary, or the indulgence of a protector. And in this new battle, they follow neither the laws of honor nor those of kindness.

If a woman were to achieve remarkable fame in a time of political dissent— the apex of misfortune—one is likely to think that her influence knows no limits, even if in fact she has none. She would be blamed for the actions of her friends and hated for everything that she loves. She—a defenseless object— would be attacked well before those whom one should really fear.

Nothing promotes vague assumptions more than the uncertain existence of a woman whose name is well known but whose life [*carrière*] is obscure. If a vain man inspires contempt, if a vile one ends up having to succumb to the weight of public scorn, if a mediocre man is rejected, they would all blame their fates on the mysterious power called woman. The ancients persuaded themselves that fate had thwarted their aims when they could not achieve them. In our day, *amour propre* explains our inability to achieve our aims by pointing the finger at secret causes, but it never looks at itself. And at times this secret cause may be well-known women.

Women have no means by which to demonstrate truth or shed light on their lives. While it is the public who hears scandal, it is intimate society alone who can discern the truth. How can a woman genuinely demonstrate the inaccuracy of false charges leveled against her? A man mired in scandal can respond to the world via his actions. He can say, "My life is a witness to whom you must also listen." But does a woman have this witness? [All she has are] some private virtues, some obscure services, some hidden sentiments in the narrow circle in which she moves, some writings which have made her known in countries where she does not live, in eras where she will no longer exist.

A man can, even in his writings, refute scandals of which he is the object. By contrast, a woman who defends herself will only incur further harm, her self-justification regarded as nothing but a new noise. Women feel that there is something in their nature which is pure and delicate, something which quickly withers under the gaze of the public. Spirit, talents, a passionate soul—all of these allow women to leave behind the clouds which usually envelop them. But women do not stop regretting leaving these clouds, as though they were their true refuge.

However distinguished they may be, women tremble at malevolence. Courageous in times of sorrow, they are nonetheless timid toward enmity. Thought exalts them, but their character remains fragile and sensitive. The majority of women whose higher faculties inspired in them the desire to become renowned are like Hermione dressed in the arms of combat—the soldiers see the helmet, the spears, the glowing feathers, and think they have just encountered a force. They launch a violent attack, and from the first shot they reach the heart.

These injustices do not only completely transform the happiness and well-being of a woman. They can also distance her from the objects of her greatest affections. Who knows whether a scandalous image may not also undercut true memories? Who knows if these scandals, after having torn apart a woman's life, do not also remain with her to her death, robbing her of those sensible regrets [*regrets sensibles*] which should accompany the memory of a loved woman?

In this account, I have only spoken of the injustice of men toward distinguished women. But isn't the injustice of women against women also something to fear? Don't women get secretly excited when a man displays malevolence toward [a distinguished woman]? Do women ever develop an alliance with a famous woman in order to encourage and defend her, to support her in her difficult path?[13]

But this is not all. Public opinion appears to free men of all their duties toward a woman if she is known to be a superior spirit. Men are allowed to be ungrateful, perfidious, and mean toward her, and public opinion will do nothing to avenge her. *Isn't she an extraordinary woman?* Everything is said in these words and the woman is abandoned to look after herself. She is left to struggle with her pain. The interest which inspires a woman, the power which safeguards a man, all of a sudden fail her. Like an untouchable in India, she is no longer admitted into any social classes, which regard her as being fit to live alone, an object of curiosity, maybe of envy, meriting only pity.

---

[13] [This topic—along with the problem of implicit and explicit bias—is further explored in *Corinne*, especially Corinne's letter.]

Kant

Kant lived to a very advanced age and never left Königsberg. There, in the midst of the northern ice, he spent his life meditating on the laws of human understanding. An indefatigable thirst for study led him to boundless knowledge. Sciences, languages, and literature were all familiar to him. He did not seek fame [*gloire*], which he did not enjoy until late in life, not having been aware of his renown before then. He was content with the silent pleasure of reflection. All alone, he contemplated his mind closely: the examination of his thoughts endowed him with a new strength in cultivating virtue, and although he never meddled with ardent passions, he knew how to provide weapons for those who were called to combat those passions.

With the exception of the Greeks, we have hardly any examples of such a strictly philosophical life, a life that answers to the good faith of the writer. And to this purest of good faith, we must add an acute and exacting understanding, which served to keep his genius in check when he tried to carry it too far. It seems to me that this is enough for us to judge, at least impartially, the perseverance of such a man.

Kant's first publications were several works in the natural sciences, and his wisdom in this branch of study was such that he was the first to predict the existence of the planet Uranus. After having discovered it, Herschel himself acknowledged that it was Kant who had announced its existence.[14] His treatise on the nature of human understanding, entitled the *Critique of Pure Reason*, appeared nearly thirty years ago,[15] and remained unknown for some time. But when at length the intellectual treasures that it contains were discovered, it produced such a sensation in Germany that almost everything that has appeared since, in literature as well as in philosophy, has been inspired by this work.

This treatise on human understanding was followed by the *Critique of Practical Reason*, which dealt with morals, and the *Critique of the Power of*

---

[14] [Sir Frederick William Herschel (1738–1822) was an English-German astronomer, who built a twenty-foot telescope with a twenty-inch aperture. This instrument allowed Herschel to observe fuzzy patches of light which he called nebulae. By the end of his career, Herschel had cataloged five thousand of these nebulae. Herschel's work inspired Kant to speculate on a number of issues in his 1755 *Universal Natural History and Theory of the Heavens*, including the existence of the planet Uranus. When Herschel's 1781 book announcing his own discovery of the planet was published in a German translation in Königsberg in 1791, an extract of Kant's 1755 text was published alongside it—at Kant's instigation.]

[15] [Kant's *Critique of Pure Reason* was published in 1781 (second edition 1787)].

Judgment, which had beauty as its subject.[16] The one theory serves as the foundation for the three treatises, which cover the laws of the intellect, the principles of virtue, and the contemplation of the beauty of nature and that of the arts.

I shall endeavor to give a sketch of the central ideas of this doctrine. In so doing I wish to emphasize that no matter how much care I take in attempting to explain Kant's doctrine clearly, in order for it to be properly understood, we must continue to pay careful attention to it. A prince, who was learning mathematics, grew impatient with the labor that its study required. "It is necessary," his instructor said, "for your royal highness to take pains to study in order to understand the science, for there is no royal road in mathematics." The French public, which has so many reasons to consider itself a prince, will permit me to suggest that there is no royal road in metaphysics, and that, in order to arrive at any theory, one needs to pass through the intermediate stages that the author himself followed in coming to the results that he sets out.

Materialist philosophy gave up human understanding to the empire of external objects, morals to personal interest, and reduced the beautiful to the agreeable. Kant wanted to re-establish fundamental truths and spontaneity in the mind [*âme*], conscience in morals, and the ideal in the arts. Let us examine how he satisfied these different ends.

At the time that the *Critique of Pure Reason* appeared, there were only two systems concerning human understanding among thinkers: Locke's, which attributed all our ideas to sensations; and that of Descartes and Leibniz, which attempted to demonstrate the spiritual nature of the activity of the mind, its free will, in short the doctrine of idealism. But these two philosophers rested their case on purely speculative demonstrations. In the previous chapter, I enumerated the problems that arise from these attempts at abstraction, which, if I may use the expression, inhibit the flow of blood in our veins so that at last our intellectual faculties alone reign with us.[17] When applied onto objects that cannot be grasped by reason alone [i.e., non-mathematical objects], the algebraic method leaves no lasting trace on the mind.[18] While

[16] [Kant's *Critique of Practical Reason* was published in 1787, and the *Critique of the Power of Judgment* was published in 1790.]

[17] [The preceding chapter of the third volume of *Germany*, which is titled "General Observations on Philosophy in Germany," contains a discussion as well as a critique of Leibniz. Staël argues that the fundamental problem is that Leibniz's philosophy is "founded solely on reasoning" rather than on immediate knowledge of the self (as in, for instance, Descartes or Fichte).]

[18] [In the preceding chapter on Leibniz, which discusses his reliance on the mathematical method, Staël writes that while "the knowledge of mathematics is useful in metaphysics," this sort of reasoning is "unsuitable when we attempt to apply it onto a subject that is in any way connected to sensibility."]

we are perusing these abstract philosophical writings, we believe that we understand them, but the arguments that once seemed so convincing very soon escape from memory.

If, wearied by these efforts, we were to confine ourselves to what can be known by the senses, our mind would come to grief. Would we have any idea of immortality when the forerunners of destruction are so deeply engraved on the faces of mortals, and living nature incessantly returns to dust? When all the senses speak of death, what slim hope can we have of resurrection? If we consulted only our sensations [*sensations*], what idea could we form of supreme goodness? So many afflictions battle to master our lives, so many hideous objects disfigure nature, that the unfortunate created being curses their existence a thousand times over before the last convulsion snatches it away. If we reject the testimony of the senses [*sens*], how will we be guided on earth? And yet, if we trust them alone, what enthusiasm, what morality, what religion is able to resist the repeated assaults to which pain and pleasure alternately expose us?

Reflection wandered in this immense uncertainty when Kant endeavored to trace the limits of the two empires, that of the senses and that of the mind [*âme*]: of external nature and intellectual nature. The strength of thought and the wisdom with which he mapped these limits were perhaps unprecedented. He recognized the boundaries that the eternal mysteries set to human understanding, and—what will perhaps be new to those who have only heard of Kant—there is no philosopher more averse, in numerous respects, to metaphysics: he made himself so deeply learned in this science so as to use the means it afforded him to demonstrate its insufficiency. We might say of him, like the new Curtius, that he threw himself into the gulf of abstraction only to fill it up.[19]

Locke fought victoriously against the doctrine of innate ideas, because he always represented ideas as making up a part of our experiential knowledge. The examination of pure reason, that is, the primordial faculties of which the intellect is composed, did not engage his attention. Leibniz, as we noted above, announced the sublime axiom that "there is nothing in the intellect which does not come from the senses, except the intellect itself." Kant

---

[19] [Marcus Curtius is a legendary Roman hero, who in 362 BCE, when a deep chasm suddenly opened in the Roman Forum but could not be filled, told the Romans that what was needed to fill it was a courageous citizen. Curtius rode into the pit on his horse, and it immediately closed. Afterward, the area was covered by a pond, which is known as Lacus Curtius. Kant makes reference to Curtius in *The Metaphysics of Morals*, arguing that although his suicide saved Rome, as suicide it remains immoral.]

acknowledged, as much as did Locke, that there are no innate ideas, but he endeavored to penetrate the meaning of the above axiom, by asking what the laws and feelings [*sentiments*] are that constitute the essence of the human mind, independently of all experience. The *Critique of Pure Reason* strives to demonstrate the nature of these laws and their area of application.

Skepticism, to which materialism almost always leads, was pursued so far that Hume ended up overturning the foundations of rationality in his search for arguments against the axiom "there is no effect without a cause." Such is the volatility of human nature that, when we fail to place the principle of all conviction at the center of the human mind, that incredulity which starts by attacking the existence of the moral world ends up also getting rid of the material world—which it first used to destroy the other.

Kant wanted to know whether the human understanding could attain absolute certainty, and he found this only in our necessary concepts, that is, in the laws of the understanding which are of such a nature that we cannot conceive anything to be otherwise than how those laws represent it.

The first level of the imperative forms of our mind is space and time. Kant demonstrates that all our perceptions come under these two forms, concluding that they are in us and not in objects, and hence that it is our understanding that provides external nature with laws, rather than the other way around. Geometry, which measures space, and arithmetic, which divides time, are completely certain sciences because they rest on the necessary forms of our understanding.

Truths acquired through experience are never absolutely certain. When we say "the sun rises every day," "all men are mortal," etc., the imagination could think to itself an exception to these truths, which experience alone makes us consider indubitable. However, the imagination cannot suppose anything which is not in space or time; and we cannot suppose those forms of our thought that we impose on things to be the result of habit (i.e., of the constant repetition of the same phenomena). Sensations may be doubtful, but the prism through which we receive them is immutable.

To this primitive intuition of space and time we must add, or rather give as a foundation, the principles of reasoning, without which we are unable to comprehend anything, and which are the laws of our understanding: the connection between causes and effects, unity and plurality, totality, possibility, reality, necessity, and so on.[20] Kant considers them all to be equally necessary concepts, and he only treats whatever can be immediately founded on these

[20] Kant gives the name *categories* to the necessary concepts of the understanding which he presents in the form of a table.

concepts as being real sciences, because it is in them [i.e., these concepts] alone that certainty can exist. The concepts of the understanding are effective only when they are applied through judgment onto external objects, in which case they are subject to error. But in themselves they are necessary, that is, we cannot do without them in any of our thoughts. It is impossible for us to think of anything outside the realms of cause and effect, of possibility, of quantity, etc. These concepts are as inherent in our conceptions as are space and time [in our apprehension]. We perceive [*apercevons*] nothing except through the medium of the immutable laws of our way of reasoning, and therefore these laws are located in ourselves, not outside us.

In German philosophy, ideas that have their origin in the nature of our reasoning and its faculties are called *subjective*, and all those ideas that have their origin in sensations are called *objective*. Whatever nomenclature we employ in this respect, it seems to me that the examination of our intellect agrees with the dominant thought in Kant, namely the distinction that he establishes between the forms of our understanding and the objects that we know by means of those forms. Moreover whether he adheres to abstract conceptions, or whether he appeals, in religion and morals, to sentiments which he also considers to be independent of experience, nothing is more illuminating than the line of demarcation that he traces between what comes to us via sensation and what belongs to the spontaneous action of our mind.

Some expressions in Kant have been misinterpreted; thus it has been claimed that he believed in a priori knowledge, that is, knowledge engraved on the mind before we have discovered it. Other German philosophers, closer to the system of Plato, have in fact thought that the form of the world was in the human understanding, and that one would not be able to conceive of the universe unless one had an innate image of it in oneself. But there is no question of this doctrine in Kant: he reduces the intellectual sciences to three, namely logic, metaphysics, and mathematics. By itself, logic teaches nothing. However, since it rests upon the laws of the human understanding, its principles are undeniable when abstractly considered. This science cannot lead to truth unless it is applied to ideas and things. Its principles are innate, and its application is experiential. As for metaphysics, Kant denies its existence, claiming that reasoning cannot go beyond the sphere of experience. Mathematics alone seems to him to depend immediately on the notions of space and time, i.e., upon the forms of our understanding anterior to experience. He sets out to show that mathematics is not simply analytic, but is a synthetic, positive, creative science, certain in itself without any need to appeal to experience to be assured of its truth. We may study in Kant's work the arguments that he uses to support this way of thinking, but at the very least it is the case that there is no one more averse to what is called the philosophy of dreamers, and that on the contrary he has a dry and didactic way of thinking, even though the aim of his doctrine is to save the human species from the degradation in which the spell of materialist philosophy has put it.

Far from rejecting experience, Kant considers our lives as being nothing other than the exercise of our innate faculties on externally derived knowledge. He believes that experience would be wholly chaotic without the rules of the understanding, but that these rules have as their sole object the elements of thought afforded by experience. It follows that metaphysics can teach us nothing beyond the limits of experience, and that it is to feeling alone that we should attribute our foreknowledge and our conviction about anything that goes beyond the visible world.

When one uses reason alone to establish religious truths, it becomes a pliable instrument, in that it can be used either to defend or attack these truths. For in this context we have no foothold in experience. Kant lines up arguments for and against human freedom, the immortality of the soul [âme], the limited or eternal duration of the world, and it is to feeling that he appeals to establish one or the other, because metaphysical demonstrations seem to him to be of equal strength on either side.[21] Perhaps he was wrong to push skeptical reasoning to such an extent, but it was in order to extinguish this skepticism with a greater degree of certainty, by removing certain questions from the abstract discussions that gave rise to skepticism in the first place.

Simply because Kant balanced arguments for and arguments against the great questions of metaphysics, it would be unjust to suspect the sincerity of his piety. On the contrary, it appears to me that there is candor in this way of presenting things. So few minds are able to understand rational arguments, and those who are able are disposed to quarrel with one another. As such it is a great service to religious faith to banish metaphysics from all questions that relate to the existence of God, to free will, and to the origin of good and evil.

Respectable people have suggested that we ought not to neglect any weapon, and that metaphysical arguments also ought to be deployed to persuade those over whom we have power. These arguments, however, lead to discussion, and discussion in turn leads to doubt on any subject.

---

[21] [Staël is referring to Kant's antinomies of reason.]

The greatest eras for the human race have always been those in which the truths of a certain class were uncontested in writing or discourse. The passions might have seduced them into culpable acts, but no one called into question the truths of that religion which was thereby disobeyed. Sophisms of every kind and the abuses of a certain philosophy have, in different countries and different ages, destroyed that noble security of belief which was then the source of devotion for heroes. Is it then not a fine idea for a philosopher to shut the door of the sanctuary to the very science which he professes, and to use all the power of abstraction to show that there are areas from which it ought to be banished?

Despots and fanatics have tried to prevent human reason from examining certain subjects, and reason has always burst these unjust fetters. But the limits which reason imposes on itself, far from enslaving it, give it a new strength, which always results from the authority of laws that are freely agreed to by those who are subject to them.

Deaf-mutes, before they were under the discipline of the Abbé Sicard,[22] might experience a full conviction of the existence of the Divinity. Many people are as far removed from those who think deeply as a deaf-mute is from other human beings, and still they are not any less able to experience (if we can be allowed this expression) within themselves primitive truths, because such truths spring from feeling.

In their physical study of the human, medical doctors recognize the principle that animates us, and yet no one knows what life is; and if anyone were to think about it, it would be easy to prove—as several Greek philosophers have done—that they do not live at all. It is the same with God, conscience, and free will. You must believe in them because you feel them: no argument will change this fact.

Anatomical study cannot be undertaken on a living body without destroying it. Analysis, when one tries to apply it to indivisible truths, destroys them, because its first attempts are directed against their unity. We need to divide our mind in two so that one half may contemplate the other. However this division takes place, it deprives our being of that sublime identity without which we would lack sufficient strength to believe in that which consciousness alone can affirm.

---

[22] [Roch-Amroise Cucurron Sicard (1742–1822) was a priest and principal of a school for the deaf, first in Bordeaux and then from 1789 in Paris.]

GERMAINE DE STAËL   45

Let a great number of people be assembled at a theater or some public place, and let some truth of reason, however general, be proposed to them. There will be as many different opinions formed as there are individuals gathered. But if any features showing a greatness of soul [âme] are recounted, it will be unanimously proclaimed that we have touched upon that instinct of the soul, which is as alive and powerful in our being as the instinct that preserves our existence.

By referring to feeling, which does not admit of doubt, and to the knowledge of transcendental truths in his endeavor to show that reasoning is only valuable when applied within the sphere of sensations, Kant is very far from regarding the power of feeling as illusory. Quite the contrary, he assigns it to the first rank in human nature; he makes conscience the innate principle of our moral existence; and the feeling of right and wrong is, on his account, the primordial law of the heart, just as space and time are of the understanding.

Has humanity not been led by reasoning to deny the existence of free will? And yet, even as we are convinced of this, do we not find ourselves surprised to experience esteem or dislike for the animals around us, on account of our belief that all beings express a spontaneous choice between good and evil?

The certainty of freedom that we possess is just the feeling that we have of it, and this freedom is the foundation of the doctrine of duty. For if humanity is free, we ought to be able to motivate ourselves sufficiently to combat the effects of external things, and to set our will against egoism. Duty is at one and the same time the demonstration and the guarantee of the metaphysical independence of the human being.

In the following chapters we shall examine Kant's arguments against a morality based on self-interest, and the sublime theory that he substitutes for this hypocritical sophism or perverse doctrine. Different opinions may be entertained regarding Kant's first work, the *Critique of Pure Reason*, because, having himself acknowledged reasoning to be insufficient and contradictory, he ought to have anticipated that it would be used against him. But it seems to me to be impossible not to read with respect his *Critique of Practical Reason*, as well as the other works that he has written on morality.

Not only are Kant's principles of morality austere and pure, as might be expected from a lack of philosophical compromise, but he also constantly connects the evidence of the heart with that of the understanding, and is quite happy to make his abstract theory on the nature of the understanding serve to support the simplest and most powerful feelings.

A conscience that has been developed from sensations may be stifled by them, while the dignity of duty is degraded if it is made to depend on external objects. Kant therefore constantly tries to show that a profound feeling of dignity is a necessary condition for our moral being, that is, the law by which it exists. The realm of sensations and the evil actions that they bring about can no more destroy in us our notions of good or evil than the idea of space and time can be changed through mistaken application. There is always, in whatever situation we are in, a power to react against circumstances, which springs from the depth of the soul [âme], and we feel that neither the laws of the understanding, nor moral freedom, nor conscience, are the result of experience.

In his treatise on the sublime and the beautiful, the *Critique of the Power of Judgment*, Kant applies to the pleasures of the imagination the system from which he has derived such fruitful deductions in the spheres of intelligence and feeling. Or, rather, he examines the same mind [âme], as manifested in the sciences, in morality, and in the fine arts. Kant holds that there are, in poetry and in those arts which, like poetry, are able to depict feelings by images, two kinds of beauty: one which may be referred to the temporal and to this life, the other to the eternal and the infinite.

Accordingly, one cannot say that what is infinite and eternal is unintelligible. It is the finite and the transient that one is often tempted to regard as a dream. For thought is unable to see any limits to anything, and being cannot be conceived as nothing. We cannot search the exact sciences in depth without encountering even there the infinite and the eternal. And the most evident things belong, under some descriptions, to this infinity and eternity as much as to sentiment and imagination.

Through the application of the feeling of infinity to the fine arts arises the system of ideal beauty, that is, of beauty considered not as the bringing together and imitation of whatever is most worthy in nature, but as the realization of an image of what our mind represents to itself. Materialist philosophers judge the beautiful according to the agreeableness of the impression that it causes, and therefore place it in the realm of sensations. Immaterialists, who ascribe everything to reason, see perfection in beauty, and they find there an analogy to the useful and the good, which they take to be the highest degrees of perfection. Kant rejects both of these accounts.

Beauty, considered simply as something agreeable, would be confined to the sphere of sensations, and would consequently be subject to differences in taste. It could never claim that universal recognition which is the true character of beauty. Beauty defined as perfection would require a form of judgment similar to that on which esteem is based. However, the enthusiasm that ought to be inspired by the beautiful belongs neither to sensations nor to judgment, but is an innate disposition, like the feeling of duty and those concepts essential to the understanding. We discover beauty when we see it, because it is the outward image of that ideal beauty, the type which exists in our intelligence. Differences in taste are appropriate to what is agreeable, for our sensations are the source of this kind of pleasure. But we must all admire what is beautiful, whether in art or in nature, because we have in our mind feelings of heavenly origin, which beauty awakens, and which excite enjoyment.

Kant passes from the theory of the beautiful to that of the sublime, and the second part of the "Critique of Aesthetic Judgment" is even more remarkable than the first: he makes the sublime consist in moral freedom, in a struggle between destiny and nature. Unlimited power causes us dread, greatness overwhelms us, yet by the power of our will we escape from our feeling of physical weakness. The power of destiny and the immensity of nature stand in endless opposition to the miserable dependence of creatures on the earth, but one spark of that sacred fire in our breasts triumphs over the universe, since with that one spark we are able to resist all the powers in the world that could act on us.

The first effect of the sublime is being overwhelmed, while the second is exaltation. When we contemplate a storm raising the waves of the sea, seeming to threaten both heaven and earth, at first terror takes possession of us, even though we may be free from personal danger. But when the clouds that have gathered burst over our heads, when all the fury of nature is displayed, one feels an inward energy that frees us from every fear, whether through the will or through resignation, whether through the exercise of one's moral freedom or through giving it up: and this consciousness of what is within us animates and encourages us.

When we hear of a generous action, when we hear of individuals who have faced great hardship in remaining faithful to their beliefs, without the smallest compromise, we are at first confused by the description of the miseries that they have suffered. But by degrees we regain our strength, and the sympathy that we feel—excited within us by this greatness of soul—makes us hope that we ourselves would be able to triumph over the miserable sensations of this life, in order to remain faithful, noble, and proud to our last day.

Furthermore, no one can define what—if I can put it in these terms—is at the summit of our existence: "Our self-respect is too great for us to be able to comprehend ourselves," says St. Augustine. Anyone who thought himself able to exhaust the simplest flower in contemplation must have a very poor imagination. How then could we arrive at the knowledge of everything that is included in the idea of the sublime?

I certainly don't flatter myself that, in a few pages, I have been able to give an account of a system which, over twenty years, has occupied all the thoughtful minds of Germany, but I hope to have said enough to show the general spirit of Kant's philosophy, and to enable me to explain, in the following chapters, the influence that it has had upon literature, the sciences, and morality.

In reconciling experimental and idealist philosophy, Kant has not subordinated the one to the other, but has instead empowered them both. Germany was threatened by that arid doctrine, which regarded any enthusiasm as an error and which classified as prejudiced those sentiments that form the consolations of our existence. For individuals who were both philosophical and poetical, who were both capable of study and of being uplifted, it was a great satisfaction to see all the fine affections of the mind defended with the rigor of the most abstract thinking. The force of the mind can never be in a negative state for long, that is, it cannot consist principally in a state of unbelief, in lack of understanding, in what it disdains. We must have a philosophy of belief, of enthusiasm, a philosophy that confirms by reason what feeling reveals to us.

Kant's adversaries have accused him of having merely repeated the arguments of the ancient idealists. They have claimed that the doctrine of the German philosopher was just an old system in a new language. But this criticism lacks foundation: there are not only new ideas but also a distinctive character in Kant's doctrine.

Kant's doctrine has the flavors of the philosophy of the eighteenth century, despite the fact that it was designed to refute the doctrines of that philosophy, because it is human nature to be caught up in the spirit of the age in which one lives, even when one's intention is to oppose it. The philosophy of Plato is more poetical than that of Kant, the philosophy of Malebranche more religious, but the great merit of the German philosopher has been to raise up moral dignity by setting all that is fine in the heart on the basis of a strongly argued theory. The opposition which some seek to establish between reason and feeling attempts to reduce reason to egoism and feeling to madness. By contrast, Kant, who seemed to have been destined to complete all the great intellectual alliances, made the mind a single focus in which all our faculties harmonize.

The polemical part of Kant's works, where he attacks the philosophy of the materialists, would be a masterpiece in its own right. That philosophy, which has become so deeply rooted in our minds, has led to so much irreligion and selfishness, such that one ought to regard those who have combated this pernicious system—by reviving the ideas of Plato, Descartes, and Leibniz—as benefactors to their country. But the philosophy of the new German school contains many ideas that are its own. It is thoroughly grounded in scientific knowledge, which has been increasing daily, and upon a singularly abstract and logical mode of reasoning. For although Kant criticizes the use of such reasoning in the examination of truths that fall outside the realm of experience, his writings in metaphysics demonstrate a power of mind that places him in the first rank of thinkers in that respect.

It cannot be denied that Kant's style, in his *Critique of Pure Reason*, deserves all the criticism that his opponents have directed against it. He has employed a terminology that is very difficult to understand, as well as tiresome neologisms. He lived alone with his thoughts and convinced himself that he needed new words for new ideas, even though these words already existed.

In those areas that are clear in themselves, Kant is frequently guided by a very obscure metaphysics, and it is only in those areas of thought where darkness generally prevails that he carries a luminous torch: like the Israelites, who were guided by a column of fire by night, and a pillar of cloud by day.

No one in France would take the trouble to study writings as suffused with difficulties as those of Kant, but he needs patient and persevering readers. Without a doubt, this was not the reason for his abusing their patience, but perhaps he would not have been able to search so deeply into the science of human understanding had he attached more importance to the choice of expressions that he employed in explaining it.

In his metaphysical treatises, he uses words as if they were arithmetical expressions, giving them whatever meaning he pleases without troubling himself with their customary meanings. This seems to me a great error, for the reader's attention is exhausted in trying to understand the language before arriving at the ideas, and what is known never serves as a step up to what is unknown.

Nevertheless, we must give Kant the credit he deserves, even as a writer, when he lays aside his scientific language. In his discussion of the arts, and even more so in the case of morality, his style is always perfectly clear, energetic, and simple. How excellent his doctrine then appears—in its expression of the sentiment of beauty and the love of duty, and in the force with which he separates them both from all calculations of interest or utility! How well he enables actions by their source, not by their success! In sum, what moral greatness does he grant to the human being—the exile from heaven, the prisoner upon the earth—when he examines us in ourselves or considers us in our relations to one another. So great an exile, so miserable a captive!

We could extract from Kant's writings many brilliant ideas on all subjects, and it is perhaps to this doctrine alone that even now we must look for conceptions that are both ingenious and novel, for the materialists' point of view no longer offers anything interesting or original. Cleverness in wit against what is serious, noble, and divine is left behind, and in the future it will be impossible to restore to humanity any of the qualities of youth except by returning to religion via the route of philosophy, and to feeling via reason.

On the Influence of the New Philosophy on the Sciences

There is no doubt that idealist philosophy leads to an increase in knowledge, and by encouraging the mind to turn back on itself, it strengthens its penetration into and perseverance in intellectual labor. But is this philosophy equally favorable to the sciences, which consist in the observation of nature? The following reflections are devoted to an examination of this question.

The progress of the sciences over the last century has generally been attributed to experimental philosophy; and, as observation is of great importance for this area, it has been believed that the more importance one attaches to external objects, the greater the certainty of reaching scientific truths. Yet the country of Kepler and Leibniz is not an object of disdain for its science.[23] The significant modern discoveries—gunpowder and the art of printing—have been made by the Germans. However, the tendency in Germany has always been toward idealism.

Bacon compared speculative philosophy to the lark that rises into the sky and descends again without bringing back anything from its flight; and experimental philosophy to the falcon, that soars high but returns with its prey.[24]

In our day, Bacon would perhaps have been aware of the disadvantages of a purely experimental philosophy. It has turned thought into sensation, morality into self-interest, and nature into mechanism, for it tends to degrade everything. The Germans have fought against its influence in both the physical sciences and the sciences of a higher order. For while submitting nature to observation, they consider the phenomena of nature in general as something vast and animated [*animée*]. There is always a presumption in favor of a view that bases its investigations on the imagination, for in the sublime conception of the universe everything tells us that the beautiful is also the true.

The new philosophy has already exerted its influence in a number of ways on the physical sciences in Germany. First, that spirit of universality that I have already remarked on in literary and philosophical figures is also evident in scientists. Humboldt, as an exact observer, relates the voyages in which he braved dangers as a gallant knight, and his writings have been

---

[23] [Johannes Kepler (1571–1630), German astronomer, mathematician, and theologian, was most well known for his laws of planetary motion.]

[24] [Francis Bacon (1561–1626) was an English philosopher, the attorney general of England, and a critic of mathematical philosophy. His experimental methodology is credited for the development of the scientific method.]

of equal interest to natural philosophers and poets.[25] Schelling, Baader, Schubert, among others, have all published works in which the sciences are presented from a point of view that engages both our reflective thought and our imagination.[26] Furthermore, well before the existence of modern metaphysicians, Kepler and Haller were able to observe and divine nature at the same time.[27]

The attractions of society are so great in France that it does not allow people much time for work. Consequently it is natural not to place too much confidence in those who try to combine many different types of study. But in a country where one's whole life can be given over to contemplation, it is reasonable to pursue many kinds of study, subsequently confining one's attention to those one prefers; though it is perhaps impossible to gain a thorough understanding of one science without touching upon all of them. Sir Humphry Davy, now the premier chemist in England, cultivates letters with as much enthusiasm as success.[28] Literature throws light on the sciences as the sciences throw light on literature, and the connection that exists between everything in nature must have a place in the realm of ideas.

The universality of knowledge necessarily leads to the desire to discover the general laws of the physical realm. The Germans descend from theory to experience whereas the French ascend from experience to theory. In literature the French reproach the Germans for having no beauty except in the detail of their work and for failing to understand the composition of the work. The Germans reproach the French for only considering particular facts in the sciences and failing to refer them to a system. This is the principal difference between German and French scientists.

In fact, were it possible to discover the principles governing the universe, there can be no doubt that this would be the point from which we should start, i.e., by studying everything that can be derived from them. But we

---

[25] [Staël is speaking of Alexander von Humboldt's voyage to South America (1799–1804). Humboldt writes of his voyage in *Personal Narrative of Travels to the Equinoctial Regions of America, during the Years 1799–1804*, which he coauthored with Aimé Bonpland, the French scientist with whom he traveled, and which was originally published in French in three volumes between 1814 and 1825 under the title *Relation historique du voyage aux régions équinoxiales du nouveau continent.*]

[26] [Friedrich Schelling (1775–1854) was a German philosopher who composed three works in the philosophy of nature between 1797 and 1799; Franz von Baader (1765–1841) was a physician, engineer, and philosopher whose philosophy of nature was influenced by Schelling's; Gotthilf Heinrich von Schubert (1780–1860) was also a physician and philosopher influenced by Schelling. Women philosophers interested in Schelling's philosophy of nature included Karoline von Günderrode.]

[27] [Albrecht von Haller (1708–1777) was a Swiss anatomist, naturalist, physiologist, and poet.]

[28] [Davy (1778–1829) was a chemist (who isolated elements for the first time) as well as a poet.]

know very little of the whole, and what we know we gained from the details. Nature, for human beings, is like the scattered leaves of Sibyl, out of which no one has been able to compose a book to this day. Nevertheless, German scientists, who are at the same time philosophers, show a prodigious interest in contemplating the phenomena of the world. They do not examine nature fortuitously, following the accidental course of their observations, but they use reflection to predict what observation must confirm.

Two great general ideas serve to guide them in the study of the sciences: the one, that the universe is made on the model of the human soul; the other, that the analogy between the parts of the universe and the whole is such that the same idea is constantly reflected from the whole to all the parts and from every part to the whole.

It is a fine conception that seeks to discover the resemblance between the laws of human understanding and those of nature, and to regard the physical world as the moral one in relief. If the same genius were able to compose the *Iliad*, and to carve, as Phidias did, the sculpture of Jupiter so as to resemble the Jupiter of the poet, then why should the supreme intelligence, who has formed both nature and the soul, not have made the one the symbol of the other?[29] There is no vain flight of the imagination in these continual metaphors, which help us to compare our feelings with external phenomena: sadness with the clouded heavens, composure with silver moonlight, anger with the stormy sea. They express the same thought of the creator translated into two different languages, the one serving to interpret the other. Almost all the axioms of physics correspond to the axioms of morals. This kind of parallel progress can be perceived between the world and the mind, and indicates a great mystery. All minds would be struck by it if positive discoveries had been drawn from it. But the uncertain luster that comes from it still carries our views to a great distance.

The analogies between the different elements of external nature together constitute the supreme law of creation: variety in unity, unity in variety. What is more astonishing, for example, than the relation between sounds and shapes, and between sounds and colors? A German, Chladni, has lately

---

[29] [Phidias (480–430 BCE) was a Greek sculptor, painter, and architect, whose statue of Zeus (i.e., Jupiter) at Olympia was considered to be one of the Seven Wonders of the ancient world. According to legend, when Phidias was asked what inspired him, he replied that it was the depiction of Zeus in Book 1 of Homer's *Iliad*. Staël's point is that if Phidias had been inspired by Homer's lines, then the two portraits of Zeus (Jupiter) are connected (one functions as the inspiration of the other). In turn, if art works are connected in this way, might it not also be fathomable that other productions are also connected—for instance, the productions of nature and those of the mind?]

proved by experiment that sound vibrations put grains of sand in motion on a glass plate in such a way that, when the tones are pure, the sand is arranged into regular forms, and when the tone is discordant, there is no symmetry in the shapes traced.[30] Saunderson, who was blind from birth, said that in his mind the color scarlet was like the sound of a trumpet, and a scientist wanted to make a harpsichord for the eyes, which we might imitate, through the harmony of colors, the pleasure excited by music.[31]

We incessantly compare painting and music, because the motions that we experience reveal analogies where cold observation would only have perceived differences. Every plant, every flower, contains within it the entire system of the universe. One instant of life conceals eternity within it. The most feeble atom is a world, and the world itself is perhaps only an atom. Every part of the universe appears to be a mirror in which the whole of creation is represented, and we do not know whether it is thought, which always remains the same, or form, which is always different, that is most worthy of our admiration.

One can divide the scientists [*savans*] among the Germans into two classes: those who devote themselves wholly to observation, and those who claim the honor of predicting the secrets of nature. Of the former, first mention must go to Werner,[32] who has drawn from mineralogy the formation of the earth and historical epochs; Herschel and Schroeter,[33] who are constantly making new discoveries in the heavens; the calculating astronomers such as Zach and Bode;[34] the great chemists such as Klaproth and

[30] [Ernst Chladni (1756–1827) was a German physicist and musician, who is known for his research on vibrating plates and for calculating the speed of sound on different glasses.]

[31] [Though this particular example of the rare phenomenon of synesthesia—in which a stimulus (e.g., a sound) evokes a different, unrelated stimulus (a color)—was already used by Locke in the *Essay Concerning Human Understanding* (1690), it was Staël who revealed the identity of the blind man as the famous English mathematician Nicholas Saunderson (1682–1739), thereby giving substance to what might otherwise seem like an invented scenario. See Erika von Erhardt-Siebold, "Harmony of the Senses in English, German, and French Romanticism," *PMLA* 47, no. 2 (1932): 577–592.]

[32] [Abraham Gottlob Werner (1749–1817), was a German geologist who in the eighteenth century was most well known for his theory that rocks are formed from crystallization of minerals in the oceans (Neptunism) and his demonstration of geological succession in rocks. Werner was an inspector and teacher at the Freiberg Mining Academy, and his students included Friedrich von Hardenberg (Novalis) and Alexander von Humboldt.]

[33] [For Herschel, see note 14 above; Johann Hieronymus Schroeter (1745–1816) was a German astronomer who drew extensive detailed maps of the physical surface of the moon.]

[34] [Franz Xaver von Zach (1754–1832) was a German-Hungarian astronomer who played a significant role in stimulating German astronomers to look for a planet between Mars and Jupiter—a search that was originally motivated by Johann Elert Bode's (1747–1826) claim that the mathematical law of planetary spacing (proposed by Titius) required that there be a planet in that space. The search resulted in the discovery of the asteroids. Bode was himself involved in the discovery of Uranus in 1781.]

Bucholz;[35] and in the class of philosophical naturalists we must include Schelling, Ritter, Baader, Steffens, etc.[36] The most distinguished geniuses of these two classes approach and understand one another, because the philosophical naturalists are not able to deny experience, and the profound observers do not deny the possible results of sublime contemplations.

Attraction and impetus have already been the subject of novel inquiry, and they have successfully been applied to chemical affinities. Light, considered as an intermediary between matter and mind, has initiated several very philosophical insights. Goethe's work on color is highly spoken of.[37] In short, throughout Germany emulation is excited by the desire and the hope of uniting experimental and speculative philosophy, thereby enlarging our knowledge of humanity and of nature.

Intellectual idealism makes the will, which is the soul, the center of everything. By contrast, the principle of physical idealism is life. One reaches the highest degree of analysis in chemistry, as one does in reasoning; however, life escapes us in chemistry, as does feeling in reasoning. A French writer has claimed that thought was just "a material product of the brain."[38] Another scientist has said that when we become more advanced in chemistry we will be able to determine "how life comes about." The one insults nature, the other the soul.

"We must grasp what is incomprehensible as such," said Fichte. This singular remark contains a profound meaning: we must sense and recognize what will forever remain inaccessible to analysis, but that the soaring flight of thought alone can approach.

We find in nature three distinct modes of existence: vegetation, irritability, and sensitivity.[39] Plants, animals, and human beings are included in these

---

[35] [Martin Heinrich Klaproth (1743–1817), was a German chemist known for his discovery of uranium; Christian Friedrich Bucholz (1770–1818) was a German pharmacist and chemist.]

[36] [Schelling was the first among these philosophers to develop the philosophy of nature, i.e., *Naturphilosophie* (see n. 26 above). Johann Wilhelm Ritter (1776–1810) was a German chemist, physicist, and philosopher, with whom Schelling collaborated and who adopted Schelling's schema for understanding nature. Baader (see n. 26 above) became an increasingly significant collaborator for Schelling after 1806. Henrik Steffens (1773–1845) was a mineralogist who studied with Schelling in Jena. He is known for his work in the philosophy of nature, but also in other areas.]

[37] [*Theory of Colors* (1810) by Johann Wolfgang von Goethe (1749–1832).]

[38] [Staël is likely referring to Julien Offray de La Mettrie (1709–1751), and in particular his book *Man a Machine* (1747).]

[39] [Staël is likely referring to the different "drives" which, in the eighteenth century, were used to understand and distinguish living beings from nonliving beings. Johann Blumenbach (1752–1840), for instance, regards irritability and sensitivity as vital powers of living beings and by "vegetative" functions understands the processes of nutrition, secretion, and digestion. See Nicholas Jardine,

three types of life, and if one chose to apply to individuals of our species this ingenious division, we would recognize it in their different characters. Some vegetate like plants, others enjoy themselves or are stimulated in the way animals are, whereas the most noble possess and develop in themselves the qualities that distinguish our human nature. However this may be, volition, which is life, and life, which is also volition, comprehend the whole secret of the universe and of ourselves, and as we can neither deny nor explain this secret we must of necessity arrive at it by a kind of divination.

What an exertion it would be to overturn, with a lever made on the model of an arm, the weight lifted up by the arm! Do we not every day see anger, or some other emotion, augmenting, as if by a miracle, the power of the human body? What is this mysterious power of nature that manifests itself in the human will, and how, without studying its causes and effects, can we make any important discovery in the theory of physical forces?

The doctrine of the Scottish writer, Brown, which has been analyzed more profoundly in Germany than elsewhere, is based on this same system of central action and unity which has such fruitful consequences.[40] Brown believed that the state of suffering and the state of health did not depend on partial maladies but on the intensity of the vital principle, which is diminished or augmented depending on the vicissitudes of existence.

Among English scientists, there is no one save Hartley and his disciple Priestley who regarded metaphysics as physics, interpreting it from a wholly materialist point of view.[41] It will be said that physics can only be materialist. However, I do not hold that view. Those who make the soul itself into a passive being have the strongest reason to exclude any spontaneous action of the human will from the positive sciences, and yet there are many instances in which this volition acts on the intensity of life, and life on matter. The principle of existence is, as it were, intermediary between physics and morals, a power that cannot be calculated; but nor can it be denied unless we are ignorant of what constitutes animated nature and reduce its laws to those of mechanism.

The Scenes of Inquiry: On the Reality of Questions in the Sciences (Oxford: Oxford University Press, 1991), 27.]

[40] [John Brown (1735–1788) was a Scottish physician who influenced, among others, Schelling.]
[41] [David Hartley (1705–1757) was an English philosopher and a close friend of Joseph Priestley (1733–1804), who discovered oxygen.]

However we may judge the system of Dr. Gall,[42] he commands the respect of all scientists for his anatomical studies and discoveries, and if we consider the organs of thought as distinct from thought itself, that is, [as distinct] from the faculties that it employs, it seems to me that we can admit memory and the power of calculation, the aptitude for this or that science, the talent for a particular art, in short everything that the understanding uses as an instrument, to depend to some extent on the structure of the brain. If there exists a graduated scale between a stone and human life, then there must be certain faculties in us that partake of body and soul at the same time, and among these are memory and the power of calculation, the most physical of our intellectual and the most intellectual of our physical faculties. But the moment we attribute an influence over our moral qualities to the structure of the brain we begin to err, for the will is absolutely independent of our physical faculties: it is in the purely intellectual action of this will that conscience consists, and conscience is and ought to be free from the influence of corporeal organization.

A very talented young physician, Koreff,[43] has already attracted the attention of those who understand his work in virtue of some entirely new observations on the principle of life, and in relation to the causes of insanity. All of this intellectual activity [*mouvement dans les esprits*] portends a revolution of some kind in the very way in which the sciences are studied. As yet, it is not possible to foresee the results of this change, but we may rightly assert that if the Germans use imagination to guide them, they spare themselves no labor, or research, or study; and that they unite, to the greatest extent possible, two qualities which seem to preclude one another, namely patience and enthusiasm.

Some German scientists, pursuing their physical idealism too far, challenge the truth of the axiom that there is no action at a distance.[44] They wish, on the contrary, to re-establish spontaneous motion throughout nature. They reject the hypothesis of fluids [vortices], the effects of which depend in many respects on mechanical forces, pressing and compressing one another without external guidance.

---

[42] [Franz Joseph Gall (1758–1828) was a German physician and anatomist who is regarded as the founder of phrenology.]

[43] [David Ferdinand Koreff (1783–1851) was a German physician and a professor of animal magnetism.]

[44] [Isaac Newton rejected the idea that action at a distance can offer an explanation of gravity, and Newtonians generally rejected action at a distance as absurd. Roy Porter, ed., *The Cambridge History of Science*, Vol. 4, *Eighteenth Century* (Cambridge: Cambridge University Press, 2003), 273.]

Those who consider nature as an intelligence do not give to this word the same meaning that is customarily given to it. For human thought consists in the faculty of turning in on itself, and the intelligence of nature advances linearly, like animal instinct. Thought has self-possession, for it can judge itself, whereas intelligence without reflection is a power that is always attracted to external things. When nature performs the work of crystallization according to the most regular shapes, it does not follow that it thereby understands mathematics; or, at all events, nature is ignorant of her own knowledge, lacking self-consciousness. German scientists attribute a certain individual originality to physical forces, yet it appears, from their way of presenting some of the phenomena of animal magnetism, that the human will, without any external action, exerts a great influence over matter, and especially over metals.

Pascal said that "astrologers and alchemists have principles, but they abuse them."[45] In earlier times, there were perhaps more intimate relations between human beings and the natural world than there are now. The mysteries of Eleusis, the cult of the Egyptians, the system of emanations of the Indians, the worship of the elements and the sun by the Persians, the harmony of numbers at the basis of the Pythagorean doctrine: these are vestiges of some peculiar attraction which united the human being with the universe.

By strengthening the power of reflection, spirituality has further separated human beings from physical influences, and the Reformation, by carrying the tendency toward analysis still further, has guarded reason against the first impressions of the imagination. When they seek to awaken the inspirations of nature by the light of thought, the Germans are aspiring to the true perfection of the human mind.

Every day, experience leads scientists to recognize phenomena which they had ceased to believe because they were mixed with superstitions and had been the subject of portents. The ancients related that stones fell from heaven, and now the accuracy of this fact, which had been denied, has been established. They spoke of showers red as blood, and of terrestrial lightning: we have lately been convinced of the truth of these reports.

Astronomy and music are the science and art which have been known since antiquity: why should not sounds and the stars be connected by relations

---

[45] [Blaise Pascal (1623–1662) was a French mathematician, physicist, and philosopher who developed a philosophical argument concerning the existence of God, often referred to as "Pascal's wager."]

which the ancients perceived, and which we may yet rediscover? Pythagoras maintained that the distance between the planets was in proportion to that of the seven strings of the lyre; and it is said that he predicted the new planet that has been found between Mars and Jupiter.[46] It seems that he was not ignorant of the true system of the heavens, with the sun stationary, since Copernicus offers support of his own view on the opinion of Pythagoras, as reported by Cicero. How then did these astonishing discoveries arise without the aid of experience or the new devices which the moderns possess? The answer is that the ancients proceeded boldly, lit by the sun of genius. They used reason, the resting place of the human intellect, but they also consulted the imagination, the priestess of nature.

That which we call error and superstition may perhaps depend on laws of the universe which are unknown to us. The relations between planets and metals, the influence of these relations, even oracles and presages—may they not be caused by occult powers which we are unable to grasp?[47] And who knows whether there might be a germ of truth hidden under every fable, and under every belief which has been stigmatized under the rubric of madness? This certainly does not imply that we should renounce the experimental method, which is so necessary in the sciences. But why not develop—as a supreme guide for this method—a more encompassing philosophy, one that would embrace the universe in its totality, and which would not scorn *the nocturnal side of nature*, expecting instead to illuminate it?

It will be replied that it is the responsibility of poetry to consider the physical world in this way. But we can arrive at no certain knowledge except through experience, and while those things not susceptible to demonstration may amuse the mind, they cannot facilitate progress. Doubtless the French are correct in recommending to the Germans that they respect experience, but they are mistaken in ridiculing the presages of reflection, which will perhaps later be confirmed by the knowledge of facts. Most great discoveries initially appeared absurd, and a genius will never do anything if he fears being exposed to ridicule. Ridicule is impotent when it is disdained and

---

[46] M. Prevost, professor of philosophy in Geneva, has published on this subject in a brochure of great interest. This philosopher is as known in Europe as he is in his own country. [See also n. 34 above.]

[47] [Newton regarded gravity as an "occult power," and the use of the term to describe unknown causes became widespread in the eighteenth century. See Charles T. Wolfe, "On the Role of Newtonian Analogies in Eighteenth-Century Life Science: Vitalism and Provisionally Inexplicable Explicative Devices," in *Newton and Empiricism*, ed. Zvi Biener and Eric Schliesser (Oxford: Oxford University Press, 2014), 223–261.]

increases its influence in proportion to how much it is feared. We see in fairy tales the phantoms that oppose themselves to the work of knights and that torment them until the knights have passed beyond them. Then all the spells vanish, and the rich countryside opens up before their sight. Envy and mediocrity also have their spells, but we ought to march onward toward the truth without worrying about the seeming obstacles that impede our progress.

When Kepler discovered the harmonic laws that regulate the motion of the heavenly bodies, he expressed his joy thus: "At length, eighteen months after a first dawn shone on me, but a very few days after I saw the pure rays of sublime truths, nothing now holds me back. I dare to yield myself up to my divine enthusiasm; I dare to taunt mortals by acknowledging that I have turned terrestrial science to advantage, that I am stealing the golden vessels of the Egyptians in order to erect a temple to the living God. If you forgive me, I shall rejoice; if you blame me, I shall endure it. The die is cast, I have written the book. Whether it is to be read by the people of the present or of the future is of no consequence. Let it await its reader for a hundred years, if God himself had waited for one to study him such as myself."[48] This bold expression of proud enthusiasm reveals the external force of genius.

Goethe has remarked on the perfectibility of human understanding in wise words: "It is always advancing, but in a spiral motion."[49] This comparison is all the more appropriate in that the improvement of humanity seems to move backward in many eras, and then returns upon its path, having advanced some degrees further. There are moments when skepticism is necessary to the progress of the sciences, and there are others when, as Hemsterhuis says, "the wondrous spirit must supersede the geometrical one."[50] When a person is swallowed up, or rather reduced to dust, by unbelief, this wondrous spirit [*l'esprit*] alone is able to restore to the mind [*âme*] the power of admiration, without which we cannot understand nature.

The theory of the sciences in Germany has given to those who possess genius an impulse like that which metaphysics had excited in the study of the mind: life holds the same rank in physical phenomena that the will has in the moral order. If the relations between these two systems have led certain

---

[48] [Reported to have been said by Kepler after discovering the third of his planetary laws. See Max Kasper, *Kepler*, ed. and trans. C. Doris Hellman (London: Dover, 1959), 267.]

[49] [A statement Goethe makes about the way in which science proceeds in the "Historical" part of his *Theory of Colors*.]

[50] [Franz Hemsterhuis (1721–1790) was a Dutch philosopher who was influenced by Plato and Platonism, and who in turn influenced a number of romantic thinkers, including Hardenberg (Novalis) and Günderrode.]

persons to forbid them both, there are those who will discover in these relations the twofold guarantee of the same truth. It is at least certain that the
interest of the sciences will be singularly increased by reconnecting the sciences to some fundamental ideas. If the sciences communicated with each
other on philosophical questions concerning the [nature of the] universe,
and if this philosophical inquiry into the universe, instead of being abstract,
were animated by an inexhaustible source of feeling, then poets might find in
the sciences many useful ideas.

The universe is more like a poem than a machine, and if, in order to form
a conception of the universe, we were compelled to avail ourselves of either
the imagination or of a mathematical spirit, the imagination would bring us
closer to the truth. But let me repeat again that this is not a choice that we
must make, because it is the totality of our moral being that ought to be employed in a meditation of such an important kind.

The new system of physics, which in Germany serves to guide experimental physics, can only be judged by its results. We need to see whether it
will lead the mind to new notable discoveries. But what cannot be denied are
the connections that it has demonstrated between the different branches of
study. One usually studies the one or the other because one's preoccupation
differs and the two are mutually antagonistic. The scholar has nothing to say
to the poet, the poet to the natural philosopher, and even those concerned
with the sciences, if they are differently occupied, will avoid one another,
taking no interest in what falls outside their own concerns. This would not
happen if a central philosophy established connections of a sublime nature
between all our thoughts. Scientists penetrate nature with the aid of the imagination. Poets discover in the sciences the true beauties of nature. Erudites
enrich poetry with their stores of recollection [*souvenirs*], and scientists with
analogies.

Presented as isolated and as a domain alien to the soul, the sciences do not
attract the exalted mind. With some honorable exceptions, the majority of
those who have devoted themselves to the sciences have provided our times
with a bias toward calculation, which is very useful for discerning what is the
strongest in every case. German philosophy introduces the physical sciences
into that universal sphere of ideas, where both the most minute observations
and the most important results are held together in the interests of the whole.

2

Karoline von Günderrode (1780–1806)

Introduction

Karoline von Günderrode (1780–1806) was a writer, philosopher, and poet who made distinctive contributions to German romanticism and idealism. In her writings, Günderrode engaged with some of the most discussed philosophical issues of the time, including the question concerning the "human vocation" (e.g., what is the meaning of human life, and what should human beings aspire to achieve?), and the related questions of (female) self-determination, autonomy, and cross-cultural understanding. In thinking through these matters, Günderrode reached conclusions that departed from those of her (male) contemporaries. Most strikingly, she argued that the human vocation must not be understood in purely human terms—i.e., in terms of what is good for human beings—but must also take into account the larger community of which human beings are part: the earth and all its inhabitants.

During her lifetime, Günderrode was primarily known as a poet and playwright, whose writings were praised not only by friends and collaborators but also by significant cultural figures, including Goethe.[1] But it was only after her suicide that Günderrode gained widespread attention and fame: first through Bettina Brentano von Arnim's 1840 publication of their correspondence (see the introduction to chapter 3 in this volume) and more recently through Christa Wolf's 1979 novel, *No Place on Earth*.[2] The novel,

---

[1] In a letter from 1804, Goethe writes that Günderrode's poems are "really a peculiar phenomenon and demand a review." Karoline von Günderrode, *"Ich Sende Dir ein zärtliches Pfand." Die Briefe der Karoline von Günderrode*, ed. Birgit Weißenborn (Frankfurt am Main: Insel Verlag, 1992), 379. As Renata Fuchs notes, this remark sparked a heated discussion between Günderrode's supporters, including Friedrich Creuzer and Friedrich Carl von Savigny, and her critics, in particular Clemens Brentano and his wife, Sophie Mereau-Brentano. Renata Fuchs, *" 'Dann ist und bleibt eine Korrespondenz Lebendig'*: Romantic Dialogue in the Letters and Works of Rahel Varnhagen, Bettina Brentano von Arnim, and Karoline von Günderrode" (PhD diss., University of Illinois–Urbana Champagne, 2015), 194 n792. For a summary of the reception of Günderrode's works, see Anna C. Ezekiel, "Introduction," in Karoline von Günderrode, *Poetic Fragments* (Albany: SUNY Press, 2016), 1–37, here 3.

[2] Christa Wolf, *No Place on Earth*, trans. Jan van Huerck (New York: Farrar Straus Giroux, 1982).

Women Philosophers in the Long Nineteenth Century. Dalia Nassar and Kristin Gjesdal, Oxford University Press.
© Oxford University Press 2021. DOI: 10.1093/oso/9780190868031.003.0004

which imagines a meeting between Günderrode and her contemporary, the writer Heinrich von Kleist, is partly responsible for the popular interest in Günderrode's life and legacy today.[3]

Like Germaine de Staël, Günderrode was a critic of the fact that bourgeois society offered no space for intellectual women and their aspirations. While in the late eighteenth century it had become possible for women to publish, they often felt forced to limit themselves to a particular style (pleasing or associative) and a particular genre (letters, novels, drama, and poetry) in order to find a publisher. Women who had immersed themselves in philosophy and composed philosophical essays and creative works inspired by philosophical questions faced a number of obstacles on the way to publication—and often ended up publishing their works under (male) pseudonyms. Günderrode published a number of works under the pseudonym "Tian."

While Günderrode received assistance from (male) friends,[4] these friends also at times questioned her desire to publish particular pieces and in one case outright hindered publication. The philologist and historian Friedrich Creuzer (1771–1858)—who became Günderrode's lover in 1804 and was often the first to read and comment on her writings—hindered the publication of "Idea of the Earth." This is particularly unfortunate, not only because Creuzer himself regarded the essay as a milestone in Günderrode's thinking[5] but also because it has recently come to be widely regarded as one of Günderrode's most significant philosophical contributions.[6]

Günderrode grew up in an intellectually stimulating and highly literate environment. Her mother, Louise von Günderrode, was herself a poet and writer—though she published under a pseudonym—and was interested in philosophy, particularly in the writings of Johann Gottlieb Fichte. It was, in fact, through her mother that Günderrode first became familiar with Fichte's thought. Though of aristocratic lineage, Günderrode's family was not well-off,

---

[3] In addition, Wolf published an edited volume of Günderrode's works and letters in 1979. Christa Wolf, *Karoline von Günderrode. Der Schatten eines Traumes* (Darmstadt: Luchterhand, 1979).

[4] These include Sophie von La Roche, who published Günderrode's "Story of a Brahman" in 1805, and Lisette Nees von Esenbeck, as well as Bettina Brentano von Arnim and her sister Gunda Brentano. In addition, Christian Nees von Esenbeck, Friedrich Creuzer and Friedrich Carl von Savigny supported Günderrode by offering editorial advice and helping her find suitable publishers.

[5] As Creuzer puts it in a letter from December 1805, "It's been a long time since I've liked anything as much as I like your 'Idea of the Earth.' " Friedrich Creuzer and Karoline von Günderrode, *Friedrich Creuzer und Karoline von Günderode. Briefe und Dichtungen*, ed. Erwin Rohde (Heidelberg: Winter, 1896), 78.

[6] Wolfgang Westphal, for instance, argues that "Idea of the Earth" contains the kernel of Günderrode's "thinking about nature." Wolfgang Westphal, *Karoline von Günderrode und "Naturdenken um 1800"* (Essen: Blaue Eule, 1993), 99.

and as an adult, Günderrode lived in a Protestant convent for poor aristocratic women in Frankfurt am Main. Günderrode's limited resources meant that she, unlike many of her friends, could not easily travel and participate in cultural life in Berlin, Heidelberg, or Jena. Nonetheless, her connections to the most exciting intellectual movements of her time were solidified through her personal associations, her study, and her publications.

On a personal level, Günderrode was a close friend of the Brentanos: Bettina Brentano (1785–1859), as well as her older sister Gunda Brentano (1780–1863) and their brother, the poet Clemens Brentano (1778–1842). Günderrode's own brother, Hector, was a student of Creuzer and of the historian and jurist Friedrich Carl von Savigny (1779–1861), who became a strong supporter of Günderrode's writing.

On an intellectual level, Günderrode studied philosophy, world religions and mythologies, ancient languages (especially Latin), and the natural sciences (chemistry). She discussed the writings of Rousseau, Herder, Kant, Fichte, Novalis, Schlegel, Schleiermacher, and Schelling. She was particularly interested in Islam and Hinduism, wrote both creative and philosophical works inspired by them, and came to the conclusion that certain ideas in Eastern thought have the potential to revitalize European culture.

In many ways, Günderrode's syncretism, and her interest in fusing mythological and philosophical insights, exemplified the ideals of her contemporaries—among them Friedrich Hölderlin and Friedrich Schlegel—who also sought to make philosophy more poetic and poetry (mythology) more philosophical. Thus, in describing herself as a "philosophical poet" who represented the "new school," Günderrode was both aligning herself with these contemporaries and elucidating her approach to philosophy and mythology.[7] In contrast to Enlightenment approaches to mythology, Günderrode was of the view that mythological ideas and insights were not to be studied in an impersonal way but considered in all their existential and moral significance: what might they teach us about being human, and how might they help to expand our moral horizon? This last point is particularly evident in "Idea

---

[7] Quoted in Maria Lucia Licher, *Mein Leben in einer bleibenden Form aussprechen. Umrisse einer Ästhetik im Werk Karoline von Günderrodes (1780-1806)* (Heidelberg: Winter, 1996), 3. It is also interesting to note that the "new school" was the term that their contemporaries used to describe the movement that emerged in Jena and revolved around the two Schlegel brothers (Friedrich and August Wilhelm), their wives (Dorothea and Caroline), and their friends and acquaintances (including Schleiermacher, Friedrich von Hardenberg [Novalis], and Friedrich Schelling). In other words, the "new school" refers to the movement that we now call "romanticism." See Beiser, *The Romantic Imperative*, 45–46.

of the Earth," in which Günderrode draws on various philosophical and religious traditions to think about our (moral) relationship to the earth.

In addition to "Idea of the Earth," we have selected two sets of notes on philosophy that Günderrode composed sometime around 1804.[8] The first focuses on Fichte's 1800 *The Vocation of Humankind*, while the second set concerns the philosophy of nature and is connected to Günderrode's reading of Schelling's work (in particular, his 1797 *Ideas for a Philosophy of Nature* and his 1799 *First Outline for a Philosophy of Nature*). In interesting and surprising ways, "Idea of the Earth" unites the concerns of Fichte's *Vocation of Humankind* with those of the philosophy of nature. More specifically, Günderrode brings Fichte's ethical questions—questions focusing on what we, as human beings, ought to achieve—to bear on the philosophy of nature, asking what it means to be moral in relation to the earth. In posing and attempting to answer this question, Günderrode develops an account of human responsibility to the earth and its inhabitants that significantly departs from the accounts given by her contemporaries, whether Fichte, Schelling, or Hardenberg (Novalis). Her work, moreover, prefigures recent contributions to the field of environmental ethics.

To begin with, it is worthwhile to note that Günderrode chooses to focus on Fichte's *Vocation of Humankind*. The text was written three years after Fichte's *Foundations of Natural Right*, in which he had argued that women do not have the capacity to pursue philosophy or the ability to determine themselves. Though Günderrode's notes do not directly address female self-determination, the theme is present in a number of her creative works, in particular her play *Hildgund*, which was published in 1805. By portraying a strong female character (Hildgund) who must make far-reaching political decisions, Günderrode offers a significant counter-image to Fichte's view of women as irrational or petty. In her notes on Fichte, she takes up the challenge, but from a different angle.

Vocation of Humankind discusses the question of self-determination.[9] However, in it, Fichte does not address women specifically; his main concern

---

[8] The editor of Günderrode's collected works, Walter Morgenthaler, dates her notes on Fichte to sometime before 1804, without being able to date them with any more precision, while he dates her notes on the philosophy of nature to 1804. Walter Morgenthaler, ed., *Karoline von Günderrode. Sämtliche Werke und ausgewählte Studien* (Frankfurt: Stroemfeld/Roter Stern, 1990–1991), Vol. 3, 325–330.

[9] The original (German) title of Fichte's work is *Bestimmung des Menschen*. The word *Bestimmung* can be translated as either "vocation" or "determination."

is to challenge the view (increasingly widespread at the time) that the human being is part of nature. While Günderrode concedes some aspects of Fichte's arguments and recognizes the moral significance of his views, she ultimately disagrees with his overall position, and (more indirectly) with his position on female self-determination.

At first sight, Günderrode's notes on Fichte appear to summarize Fichte's key claims in *Vocation of Humankind*. For instance, Fichte's book is divided into three sections, respectively titled "Doubt," "Knowledge," and "Faith." Günderrode's notes are organized in a similar way. Upon closer consideration, however, it becomes clear that Günderrode carefully selects her focus and offers critiques of Fichte's conclusions.

The crucial claim in Fichte's text comes toward the end of the first section, where he contends that if the self is regarded as part of nature, then human actions must follow the natural chain of cause and effect. This means that my actions would be determined not by me—by my will—but by external circumstances (my family, my culture, or, from a contemporary perspective, my genes). But, Fichte argues, this conception of the self undermines the very idea of self-determination and human morality. After all, if my actions are not mine, then how can I be held responsible for them?

In her notes, Günderrode disagrees with Fichte's conception of self-determination and his understanding of nature. To begin with, she argues that the self can only emerge in relation to others, as part of a larger whole: "That I am this and nothing else is necessarily determined in conjunction with the whole." In other words, it is only by being with others that the self comes to realize its limits—and, through these limits, recognize itself as an individual. As Günderrode puts it: "Because I am, therefore, only a part of *being* overall, and there are multiple *beings* that are not me, I become conscious of my own being in its circumscribed state, which emerges through the being of the other beings." In this statement, Günderrode is ambiguous as to what "beings" refers to: does she mean other human beings, or does she mean beings more generally, including the human being? In light of her critique of Fichte's conception of nature, one may ask if the ambiguity may have been intentional.

Specifically, Günderrode points to inconsistencies in Fichte's account: he begins by describing nature as self-directed (self-determining) but then proceeds to speak of nature as blind mechanism. It is on the basis of this latter conception that he goes on to argue against the idea of the human being as part of nature. However, Günderrode suggests, if Fichte had stuck with his first account of nature, he would not have been able to claim that the view of the human being as part of nature necessarily robs us of self-determination. After all, if nature were self-determining (if natural objects strive to achieve goals), then the idea of human self-determination *within* nature would not be paradoxical.

A key claim in *Vocation of Humankind* is that the human vocation can only be fully realized in a supersensible realm. This is because, Fichte argues, the sensible realm (the world of space, time, and sensible objects) often impedes my will, and so I regularly fail to achieve my (moral) ends. For this reason, Fichte contends, I must conceive of a realm in which my will is not impeded and my moral actions are always realized.

Günderrode is sympathetic to this idea, and at first sight her views seem to mirror Fichte's. However, an important note invites a different reading. She writes: "My best will does not work in the world if I do not have the opportunity to demonstrate it through actions; if I do not have this opportunity, what is it worth, if there is only a sensible world?" In contrast to Fichte, Günderrode regards the supersensible as significant not because my will is impeded in the sensible world but rather because the sensible world (the world as it currently is) fails to provide me with the opportunity to realize my intention. What Günderrode is pointing to is the possibility of finding oneself in a situation where one cannot even attempt to realize one's intention—a problematic far more basic than the separation between will and consequence that concerns Fichte. Importantly, for Günderrode this problematic is not simply hypothetical. Rather, she is describing the reality of women's lives in the late eighteenth and early nineteenth centuries. Thus, Günderrode reframes the basic problem as Fichte had formulated it: the problem is not simply the *realization* of one's will but rather the lack of *opportunities* to develop and act on one's will. It is for this reason that Günderrode invokes the supersensible: to provide a regulative space in which we can posit alternative realities—realities where currently impossible but fundamentally necessary ideals (such as the self-determination of women) appear realizable.

In her notes on the philosophy of nature, Günderrode offers an illuminating account of why philosophy must move away from idealism. As Günderrode explains, this move has to do with the fact that since the early modern period, philosophy has tended to separate mind and nature (subject and object)—a separation that reached its apex in Kant's notion of the thing in itself. This resulted in an isolation of the mind from the world such that the main goal of philosophy (the achievement of knowledge) became impossible. After all, knowledge aims to know the world. If, however, the mind has no access to the world, to what is beyond our subjective construction of the world, then knowledge seems impossible. The only way to overcome this subjectivism, Günderrode writes, is by positing a fundamental identity between subject and object, between mind and nature, and then going on to (philosophically) demonstrate this identity.[10] This was, in fact, the view that Schelling had expounded in his own writings on nature, and Günderrode's notes appear to largely concur with Schelling's systematic explanation of the philosophy of nature.

Thus, in agreement with Schelling, Günderrode maintains that demonstrating this identity (between mind and nature) is the crucial task of philosophy. She also agrees with Schelling (and Kant) that matter is composed of two opposing forces (attraction and repulsion) and attempts to show how these two forces re-emerge at different levels of reality (from inorganic to organic nature). Furthermore, and also in line with Schelling, Günderrode identifies the "absolute" as the synthesis of mind and nature, or what Schelling described as a "higher synthesis."[11] There are, however, important ways in which Günderrode departs from Schelling—above all, in her claim that human beings bear a moral responsibility to the natural world, as she argues in "Idea of the Earth."[12]

What these notes furnish, then, are important insights into Günderrode's reasons for embracing the philosophy of nature, her critique of Fichte, and her understanding of nature, all of which become central concerns in "Idea of the Earth." Thus, alongside her notes on Fichte, the notes on the philosophy of nature offer invaluable background for understanding Günderrode's systematic philosophy as well as the crucial argument in "Idea of the Earth."

The key premise in "Idea of the Earth" concerns the notion of "earth." According to Günderrode, the earth is an "idea" that must be realized. At first sight, it is difficult to grasp this statement. Upon closer inspection,

---

[10] On subjectivism in German idealism, see Beiser, *German Idealism*.

[11] J. G. Fichte and F. W. J. Schelling, *The Philosophical Rupture between Fichte and Schelling: Selected Texts and Correspondence (1800–1802)*, trans. and ed. Michael G. Vater and David W. Wood (Albany: SUNY Press, 2012), 61.

[12] For an account the ethical underpinnings of Günderrode essay "Idea of the Earth," see Dalia Nassar, "The Human Vocation and the Question of the Earth: Karoline von Günderrode's Philosophy of Nature," *Archiv für Geschichte der Philosophie* (2021), https://www.degruyter.com/document/doi/10.1515/agph-2019-0028/html.

however, it becomes evident that it is connected to Günderrode's argument, developed in the notes on the philosophy of nature, that nature is not an object "out there" opposed to the subject "in here." Rather, her claim is that nature (like mind) embodies both objectivity and subjectivity. By this Günderrode means that nature exhibits a certain purposiveness. Nature is not simply determined by our desires or ends; it has its own ends. On the basis of this premise Günderrode goes on to formulate her moral account of the human-nature relationship. Precisely because nature is not a random amalgamation of passive forces or inert parts but is a living and directed process, she argues that we must heed its goals and not simply force ours onto it.

In this brief but radical essay, Günderrode develops an account of the human relation to the natural world that departs from the views of her contemporaries and resounds with our current concerns. However, in some ways, Günderrode goes even further than contemporary environmental ethics. This is because her ethics is built on two key premises: that the earth is in some sense an agent and that human agency depends on the agency of nonhuman others. This leads to her main claim, that it is our responsibility, as moral agents, to achieve human virtues (such as goodness and truth), not simply for the sake of other humans but also for the sake of the earth. This is what she calls the "realized idea of the earth." From this point of view, human morality is not solely for the achievement of human ends but also for the realization of the earth's ends.

On Fichte's *The Vocation of Humankind*

Chapter One: Doubt
Chapter Two: Knowledge
Chapter Three: Faith[13]

Doubt

When I observe nature, I find that the properties of objects change every moment. But each property is necessarily determined by another one that precedes it, and so on. Therefore, in order to explain the being of these properties and determinations, I must first assume the existence of another being.[14] Because their being cannot be explained from themselves, it is incomplete. This is because these properties do not exist for themselves, but are only conditions of something conditioned, forms of something formed. That a thing of this kind, which assumes and bears a property (i.e., is a substrate of the property), should have a determinate property expresses a state of stillness in its transformations. The state of standing still, or of determinacy, is a state of passivity. Therefore, an activity is required that contains the ground of this passivity.

An active force, unique to the object and constituting its essence, must be assumed in order to grasp the emergence and change of these determinations and properties.

The essence of this force is that, by virtue of its nature, and under these circumstances, it cannot produce any other effect. The principle of its activity lies within itself; it sets *only* itself in motion. The inner determination of this force by itself, and its outer determination by its circumstances, must come together in order to effect a change. For the circumstances and the static being and subsisting of things produce no becoming, for in them lies the opposite of becoming: static subsisting. The force itself is determined in itself; but it is completed by the circumstances among which it develops.

---

[13] [Günderrode's notes in this section are on Johann Gottlieb Fichte, *Die Bestimmung des Menschen* (Berlin: Voss, 1800). The notes are a mixture of direct quotes, paraphrasing, and Günderrode's own modifications of or reflections on Fichte's text.]

[14] [Günderrode uses two terms, *Dasein* and *Sein*, that are translated with the English word "being." In this first paragraph, she uses *Dasein* consistently; subsequently, she uses *Sein* in almost all instances. It is made clear where Günderrode deviates from this practice and uses *Dasein* instead.]

The universe is one active force, if I observe it as a whole; if I observe it in its particulars, then it is several. They work partly according to their inner nature, and partly according to the *determination* that they obtain through the effect of the other forces. Everything in nature can be explained by these forces; they themselves remain inexplicable. Everything that occurs in nature occurs through its forces—therefore thought does too: it is within nature and develops according to natural laws; it *is*, therefore, through nature. Consequently, there is a thinking force [*Denkkraft*] in nature, as there is a formative force [*Bildungskraft*]. And, accordingly: there must be a force of human formation [*menschenbildende Kraft*] in nature. I unite within myself the particular determination of the formative force, like the plant, the determination of the particular force of movement [*Bewegkraft*], like the animal, and the determination of the thinking force. The unification of these three forces in one, and in one harmonious development, constitutes the distinguishing characteristic of the human species. Now, as surely as those natural forces are something, have laws and purposes, just as surely must their expressions become real, if they are not suppressed by more powerful effects.

That I am this and nothing else is necessarily determined in conjunction with the whole.—I myself am not the force of human formation but only *one* of its expressions; and as this expression I am conscious of myself as my *self*. Because I am, therefore, only a part of *being* overall, and there are multiple *beings* that are not me, I become conscious of my own being in its circumscribed state, which emerges through the being [*Dasein*] of the other beings. In short, because I perceive that the universe is not in me—that I am not it—I must conclude, by virtue of the nature of my thinking force, that there are foreign *beings*. And so, separated from the rest, I am conscious of myself. On this conclusion, the freedom of our will is lost among the necessary effects of the forces—

Knowledge

In all perceptions I only perceive my own state: I see this surface, it seems green to me, i.e., it makes an impression on me that I call green. The visual sensation green, therefore, is part of *me*.[15] The sensation *green* is simple, like the sensation *surface* that my hand gives me of the space in which it finds

---

[15] [N]ot the object.

itself. Whether these sensations really match an existing green surface I do not know, because I only know my sensations. Thus, when an object arouses a sensation, I do not sense it, but my own sensation: the sensing and the sensible are united in me. I intuit things, but they are in my intuiting: the objects of my knowledge are in *me*, in my knowledge. I am *subject* insofar as *I intuit myself in all things*,[16] *object* insofar as *I am that which is intuited* by myself.

The consciousness of a thing outside me is nothing more than the product of my capacity to represent.[17] The manifold things, with their necessary determinations, which in their interrelationship form a world system for us, can therefore also be explained by the necessary laws of our thought.[18]

By this inference, the entire sensible world disappears, for things outside us emerge only through our knowledge, are only our knowledge, and are therefore not reality. Whether my body—indeed my whole I—is anything more than my thinking and having thought *I am it* can just as little be proven as the fact that real things exist outside me. But because all things are only in me, because in everything that I see and sense I sense only my own condition, how can I fear becoming the slave of a world-system that I myself have thought up, and onto which I merely transfer the laws of my thinking?

But how do I arrive at that representing, thinking, willing (intelligent) essence? How do I become conscious of it? I become conscious of the thinking *etc.* as a determined event, but not of a capacity to do it, still less of an essence that possesses this capacity.—This happens like this: Now I intuit this determined thinking, in another moment another, and then this inner intuition comes to an end. But this inwardly intuited thinking is only half a thought, because, according to my laws of thought, for each condition I must add the thought of a ground of the condition. Thus, here, I add to the thought of what is *determined* (my real thinking) the thought of something that is *determinable* (a manifold, possible thinking). I grasp this possible thinking as a whole, which, because I cannot grasp anything infinite, seems to me to be a finite capacity, and because something independent of thinking is represented by this way of thinking, I represent to myself a *being* and essence that has this capacity. Thus, I achieve *immediate self-consciousness*.[19]

---

[16] [Günderrode originally wrote here just "I intuit things" (ms 210v; see *Sämtliche Werke*, Vol. 2, 291).]

[17] But because I receive an impression without finding its cause in myself, I stipulate an object to which I ascribe the impression; I set this object in space outside me.

[18] I.e., the laws that we believe we perceive in these things are in our own thinking.

[19] [T]he second, or mediated, consciousness is only a consciousness of that which is *not I*. The *former* (self-consciousness) always lies at the basis of the second and is its condition. It can also be said that the first, immediate, consciousness is only a *modification* of the overall consciousness that one calls *I*.

Faith

But whatever the case may be with the outer world, whether it is reality or mere representation, there still lie deep within me a faith[20] and an interest that move me to accept it as real. And a voice—that of conscience—says aloud to me: "treat people as if they were rational free entities, as if they were like you."—I could withhold my obedience from this voice, could deny to myself the existence [*Dasein*] of the entities outside me, for it is within my power to choose to think in any kind of way. But I obey: no longer blindly, but from choice and from free resolve of that interest, based deep within me, according to which rational entities exist outside me. I have faith in their existence [*Dasein*], and I obey the law within me that commands me how I have to treat them. I choose this way of thinking for myself, because it seems to me to be the most commensurate with my worth.—

A force within me urges me to act: through my activity I should produce a *condition*, a *being* outside me. Already this brings me to the thought of a *being* outside me and sets me a purpose. What is this purpose? What is my vocation? It is nothing other than to always obey the voice of my conscience: what it commands should occur (that is why I am here). I have understanding in order to recognize what it commands, power in order to do it. I should present the inner command of duty through my willing and doing.—But is the goal of this vocation found on earth? For any reasonable striving I must set a reasonable purpose.—No, for in the sensible world my free obedience does not work directly toward the command of duty; no, only an act can work, no matter what attitude it occurs with. This drives me to faith in a spiritual world, where my spirit can work immediately, i.e., by will alone. For an act and its consequences belong under the law of the sensible world, by which the expressions of our willing would be constrained, and therefore often futile.[21] And what would our vocation be if we could not achieve it by ourselves, i.e., through *firm willing*, but instead only through the facilitation of the circumstances that always (by virtue of natural laws) work on our acts? There is a spiritual world in which my *will* is the first link in a chain of consequences that runs through the invisible realm, just as in the world the *act*, an expression of my will, produces an ongoing movement of material whose first link is my act. The will is what is living and effecting in the rational world, just as movement is what is living and effecting in the sensible world. I stand

---

[20] [The German word *Glaube* can be translated as either "faith" or "belief." In this section, it has been translated consistently as "faith."]

[21] My best will does not work in the world if I do not have the opportunity to demonstrate it through acts if I do not have this opportunity, what is it worth, if there is only a sensible world?

in the middle of both worlds, I am one of the primal forces in both, and my will encompasses both. As I move my will by a resolution, I effect—change—something in the spiritual world; if I let this overflow into an act, I change something in the sensible world.

My conscience is the voice of the *spiritual world* speaking to me, the bond that binds *it* to me, and my voluntary obedience is the bond by which I tie myself to *it*. My will is the only thing that is wholly *mine*, and through it I am already a citizen of a better world; through it I grasp that better world and give myself my vocation.

If it were true that all human virtue had to have an external purpose, the attainment of which it was certain of, before it could act; if reason had to obtain the principle of its activity not from itself, but from observing the world, then our vocation would already be achieved *here* [in this world]. But the end purpose of reason is pure activity itself, independence from everything that is not reason, and the will is the living principle of this reason. It scorns all outer purposes, sets only itself as its purpose (for I should will according to laws, even if nothing but my will would be effected as a result), and thereby shows us a world where it can work simply through itself. The life-principle of that spiritual world is an infinite will, whose product is the whole spiritual world. I cannot know what the essence of this infinite will may be, for whatever I may think about it, I can only think it *finitely*. But it is this will that binds me together with all finite entities of my kind, that connects me with itself; I flow into it, it into me. Only through it (the common source of our being [*Dasein*]) do I have tidings [*Kunde*] of free spirits outside me, which otherwise, according to nature and the laws of thought, would be impossible. Only the *one* in which we are, the spiritual source from which we flow, makes it so that we recognize each other and work on each other.

And so I am related to that *will* and everything around me is related to *me*. And *its* life is (as far as I can grasp) a *self*-forming and presenting willing that flows through the whole universe in manifold forms. A force that organizes itself in the plant, moves in the animal, and presents its own world in each. The invisible bond of the spiritual world in which they all are, and which is in them, and from which all personhood [*Persönlichkeit*] emerges from the sum of the whole.[22] From this perspective, nature spiritualizes itself before my gaze, it becomes related to me, it is, like me, an expression of that will, presented in another form. And so, to me, death itself is only a wrestling of the inner life to a better life. I am part of that spiritual life force; how could I die, who am myself life?

---

[22] [Günderrode originally wrote here: "and to which all personhood returns, into the sum of the whole" (ms 215r; see *Sämtliche Werke*, Vol. 2, 297–298).]

Philosophy of Nature

Nature[23] is an eternal activity [*Tätigkeit*], a self-producing product, an ever enduring becoming—for if it were a being then its productive activity would be canceled out by this completion. But it is an activity, infinite in time, a continuum that would develop with infinite velocity (and thus have no state) if its activity were not inhibited at all points by something just as infinite: repulsion and attraction. These two activities converge so that they do not cancel each other out; instead, the inhibition changes the infinite velocity into a finite one, whereby a product emerges. And although the same thing always repeats itself under the same conditions, and thus adopts the appearance of subsisting, the activity out of which it sprang would be negated by this subsisting.[24] Thus there can be as little rest in the product as there is in the producing force of nature, which (only held chained in a determinate form by the inhibition) strives to create ever new conditions, and opposes itself to the inhibition. Both forces, therefore, are contending in all products, and all things only exist through their permanent struggle. But that pure action [*Aktion*]—the primal connection [*Urverbindung*] of the two forces—is not what appears in space; the visible appearances of nature are, rather, only the outer expression—the various connections—of the primal activities [*Urtätigkeiten*]. These primal activities contain the principle of all products, but never emerge themselves. Space is not filled, no material is brought forth by the two first dimensions of the first potency; they are ideal primal actions [*Uraktionen*]—principles of material, but yet not material.

[...]

All things are, so to speak, finite presentations of the infinite, and so to a greater or lesser extent all things have a double being: an individual limited being, insofar as they constitute an independent entity for themselves; and a universal being, insofar as they are dependent on and connected with the universe, and therefore are, at the same time, participants in the infinite.[25]

---

[23] [These notes on the philosophy of nature are from Günderrode's studies of Schelling. Their likely sources are Schelling's *Ideen zu einer Philosophie der Natur*, books 1 and 2 (Leipzig: Breitkopf und Härtel, 1797); *Erster Entwurf eines Systems der Naturphilosophie* (Jena: Christian Ernst Gabler, 1799); and "Allgemeine Deduction des dynamischen Processes oder der Categorieen der Physik vom Herausgeber," *Zeitschrift für spekulative Physik*, ed. F. W. J. Schelling (Jena: Christian Ernst Gabler, 1800), Vol. 1, issue 1, 100–136, and Vol. 1, issue 2, 3–87.]

[24] [Günderrode originally wrote here: "The productivity of nature [*Naturproduction*] has developed in all determinate products" (*Sämtliche Werke*, Vol. 2, 365; ms 133).]

[25] [In this paragraph, Günderrode consistently uses the word *Dasein*, translated into English as "being"; elsewhere in this text, she uses the related German term *Sein*, unless indicated otherwise.]

This double being is the principle of all entities. Thus, all the bodies and materials of the earth are each an individual being for themselves and also, at the same time, a universal being insofar as they are an element that belongs to the great whole of the earth.

The earth itself has this double life. Its individual movement is the movement around its own axis: it strives to break away from the sun to become entirely an individual, but the sun, with all its magnetic force, strives to draw it to itself, to unite it with itself, and thus to annihilate its singularity. The double movement of the earth around the sun and around its own axis emerges from the struggle of this attractive force of the sun with the force of the earth, by virtue of which the latter seeks to maintain its selfhood.

[...]

That is absolute which is not limited by anything else, which limits itself, and which is in itself cause and effect at once, and consequently has no ground outside itself. The universe is an absolute. All things are absolute in a certain sense, insofar as they participate in the universe; but they are also not absolute, insofar as they have a ground outside themselves (the universe).

Absolute knowledge—i.e., knowledge in general, the knowledge of everything that is—is, at the same time, real (actual, being). A spirit that knew everything, all of whose knowledge would also be real. For if I know everything, then nothing is outside my knowledge; but, also, I cannot know of anything that is not. This highest unity of the ideal (of knowledge, thinking) with the real (of what is, of the real) is again an absolute—the universe.

Nature is the ideal formed in the real.

Knowledge is a transferring of the ideal onto the real.

Acting is a transferring of the real into the ideal.

The first moment of intuition is the unity of the intuiting and what is intuited.

Reflection divides this primitive unity: it separates intuiting from what is intuited, myself from objects, spirit from material. Finally, it dissects my own life into two parts in order to observe one half with the other. It therefore makes me into object and subject at the same time.

Philosophy presupposes this division and makes it its task—through an act of freedom—to reunite in consciousness that which is separated by reflection (intuited and intuiting, thought and object, object and subject).

Philosophy, therefore, first investigates whether there are really things outside us, whether these things can affect us, and how they can do so. Thus, concerning the first question, in order to learn whether there are things in themselves, that means things that would exist without our representation, if these so-called things outside us were stripped of all that our representation transfers onto them. And all concept of succession[26] of cause and effect, of space and time, belongs to representation. But if things are stripped of everything that my representation transfers onto them, what do I have left of them? Nothing, i.e., no more representation—and what are they to me if I cannot represent them to myself?

However, our representations would be absolutely empty, mere forms, if there were not things that corresponded to them. Accordingly, things without representations are not thinkable for us, and representations of things without the things are nothing: empty, insubstantial concepts. But in order for things to have reality for us, and in order for our representations to have reality, philosophy seeks their absolute unity, the identity of the object and subject. But it can take no other path toward this than self-observation: it must descend into the depths of its own mind[27] and seek the ground of our representations within it, find the necessity of their emergence and their unity with their objects there.

Philosophy is therefore nothing other than the natural doctrine of our spirit. It allows the whole system of our representations to develop in front of us, and with it, at the same time, the whole system of outer appearances, or of objects outside us. This philosophy wants to show how nature coincides (not accidentally) with the laws of our spirit and realizes them. Thus, as nature is visible spirit, spirit is invisible nature. If this is demonstrated in the following, the question "how can things outside us work on our representations and generate them?" will need no further discussion.

The insight that the *absolutely ideal* is at the same time also the absolutely real is the condition of all higher scientificity [*Wissenschaftlichkeit*]—not only philosophical scientificity but also mathematical and astronomical scientificity—for this unity is the ground upon which they are built.[28]

We first ask: what is the absolute ideal? It is an absolute knowing (a knowing that knows everything), an absolute act of knowledge.

In absolute knowing, the objective must therefore be wholly subjective and the subjective must be wholly objective.

But how does this highest unity of the objective and subjective, the ideal and real, come to be divided?

[26] Succession is a concept that necessarily emerges from the finitude of our spirit, by virtue of which we cannot survey a thing at once and at one point, but are compelled to let our representations follow each other.

[27] Since, whatever we may perceive and investigate, we perceive only our selves, i.e., our states, in our own mind we can only find constructions of things.

[28] The astronomical calculations apply without one having previously experienced their accordance with the movements of the heavenly bodies.

The absolute in its highest unity (where it is object and subject, ideal and real) is an eternal act of knowledge which is itself matter and form; an eternal producing that produces itself, that is itself essence and form. For because this absolute is everything, nothing is outside it, and there is no cause of its being but itself. It can therefore only produce itself, can only itself be matter and form.

This absolute (the highest unity) is an eternal, active act of knowledge, the concept of which is at the same time a creating, i.e., the essence of which is that its thought is at the same time real, a *being*.

In this absolute, three actions can be distinguished:

1) Where it brings forth its essence (subject), the general or infinite, as a particular, finite form (object). (But every form is finite, as form, i.e., as limited.) Thus, in this act the subjective objectivizes itself.
2) Where the objective, the form, the particular finite thing, is dissolved again in the essence of the general or infinite. This act is the subjectivization of the objective.
3) Where the object is not separated from the subject, and the form is not separated from the essence. Thus, in the third act an absolute emerges again, i.e., a unity of the object and the subject, of the form and the essence, of the particular and the general, of the finite and infinite.[29]

Now, because the absolute is everything (the ideal and real at the same time), everything that exists must proceed from the absolute. But because the absolute can only produce itself, all its productions must also be an absolute, and these three acts of the absolute must be expressed in everything: (1) the objectivization of the subjective, (2) the subjectivization of the objective, and (3) the indifference of both (absoluteness).

Because it is our purpose to ascend from the real to the ideal, we must first pay attention to the former.

The real side of that eternal acting of the absolute infinite is nature in itself.

Eternal nature,[30] the basic force or the type from which all individual appearances (bodies) proceed, is the spirit of God born in form (objective). This is the general, or the essence, whose particular, or form, all individual appearances of nature are (the body, so to speak, of this invisible force of nature).

---

[29] But this unity is not that primal unity, or the eternal, in which the ideal and the real rested, still undivided and indivisible; it is a synthesized unity, a product of opposed activities, an absolute in second potency, the universe.

[30] The ancients called nature the birth of things, because the eternal things, the ideas, are, so to speak, born in nature.

Philosophy of Nature

Now, this eternal nature is neither only real nor only ideal, neither only essence nor only form, but, again, an absolute unity of both: a realized idea, an essence that molds itself in forms, forms that dissolve themselves in essence, and a unity of both.

In order to further investigate these three acts in nature and in natural appearances, we must consider the invisible type of nature, the all-pervading nature-spirit, as the general.[31] And so we find out how it (1) expresses, molds itself in forms (appearances of nature), (2) how these forms return to and dissolve themselves in the essence, (3) how form and essence are one.

In order to detect these three acts in all particular appearances, we must seek the potencies that are always subordinated to the three acts.[32] So, for example, in order to construct nature according to this idea, we must completely abstract from the absolute ideal, and instead of this posit the universal (the force of nature) as its factor (representative). And thus we must say: (1) The general force of nature presents itself in particular appearances (forms). (2) The appearances return to the general force of nature. (3) The force of nature and its forms (appearances) are indifferent. If we want to pursue this idea further in terms of how it presents itself in detail, then we must posit, as the factor of the general, a subordinated, relative general (one that is not absolute, but only general within its class) and a relative particular.

[...]

Where we see the forces fully equalized (one, so to speak, bound and canceled out by the other), there is no activity, no movement, no life, but only a being, a constant subsisting in itself. But where the forces are in a certain conflict (in active opposition) there is activity, movement. Where this conflict becomes permanent in a determinate form, there is life.

But the form is the result of this conflict, and the conflict ends with it.

[...]

Nature is the real side of absolute knowledge. Its products are thoughts congealed to being, dark dreams out of which it progressively awakens to consciousness. It presents the laws of our spirit in realities, in being. Just as we must

---

[31] [Günderrode originally wrote here: "as the essence, subject, of the all" (ms 165; see *Sämtliche Werke*, Vol. 2, 379).]

[32] [Günderrode originally added a description of these three acts here: "of the absolute, ideal: (1) the formation of the ideal in the real, (2) the returning of the real to the ideal, (3) the indifference point of both" (ms 166; *Sämtliche Werke*, Vol. 2, 389).]

think of matter as the result of the opposed forces[33] of repulsion and attraction, so the conflict of these opposed activities (among other forms) is the condition of nature, of life, and of spirit. We define repulsion as that force by virtue of which a thing strives to extend itself, unconstrained, into the infinite on all sides and to push away everything that resists it. This force is a positive, active, infinite one.

Attraction resists the infinite expansion of repulsion; it seeks to draw the expansion back to one point. It is, therefore, a negative, constraining, finite force.

All forms have proceeded from the conflict of these forces: the first gave things extension, the second gave them limitation, determination. But the product of opposed activities is always a finite, constrained thing. Repulsion strives to fill space on all sides; attraction wants to bring the filling of space back to one point; what emerges from the activity of the two together is the filling of space under determinate limits.

The positive, infinite activity of spirit strives to extend itself on all sides; if left alone to do this it would dissolve in the infinite, so to speak. The negative, finite activity strives to draw its activity back to one point (it is a striving for the center, a leading back into itself, consciousness). From the conflict of the two activities emerges a constrained activity, a determinable, finite thing, an indifference of the infinite and finite: our spirit.

Repulsion is, so to speak, the factor of space, or of unlimited extension, and attraction is the factor of time, or of constraint in successive points (moments of time). Time only exists where circumstances follow each other, where something becomes, is, and was. Time is therefore finite in everything. But where nothing becomes and was, where everything is and remains unchanged, there time cannot be imagined.

---

[33] Without these forces, no material, no filling of space, would be conceivable: without attraction there would be no connection at all, without repulsion no expansion.

The Idea of Nature

Nature is an infinite activity, a self-producing product, an ever enduring becoming; if it were a *being* then its productive activity would be canceled out. But if it were only pure activity then it would develop at infinite velocity, and would therefore have no state and would not bring about any product. But at all points its pure positive activity is opposed by an equally infinite negative activity as an inhibiting factor, and through this opposition products become possible.

The positive and negative activities must be thought of as equal to each other, for nature cannot exist through the victory of either one or the other, but only in their equilibrium. If both activities—equal to each other, different only in their direction—were to meet in one point then they would necessarily cancel each other out (make null), and a common effectiveness, a product, would not be possible. Their meeting must therefore be thought of as occurring in many points, and in each point in a different proportion, so that the necessary equality in the whole does not cancel out the necessary difference in the products.

Thus, the way in which the two activities meet is one that changes the infinite velocity of the first one into a finite velocity, i.e., makes a product possible. But within the products there is as little rest as there is in the productive nature-spirit, which strives to present itself in ever new states, and is only held chained in a determinate form by the inhibition, which it resists and from which it seeks to tear itself away. The permanence of this struggle in the whole ensures nature its infinity in time, for time is the succession of the developments of this struggle, and only infinite time (and within it an infinite evolution of its capacity to present itself) is commensurate to it. But, because nature presents itself in all forms and in all times, no single *form* can suffice it, and, because its activity is infinite, it can persist in *none* of these forms. Therefore, the individual product is dissolved by the victory of one of the two activities in it, and its essence returns to that from which it sprang, which develops ever new forms from out of its abundance.

The Idea of the Earth

The earth is a realized idea, one that is simultaneously effective (force) and effected (appearance). It is thus a unity of soul and body. We call the pole of its activity that it turns outward extension, form, body; the one turned inward intensity, essence, force, soul. Now, as the whole of the earth only exists through this unification of soul and body, so, too, the individual and smallest things only exist through it and cannot be conceived as split in two, for an outer without an inner, an essence without form, a force without some sort of effect, is not comprehensible. Thus, the elements are the poles of this identical earth-essence, and each individual is in itself body and soul, yet in various proportions of both, so that either the spiritual pole or the bodily pole can predominate. The most intimate mingling of different elements with the highest degree of contact and attraction we call life. To whatever perfection it may have developed it is still only the product of the synthesis of the elements that gestate life. With the dissolution of this synthesis the product also ends, but the life-principle in the elements is immortal; it requires only contact and connection again like before and new life blossoms with all the blooms that we call thought and sensation, and organism and body and soul.

Thus, life is immortal and surges up and down in the elements, for they are life itself. But determinate and individual life is only a life-form given through this determinate connection, attraction and contact, which can last no longer than the connection.

Now, when a person is dead, their mixture returns to the substance of the earth, but that within them which we called force, activity, or rather that of its materials in which the more active pole predominated, reverts to that which is related to it in the earth; the coarser elements likewise seek what is similar to them according to laws of affinity. But once these elements have been driven to life in the organism, they become different from what they were before they entered into this organic connection. They have become livelier and increase the earth's life in returning to the earth, like two who have increased their strength in long struggle are stronger when the struggle has ended than they were before. The elements are like this, for they are alive, and the living force is strengthened in every exercise.

But each form that they produce is only a development of their life-principle. The earth bears the life-material given back to it again in ever new appearances, until through ever new transformations everything capable of life in it has come to life. This would be when all mass would become organic; only then would the idea of the earth be realized.

So each mortal gives back to the earth a raised, more developed elemental life, which it [the earth] cultivates further in ascending forms, and the organism, by assimilating ever more developed elements, must thereby become ever more perfect and universal. Thus, the All [*Allheit*] comes to life through the downfall of the particular, and the particular survives immortally in the All whose life it developed while alive, and elevates and increases even after death, and so by living and dying helps to realize the idea of the earth. Thus, however my elements may be dispersed, when they join to what is already living they will elevate it; when they join to those things whose life resembles death, they will animate them. The Indian notion of the transmigration of souls corresponds to this opinion, and the life-elements may wander and search no longer only when the earth has thoroughly attained its proper existence, the organic. But all forms of the organism that have been produced until now must not suffice the earth-spirit, for it always breaks them up again and seeks new ones; whereas a form that was totally identical to the essence could not be broken apart from it, for it would be entirely the same as it and inseparable from it.

This perfect unity of essence and form cannot be achieved in *separation* and multiplicity, for through precisely *these* the form is different from the essence, because the essence can only be one but the forms are various. The earth can therefore only attain its proper being [*Dasein*] when its organic and inorganic appearances dissolve in a collective organism, when both factors—being (body) and thinking (spirit)—penetrate each other to the point of indistinguishability, where all body would also at the same time be thought, all thinking at the same time body, and a truly transfigured body, without lack or illness and immortal, and thus wholly different from what we call body or material and to which we attribute transience, inertia, illness, and deficiency, for this kind of body is, as it were, only a failed attempt by nature to produce that immortal ideal body. I do not assert whether the earth will be altogether successful in organizing itself immortally like this; there may be a disproportion of essence and form in its primal elements that always hinders it from this; and perhaps the totality of our whole solar system is needed to resolve the task of such an equilibrium of essence and form, and perhaps even this does not suffice for it and it is a task for the entire universe.

Truth is the expression of what *is always the same* as itself; justice is the striving of the All in the particular to be the same as itself; beauty is being the same as oneself and harmonious; love, benevolence, compassion are the longing of the particular to enjoy itself in the All, i.e., to become aware of the All in the particular, and, renouncing personhood, to surrender itself to the All. But what is always the same as itself, harmonious with itself, not torn asunder into the particular, that is immortal, without change and illness; in short, it is that which I have called the realized idea of the earth (or of the universe). All single virtues and excellences are therefore mere attempts by the earth-spirit to bring itself nearer to this state (as much as can occur in the particular). Through any kind of truth, justice, beauty, and virtue it becomes more like itself, more harmonious, and freer of the bonds of personhood; through every act of injustice, untruth, and selfishness this state is made more distant and the god of the earth, who expresses his longing for a better life in every mind through receptivity to what is admirable, is bound in chains.

3

Bettina Brentano von Arnim (1785–1859)

Introduction

Bettina Brentano von Arnim (1785–1859) was a known iconoclast, an out-spoken political reformer, and a *salonnière*, whose publications in the 1830s and 1840s reignited philosophical romanticism. In her writings, she challenged philosophy's tendency to abstraction and sought to make philosophy more capacious and expansive in its concerns. This can be seen, for instance, in her contention that a proper understanding of the human being requires that we take into account not only our intellectual capacities but also our sensual and emotional lives. It can also be seen in her view that philosophy is a fundamentally dialogical enterprise and can only be properly carried out through the activity of "sym-philosophy."[1] Importantly, in Brentano von Arnim's case, "sym-philosophy" was not only an ideal to strive to achieve but a realized accomplishment. Her writings emerged in and through actual correspondence with fellow thinkers and thus bear witness to the role that dialogue plays—or ought to play—in philosophy.

Brentano von Arnim was born in Frankfurt am Main into a well-to-do family. The granddaughter of one of the most significant female authors of the eighteenth century, Sophie von La Roche (1730–1807), and the sister of the poet Clemens Brentano (1778–1842), Brentano von Arnim was, from early on, surrounded by a lively and intellectually stimulating atmosphere. Brentano von Arnim spent a number of years living at her grandmother's home, and the uniqueness of her life might have had much to do with her grandmother's influence. For one, she received a private education in mathematics, history, art, music, and botany. Furthermore, she was not forced to marry early but waited until she found the right partner.[2] At the age of

---

[1] Brentano von Arnim shared this with the romantic philosophers Friedrich Schlegel, Friedrich Schleiermacher, and Friedrich Hardenberg (Novalis).

[2] This contrasts with other well-known women of the romantic salons, such as Henriette Herz, who married (by arrangement) at the age of sixteen; Dorothea Schlegel, who married the banker Simon Veit (also by arrangement) when she was eighteen; and Germaine de Staël, who at the age of twenty married (by arrangement) Erik Magnus Staël von Holstein.

Women Philosophers in the Long Nineteenth Century. Dalia Nassar and Kristin Gjesdal, Oxford University Press.
© Oxford University Press 2021. DOI: 10.1093/oso/9780190868031.003.0005

twenty-six, Brentano von Arnim married the poet and novelist, Achim von Arnim (1781-1831), whom she met through her brother and the romantic circles of which they were both part.

In 1809, Brentano von Arnim moved with her husband to Berlin, where she became a regular attendee of the salons of Henriette Herz and Rahel Levin Varnhagen, with whom she was close. From the 1820s onward, Brentano von Arnim hosted her own salon, which was one of the longest-running and most politically engaged of the romantic salons. For Brentano von Arnim, political engagement and intellectual activity were fundamentally connected. She criticized philosophers who do not pay heed to the world around them—whether the natural world or the social and political world. Brentano von Arnim's concern with social and political questions intensified with age, and in the last decade of her life, she became increasingly concerned with social and economic inequality, and with poverty in particular. She wrote about poverty and also worked to improve the lives of the poor. Her *This Book Belongs to the King* (1842) was banned in Bavaria and Austria for, among other things, its call for a king who would be susceptible to the plights of the people. It received a glowing anonymous review that was likely written by Friedrich Engels. Brentano von Arnim had met with Karl Marx a year earlier.

On account of her publications, Brentano von Arnim was sentenced to prison for two months in 1847. This event crystallized the growing tensions between Brentano von Arnim and the Prussian state, convincing her not to publish her provocative *The Book of the Poor*, which only appeared in 1962, more than a century after her death.

However, it was well before then that Brentano von Arnim's publications had gained political attention. This is especially the case with her influential work, *Günderode* (1840), selections of which are translated for this volume. The book was dedicated to students—a dedication that could only be read as a provocative gesture. Some ten years before its publication, the Prussian state had banned student associations, and in December 1836, the Prussian High Court sentenced thirty-nine students who were members of student associations, first to death and then to thirty years' imprisonment.[3] Upon the

---

[3] For more background on the student associations and their ban in Prussia in the 1830s, see Robert Justin Goldstein, *Political Repression in 19th Century Europe* (New York: Routledge, 1983), esp. 144–150.

publication of *Günderode*, students in Berlin held a torch parade in honor of
Brentano von Arnim.[4]

Günderode was Brentano von Arnim's second work, following a book based
on a correspondence with Johann Wolfgang von Goethe, which appeared in
1835, just a few years after Goethe's death.[5] Though Brentano von Arnim was
much younger than Goethe, she regarded herself as a close friend of the poet
and his mother, herself an intellectual of significant proportions. The publication of their exchange (which is largely composed of letters by Brentano
von Arnim to Goethe) attempts to consolidate this friendship for posterity.

The same can be said of *Günderode*, which was published thirty-four years
after Brentano von Arnim's friend, Karoline von Günderrode, had committed suicide (a fact not mentioned in the text). *Günderode* is loosely based
on the letters exchanged between the two women in the years 1804–1806.
During this time, Günderrode was intensively engaged in a number of philosophical debates (including debates on the relation between the human being
and the natural world, on the idea of [female] self-determination, and on the
relation between philosophy and mythology). Brentano von Arnim's work
bears further witness to Günderrode's contributions to romantic and idealist
philosophy. But it does a lot more than that: it demonstrates the extent to
which Günderrode and Brentano von Arnim learned from each other and
the ways in which their views developed through their exchange. As such,
it is no exaggeration to say that *Günderode* offers one of the best examples
of sym-philosophy and the romantic ideal of sociability—of enacting on the
page a conversation in which both partners develop their points of view and
arrive at a higher understanding.[6]

While *Günderode* is based on letters exchanged between the two friends
(and includes some of Günderrode's published writings), it is ultimately a
work composed by Brentano von Arnim and clearly bears her authorial and
editorial stamp. In *Günderode*, Brentano von Arnim uses the names Bettine,

---

[4] See Christa Wolf, "Your Next Life Begins Today: A Letter about Bettine," in *Bettina Brentano-von
Arnim: Gender and Politics*, ed. Elke P. Frederiksen and Katherine R. Goodman (Detroit: Wayne State
University Press, 1995), 35–70.

[5] On Brentano von Arnim's relationship to Goethe—whom she met in 1807—their letter exchange,
the ways in which she helped him with his autobiography, and their falling out and eventual reconciliation, see Miriam C. Seidler, "Johann Wolfgang von Goethe," in *Bettina von Arnim Handbuch*, ed.
Barbara Becker-Cantarino (Berlin: De Gruyter, 2019), 178–187.

[6] On romantic sociability, see Jane Kneller, "Sociability and the Conduct of Philosophy: What We
Can Learn from Early German Romanticism," in *The Relevance of Romanticism: Essays on German
Romantic Philosophy*, ed. Dalia Nassar (New York: Oxford University Press, 2014), 110–124.

as opposed to Bettina, and Günderode, rather than Günderrode.[7] In this way, she signals the fictional selves of the two main characters and the editorial work that went into the creation of the text. In some cases, the editorial work is slight and involves simplifying Günderrode's syntax or changing the tense of her sentences. For instance, although Brentano von Arnim altered aspects of Günderrode's fragment "The Manes" (included in this selection), the content of the work remains the same.[8]

In other cases, however, the authorial and editorial hand is heavier. This involves adding passages from preceding letters—for instance, a letter from Günderode would include a passage from a letter sent to her by Bettine—and clear and direct responses to claims made by the other. Günderode, for example, offers a lengthy retort to Bettine's statements about her dislike of history. It also involves posing questions at various points in a letter in order to invite a response from the other and in this way perform, on the page, the kind of dialogue that one might expect in a conversation.

Through these various editorial interventions, Brentano von Arnim's aims are to heighten the sense of dialogue, demonstrate the extent to which the two friends were responding to each other's ideas, report conversations between them that were never written down, and also, in some ways, establish Günderrode as a thinker of lasting importance.[9]

---

[7] Accordingly, when references are made to the authors of the letters that appear in *Günderode*, their names will be spelled according to Brentano von Arnim's spelling, rather than their actual spelling. Thus, instead of Günderrode, reference will be made to Günderode, and instead of Bettina or Brentano von Arnim, reference will be made to Bettine.

[8] There are, however, ways in which this different form, especially the different syntax, may affect the meaning and content. As Lorely French notes, in her version of "The Manes," Brentano von Arnim eliminates expressions of time, making the pupil's experience timeless—an alteration that could carry philosophical significance. Other editorial changes include Brentano von Arnim's elimination of Günderrode's use of *and* and *but*, with the result that the 1840 text is largely composed of long, uninterrupted sentences broken only by the slight pauses of commas or semicolons. Lorely French, *German Women as Letter Writers: 1750–1850* (London: Associated University Presses, 1996), 229–231.

[9] The German author Christa Wolf, whose interest in Günderrode led her to Brentano von Arnim, puts the matter as follows: "The fact that Bettine treated her material freely, shortened letters, included letters from other correspondences, and invented some things has been held against her. This book is nonetheless authentic, in a poetic sense: as a witness for a friendship between two women, but also as a document of an era's social forms and customs and a powerful criticism of these customs." Wolf, *Karoline von Günderrode*, 25. See also Elke Frederiksen and Katherine Goodman, "'Locating' Bettina Brentano-von Arnim, A Nineteenth Century German Woman Writer," in *Bettina Brentano-von Arnim: Gender and Politics*, ed. Elke Frederiksen and Katherine Goodman (Detroit: Wayne State University Press, 1995), 13–34; and Patricia A. Simpson, "Letters in Sufferance and Deliverance: The Correspondence of Bettina Brentano-von Arnim and Karoline von Günderrode," in *Bettina Brentano-von Arnim*, 247–277.

Günderode was a hit in Germany, and translations into other languages quickly began to appear.[10] Margaret Fuller translated *Günderode* into English the same year it was published, under the title *Correspondence of Fräulein Günderode and Bettine von Arnim*. Although Fuller published her translation anonymously, she later wrote an essay on *Günderode* for *The Dial*. *The Dial* had been cofounded by Fuller and Ralph Waldo Emerson to serve as the mouthpiece of the ideas and ideals of those writers whom we might call the American romantics—i.e., the writers and thinkers who congregated in Concord (and Boston) and included (in addition to Fuller and Emerson) Henry David Thoreau, Nathaniel Hawthorne, and Bronson Alcott. What attracted the Concord circle to Brentano von Arnim's *Günderode* was its representation of an intellectual (Platonic) friendship and, for Fuller in particular, its expression of an intellectual friendship between women.

Brentano von Arnim and Günderrode first met in Frankfurt in 1803. While Brentano von Arnim was five years Günderrode's junior and often deferred to her in their correspondence, in the letters their relation is ultimately one of equals: Brentano von Arnim takes the advice of Günderrode but also challenges her. In particular, she takes aim at Günderrode's interest in abstract philosophy and what Brentano von Arnim critically describes as "the hocus pocus of [the philosopher's] superlative machine." As Brentano von Arnim saw it, the majority of philosophers and philosophies were too obtuse to be able to say anything significant about lived experience—"that which moves our senses," that which invites us to "live together, create together," and enable us "to be active." In her letters, Brentano von Arnim repeatedly argues that philosophers fail to take account of sensuality. In this way, she reiterates Friedrich Schiller's and Goethe's critiques of philosophy but also gives their critiques a new twist. While Schiller argued that philosophy fails to reconcile our rational and sensual drives, Goethe regarded philosophy as incapable of properly educating (transforming) our perception. For Brentano von Arnim, however, the chief problem with philosophical abstraction has to do with the fact that it fails to grasp the essentially poetic character of human life. Brentano von Arnim's claim is that human beings are born poets, even if

---

[10] As a writer for the American magazine *The Atlantic Monthly* put it in 1873: *Günderode* "had great popularity, and the young German 'girls of the period,' the young and sentimental wives, the flaxen-haired, blue-eyed 'femmes incomprises,' of all Germany, wept over it as their grandmothers had wept sixty years before over the 'Sorrows of Werther.'" M. E. W. S., "A Curiosity of Literature," *Atlantic Monthly* 31 (1873): 210–217, here 211.

they cannot or do not write poetry.[11] In her view, human beings are funda-mentally creative—in the same way that nature is creative. Thus, to become fully human, to fully actualize one's capacities and experience human life to the utmost, it is necessary, she contends, to live poetically. It is only by living poetically that we are able to pay full attention to what appears before the senses: we see it in a new light, recognize its connection to other things, are enlivened by it.

Historically, philosophy admonished poetry on account of poetry's ten-dency to employ imagination, in contrast to philosophy's search for truth through reason (Plato comes to mind). For Brentano von Arnim, how-ever, the crucial difference between philosophy and poetry has to do with the fact that philosophy tends to speak only in the most general terms. For this reason, philosophy often fails to capture the most significant life experiences, which are usually singular (in that they occur only once or pertain to the specific individual) and non-discursive (cannot be reduced to any one concept or proposition). To make her point, Bettine invites Günderode to imagine "a philosopher who lived entirely alone on an island where it was as beautiful as only spring can be. Everything bloomed free and alive and birds sang, and all that nature bore was perfectly beautiful." But, she adds, the philosopher is disappointed in this beautiful and full ex-perience because "there were no creatures there out of which the philo-sopher could make anything wise." In other words, the philosopher—and philosophy more generally—is incapable of appreciating precisely those things that make us fully human, those things that speak to our whole selves, rather than our intellect alone.

Bettine's exchanges with Günderode are not, however, only critical. She invites Günderode to offer advice or to engage in a genuine exchange of ideas that allows both women to rethink their original positions. This is evident, for instance, in their discussion of history. To begin with, Bettine relates to Günderode her disdain of history, claiming that historical knowledge is of no use. Günderode, who is shocked by her friend's claims, admonishes Bettine

---

[11] This view is also found in Hölderlin's work. In his 1808 poem "In Lieblicher Bläue," Hölderlin writes: "but poetically, / dwells the human being." Friedrich Hölderlin, "In Lieblicher Bläue," *Sämtliche Werke*, Vol. 2, ed. Friedrich von Beißner (Stuttgart: Cotta, 1953). While this poem was composed after Brentano von Arnim's original letter to Günderrode, it appeared in print in 1823, i.e., before the publication of *Günderode*. Thus, it is not unlikely that Brentano von Arnim was familiar with it by the time she published *Günderode*. Furthermore, Brentano von Arnim learned a great deal about Hölderlin's thought and writings through her connection to his close friend, Isaac von Sinclair, whom she calls St. Clair in *Günderode*.

and goes on to demonstrate precisely that which Bettine denies, the signifi-cance of historical knowledge for life, concluding that "history seems essen-tial to revive the sluggish plant-life of your thoughts; within it lies the strong force of all education.—The past drives forward; all seeds of development in us are sown by its hand."

A similarly intense philosophical engagement takes place when the two discuss the nature of a philosophical proof or demonstration. Günderode begins by offering a difficult thought, one that resounds with Baruch Spinoza's view that truth is its own standard, or, in Günderode's words, "the truth itself is proof." Her claim is that truth cannot be proven, in the same way that a first principle is self-evident and requires no demon-stration (it is its own demonstration). Bettine latches onto this thought, quoting Günderode's claim that "to think without proof is to think freely," and cheekily adds her own "proof" of this statement. Ultimately, however, Bettine comes to conclude that the most relevant "proof" of truth is to be found not in a narrowly philosophical demonstration but in the fact that someone has been fundamentally changed by truth. In other words, truth transforms us. And *this* transformation is the greatest proof of a truth. Thus, in some significant instances, the proof of truth is not logical at all but is to be found in the life that one leads.

This emphasis on the transformative aspects of truth goes hand in hand with Brentano von Arnim's general view that intellectual activity is insepa-rable from praxis, a view she shared with many of the philosophers whose writings are collected in this volume. It is also reflected in Brentano von Arnim's social engagement—from her politically engaged salon to her re-lief work with the poor. Through her work, Brentano von Arnim sought to realize her ideal of the unity of theory and practice. Like her friend Alexander von Humboldt, who supported her social and political activity, Brentano von Arnim never strayed from her socially and politically rad-ical early romantic roots, and indeed her "return" to romanticism late in life distinguishes her from the majority of her romantic contemporaries, who by the 1840s had largely forgotten their early zeal for the ideals of the French Revolution. Her distinctive life and work shed new light on German romanticism, including on the early romantic interest in social and polit-ical questions and concerns.

Selections from *Günderode*

The Manes

Student. Wise master! I was in the catacombs of the Swedish kings, and I approached the casket of Gustav Adolph with a peculiar painful feeling. His deeds passed before my spirit: I saw at the same time his life and his death, his exuberant vigor and the deep peace in which he has slumbered for almost two centuries. I recalled the grim time in which he lived, and my mind resembled a crypt out of which climb the faltering shadows of the past. I wept hot tears for his death as if he had only fallen today. Gone! Lost! Past! I said to myself; are these all the fruits of a great life?—Ah!—I had to leave the crypt.

I sought distraction, I sought other kinds of pain, but the gloomy underground spirit haunts me. I cannot be rid of this melancholy that lays itself like a mourning band over my present. This age seems futile and empty to me; longingly and violently I am drawn toward the past. Past: so calls my spirit. Oh, if only I were gone too and had never seen this poor time, in which the earlier world vanishes, in which its greatness is lost.—

Teacher. Nothing is lost, young student, and in no way; only the eye cannot survey the ground's unending chain of consequences. But even if you don't want to think about that, still you cannot call something lost and gone that works so powerfully upon you.—Your own fate, the present, does not move you so intensely as the memory of this great king; does he not live more powerfully in you now than the present? Or do you only call life that which lives on in flesh and in what is visible? And is that gone and lost to you which still works in your mind and is there?

Student. If that is life, then it is no more than a shadow-life, for the memory of what has been is more than this pale shadow-reality!

Teacher. The present is a fleeting moment, it passes away as you experience it; the consciousness of life lies in memory. Only in this sense can you observe what is past, whether it happened long ago or just now.

Student. You speak truthfully!—Thus a great man lives on in me not according to *his* way, but according to mine, as I absorb him. [According to] how—and whether—I want to remember him?

Teacher. Indeed, only that lives on in you which your mind [*Sinn*] is capable of absorbing, insofar as it has similarities to you. Anything in you that is unlike it does not connect with it—it cannot work on it. All things work only with this limitation. That which you have no sense for is lost to you, like the world of colors is lost to the blind.

Student. So I must believe that nothing is lost, since all causes live on in their consequences, but that they only work on that which has receptivity or sense for them.—The world may be satisfied by this *not being lost*, by this kind of living on, but to me it is not enough. I want to go back into the womb of the past; I long to be immediately connected with the Manes of great antiquity.[12]

Teacher. Do you think that is possible?

Student. I had thought it impossible before longing drew me there. Yesterday I would have considered any question of this sort to be foolish. Today I wish the connection with the spiritual world were possible—yes, it seems I would be inclined to find it believable.

Teacher. It seems to me the Manes of the great Gustav Adolph have helped bring light to your inner eye. So hear me, then. As surely as all harmonious things are connected, whether they are visible or invisible, just as surely we, too, are connected with the part of the spiritual world that harmonizes with us. Even if they never know of each other, people with similar thoughts are, in a spiritual sense, connected. The death of a person connected with me in this way does not cancel out this connection; death is a chemical process, a separation of forces, but no annihilator: it does not tear the bond between me and similar souls. But the progress of one soul while another remains behind can cancel out this fellowship, as someone who has advanced in all virtues will not harmonize with a friend of their youth who remains ignorant. You will easily be able to apply this in general and to particular cases.

Student. Perfectly!—You say harmony between forces is connection, and death does not cancel out this connection, as it only divides and does not annihilate.

Teacher. I added to that: the canceling out of that which determines this harmony must also necessarily cancel out this connection. A connection with the dead can therefore take place, if they have not stopped harmonizing with us.

Student. I can grasp that.

---

[12] [The Manes are ancient Roman deities who have sometimes been thought of as the souls of the dead. The text, "The Manes," was originally composed by Günderode between 1802 and 1804 and was included by Brentano von Arnim in *Günderode*. Günderrode had published "The Manes" before her death, and the version that Brentano von Arnim includes in her book is edited.]

Teacher. It just comes down to becoming aware of this connection. Forces that are only spiritual cannot be revealed to our outer senses; they do not work through eyes and ears, but through the only organ by which a connection with them is possible: through the inner sense [*innern Sinn*]—on this they work immediately. This inner sense, the deepest and finest organ of the soul, is undeveloped in almost all people and only there in seed form.—The noise of the world, human doings and dealings, which touch only the surface and only superficially, do not allow this organ to develop, to become conscious. For this reason, [this organ] is not recognized, and what is revealed in it in all ages has encountered many doubters and vilifiers, and until now it has only been received by and had an effect in rare people, people of the most individual rarity.—I don't want to argue for unspiritual visions and spiritual apparitions, but I can think clearly that the inner sense can become so highly animated that inner appearances can come before the bodily eyes, just as, conversely, outer appearances come before the spiritual eye [*geistige Auge*]. So I do not need to explain everything miraculous as fraudulent or as a deception of the senses. Still, I know that in everyday speech one calls this inner development of the senses "imagination."

Someone whose spiritual eye picks up the light sees things that are invisible to others, which are connected with that person. Religions emerged from this inner sense, and many apocalypses of ancient and modern times.[13] Out of this sensory capacity to perceive connections, which those whose spiritual eye is closed do not grasp, emerges the prophetic gift of connecting the present and the past with the future, of seeing the necessary connection of causes and effects: prophecy is the sense for the future. One cannot learn the art of divination; the sense for it is mysterious, and it develops in a mysterious way. It often reveals itself only like a quick flash that is then buried again by dark night. One cannot call spirits through incantations, but they can reveal themselves to the spirit, the sensitive can feel them, they can appear to the inner sense.—

The teacher fell silent and his listener left him. Various thoughts moved his inner being and his whole soul strove to take possession of what he had heard.

---

[13] [Although *apocalypse* is often associated with the end of the world, its original meaning is "uncovering" or "revelation." Here Günderrode is using "apocalypse" in this sense, to mean religious revelations.]

The Correspondence between Bettine and Karoline

[Letter from Bettine to Karoline]

[. . .]

People are good, and I feel that way toward them from my heart, but why is it that I can't talk to anyone?—God willed that I'm only at home with you.—I read "The Manes" again and again: it really awakens me to contemplation. You say you don't like the language in it?—I believe that great thoughts, which you're thinking for the first time, are so surprising because the words by which you absorb them, with which you seek to express them, seem too trifling. It's as if we're too timid to use a word that's not yet customary. But why is that? I would always like to talk in a way that isn't permitted if, in that way, my speech more closely reflected my soul.

I certainly believe music must prevail in the soul: mood without melody is not fluent thinking; there must be something inborn in the soul within which the stream of thoughts flows.—Your letter is wholly melodious to me, like your conversation. *"If you aren't coming to us again, then write to me again, for you are dear to me."* These words have a melodious cadence, and then: *"Over time I have thought of you so often, dear Bettine! A few nights ago I dreamed you had died. I wept very much about it and the whole day there was a sad resonance from it in my soul."* I, too, dearest little Günderode, would weep very much if I should have to leave you here and go to another world; I can't imagine that I might come to myself somewhere without you. The musical sound of those words expresses itself like the heartbeat of your feeling: it is living love that you feel for me. I'm really happy. I also believe that without music nothing can exist in the spirit, and that only *those* spirits feel free for which the mood remains true.—I can't say it very clearly yet: I think you can't read a book, understand one, or absorb its spirit, if it doesn't carry an inborn melody. I believe that everything must be immediately graspable or touchable if its melody flows. And, because I think that, it occurs to me to wonder whether everything that is not melodious may also actually be untrue. To me your Schelling and your Fichte and your Kant are wholly impossible fellows. What effort I put in, and in fact I only ran away here because I wanted a break. Repulsion, attraction, highest potency.—

Do you know how it seems to me?—Spinning—My head gets dizzy and then do you know what else?—I'm ashamed—yes, I'm ashamed to drive into language like that with picks and crowbars in order to drill something out of it, and that a person who is born healthy must think their head is covered in lumps and imagine all kinds of illnesses of the spirit.—Don't you think a philosopher is terribly arrogant?—Or, if he has even one thought, does that make him clever?—Oh no, thoughts fall from him like shavings from a lathe, such a wise master isn't clever just because of that. Wisdom must be natural; why would it need such obnoxious tools to get started? Wisdom is living—it won't put up with that.—The man of the spirit must love nature above all, with true love; then he blossoms—then nature plants spirit in him. But to me, a philosopher doesn't seem to be someone like that, who lies at nature's bosom and trusts in her and devotes himself to her with all his forces.—It seems to me much more that he steals whatever he can from her, which he mashes up in his secret factory, and has a hard time making sure it doesn't falter: here a wheel, there a weight, one machine connects with another; and he shows students how his perpetual motion machine goes, and sweats a lot doing it, and the students are astonished by it and become very stupid from it.

—Forgive me that I say such fabulous stuff; you know I've never gone further with my revulsion than getting hot and dizzy from it. And when the great thoughts of your conversation appear before me, which are philosophical, then I know that nothing is spirit except philosophy. But turn it around and say: nothing is philosophy except ever-living spirit, which cannot be grasped or inspected or surveyed, but only felt, which works anew and as an ideal in everyone, and, in short, that's like the ether around us. You cannot grasp it with your eyes; you can only feel yourself illuminated, surrounded by it; you can live from it, but not generate it for yourself. Isn't the spirit of creative nature more powerful, then, than the philosopher with his triangle,[14] poking at its creative forces here and there—what does he want?—Does he think this thought-performance is a compelling way to approach the spirit of nature? I don't believe nature can stand someone who has shrunken himself into a philosopher. *"How lovely and good nature is, holding me to her bosom"*—that sounds like a joke to a philosopher. But you are a poet and everything you say is true and holy. *"One cannot call spirits through incantations, but they can reveal themselves to the spirit, the sensitive can sense them, they can appear to the inner sense."* Yes! Even if the whole of today's world doesn't grasp what you say, which I believe is the case, even if it's spoken in vain to the world, I am still the student whose whole soul strives to take possession of what I have heard.— From this teaching my future happiness will bloom, not because I learned it,

[14] [Brentano von Arnim refers to the "triangle" at several points in this text, always in a negative sense. As a measuring instrument, the triangle represents what she sees as the "philosophical" tendency to measure, calculate, and reduce the rich natural world to simple shapes and numbers.]

but because I feel it. It has become a seed in me and is deeply rooted. I can even say it expresses my nature, or rather it is the holy word "Let there be" [15] that you speak over me.—I've read it every night in bed, and no longer feel alone and for nothing in the world; I imagine that because spirits can reveal themselves to a person's spirit they might speak to mine. And what the world calls "oversensitive imagination"—I will silently make sacrifices to that, and protect my mind against anything that could make me incapable of it, for I feel my conscience secretly warning me to avoid certain things.—And, as I talk with you today, I feel there is an unconscious consciousness, which is feeling, and that the spirit is animated unconsciously—it must be like that with spirits.
[. . .]

    Bettine.

[Letter from Bettine to Karoline]
[. . .]

   Imagine a philosopher who lived entirely alone on an island where it was as beautiful as only spring can be. Everything bloomed free and alive and birds sang, and all that nature bore was perfectly beautiful, but there were no creatures there out of which the philosopher could make anything wise. Do you believe he'd come up with [mental] leaps like the ones I can't compel from you?—Listen, I believe he would gladly bite into a beautiful apple, but he wouldn't manage to build such a strange wooden framework for his own edification from the high cedars of Lebanon. The philosopher connects and transfers and changes and considers and unites only his work of thought. He does this not in order to understand himself—then he wouldn't make such an effort—but in order condescendingly to make others think how high he has climbed. And he doesn't even want to share his wisdom with his companions below; he only wants to propound the hocus pocus of his superlative machine, the triangle that connects all parallel circles, the isosceles and offset angle, how they connect with each other and bear his spirit, hovering, to those heights. That's what he wants, but only an idle person, still unknown to themselves, would be caught by it; anyone else is lying if they deny nature and depend on this framework and climb up too. It is vanity, and up there it becomes pride, and he breathes sulfur fumes down upon the spirit;

---

[15] [In the original German, this is *Es werde*. Brentano von Arnim is referring to the creation story in Genesis 1:3, in which God creates the world with his word.]

there in the blue haze people delude themselves that they perceive the high motivating ground [*Beweggrund*] of being. [...]

[Letter from Bettine to Karoline, and Karoline's response to Bettine]
[...]

On Monday.

The history teacher comes three times a week, Tuesday, Wednesday, and Thursday, bracketed behind and in front by two lazybones: Friday-Saturday at the end, Sunday-Monday at the beginning.—He instructs me in a way that means I will probably forever turn my back on the future, and would also be cheated of the dear present if the unripe apricots in Grandmother's garden didn't awaken my thievery, with which I intend to obtain something more tangible for my understanding than: "The history of Egypt in its earliest times is dark and uncertain." That's a piece of luck, otherwise we'd also have to bother with *that*;—"Menes is the first king we know of"—also fine with me, if only we heard something intelligent about him.—"He built Memphis and guided the Nile into a safe bed. Moeris dug Lake Moeris, to hinder the harmful flooding of the Nile.—Then follows Sesostris the conqueror, who killed himself."—Why?—Was he beautiful?—did he love?—was he young?—was he depressed?—No answer from the teacher follows all this, only the remark that one might better imagine Sesostris as old.—I prove to him that he was young, merely in order to set the wheel of time in motion, which always gets stuck in the historical dirt of boredom.

He also rumbled on about Busiris, who built Thebes, Psammitichus, who took the divided states under his wing, then the wars with Babylonia, Nebuchadnezzar, from whom Cambyses, Cyrus's son, takes Babylonia again. The Egyptians unite with Libya, set themselves free again, war with the Persians, until Alexander makes an end to the fight and, to my satisfaction, to the story.

That's the content of the first hour—you see that I paid attention. But had I not had the spurs to hunt down boredom and show you how useless it is to stoke the ashes again, from which nature cannot consume the salt[16]— there's no more life in it—I'd have thought we'd let the old rulers molder on in their pyramids.—Spring makes the earth swell, all around it urges on the

---

[16] [In analytic chemistry, ash is defined as the dry residue of burning, which contains metal salts. After a material has been completely burned, and cannot be burned any more, this is what is left.]

sprouts—and turns green in unfolded leaves—it also urges on my senses, swellingly intoxicates my lips, so that the brittle wrappings and buds of my thoughts burst open in the renewed sun.

[...]

Saturday.

[...]

This morning Hoffmann said: "The simple harmonic jump is when a harmony between two successive chords is heard in the mind."[17]—I don't hear this harmony in my mind; I'm wholly penetrated by what I feel, not by what I understand.—Believe it: music works, enthuses, delights not through the fact that we hear it, but through the power of the intermediate harmonies that are passed over; *these* bind the audible bodily spirit of music to themselves, with their inaudible spiritual power.—*That* is its tremendous influence upon us: that we are aroused by what is heard to what is unheard. For through *one* tone we are related to them all, and through them all we are related to every single one in particular. I can only say: during the music rehearsal I fell with certainty upon the thought of how God created the world.—The great word: *Let there be*, is clear to me. Without the one, everything is nothing; without everything, the one does not exist. All creation surges in breath: fire, earth, air, and water, and all life and all being is the marriage of these four spirits, which are the life of the cosmos. These four also create and generate themselves in spirit, which they unite in each other. Music is the self-generation of these four elements in each other. In each creature that lives, these elements generate themselves; that's spirit, that's music. The animal, too, has music; it is sensuously penetrated by water, air, earth, and fire, by their spirit, which generates itself in it. That's why it's so excited by music, because its senses slumber, dream in it, and everything has the same right to divinity that's raised to spirit by the self-generation of the elements within it.

—I wrote this; I stare at these lines and don't know what I wanted to say.—

In the light of day the spiritual host of the mind disperses, but there under the linen, where the sun dripped upon me through the gathered drops of water, where I lay caught in the net of all the blooming grasses, there it was clear to me: No, not that which we perceive with the senses is true sensuality—but rather that which moves our senses—to live together, create together: that is life, that is sensuality—to be active!

---

[17] [Brentano von Arnim is referring to Philipp Carl Hoffmann, her music tutor.]

Enough; the spirits were mighty in me during the music. They called to me clearly: Take a violin and join in however you feel, so you can contribute to the unfolding of the stream of harmony, and can enhance it and assert yourself in roaring out your enthusiasm;—and there on the heights expand, feel yourself in each tone, through the relationship of your voice with it.—If someone were to understand the theory of harmony and apply it rationally, they would secretly master the world, without anyone noticing, and the whole universe would sound to them like *one* symphony, and the whole of world history would drum and whistle and pipe for their great worldly pleasure.

Yes, I understand, I will not say this to Hoffmann; to him I will expound the first, second, and third degrees of all relationships, and how everything is subjugated to serve me, how I can transfer dominance to anything and take it away again, and how I therefore rule, as long as I swim with the stream of divine harmony.

Adieu! I stretch my pincers out like a crab from the shallow ground of my perceptions and seize what I first grab hold of, in order to unwind myself from my own ignorance.

To Bettine,

Hold out a little while longer with your history teacher; it's essential that, as briefly as possible, he outlines to you the physiognomy of the various peoples. You now know that, at various times, Egypt was at war with Babylonia, Media, and Assyria; from now on this people will no longer be a stagnant bog in your imagination. Active and vigorous at each task—their undertakings were almost too mighty for our comprehension; they did not hesitate to get started for fear they wouldn't reach the end. In their daily work, they put their lives into the buildings of their cities, their temples. Their rulers were sensible and thoroughly heroic in their plans. The little that we know of them gives us an idea of the force of their strength of will, which was stronger than is possible today, and allows us to imagine what the human soul could be, if it developed ever onward in simple service of itself.

The nature of the soul is probably like that of the earth: a vineyard planted on a barren mountain. Through the wine, the power of the soil works on your senses; the soul, too, will work on your senses: the wine, permeated by spirit, bestows upon you art or poetry or even higher revelation. The soul is like a stony field, which perhaps only gives the vines the peculiar fire to awaken hidden powers and achieve what we dare not expect of genius.

But you stand like a lazy youth before the day's work: you're disheartened because you don't dare to make arable the stony terrain, over which speed the winged seeds of thorns and thistles. Meanwhile, the wind has embedded many a noble seed in this wild steppe, which sprouts to flaunt itself a thousandfold.—Your shy gaze doesn't dare grasp the spirit within yourself. You pass defiantly by your own nature, you dampen its ample power with willful conspiracy against its spirit of perception, which then whisks it away again over your head, for in the middle of your litany of desolation you spark with fire. Where does this fire come from?—have the earth-spirits breathed upon you?—does it fall to you from heaven?—do you suck it into you with the air?—I do not know; should I admonish you, or should I silently let you do as you like?—and trust in the writing in your face? Again, I do not know.—I'd like to, but then sometimes I'm so anxious, when, like in your last letter, I become aware of the ability in you, how, clasped loosely within itself, it says not a word, as if sleep held it bound and when it stirs then it's like it's in a dream, but you yourself sleep all the more firmly after such explosions!

Do I do right, to say this to you?—That also torments me: one should not wake someone who sleeps through the storm!—You always seem to me as if electrical clouds discharge over your sleeping head in the sluggish air, the lightning reaches you through your sunken lashes, brightens your dream, crisscrosses it with enthusiasm, so that you speak aloud, without knowing what you say, and sleep on.—Yes, so it is. For your curiosity must be excited to the utmost about everything your genius says to you, despite the fact that you often don't dare to understand it. For you are cowardly—genius's inspirations prompt you to think; you don't want that, you don't want to be woken, you want to sleep. It will avenge itself upon you—do you want to reject your lover like that?—who fierily draws near to you?—is that not a sin?—I don't mean me, nor Clemens, who watches your movements with concern; I mean yourself—your own spirit, which watches over you truly and which you so petulantly rebuff.

The closer the mountains, the greater their shadows, perhaps so that the present doesn't satisfy you: what lies closer to us throws shadows onto our vision, and therefore it's good that the light of the past illuminates the dark present. To me, therefore, history seems essential to revive the sluggish plant-life of your thoughts; within it lies the strong force of all education.—The past drives forward; all seeds of development in us are sown by its hand. It is one of the two worlds of eternity that surge in the human spirit; the other is the future. From the one comes every wave of thought, and to the other they hurry! Was thought born in us just this moment?—It was not. Your genius belongs to eternity, yet it strides toward you through the past, which hurries over into the future in order to pollinate it.

That's present, actual life; each moment that doesn't grow into the future, pervaded by it, is lost time for which we must give a reckoning. This reckoning is nothing other than retrieving the past, a means of bringing back what is lost, for, with the recognition of what has been missed, the dew falls on the neglected fields of the past and revives the seeds to grow into the future.—Did you yourself not say last fall in the convent garden how the thistle bush at the steps, around which we saw so many bees and bumblebees swarming in the spring, scattered out its fluffs of seed: "There the wind drives the seeds of the past into the future." And on the green castle at night, where we couldn't sleep because of the storm—did you not say then: "The wind comes from the distance, its voice sounds over here from the past; and its fine whistling is the urge to hurry on into the future."

Among the many things that you babbled, laughed, yes spoke outrageously that night, I held onto these, and can now offer you as a treat your own big ideas,[18] which you scatter around so thoroughly in your musical abstractions.—You remind me of the fable of the stork and the fox,[19] except I, poor little fox, completely innocently offered you the shallow dish of history, but you, long-beaked, chose with diligence the long-necked flask of mysticism in figured bass and theories of harmony, while I of course stand by, sober and ravenous.

[…]

Karoline.

[Letter from Karoline to Bettine]

[…]

You are not self-determining [selbsttätig], but completely surrendered to the unconscious; all reality dissolves out of you like fog. Human deeds,

---

[18] [Brentano von Arnim uses the German phrase große Rosinen, which literally means "large raisins." Raisins could be served for dessert and scattered around; but in German, "having raisins in one's head" also refers to someone who has overinflated ideas.]

[19] [In one of Aesop's fables, a fox offers a stork soup in a bowl so shallow the stork can't get its long beak into it to drink it. The stork retaliates by offering the fox a meal in a bottle with a neck too narrow for the fox to get at the food. The moral of the story is to treat others as you would like them to treat you, but here Günderode claims that, unlike the fox, she offered the shallow bowl innocently, not intending to trick her friend.]

human feelings—you were not born for that, and yet you're always recklessly ready to rule everything, to appropriate everything for yourself. Icarus was a careful, considered, testing lad compared to you: he tried to sail through the solar ocean with wings, but you don't need your feet to stride, nor your ideas to comprehend, nor your memory to experience or to infer. Your armor-plated fantasy, which scatters all reality in the storm, stops in rapture at a black salsify.[20] [...]

I'm intimidated by your claims, held to the fire by your exuberance. Here at the writing desk I lose patience with my dull attempts at poetry, when I think of your Hölderlin. You cannot write poetry, because you are that which the poets call poetic: material does not form itself; it is formed. You seem to me to be the clay that a god sets foot upon to form, and what I notice in you is the fermenting fire which his supersensible touch kneads so strongly into you. So let us surrender to him; he who prepares you will also form you.—I must form and make myself, as well as I can.

I wrote the little poem I'm sending here for Clemens with an inward gaze.[21] There's a truth in poetry which I've always believed in till now. To thrust this irksome earthly world from us like old sourdough, to strive toward a new life in which the soul may no longer deny its higher properties—I think poetry is suitable for that. [...]

[Bettine's response to Karoline]
[...]

You choose a beautiful thought and set it in rhyme as a robe of honor for Clemens, oh, what a beautiful virtue you have there, you raise spirit from earthly life.

God created the world from nothing, the nuns always preached—and I always wanted to know how.[22] They couldn't tell me that and told me to be quiet, but I walked around and looked at all the plants as if I had to find out what they were made out of.—Now I know: he didn't create them out of nothing; he created them out of spirit—that I learned from the poets, from you: God is a poet—yes, I think of him like that.

---

[20] [*Scorzonera hispanica*, a root vegetable in the sunflower family, was (wrongly) considered in medieval times to guard against snake bites and bubonic plague.]

[21] [The poem Günderode is referring to is "To Clemens." According to Walter Morgenthaler (the editor of Günderrode's collected works), the evidence that this poem was actually written by Günderrode is inconclusive (see Günderrode, *Sämtliche Werke*, Vol. 2, 278).]

[22] [As a child, Brentano von Arnim was educated in a Catholic convent.]

Today I read to Grandmama from Hemsterhuis:[23] Choiseil[24] said, "God must have the form of a man because he created him in his image";[25] d'Allaris reckoned: "It is most singular, sir, to imagine the figure of God with a human face, as the latter is made for earthly needs and functions with which God can have no connection; because of his strength and his great courage the whole world would depart in dust if the good Lord just once enjoyed a hearty sneeze."[26]—If God created humans in his own image (so I understand this), God has personhood, which, however, only he can grasp, for he faces himself alone, but as a poet his personhood vanishes, it dissolves in the fabrication of his creation. So God has and does not have personhood. The poet represents this—he has and does not have personhood, entirely according to God's image, because he creates with the spirit what lies wholly outside sensuous being; but it is still sensuous, for the senses grasp it and feel nursed and nourished by it. And because nourishment of the senses is their higher development, the poet, like God, dissolves his personhood into a higher form through his thinking, and develops himself in a higher form.

What am I saying to you there?—Ah, for a moment I understood what God is, as if I could read it in the clouds, and then I saw in the sky how the moon sweeps forth and scatters my thoughts so I cannot read any more; everything melts, and the words there above, in which I wanted to hold it fast, are blurred. I had to speak with other words; it's not exactly as I meant it. Yes, God does not let himself be caught; I thought I had him.—But that one thing I retained, that God is poetry, that the human being is created in his image, that the human being is therefore born a poet, but that all are called and few chosen, which I must, sadly, experience in myself. Still, I am a poet, although I can't make rhymes: I feel it when I go into the free air, in the forest or up

---

[23] [Franz Hemsterhuis (1721–1790), a Dutch philosopher.]

[24] [Choiseul (which Brentano von Arnim also spells "Choeseil") and d'Allaris are friends of Brentano von Arnim's grandmother, La Roche. Later in the book, Brentano von Arnim describes them as "emigrants" (*Emigranten*)—most likely, they are French aristocrats who left France after the Revolution. Here they are commenting on Brentano von Arnim's reading from an unnamed book by Hemsterhuis in which, judging from their comments, Hemsterhuis claims that God made human beings in his image.]

[25] [Brentano von Arnim quotes here in French: *il faut que Dieu ait la figure de l'homme comme il l'a créé d'après son immage.*]

[26] [Brentano von Arnim writes here in (not always correct) French: *C'est fort singulier monsieur de se figurer la figure de Dieu avec un visage humain, comme celui la est fait pour des besoin et des fonctions terrestres auquelles dieu ne doit avoir aucun raport, en raison de sa force et de son grand courage le monde entier devrait s'en aller en poussière si par exemble le bon Dieu s'amusait une seule foix a eternuer de bon coeur.*]

on the mountains. There is a rhythm in my soul, according to which I must think, and my tune changes in its cadence.

And then, when I'm among people, and let myself be swept along by their cadence or meter, which follows the popular melody, then I feel wretched and know nothing but silly stuff. Do you also feel that silly people make one much sillier than they are themselves? So they're not wrong when they say I'm silly. But you, heart that understands me, only come and I'll give you a banquet that honors you.—But only listen a little longer:

All great action is poetry, is transformation of personhood into divinity, and any action that is not poetry is not great, but everything is great that is grasped with the light of reason. That means: everything you grasp in its true sense must be great, and it's certain that every such thought must have roots planted in the soil of wisdom and a flower that blooms in divine light. To proceed from the ground of the soul, in God's image, out, up to our source. Isn't it? Am I right?—And if it's true that human beings can be like that, why should they be any other way?—I don't understand it, people are all different from how it would be so easy to be;—they cling to what they shouldn't heed, and scorn what they should cling to.

Ah, I long to be clean from these failings. [...]

[Letter from Bettine to Karoline]
[...]
—Only yesterday in the copse, among various new pieces of music that really didn't excite me, a symphony by Friedrich the Second was performed.[27] Right in front of me he mounts bravely in stiff boots with clanking spurs, resounding back to him from all sides; he must boldly gallop away over timid humanity and soon he doesn't worry about that anymore; only the one muse, the art of tones, confronts him firmly. His steed has borne him into the loneliest wasteland, far from the people he leads with a whistle like a pack of dogs. Here he kneels before the only overpowering one, here he confesses the wide emptiness of his mind, here he wants to have balm laid on all wounds; impatient and tender, full of humility, he kisses the traces of her wandering, and with trust bends his crowned head under her blessing.—Purified, consoled, as if nothing had happened to him, he turns from this flute adagio back to

---

[27] [Brentano von Arnim may be describing Johann Sebastian Bach's piece *Das musikalische Opfer*, which Bach wrote on the basis of a musical theme given to him by King Friedrich II of Prussia (also known as Frederick the Great) in 1747.]

his people in the brilliant clashing of the violins and oboes.—But I feel how art serves wisdom. Where no hand reaches, where no lips open, no thought ventures, there she appears as a priestess, and one's heart breaks before her, declares its confessions pleadingly, wants to accuse itself of every fault, wants to be wholly taken up into her bosom. Yes, music—she crushes gold and steel; no helmet sits so firmly upon the head, and no armor on the breast; she penetrates them, and the king, like the vassal, pledges himself to *her*.

But what about the symphony by Beethoven that immediately followed that?—Would you go with me among that olive wood's uniform trunks with foliage like velvet, swimming in the wind that strikes waves in their green veils and gently whispers around your lonely silent step on the flocked sward!—Come!—look at the sun in its fiery shell, its arrow beams streaming from the arc into the eternal blue.—Soon, carried by the changing waves, the unending ocean sways under you. The wind travels there between towering waves—blazes trails for silver gods that rush off, entwining themselves with you according to heavenly rhythms born from your breast. So closely is everything related to you.—Yet without end this ocean changes, it bowls along, in its moody rapture coloration upon coloration slips through its play of waves, fetters your gaze—penetrates your senses, languishing and then fiery, laughing, weeping, blindingly and again enveloped—so rapidly it streaks past like enthusiasm's gaze from beloved eyes; you cannot grasp it, cannot leave it.—Pure from the clouds of heaven, its breath gently chases little waves before it—innumerable—one upon the other, and all die on the shore with soft sighs.—Ah!—sweet moment ruling over passion's ocean!—There your breath falters, and wants to hold—wholly and forever—everything that, each moment, without ceasing, disappears from you.—

What is it, the soul in the ocean of music?—Does it feel pain?—Does it have desires, this wonderfully moving one?—No thought may follow it—Does it feel, by reaction, everything it stirs?—Does it love when we love?—Does it flatter its seething when our tears mingle with it?—Oh, I would throw myself into the emerald lagoons, over which, borne lightly through the monstrous ocean to its heights, the boat rocks us, we two related souls, harmoniously to the last note.—And then—the same stillness of air, the same heavenly purity, the same breath, sweet—untouched,—the same sunlight in the spirit,—drunk from sweet swaying of the tones that stir through the breast. Yet soon it ascends! The great spirit of creation—in the roaring you hear its voice, which nestles everything to itself, breathe out—then in the awe of your breast its breath rises again—and now—violently—in inexhaustible rising and falling it streams frothing against the winds, which—agitating in the abyss—blast it back.—Yes, that is Beethoven's ocean of music, from heaven to heaven the tones rise and more boldly the more often they stream down again, and you feel yourself secure on the free cliff high over this double sound, encircled by those raging hurricanes, those waves, that without end rise in your heart and without end are thrown back, without ceasing return with renewed might, blaring around you, overwhelming each other and yet dividing again in the solar ocean of harmony. And, finally, all the longing voices, tumbling in joyful confusion of the jubilation of woe, and the thousand feelings, that at a single light sign from his masterful hand—all at the same time agree: now it is enough!—

Ah, what is it like, there in your breast?—yes, confess!—is it not the ocean, music?—and he, Beethoven, is it not he who commands it?—And do you not also feel here: the divine, which grants the spirit of creation, is unbridled passion?—And do you not believe that God's spirit is just sheer passion?—What is passion but life intensified by the feeling that the divine is near to you, that you can attain it, that you can flow together with it?—What is your happiness, your soul's life, but passion? And how is the power of your activity increased? What revelations occur in your breast, that you previously had not dreamed of? What is too difficult for you?—Which of your limbs would not stir themselves in its service?—Where is your thirst, your hunger?—You see, already you're beginning to live from the air; lightly like a bird you surmount the insurmountable, and out into the distance you send flames of your immortality, and they kindle the eternal, and it devotes itself to your service, pours out in streams of passion, in the great ocean over which the eternal stars shine for you and the night pales in their luster and dawns joyfully awaken.

Yes, for this reason, the error of the church fathers, that God is wisdom, is really offensive; for *God is passion.*—Great, encompassing everything in his bosom, which reflects all life like the ocean, and all passion pours itself out in it like streams of life. And encompassing it all is passion, the highest peace.

[…]

[Letter from Bettine to Karoline]

[…]

God is poetry, I said in my last letter, and wisdom, the church fathers say. I denied that and said God is passion; wisdom serves him well to sustain the world of passion, but it is not him. My reasons: what should God do with all his wisdom if he can't apply it? If something new is generated from every-thing that is created, if no power, no force is superfluous, but for the sake of its highest development must eternally increase, stimulating itself, then God's wisdom can't want to lay its hands idly in its lap.—To govern heaven and earth where the sun and the moon and all the stars are already fixed for eternity—that can have no allure for wisdom. To meddle in human af-fairs, to answer human prayers, which are all perverse—that must surely go on by itself at the heavenly court. Should God take things on himself, that would be unwise, for if the breath of God outweighed all the spiritual labors of humanity, then these would never be able to release the seed of their own wisdom in themselves.

Our spirit is powerful like fire: it should stoke itself. We have passion: it should rise in spiritual fire toward heaven, to its eternal creator, pass over with everything into his passion's glow. The mighty spirit of immortality does not ascend in passion in vain; each breath, each gaze should last forever, so says an inner voice. I swear eternal fidelity to everything that delights me in nature: the breezes' caresses, how could I refuse them my hot breath, which is only hot so it can cool itself in the breezes' love? The clear wavering waters, how could I not entrust myself to them, which bear me, quietly bedded, upon eternally stirring life, like love bears the beloved? And the gentle soft earth, how could the senses turn from her, who leaves no impulse unborn, bears each seed in the winds, and, secretly in the cradle of all creation, gives wings so that one day the spirit will unfold mightily toward heaven when it has ripened through her bounty? She, the heavenly earth—upon which all life tumbles jubilantly and who bears everything in her breast and over it—who lets all living beings trample around—and gives them the milk of her herbs and fruits that spring from her bosom in such great fullness—yes, how could I not love her, the twice-loving, with hot love?—And then—the light that descends into the darkness to play there, lonely:—and breathes into the lone-liness, and nourishes and drenches earth's forces, which then play around the spirit so that, in its own sealed darkness, it remembers light's passion for it and grows toward it to kiss it.

If all of you poeticize from these truths, so mighty, so alive in themselves that they move the poet's breast so that the poet becomes their element and utters them eternally, oh, then let them be born for me so that I trust them, so that I surrender myself to them and enjoy them. Why do they press them-selves eternally into your spirit, why do they move your lips so that you utter them, if they are not true living life that, through you, shall be born again in the human senses? Now my senses are a fruitful field, they have taken up your seed, oh, everything that was intuited by you, everything that you read in the clouds, has come to life for me. That is it!—And what, after all, did I want to say?

Ah, how far I have strayed, and I only wanted to speak about God, and say that he could not be wisdom, but passion, which wisdom uses in order boldly and bravely to produce that which seethes within it.—Yet how do I tell you this if you don't understand it from yourself, if you don't understand that all being wants to be expressed by passion? Yes, even repose is nothing other than passion. That the human being is created with a god's breast, in which the passions have their hearth upon which to offer an eternal living blaze to the divine.—If you don't say yes to that, how can I force it from you?—So come and let us gather wisdom, in order to stoke the blaze of our passions with it.—

We have protested against the idea that God is wisdom. However, that wisdom and valor are in love with each other—but not the wisdom and valor of the church fathers—that is *our* teaching. These are the hearth upon which the passions flame; without them passion cannot breathe.—And if there were no burning passions between force and spirit, where should their fire come from? For nothing comes from nothing.—They would lie down to sleep and die out, the forces and the spirit—but the ardent drive to revel in each other, to possess each other, stoke the fire of life in them, constant inner movement toward each other. Feeling, sensed by the other in every impulse—that is inner living life and everything else is not living in us.

Why would one feel shame if not for this inner tyrant of love that calls feelings to account for having broken the trust of one of the inner powers, or for surrendering oneself to a weakness in front of one's beloved? What is conscience other than the court of the spirit for the senses—where they surrender to each other and perform sacrifices, heroic deeds for each other, and receive inner tokens of love? And then that voice [*Stimme*] that tests each mood [*Stimmung*]: the more deeply and broadly this life is cultivated, the more firmly it grounds its claims and justifications, the more easily it is damaged.

Ah, I say to you, there is a nobility, a heightened drive in the soul that streams back to what is outside life, all from the passionate contact of the senses with the spirit. When you walk, when you turn, when you raise your voice—whatever removes you, even for a moment from the present (influence) of those stirrings of life, do you not feel reproach?—a faltering, a powerlessness within you?—does your heart not beat in torment as if it must turn back?—to there, where the senses imagine themselves beloved by spirit, tenderly embracing it.—Ah, I must speak such nonsense—with tears, for I am so deeply moved, but how should I tell you that?—The noble human a hotbed of passions, crude forces that aspire to life through love among themselves!—

[Letter from Bettine to Karoline]
[...]

Kissing is the form, and absorbing the spirit of the form as we touch it, that's the kiss—yes, the kiss is the form born within us.

For this reason, language is also kissing. Every word in a poem kisses us, but everything that isn't poeticized isn't spoken; it's only barked like dogs. Yes, what do you want from language other than to touch the soul, and what else does the kiss want? It will suck the form into itself and touch the soul; all that is the same. I've learned this from nature, she kisses me constantly—I may go or stay wherever I want; she kisses me, and I'm so used to it that I come to meet her with my eyes, for the eyes are the mouth that nature kisses. Do you see? And so I also feel that a bud kisses me differently from a flower—why? They are different in form, but this kissing is speaking—I could say: nature, your kiss speaks to my soul.—Yes, I also wrote that thought in my book, but I wanted to leave it, I can add further to it.

Ah, when I look around myself like that, how all the branches stretch toward me and talk with me, that means kiss my soul, and everything speaks, everything that I look at hangs with its lips upon my soul's lips, and then the color, the form, the fragrance, everything wants to assert itself in language. Now, the color is the tone, the form is the word, and the fragrance is the spirit, so I can say the whole of nature speaks into me, that means she kisses my soul.

The soul must grow from that, it is its element, for everything alive has its element in nature. The element of the soul is therefore looking, which is listening; it imbibes all forms, that's the language of nature. But nature herself also has a soul, and this soul also wants to be kissed and nourished, just like my soul is nourished by nature's language, when I'm pervaded by it (for there are moments when the soul is like a fire from life, when it is wholly and completely only that which it has absorbed into itself, namely nature talking to herself; there it recognizes nature as needing nourishment). So I have stood before her and spoken back into her, I have kissed her with my soul's lips.

See, that was spirit, that was not thought; that was original life-spirit without earthly form. Thought is the earthly form of spirit—but my spirit did not absorb this form when it spoke with it; it was not thought, it was not feeling or sensation, for that also seems different to me; it was will—yes, it was will that looked at nature so swiftly and firmly as if it wanted to give her back everything that she gave to it, namely life.—That's it, everything is recip-rocal action, everything that lives gives life and must receive life.

But just don't believe that all people are alive; they live but they are not alive. I feel that in myself: I am only alive when my spirit is in this reciprocal action with nature.—Thus I also know that tears need not be the consequence of pain or pleasure—they can also be a natural consequence, like sleep can be the consequence of excited spirit.—For I must often suddenly weep without having previously been emotional: that's when nature has seized me, secretly shaken my soul, so that I must weep. And often I even lie on the ground, on the velvet-black plowed-up earth that so warmly steams from below, and that warms me because I am freezing—yes, the spirit freezes in me. I lay myself down on the ground, and my whole spirit will immediately be warm again, I feel how it moves through my head and through my breast and then I must immediately hold my hands prayerfully together. You see, all that is not thought and yet is spirit.—Spirit that is in reciprocal action with nature.—

I'm really happy I found the words today; I would have spoken with you about it earlier but I didn't find the words. [. . .]

[Letter from Bettine to Karoline]

[. . .]

It certainly seems to me with this Hölderlin as if a divine power must have overflowed him like floodwaters, namely language, pouring over his senses in overpowering swift plunging, and drowning them; and when the currents had run themselves out, his senses were weakened and the power of his spirit overwhelmed and deadened.—And St. Clair[28] says: yes, so it is—and he also says: but listening to him is like the raging of the wind, for he always blusters on in hymns that break off like when the wind turns—and then he is seized as if with a deeper knowledge, at which the idea that he is insane totally vanishes, and one listens to what he says about verse and about language as

---

[28] [Isaac von Sinclair (1775–1815) was a writer, politician, and friend of Hölderlin as well as of Brentano von Arnim's family. The nickname Sinclair is often given to people with the name St. Clair; perhaps for this reason von Arnim spells Sinclair "St. Clair."]

if he were close to illuminating the divine secret of language, and then everything vanishes from him again in the dark, and he languishes in confusion and it seems he won't be able to make himself comprehensible.

And language forms all thought, for it is greater than the human spirit, which is only a slave to language, and the human spirit will not be perfect so long as language alone doesn't call it forth. But the laws of the spirit are metric, one feels that in language; these laws throw their net over the spirit which, caught in this net, must express the divine, and as long as the poets still seek regular verse and are not swept away by rhythm, their poetry will have no truth, for poetry is not foolish senseless rhyming, in which no deeper spirit can take pleasure. Rather, poetry is *this*: that the spirit can only express itself rhythmically, that its language lies only in rhythm, while what is without poetry is also without spirit, and consequently unrhythmic. Is it, then, worth the effort to try to force feelings into rhymes with words so poor in the spirit of language, where nothing is left except to rhyme the laboriously sought artifice, so that the spirit chokes in one's throat? Only *that* spirit is poetry that bears within itself the secret of rhythm, and only with this rhythm can it become living and visible, for this is its soul. But poems are mere specters, not spirits with souls.—

There are higher laws for poetry. Each stirring of emotion develops according to new laws that cannot be applied to others, for all truth is prophetic and flows over its time with light, and it is entrusted to poetry alone to spread this light. For this reason, the spirit must and can only emerge through poetry. Spirit emerges only through enthusiasm.—Rhythm acquiesces only to those in whom spirit becomes alive!—Again:—

"Anyone who is educated for poetry in the divine sense must acknowledge the highest spirit as lawless over them, and must surrender the law to it. *Not as I will, but as you will!*—and so they do not need to construct laws, for poetry will never let itself be constrained, and the creating of verse will eternally remain an empty house in which only ghosts linger. But because human beings never trust enthusiasm, they cannot grasp poetry as God.—In poetry, law is the form of an idea; spirit must move in it, and not stand in its way. Laws, which human beings want to make divine, deaden the form of the idea, and the divine cannot form itself in the body through the human spirit. The body is poetry, the form of the idea, and this, if it is seized by the tragic, becomes deadly real, for the divine pours murder from words; the form of the idea, which is the body of poetry, murders—but as such it is a tragic thing that pours life out into the form of the idea (poetry)—for everything is tragic.—For life in the word (in the body) is resurrection, (vitally real [*lebendig faktisch*]), which merely emerges from what is murdered.—Death is the origin of the living.—[29]

To want to capture poetry in law, that's just swinging spirit on two ropes to give the impression that it flies.

[...]

The enthusiasm that emerges through contact with a beam of light moves it, makes it waver; and that's the poetry that creates from the primordial light and pours down all rhythm in supremacy over the spirit of time and nature, which carry the sensuous—the object—to meet it. Then, at a touch of the heavenly, enthusiasm awakens mightily in the wavering point (human spirit), and the poetic spirit must hold fast to this moment and, quite openly, without holding back, abandon its character to it.—And so this primary ray of divine poetizing is always accompanied by the peculiar nature of the poet, here languishing tragically, there mercilessly bearing down on the fire stirred by divine heroism—like the eternally still unwritten world of the dead, which maintains its circle by the inner law of spirit; there, too, a dreamy naive abandonment to the divine poetic spirit, or amiable composure in misfortune. And this objectifies the original nature of the poet with it, into the superlative of the heroic virtuosity of the divine.

I could write you many more sheets full of what, in these eight days, St. Clair wrote down in broken-off sentences from what Hölderlin said, for I read all this there, along with what St. Clair added verbally. Once, Hölderlin said: everything is rhythm, the whole destiny of human beings is one heavenly rhythm, as every work of art is also a single rhythm, and everything resonates from the poetic lips of God. And, where the human spirit acquiesces to it, there are transfigured destinies in which genius shows itself. Poetry is a struggle for truth, and here it is in the plastic spirit, there in the athletic, where the word seizes the body (poetic form), there again in the Hesperian, which is the spirit of observation and engenders the delights of poets, where among joyful feet the sound of poetry resounds, while the senses are immersed in the necessary forms of the ideas, of the spiritual power that exists in time.—This last poetic form is a celebratory nuptial enthusiasm for marriage, and now it plunges into the night and becomes clairvoyant in the

---

[29] [Brentano von Arnim seems to be recounting St. Clair's description of his meeting with Hölderlin; however, she does not include the closing quotation marks to indicate where she finishes quoting or paraphrasing St. Clair. It is likely that this is all St. Clair's account, up to the end of the paragraph just before "I could write you many more sheets full of what, in these eight days, St. Clair wrote down."]

dark; then, too, in the daylight it pours over everything it illuminates.—In contrast to that, in human time, is the terrible muse of the tragic period.—And whoever does not understand this, he said, could never understand the high Greek works of art, whose construction is divinely organic, which could not arise from human understanding but are consecrated to the *unthinkable*.

And so God has used the poet as an arrow to speed his rhythm from his bow, and those who do not feel this and adhere to it will never have the skill or the athletic virtue to be a poet, and will be too weak to compose themselves either in substance or in the worldview of the old or the new way of representing our inclinations, and no poetic forms will reveal themselves to them. Poets who rehearse given forms can only repeat spirit as it has already been given: they sit like birds on a branch of the tree of language and sway upon it according to the primordial rhythm that lies in its roots, but someone like that doesn't take wing as the eagle of spirit hatched from the living spirit of language.

I understand everything, although there is much there that is strange to me concerning the art of poetry, of which I have no clear—or even no—idea, but I've grasped spirit better through these intuitions of Hölderlin's than through what St. Clair has taught me about it.—To you, all this must be holy and important.—Ah, someone like Hölderlin, who is passionately swept away in labyrinthine quests, we must face him somehow, if we pursue the divine with such pure heroism as he does.—To me his sayings are like the sayings of oracles, which he calls out in madness as the priest of God, and certainly all worldly life is mad in relation to him, for it does not understand him. And yet how is the spiritual essence constituted of those who do not seem mad?—Is it not also madness, but a madness in which God does not participate?—We call that madness, I notice, which has no echo in the spirit of others, but all of this echoes in me, and I feel an answer to it resounds in yet deeper depths of my spirit, if only in outline. Still, in my soul it is like in thundering mountains: one echo wakes another, and so this speech of the mad will echo eternally in my soul. [...]

[Letter from Bettine to Karoline, and Karoline's response]
[...] and when in the evening I come to write, and must think the impossible, which is impossible to express, then I'm really dream-drunk, and I'm dizzy when I open my eyes: the walls spin and human activities spin with them.—And aren't there still hidden powers in language that we don't yet have?—don't yet understand how to govern?—Write to me whether you

also believe this, and whether we could push through to express what is un-spoken, for surely where language yields, spirit must stream in, for the whole spirit is only a translation of the spirit of God in us. Good night.

Bettine.

To Bettine.

You think when you reel and are a bit drunk that that's inexpressible spirit?—Then you're far too easily drunk.—Because you can't tolerate wine, you think new sources of language must open up to illuminate your ideas. Become a bit stronger, or don't drink so much at once; if you focused your eyes more firmly, language wouldn't leave you stuck.

Regarding language, I certainly believe that it's part of human life to learn how to grasp it completely, and that its yet undiscovered sources, which you seek, spring only from its simplification. The advice I'd like to give you is to relinquish proofs from your expressions of thought; this will very much un-burden you. The simple line of thought flows into its proof by itself, or, in other words: the truth itself is proof. To think without proof is to think freely; you make the proofs help you out. Such free thinking simplifies language, through which its spirit becomes more powerful. One must not shy away from that which wants to express itself, even giving it in the most unremark-able form, the deeper and more incontrovertible it is[. . . .]

[Letter from Bettine to Karoline]

On Monday.

[. . .] Do you know what makes me so attached to nature?—That it's some-times so sad.—Others call it ennui, which sometimes, in the middle of sunshine, falls upon you like a stone on your heart, but I interpret it like this: suddenly, without wanting to, one faces her, the goddess of everything [*All-göttin*]; a secret feeling of the care that she devotes to us, infinitely more tender than to all other creatures, makes us shy. Everything thrives, every little shrub, every little beetle testifies to such deep, finely articulated for-mation; but also, is there even one little bud in our spirit that isn't gnawed by worms, are we not stained by dust, and does even one little leaf of our soul show itself in its shining green?—When I come across a tree that's sick-ened by mildew or damage from caterpillars, or a shrub that's gone to seed, then I think: that's the language of nature, which shows us the image of an ungenerous soul.—And if all spirit's faults were overcome, if its powers were in full bloom, who knows if there would then still be such misgrowth or harmful weeds in nature, if the blight would still come to the cornfield, if poisonous umbels would still grow; who knows whether there would still be such sad moments in nature that cleave the heart; and make us turn away because we don't want to sense what, deep in our hearts, wails painfully with her. No, she finds no audience, the mother, although her reproaches are as tender as if she wanted to wrap us in her veil, and suck out the poison of illness with her lips, and mix balm from her blood to heal us.

"*To think without proof is to think freely!*" Let me reinforce just this one thing for you with a demonstration, as proof that I understand you!—Thinking is nourishing oneself with the truth, otherwise it would be drivel and not thinking. Thinking is drinking that balm that the mother mixes from her blood, which heals us from weaknesses, yes, thinking is listening to her tender reproaches. And to want, by proofs, to lay before one's own heart the love she gives us without reserve is proof enough that this love didn't touch the heart.—Truth touches the heart, is spirit, which instantly rises higher in receiving the truth, and looks around for something higher. You have risen higher through this recognition of the purer spiritual form, you have thrown its crutches away.—They say: how will the spirit advance without crutches?—it has no feet!—it also throws off propriety's tight coat.—"Look I have wings!" And your defense—how will you conduct it when you have no weapons? the philistines ask.—"I am a divine athlete, whoever wrestles with me may feel my triumph without weapons all the more deeply; for I am, and *they* are no more, those who wrestle with me; and if I don't overcome someone it's because they didn't even touch me to fight me."—Yes, I feel distinctly how deeply right you are: there is one pure and holy source of language that ushers in truth without proof. Language and spirit must love each other, and there's no need of proof for either of them; their mutual understanding is love, which raises itself to the stars in eternal feelings.—You are overcome, you are a prisoner of spirit—it possesses you and steps forth, and expresses you.

—Good night! Already very late.—

[Letter from Bettine to Karoline]

[...]

Grandfather wrote another beautiful letter about religion and politics, which I didn't keep, but in which every word rang like gold.—He says: in a great heart politics must arise only from religion, or rather they must be entirely the same; a busy person who spends his time on what that time was given him for doesn't have time to spare to separate them, so his religion must be revealed in him as perfectly cosmopolitan—etc.—

This letter is so magnificent, so pure-souled, so elevated over everything that petty people aim at, but also so alive, that I must believe that all philosophy arises from a living heart, with flesh and bone and a heart beating for the good, which stirs eternally and purifies earthly, worldly life and makes it healthy, like a stream of fresh herb-scented air.—But the kind of philosophy that's based on the triangle doesn't do this, but carries out a dangerous dance between attraction and repulsion and highest potency, which batters in the ribs of healthy common sense and must eventually withdraw as a crippled invalid.

And the natural history of our lives is also our task, and I think that if ingenuity would release itself from pride's disembodied speculation and turn itself fully to the state of sensory daily history, then no thought would be so deep or so sublime that it could not have a place in earthly activities, and grow and affirm itself in the moral sense.

I would like to be like Grandfather, to whom all people were equal, who appealed similarly to the minds of lords and peasants and got along with them just because of this, to whom a thing was never indifferent even if it lay outside his sphere. He said: "Whatever I can judge with my understanding belongs under my power, under my jurisdiction, and I must decide aloud and publicly, if I want to answer to God for having given me understanding for that purpose. Whoever uses his pound will receive more, and will be made lord over everything."

Yes, I'm convinced of that, but I don't believe that philosophers will achieve this goal. I believe, rather, that my Grandfather's way is the way to acquire the deepest philosophy, namely peace, the unification of the deepest spiritual knowledge with an active life.—

Grandfather wrote in another letter to the prince elector about the misuse of the many feast days and of the veneration of the saints; he wanted a purer foundation for an improved religion.—Instead of venerating so many stories of saints and miracles and relics, venerating all great acts of human beings, making their noble purposes, their sacrifices, their errors comprehensible from the pulpit, not interpreting them in a false sense but in the true sense—in short, making clear to people the history and the needs of humanity as an object of essential contemplation—would be better than them spending every Sunday afternoon with brotherhoods where they drone out meaningless little prayer verses and other nonsense.—And he suggests to the prince elector that, instead of taking all these faint-hearted, time-wasting beings under his protection, he should found a brotherhood where people's understanding would be awakened, instead of making them into idiots through meaningless exercises[. . . .]

[Letter from Bettine to Karoline]
[. . .]

Knowledge [*Wissen*] and being aware [*Wissendsein*] are two different things: the first is to gain self-sufficiency in knowing [*Kenntnis*], to become a personality through it. A mathematician, a historian, a teacher of law—all this is part of a fossilized world, is philistinism in a certain deeper sense. To be aware is to thrive in the healthy soil of the spirit, where the spirit blossoms. Then there's no need of memorization, then there's no need to separate fantasy from reality; then the desire for knowledge itself seems to me like the soul's kiss with spirit; tender touching with truth, becoming energetically animated by it, like lovers by their lover, by nature.—Nature is loved by the mind; spiritual nature must be loved by spirit; through continual life with her [nature], through enjoying her, spirit passes over into her, or she into him [spirit].

[. . .]

To know is to be an artisan [*Handwerker*], but to be aware [*Wissendsein*] is the growth of the soul, the life of the spirit with the soul together in nature; and life is love.—Be indulgent with me: I must call out everything to you, dear echo; don't worry about me if this doesn't seem to you like sound common sense.

[. . .]

[Letter from Karoline to Bettine]
[. . .]

You shut yourself off to philosophy, and yet your nature expresses it so personally, as spirit and soul and body. I don't mean this only to apply to you; it's a remark I make in the mirror. You can immediately flee from it and leave the mirror empty, but it still proves you right. For if your organic nature is wholly philosophy, then it is not first acquired by intuition.—It will have a youthful body that meets another spring, and another understanding with the spiritual things of the world.

—All the more it seems a mistake to encounter the real and want to measure your spirit against it. I seek in poetry what I also seek before a mirror: to gather myself, see myself, pass through myself to a higher world, and my poems are attempts at that. To me, the great events of humanity all seem to have the same purpose. I would like to connect with them, enter into community with them and, in their midst, under their influence, wander the same course, stride ever forward with a feeling of self-elevation, with the purpose of simplification, and of the deeper knowledge of and entry into the practice of this art. Then, just as the high artworks of the Greeks perhaps outwardly counted as perfect divine inspiration and reverberated through the crowds as such, and in this sense were formed by the masters with this concentration of all spiritual forces, so my activity gathers itself in my soul; it feels its origin, its ideal: it does not want to leave itself behind, but to cultivate itself further.

But you are the child born in the land where milk and honey flow: worry is superfluous there, the grapes hang down into your mouth, everything flourishes and is the climate of your cradle, everything sustains you and nourishes and protects you, as long as you don't change the climate. And whether the things you obtain in this way can be enjoyed by the world, that really isn't what matters most here, if only you aren't disturbed in your development by your own sins, for that is the only sin.—Be quiet about yourself and let them view you as they want, promise this to me sacredly, for otherwise they would transplant you from your original land, they would raise you up out of your childhood and want to make something of you.—And how lamentable it would be if by your own fault you alienated yourself from your inner life, your own religion, which so gently, so happily serves you! Oh no, I won't hope for it; remain forever with your spirits in the union that brings you nourishment, and don't discard them for strange fare.

I have often been reproached about you; how could I have fought back? It would have been a betrayal of you; no, I left you undisturbed by their eyes. And what are you?—Nothing but the way nature expresses itself a thousandfold—like that butterfly cocoon you brought with you from Schlangenbad this summer, which was so firm on the outside that nothing foreign could injure it, but with the slightest touch from the butterfly opened to let it out, and then closed again. If nature applies itself so particularly to protect each of its forms from any disturbance, even closing the empty chamber from which it let out its winged creature, then how greatly must the instinct be impressed on this living being that it does not submit to any foreign power.—You understand nature in manifold ways, so you will also understand me here: you don't seem *better* to me, no *more* than everything that lives in nature, for all life has equal claim upon the divine; just take care that you don't injure your own natural life and that it develops without disturbance.

The little poem that you wrote about ennui proves to me that we're both right. If it were by anyone else, I'd count it as a poem, but for you it's not a poem; because you express an external situation in it, not an internal one, and a poem is really only living and effective when it makes what is inner-most come forth as living form. The more purely, the more decisively this inner life expresses itself, the deeper is the impression, the power of the poem. Everything depends on this power. It throws all criticism to the ground and does what it wants. What *then* does it matter whether it's constructed in a way that doesn't violate the accepted understanding of art?—Power creates higher laws that, perhaps, no one intimated earlier or was able to express; higher laws always overthrow all the old ones, and—we're still not at the end!—If the playground where the forces now practice according to conventional princi-ples were freed up to make it easier for nature to change its laws . . .! I don't want you to apply what I say here to my products in poetry; I also had to learn to compose and obey myself; and it was good, for it gathered my material in my spirit, which perhaps would not have sufficed me for content if the form that I strove to weave grace into had not lent me its value. I believe that nothing is more essential in poetry than that its seed arises from within; a spark generating itself from the nature of spirit is enthusiasm, from whatever deep ground of feelings it may come, no matter how slight it may seem. The important thing in poetry, as well as in speech, is the true immediate feeling that is really in the soul. If the soul just feels clear, and you were to try to en-hance this feeling, then its spiritual effect would be lost.—

The greatest master in poetry is the one who needs the simplest outer forms in order to give birth to the most deeply felt things, the one for whom the forms are generated together in the feeling of inner agreement.

As I said, don't apply anything I say here to me, or you could fall into error. Have I indeed learned to understand all this in this way just through my inner being? I myself often had to recognize the meagerness of the images in which I conceived of my poetic moods; I sometimes thought to myself that close be-side them more sumptuous forms, more beautiful garments lay ready, even that I would easily have had more significant material to hand, only it didn't emerge as the primary mood in my soul. So I always rejected it, and kept my-self to that which least diverged from what was really stirring within me. It was also due to that that I dared to have them printed, they had that value for me, that sanctity of minted truth; all little fragments are in this sense poems to me. You'll probably also have experienced this simple phenomenon in yourself, that tragic moments go through your soul that capture an image in history, and that in this image the circumstances are connected so that you undergo something deeply painful or highly uplifting with them; you fight against injustice, you win, you become happy, everything bows down to you, you develop mighty great powers, you succeed in extending your spirit over everything; or: a hard fate stands facing you, you endure, it becomes more bitter, it encroaches into the consecrated places of your bosom, into loyalty, into love; then genius leads you by the hand out from the land where your higher moral worth was threatened, and you leap to its call, under its protection to where you hope to escape suffering, to where an inner spirit of sacrifice claims you.

Through imagination the spirit experiences such events as destiny. It tests itself in them, and it is certain that it thereby often internalizes the experiences of a hero. It feels itself penetrated by the sublime, which it would be too weak, sensually, to withstand, but imagination is the place in which the seed for this is laid and takes root, and who knows how or when it will blossom within you as a mighty and pure power.—How else should the hero in us come to be?—Otherwise there is no such workshop in the spirit, and however a power activates itself externally, its inward vocation is certainly the most essential.—Thus I feel a kind of reassurance in what is unremarkable and negligible in my poems, because they are the footprints of my spirit, which I do not disown, and even if one could object that I should have waited until riper and tastier fruits were gathered, still it is my conscience that moved me to this, namely to disown nothing. For if even one pure, self-aware form develops, then that's also part of it, and what I have experienced up till now within myself in this way is what led me here, to this standpoint of my firm will.—

I have now said enough to you. I did so out of love for you, like you have said and done many such things for me out of love, and apart from that you have a close share in everything, as could not be otherwise.—But I beg you urgently, don't let this influence your mood, but take care that you remain prettily, wholly yourself to me. [...]

Caroline [*sic*].

4

Hedwig Dohm (1831–1919)

Introduction

Hedwig Dohm (née Schlesinger, later Schleh, 1831–1919) started publishing at thirty six and soon became one of the most important advocates for women's rights in Germany. She wrote pamphlets, articles, novels, and short stories, which promoted women's civil rights, as well as the right to education and work. Unlike many of her contemporaries, Dohm also advocated for the rights of single women and unmarried mothers and called for a new morality.[1] Dohm's critique of the biologically based conception of "woman" prefigures twentieth-century critiques of biological essentialism, including those developed by Simone de Beauvoir in *The Second Sex* (1949).[2] Some fifty years before Beauvoir famously claimed that "a woman is not born, but rather becomes a woman," Dohm wrote: "Is my vocation born, fixed and finished with me? To be that seems almost like being stillborn."[3]

Like Beauvoir and Clara Zetkin (see the introduction to chapter 5), Dohm regarded the idea of a fixed essence of "woman" as fundamentally problematic. This is because, she argued, there is no *woman* but many *women* whose varying experiences, cultural backgrounds, and socioeconomic situations must not be overlooked. As she put it, "I am not just a woman in general; I am also a completely specific woman, whose particular way of being cannot be known at all by this or that manufacturer of natural laws."[4]

Born in Berlin, Dohm was the fourth child of Jewish parents who had converted to Christianity for political reasons. At the age of eleven, she decided to be a writer; however, her wish did not align with her family's expectations,

---

[1] On Dohm's differences from her feminist contemporaries, see Chris Weedon, "The Struggle for Women's Emancipation in the Work of Hedwig Dohm," *German Life and Letters* 47, no. 2 (1994): 182–192.

[2] For an account of the ways in which Dohm prefigures other twentieth-century feminists, including Julia Kristeva and Judith Butler, see Mikus, *The Political Woman*, chap. 7.

[3] Hedwig Dohm, "Sind Berufsthätigkeit und Mutterpflichten vereinbar?" *Die Woche. Moderne illustrierte Zeitschrift* 38 (September 22, 1900): 1667–1669; here 1668.

[4] Dohm, "Sind Berufsthätigkeit und Mutterpflichten vereinbar?" 1668.

and Dohm's intellectual interests were not supported by her parents. She did, however, manage to train as a teacher, though she never pursued teaching. In 1853, she married Ernst Dohm, with whom she had five children. Ernst, who was the editor of a satirical political paper, encouraged his wife's intellectual and literary aspirations. In the late 1880s, following the death of her husband, Dohm turned her home into a thriving salon, which became an important meeting place for women writers and activists, such as Fanny Lewald, Helene Lange, Else Lasker-Schüler, Gabriele Reuter, and Lou Salomé.

For this volume, we have chosen four philosophical texts that Dohm composed between 1898 and 1911. The earliest of these is a critical appraisal of Friedrich Nietzsche, which provides important background on Dohm's philosophical inspirations and the ways in which she both learns and departs from Nietzsche's thinking. The other three essays included here are "The New Mother," which challenges essentialist notions of motherhood; "The Old Woman," where Dohm offers a unique portrayal of the aging woman and argues that the fate of the old woman must be a concern of the women's movement (another topic to which Beauvoir later turns); and, finally, a critique of anti-feminist propaganda. In all four essays, Dohm is concerned with two related points: women's emancipation and self-transformation.

The first and fourth essays exemplify a particular form of Dohm's writing, which one might describe as refutations of anti-emancipatory (anti-feminist) arguments. Her goal is to demonstrate the problematic perspectives of the anti-feminists by showing, for instance, their logical incoherence or the fact that the arguments are based on historical inaccuracies. In "On the Agitators of Anti-feminism," Dohm draws on historical evidence to show, contra the agitators, that women have indeed been subjugated and points to important moments in which women had the intellectual acumen and courage to rise up against this subjugation. In her essay on Nietzsche, her style is analytical (but also ironic, sometimes even humorous), taking up Nietzsche's misogynistic claims and subjecting them to critical analysis. With this essay, Dohm put herself at the center of an important discussion of Nietzsche, which took place at the end of the nineteenth century and involved, among others, Salomé, Reuter, Lange, and Ellen Key.[5]

Although Dohm engaged with a number of philosophers, including Rousseau, Staël, Salomé, and Schopenhauer, it was Nietzsche who most

---

[5] For a discussion of German women's interest in, appropriation of, and response to Nietzsche, see Diethe, *Nietzsche's Women.* Diethe does not consider Key.

influenced her and with whom she engaged most directly. On the one hand, Nietzsche inspired Dohm's thinking about the self as creative—a conception that formed the basis of her argument for women's emancipation. Her novella *Become Who You Are! (Werde, die du bist!)* (1884), whose title comes from Pindar but was repeatedly used by Nietzsche in his *Gay Science* (1882/ 1886), draws on this Nietzschean conception of the self as capable of creating its own identity. On the other hand, Nietzsche's misogynistic (and essentializing) claims appeared to be deeply problematic, and Dohm's important critique of anti-feminism was, in part, first developed through a critical assessment of Nietzsche's statements about women.[6]

In "Nietzsche and Women," Dohm goes through Nietzsche's numerous misogynistic statements and, one by one, demonstrates their inconsistency. She considers, for instance, Nietzsche's statement in *Beyond Good and Evil* (1886) that women's "first and last profession [should be] the bearing of strong children." Though Dohm notes that this claim is "not entirely new," she proceeds to analyze its implications. First, she asks, if it is the case that women should be primarily concerned with childbearing, then how many should they bear? Nietzsche gives no answer, but Dohm pursues his claim to its logical absurdity: if childbearing is the sole goal of women's lives, then it follows that women should not cease doing it. This would mean that a woman would be pregnant every year, with the outcome that she would bear a total of twenty children. But, she asks, what man could support so many children? Furthermore, Dohm wonders, is such a woman, who has sacrificed herself entirely to the biological process of reproduction, the right partner for Nietzsche's *Übermensch*? Is the overman someone who seeks to have a "slave," rather than a true companion, for a partner? After all, she continues, following Nietzsche's logic in *The Genealogy of Morality* (1887), "Anyone who wants slaves is not a master." The implication is that Nietzsche's image of the man with the most superior qualities does not ultimately make sense: if his partner is reduced to a form of slavery, then the overman is no true master.

---

[6] Dohm did not limit her critique of anti-feminists to Nietzsche, even if her engagement with Nietzsche is the most sustained. She also wrote about other anti-feminists, including her friend Salomé. In an essay published in 1899, Dohm called Salomé "anti-feminist" on account of Salomé's claim that women *should* become mothers. For Dohm, any such statement denies women's freedom. Furthermore, Dohm notes that Salomé herself never became a mother—thus contradicting her own claim. Hedwig Dohm, "Reaktion in der Frauenbewegung," *Die Zukunft* 29 (November 18, 1899): 279–291. See also Diethe, *Nietzsche's Women*, 59.

By posing these questions to Nietzsche and offering their only possible answers, Dohm reveals the extent to which Nietzsche's misogyny blinded him, leading him to make problematic and often inconsistent claims. As she puts it, "he does not know what he does not know." Nietzsche, in other words, failed to meet his own standard of self-knowledge.

Nonetheless, Dohm finds inspiration in Nietzsche, and in particular his claim in the *Gay Science* that "man makes for himself the image of woman, and woman shapes herself according to this image." At first sight, Dohm's interest in this statement seems strange. For the implication is that women are passively molded by men. However, Dohm notes, what this statement shows is that "woman" is something "made" or "created"—not something "natural" and "given." Accordingly, Dohm takes the implication of Nietzsche's statement as a rallying cry for the women's movement: women are not determined by a (pre-)fixed essence and thus need not continue to be in a position of subjugation. The current conception of woman is, in other words, historical and cultural, and it is up to women to transform and become themselves. As Dohm puts it, the "belief in natural necessity has crumbled."

The theme of emancipation, whether from a predetermined essence or from cultural expectations, persists in Dohm's other writings, most clearly in "The New Mother," where she calls upon mothers and daughters to transform themselves and their relationship. Prefiguring Beauvoir's analysis of the mother, Dohm explains that the core of the problem in this relationship has to do with the fact that in becoming a mother, a woman is expected (and sometimes willingly chooses) to give up her own goals. This often means that the mother will seek to fulfill these goals through her daughter: "In her daughter, a mother wants to experience a second edition of her self." But if the daughter is not amenable to the mother's wishes, the relationship between the two is bound to be fraught with tension.

In contrast to this conception of motherhood—and of the mother-daughter relationship that emerges out of it—Dohm develops a moral account of motherhood. A mother is one who must not expect anything in return for her care, or, in Dohm's words, "The mother gives; she does not take: for this is mother-love." Mother-love, Dohm emphasizes, is not simply natural or biological love but involves acting dutifully toward the children, by, for instance, recognizing their differing needs at various stages of life and attending to them. This requires a certain level of maturity, with the implication that mothering is not a merely biological act but also a moral one—based on (and nurtured by) the moral education of the mother.

Dohm's thinking can be described as generational insofar as she is interested in and aware of what is yet to come (i.e., the coming generations).[7] This can be seen, for instance, in her claim that the mother-daughter relationship is most likely to be transformed through the "new daughter." The new daughter, Dohm notes, moves away from the old habits and ways of thinking about women, and thereby makes demands on her mother to change—to become a new mother. These "new mothers" and "new daughters," i.e., the new generation of women to come, challenge any conception of woman as an unalterable essence. For, as Dohm explains in the final essay presented here, "New people reveal new natural laws."

Dohm is also conscious of the fact that many of the goals of the women's movement—goals that she is working to achieve—will only be realized after her death, and in thinking about this future, she expresses both relief and melancholy: she will not live to experience the new reality of women's lives.

However, in the essay on the old woman, Dohm is more optimistic, celebrating the old woman and demanding that she not give up on life too early. This is because the opposite—to live as though one were dead—is to "disenfranchise the present." Dohm analyzes the condition of the old woman, comparing it to the (much better) situation of the old man, and argues that the empowerment of the old woman must be a necessary consequence of the women's liberation movement. "To limit the superfluity of the aging and old woman," she writes, "will be one of the consequences of the women's movement," for the "unconditional emancipation of women" will give women "a richer life purpose, a vocation, practical or intellectual interests," which will make the label "old woman" and its negative connotations disappear.[8]

While Dohm's arguments are largely philosophical, they also rely on a certain socioeconomic position and appear to be oblivious to the problem that privileges are unevenly distributed. In her work more broadly, she shows little interest in discussing the situation of women who are not able to hire help for household chores or those women whose vocations undermine or fail to support their self-realization. Instead, she focuses on women with bourgeois careers, i.e., careers that have a flexibility that is not

---

[7] See Birgit Mikus and Emily Spiers, "Split Infinities: German Feminisms and the Generational Project," *Oxford German Studies* 45, no. 1 (2016): 5–30.

[8] Dohm, "Die alte Frau," *Die Zukunft* 14 (January 3, 1903): 22–30; here 30.

available in (say) the daily lives of factory workers. In fact, Dohm specifically disregards the proletarian enterprises,[9] such that her argument for the significance of work in women's lives appears to only hold for women of a certain socioeconomic background, and thus fails to achieve a claim to universality.

Nonetheless, Dohm argues throughout the essays presented here that it is only if women have a life outside of the home, where they are not simply being "for another" but are also "for themselves," that true emancipation will occur—and with it a number of other advantages. These include the practical advantages—gained by men—of not having to support the old woman financially or to worry about the mother-in-law. For women, the advantages include an improved relationship between mother and daughter and, most obviously, the ability to achieve self-realization—to "become one's self," to paraphrase the title of Dohm's novel, *Werde, die du bist!*.

Dohm died on June 1, 1919. It was only in the last year of her life that German women were granted the right to vote. This fact seems to justify Dohm's generational thinking, i.e., her view that through the women's movement, the future of women's lives will be better than the present. In turn, the fact that Dohm's feminism, which appeared "unusual" to her contemporaries[10] but gained traction in the twentieth century (through the work of thinkers like Beauvoir, Julia Kristeva, and Judith Butler), similarly seems to justify her melancholic interpretation of history. But it also has a clearly positive dimension: Dohm's prefiguring of twentieth-century thinkers makes her an important and interesting interlocutor for us today— not only because she advanced many of the positions that they will advocate a century later but also because the philosophical topics she explored, including her assessment of Nietzsche, her understanding of motherhood, and her analysis of the relationship between work and self-realization, demand renewed attention.

---

[9] See, for example, Dohm, "Sind Berufsthätigkeit und Mutterpflichten vereinbar?"
[10] Helene Lange, *Lebenserinnerungen* (Munich: Herbig, 1921), chap. 11.

Nietzsche and Women

No piece of writing against the modern women's movement has yet fallen into my hands—chance may have played a part in that—that has advocated for its standpoint intelligently and with logical acuity. It is hardly miraculous that average or inferior minds come up with judgments about women that lack wisdom and depth; such little people talk and write without authority about every other area too—perhaps with the exception of their area of specialization. But there are also men of the first rank among our opponents, who have received the kiss of genius and who revolutionize the world with bold, new ideas. But when they seize the pen to write on the question of women (but why do they do it?) they give their heads a rest and juggle with feelings, instincts, intuitions, eternal truths. Devoid of all logic, scientificity, and conscientiousness, they saunter carelessly around a junk market of thoughts and peddle old trinkets they picked up cheaply somewhere, although it doesn't suit them at all, and is actually very incautious. Because if we encounter them again at their sunlike heights, we mistrust the wisdom of people who have sold us trash in the past, and we are unsure: did Zeus disguise himself as a junk seller then, or is the junk seller, disguised as Zeus, now enthroned on Olympus? Where does the amazing occurrence come from that, even with noble thinkers, as soon as the question of women surfaces, all their "gay science"[11] capsizes in sad dilettantism and they renounce and betray their logic?

[...]

In *The Gay Science* Nietzsche says: "man makes for himself the image of woman, and woman shapes herself according to this image."[12]

How true! How true!

[...]

But the ground of all grounds for the above-mentioned spiritual abnormality is provided by Nietzsche himself. He, who talks so spiritlessly about women, grounds his lack of spirit with so much spirit. In *Daybreak* it says: "Even great spirits have only their five-fingers' breadth of *experience*— just beyond it their thinking ceases and their endless empty space and stupidity begins."[13] How true! How true!

---

[11] [A reference to Nietzsche's *The Gay Science* (1882/1886).]

[12] [Friedrich Nietzsche, *The Gay Science*, ed. Bernard Williams, trans. Josefine Nauckhoff and Adrian Del Caro (Cambridge: Cambridge University Press, 2001).]

[13] [Friedrich Nietzsche, *Daybreak: Thoughts on the Prejudices of Morality*, ed. Maudemarie Clarke and Brian Leiter, trans. R. J. Hollingdale (Cambridge: Cambridge University Press, 1997), 226.]

Schopenhauer and Nietzsche are the noblest, most profound of our opponents. From the biography of his sister (whose absolute conscientiousness is not to be doubted) we may conclude that Nietzsche never had intimate relations with women. Only in the letters that he sends to Lou Andreas-Salomé does something of a commonality of souls ring through, with an almost tender sharing of minds. But, as Elisabeth Förster[14] reports, even these relationships only lasted a few months. His friendship with Malwida von Meysenbug (I don't have the impression that this was deeply rooted in his mind) had the character of a young man's admiring sympathy for a noble old woman who cared for him maternally.[15] His points of contact with other female beings were of such a fleeting, superficial kind that there is no reason to speak of them. Nevertheless, he drops his judgments about "woman in herself" with apodictic certainty.

When I read what he wrote about women, dismay, pain, deep astonishment came over me. With my head covered I might have cried out: "You too, Brutus, my son!"[16] A shudder gripped me, as if suddenly from the sublime beauty of the ocean a malformation stretched itself out and pierced the air with shrill tones.

Nietzsche, the inspired, harrowing poet, is at the same time a fiery thinker. His thoughts, which so often strike to the heart of prejudices and superstitions with razor-sharp, golden arrows, which illuminate worlds like the sun or roar forth stormily like the thunder of Zeus—the thoughts of this genius at times arm themselves with clubs to defend against women. Was it "Schopenhauer as Educator"[17] to whose suggestion he was still subject when he wrote about "woman in herself"? Or did the women's movement disgust him because it was all too timely, and he only valued and overvalued the "untimely"? It almost seems so. "Nothing," says Lou Salomé, "is more uncouth, more ignoble [to him] than what is coming to be and the bringers of what is coming to

---

[14] [Nietzsche's sister.]

[15] [Malwida von Meysenbug was the first woman to be nominated for the Nobel Prize in literature (1901). She wrote about Germaine de Staël in her *Individualitäten* (1901) and was the author of the significant *Rebel in Bombazine: Memoirs of Malwida von Meysenbug*, trans. Elsa von Meysenbug Lyons (New York: Norton, 1936); (the first volume was published anonymously in 1869). Meysenbug also authored a study on Nietzsche, with whom she remained friends and corresponded from 1872 to 1889.]

[16] [These words, attributed to Julius Caesar (100–44 BCE) upon his assassination as he recognized his betrayal by Marcus Junius Brutus, were made famous by William Shakespeare's play *Julius Caesar* as the Latin *et tu, Brute?* ("You too, Brutus?").]

[17] [An essay by Nietzsche written in 1874 and included in his *Untimely Meditations* (1873–1876). See Nietzsche, *Untimely Meditations*, ed. Daniel Breazeale, trans. R. J. Hollingdale (Cambridge: Cambridge University Press, 1997).]

be and the new: the modern human being and the modern spirit."[18] Also possible, that this great poet, this Proteus of the soul, would have come to completely different results regarding the question of women if his psychic suffering had not put an end to his mental capacities comparatively early.[19] For he always loved to revoke things in arguments.

So that no one accuses me of falling into the same error as our opponents, who make claims without proving them, I will briefly cite the key sentences in which Nietzsche outlines what woman wants and what she should do. The essence is found in *Beyond Good and Evil*. There one reads: "their first and last profession [should be] the bearing of strong children"[20] (not entirely new); and further: "someone who has the same depth in his spirit as he does in his desires [. . .] will only ever be able to think about woman in an *oriental* manner. He needs to understand the woman as a possession, as property that can be locked up, as something predestined for servitude and fulfilled by it. In this he has to adopt the position of Asia's enormous rationality [*die ungeheuere Vernunft Asiens*]."[21] And in another place: "Asian thinkers have the only right conception of women."[22] Nietzsche, who pleads for the harem following the famous examples of Schopenhauer and Napoleon! What? These nibbling, munching, gossiping, glitteringly harnessed products of the harem, makeup slapped on with an oversized brush—results of male up-bringing and "Asia's enormous rationality"—the ideal of womanhood? And widow burnings are also part of that. Does Nietzsche really believe that the harem woman "is the bow whose arrows aim at the overmen?"[23] Simply put: that she is the most suitable childbearer for the overman?

And heredity?

But perhaps a more clever mind (a male one, of course) would devise a physiological law, the force of which would be that the features of women that

---

[18] [Lou Andreas-Salomé, *Friedrich Nietzsche in seinen Werken* (Hamburg: Severus, 2013), 185.]

[19] [In 1889, at the age of forty-four, Nietzsche suffered a mental breakdown and did not recover for the remaining eleven years of his life.]

[20] [Friedrich Nietzsche, *Beyond Good and Evil: Prelude to a Philosophy of the Future*, ed. Rolf-Peter Horstman and Judith Norman, trans. Judith Norman (Cambridge: Cambridge University Press, 2002), 129. Dohm omits the word "strong" (*kräftig*).]

[21] [Nietzsche, *Beyond Good and Evil*, 127.]

[22] [This is likely a paraphrase from §238 of *Beyond Good and Evil*, 127.]

[23] [Nietzsche uses the image of a bent bow, tensed and ready to shoot arrows, at various points in his writings, including as a metaphor for the processes required to create the *Übermensch* (overman, or superman), which he views as the best possibility for human development. See, for example, "Preface" in *Beyond Good and Evil* and "Zarathustra's Prologue," §5, and "On the Friend" in Friedrich Nietzsche, *Thus Spoke Zarathustra: A Book for All and None*, ed. Adrian Del Caro and Robert Pippin, trans. Adrian Del Caro (Cambridge: Cambridge University Press, 2006).]

resist the creation of the overman would only be inherited by their daughters. Such a claim would not be any more surprising than many other witticisms that our opponents launch onto the market of thoughts.

Nietzsche calls "defeminization" the "collect[ing] together, in an inept and indignant manner, everything slavish and serflike that was and still is intrinsic to the position of women in the present social order (as if slavery were a counterargument to, rather than a condition for higher culture)."[24]

Possibly. Certainly, from the standpoint of the slave owners. But the slaves? Can one take it amiss if they think differently about it?

Woman should be property that can be locked up. She does not want to be. I cannot see that she—as Nietzsche thinks—should be so very ashamed of this enormous stupidity. Men would not much like to be eunuchs either, and yet (probably due to Asia's enormous rationality) there are also eunuchs in the harem.

There are many women among us who are property that can be locked up, not by one but by all men. I suppress the name for this harem. It is hurtful when women earn coarse words. But this is my opinion: Anyone who wants slaves is not a master.[25]

Her first and last vocation should be: to bear children. How many? The average number of children in a German family amounts, as far as I know, to three or four. If we assume that woman is to be freed from any work during the eight months of pregnancy (not counting the first four weeks) and six weeks after the birth (we hardly need to mention that this does not happen in reality), then her closed season would be accounted for in about three years. And should she lie idle for the entire remaining time? Or should she give her husband a child annually? Would he be prepared to raise and care for these twenty children in a way that befits their class? Hardly. Do the harem ladies in the Orient bear so many children?

I no longer know whether I read in Schopenhauer or somewhere else that, as a burden on society, women over forty years old should voluntarily

---

[24] [Nietzsche, *Beyond Good and Evil*, 129; Dohm uses the word "slaves" (*Sklaven*) instead of Nietzsche's "slavery" (*Sklaverei*).]

[25] [The term translated here as "master" is *Herr*, which might also be translated as "man," "gentleman," or "lord." Dohm is referring to Nietzsche's account of masters [*Herren*] and slaves [*Sklaven*] as types of human temperament (which partly depend on environment or life circumstances). The kinds of moral systems that Nietzsche claims "masters" and "slaves" respectively develop are a central aspect of his thought, elaborated most clearly in the first essay, " 'Good and Evil,' 'Good and Bad,' " in Friedrich Nietzsche, *On the Genealogy of Morality*, ed. Keith Ansell-Pearson, trans. Carol Diethe (Cambridge: Cambridge University Press, 2007), 10f.]

renounce the pleasant habit of existing. I admit, I prefer the custom of some Asian tribes who (probably pursuant to Asia's enormous rationality) simply drown their newborn female children if they exceed the number of childbearers that are expected to be necessary. I wonder whether there are also men over forty years old (as well as under it) who are a burden on society?

After Nietzsche has ascertained where nature points woman, everything else follows by itself. To her: "I want, I do not want" he opposes his: "she should, she should not." She wants to cultivate herself, become independent. She should not cultivate herself, should not become independent. The reasons? Because she thereby "degenerates, regresses,"[26] loses her charming feminine features (also not entirely new) and would be to blame for "Europe's [. . .] *increasing ugliness*."[27] And these charming features? "Women [. . .] contain so much that is pedantic, superficial, and schoolmarmish as well as narrow-mindedly arrogant, presumptuous and lacking in restraint[.]"[28] "Look out when [. . .] they start completely forgetting their discretion and their art—of grace, play, chasing-all-cares-away"—who chases away women's cares, then? Or don't they have any?—"[. . .] their subtle skill at pleasant desires!"[29] "What inspires respect and, often enough, fear of women is their *nature* [. . .] their truly predatory and cunning agility, their tiger's claws inside their glove, the naiveté of their egoism, their inner wildness and inability to be trained, the incomprehensibility, expanse, and rambling character of their desires and virtues."[30] (These women are multifaceted, at least.) "What? And that brings it to an end?"[31] (Namely, emancipation.) "The *demystifying* of women is in progress? Women's tediousness comes slowly into view?"[32]

By what is this brought to an end? By the tiger claws, the broad, sweeping desires, the inner wildness, the egoism? Would it really make Europe so ugly if some of these charming features went to the devil—that is: were withdrawn from the possession and enjoyment of men?

And all these delightful qualities are not even to the original credit of women. Praise and reward for them are due to men. "Man makes for himself

---

[26] [This is not a direct quote, but Nietzsche does state as part of a longer passage that woman "degenerates" (*entartet*) and "regresses" (*geht zurück*). See *Beyond Good and Evil*, 128.]

[27] [Nietzsche, *Beyond Good and Evil*, 124.]

[28] [Nietzsche, *Beyond Good and Evil*, 124.]

[29] [Nietzsche, *Beyond Good and Evil*, 124.]

[30] [Nietzsche, *Beyond Good and Evil*, 129. Emphasis omitted by Dohm.]

[31] [Nietzsche, *Beyond Good and Evil*, 130.]

[32] [Nietzsche, *Beyond Good and Evil*, 130. Emphasis omitted by Dohm.]

the image of woman, and woman shapes herself according to this image."[33]
How true! How true!

The men who support women in this (in their efforts for freedom) are idiots, "asses of the male sex, who [. . .] would like to bring women down to the
level of 'general education,' and maybe even of reading the newspapers and
taking part in politics"—even to the point of writing books, it says in another
place.[34]—"Every now and then, people even want to make free spirits and
literati out of women: as if a woman without piety were anything other than
absolutely repugnant or ludicrous to a profound and godless man."[35] But why
should woman be so pious, if man is impious? Only for the sake of contrast?
I would like to know what great pleasure man promises himself from her
piety; it must be that it's so much fun for him to measure his own gigantic
progressiveness against her intellectual backwardness; for religiosity does
not seem to exercise any influence on her character.

In *The Gay Science* I read: "Would a woman be able to hold us [. . .] if we
did not consider her able under certain circumstances to wield a dagger"—
may it also be vitriol?—"deftly [. . .] *against* us?"[36] In the one hand dagger
or vitriol, in the other the prayer book: that's how Nietzsche wants woman.
Or should her right hand not know what her left hand does? What use is
woman's piety to man if it doesn't protect him from daggers and vitriol? And
I also cannot make her wild, sweeping desires, her tiger claws etc. make sense
together with true religiosity. But must it make sense? Things often don't
make sense. It also doesn't make sense that the nature of woman first gave her
her untamable inner wildness and the same nature then destined her to be
the property of men that can be locked up. Should we not fear an explosion?

It also does not make sense that Nietzsche cries woe over woman because
(as a result of emancipation) she unlearns "fear" of man and thereby discloses
her feminine instincts. He says: "That in woman which instills respect and
often enough fear is her nature" (enter the tiger claws etc.). And immediately
after: "Fear and pity: these are the feelings with which men have stood before
women so far, always with one foot in tragedy which tears you apart even as
it delights you."[37] Woman should be afraid of man, but man should also be

---

[33] [Nietzsche, *The Gay Science*, 73.]
[34] [Nietzsche, *Beyond Good and Evil*, 128.]
[35] [Nietzsche, *Beyond Good and Evil*, 129.]
[36] [Nietzsche, *The Gay Science*, 74.]
[37] [Nietzsche, *Beyond Good and Evil*, 129–130. The start of Dohm's citation differs slightly from the
original: "Until now man stood before woman with fear and compassion."]

afraid of woman. Would it not be more comfortable if both disarmed themselves, man and woman, and sought, without fear, to get along with each other in peace and friendship?

"Look out when"—again as a result of her independence—"the 'eternal tedium of woman' [. . .] first dares to emerge."[38] What? Before her efforts for freedom did it not dare to come out, and was the woman imagined by Schopenhauer and Nietzsche, to whom politics, literature, any kind of knowledge was all Greek, amusing? Ah, if only it were true.

The most fleeting survey of contemporary society or of cultural or literary history teaches us that in no era was it the women who were locked up as property, the pious, the unlearned, whom the men revered. In antiquity it was the hetaerae,[39] brilliant, well-versed in literature and politics, to whom the men gave their reverence. It was the same in the time of serfdom, in the seventeenth and eighteenth centuries (remember the famous salons of the last century) and in the time of German romanticism. Eroticism was not neglected. And the strangest thing: the same man who abominates every free-thinking woman, who makes three crosses before the "woman degraded to writing books": the only woman who stood close to his mental and intellectual life, Lou Andreas-Salomé, is one of the most profound and noble authors I know. And his old friend Malwida von Meysenbug is also an intellectual and knowledgeable writer. I think it is entirely likely that his relations to Lou Salomé were only established on the basis of her full understanding of his writings. Such contradictions between word and deed do not well befit an apostle of truth.

It almost forces a laugh from us when Friedrich Nietzsche speaks so confidently of the tiger claws, of the dangerous, beautiful cat woman, of her untamable wildness—this celibate man, a stranger to women, who certainly never felt the smallest female tiger claw on his own body, never experienced how these predatory creatures, like tragedy, "delight you, while they tear you apart." Perhaps he dreamed of them precisely because of this, like Saint Anthony dreamed of the seductive she-devils: hallucinations due to too great abstinence.

Friedrich Nietzsche is no Socrates; he does not know what he does not know.

---

[38] [Nietzsche, *Beyond Good and Evil*, 124.]
[39] [The *hetaerae* (singular *hetaera*; from the Greek for "companion") were a class of courtesans in ancient Greece who were often highly educated.]

Where did he make his studies of women? Perhaps in the hospitals in the theater of war in the year 1871, where he worked as a nurse beside so many female nurses? Did he there discover women's inner wildness, their predatory cunning, their egoism? Or before Paris did he miss the beautiful opportunity to get to know "woman in herself"?

He says: "Women want [. . .] to enlighten men about the 'woman *an sich* [in herself]'—*this* is one of the worst developments in Europe's general trend toward *increasing ugliness*. Just imagine what these clumsy attempts at female scientificity [. . .] will bring to light[. . . . W]omen [should] stop compromising themselves through enlightenment[. . . .] *Mulier taceat de muliere* [Let woman be silent about women]."[40] Thank God this self-exposure could not—especially in Nietzsche—assume a threatening character, for immediately afterward he says: "She"—woman—"does not *want* truth: what does truth matter for a woman! Nothing is so utterly foreign, unfavorable, hostile for women from the very start than truth."[41] For she won't parade her ugliness, but instead graciously covers what is terrible in the depths of her soul with lies; and with that a limit is set to the uglification of Europe. She should absolutely not expose, enlighten—yes, but if she does: should men not in fact be glad if women only enlighten about women? If they put to paper their experiences about men—which are richly at their disposal—couldn't it be the case that there, too, things are exposed to the light of day that would hardly contribute to the beautification of Europe?

Woman should not emancipate herself, otherwise she loses the taste for that on the basis of which she comes most surely to her goal. (Rulership over man.) "[T]o lose control of yourself in front of men, perhaps even 'to the point of writing books,' where you used to act with discipline and subtle, cunning humility; [. . .] to dissuade men [. . .] from thinking that women must be kept, cared for, protected, and looked after like gentle, strangely wild and often pleasant house pets"[42]—he holds this to be her greatest stupidity.

Nietzsche-Machiavelli gives woman advice on how she must do this. Woe to the woman who does not lie! That's what it boils down to. Briskly and cheerfully tell men black is white, change clothes with the weather. "Their [women's] great art is in lying, their highest concern is appearance and beauty. Let us admit that we men love and honor precisely this art and

---

[40] [Nietzsche, *Beyond Good and Evil*, 124–125. Emphasis omitted by Dohm.]
[41] [Nietzsche, *Beyond Good and Evil*, 125. Emphasis omitted by Dohm.]
[42] [Nietzsche, *Beyond Good and Evil*, 128–129. Dohm omits the word "kept" (*erhalten*).]

this instinct in women[.]"[43] I really don't find that very ethical of men. Also, the piety, without which woman would be untoward and laughable, hardly corresponds well with lies and deceit. "Man makes for himself the image of woman, and woman shapes herself according to this image."[44] What? Woman, as Nietzsche characterizes her, should be constituted like this by nature and according to God's decree? Full of lies and deceit, the enemy of every truth, full of cunning humility, predatory, etc.? Is a stronger argument for the modern women's movement conceivable than this opinion of Nietzsche's?

No, women should not lie and deceive, beautiful appearances should not be their life purpose. On the contrary, women should break the habit of the vices lauded by Nietzsche. To offer them a hand in this effort is one of the goals of the women's movement. Nietzsche's combating of emancipation seems—even from his standpoint—almost like a pointless argument.[45] That is: he holds it to be a "*typical* sign of a shallow mind" to "deny the most abysmal antagonism"—between men and women—"and the necessity of an eternally hostile tension."[46] "The same affects have different tempos in men and women: that is why men and women do not stop misunderstanding each other."[47] Because they have not understood each other from the start and will never understand each other, the realization of the modern ideal of woman can hardly increase the gulf between the sexes.

"There are so many days that have not yet broken," says Nietzsche.[48] Ah yes, for him too. In his aphorisms he offers numerous glowing lights that could decorate the scrapbook of any opponent of women's rights. The best-known: "You go to women? Do not forget the whip!"[49] Slave and whip. Now those do make sense together. Otherwise not at all original, this spark of wit. Nietzsche himself cites the saying from an old Florentine novel: "*buona femmina e mala femmina vuol bastone*."[50] (The cane is for the good woman and the bad alike.)

---

[43] [Nietzsche, *Beyond Good and Evil*, 125.]

[44] [Nietzsche, *The Gay Science*, nos. 68 and 73.]

[45] [Literally, "a fight over the emperor's beard"—an expression meaning to argue over something that doesn't really matter. The expression is originally a reference to scholarly disputes about whether certain historical rulers did or did not have a beard.]

[46] [Nietzsche, *Beyond Good and Evil*, 127. Emphasis omitted by Dohm.]

[47] [Nietzsche, *Beyond Good and Evil*, 61. Dohm uses "they" (*sie*) instead of the second instance of "men and women" (*Mann und Weib*).]

[48] [Nietzsche, *Daybreak*, title page. Nietzsche attributes this statement to the Rig Veda, an ancient collection of Sanskrit hymns and commentary.]

[49] [Nietzsche, *Thus Spoke Zarathustra*, 50.]

[50] [Nietzsche, *Beyond Good and Evil*, 69.]

"Women learn to hate in the same proportion that they *unlearn* to charm."[51] Woman A and Woman B, perhaps; but "women"? The Circes, whose métier consists of enchantment, may feel struck by this glowing light.[52] They understand how to avenge themselves by changing the enchanted into . . . shall we say: into quadrupeds.

"All proper women find something shameful about science."[53] A glowing light, fit to burn a considerable hole in the admiration of Nietzsche. What? And the helotian service of love, which women have to deliver in the harem he desires, is not shameful to them?[54]

At times Nietzsche's contradictions become huge. But then they are in fact no longer contradictions, but thunderbolts of knowledge with which he surprises us. In the flash of these thunderbolts the whip, with which every man should go to women, changes into a scepter which he reverently passes to them, the back room becomes a holy grove, the kitchen stove a tripod. In *The Gay Science* it says: "A deep and powerful alto voice [. . .] suddenly raises the curtain upon possibilities that we usually do not believe in. All at once we believe that somewhere in the world there could be women with lofty, heroic, royal souls, capable of and ready for grandiose retorts, resolutions and sacrifices, capable of and ready for mastery over men, because in them the best of man aside from his sex has become an incarnate ideal."[55] Just before: "Animals think differently about females than humans do; they consider the female to be the productive being. [. . . S]piritual pregnancy produce[s] the character of the contemplative type, to which the female character is related: these are male mothers."[56]

Oh Nietzsche, you high, priestly spirit, knower of deep secrets and unknower of the simplest truths! You can speak with God and gods, with the stars, with the ocean, with spirits and specters. Only you cannot speak with and about women.

Belief seems immortal. Here someone comes from high mountains, where he lived with eagles and snakes, someone who has dispatched states and parliaments, emperors and kings with his spirit, yes, who helped kill God himself.[57] And this diver who has exhausted the oceans of knowledge, who

---

[51] [Nietzsche, *Beyond Good and Evil*, 61.]
[52] [In ancient Greek mythology, Circe was a witch or a goddess of magic.]
[53] [Nietzsche, *Beyond Good and Evil*, 66.]
[54] [The helots were a group of people subjugated by the ancient Spartans.]
[55] [Nietzsche, *The Gay Science*, 74.]
[56] [Nietzsche, *The Gay Science*, 75–76.]
[57] [A reference to Nietzsche's character Zarathustra, who is depicted in these ways in Nietzsche's book *Thus Spoke Zarathustra*.]

thinks he believes nothing that he has not explored in its depths: he has preserved one belief, one fetish. He believes in a natural law that points women to the harem, that has destined them to be the property of men that can be locked up.

He cries "woe" so often. I might too, once—no: three times I might cry woe over Friedrich Nietzsche: a crimson woe, because it is soaked with heart's blood, for I love him, the harrowing poet, the artist, who understood how to bind all arts into the versatile material of language. He wrote as a painter of words; he painted the alpine glow, the midnight suns, immeasurable yellow deserts with a hot blazing sky above, he painted the ocean in a raging storm-flood and he painted it flatteringly, smoothly. He is a sculptor. From vast stone blocks he hews forms of gods and the overman. He is an architect. From his thoughts are built churches with radiant organs, castles with bold battlements, with slender lookout towers looming high in the ether, sparkling in new suns. But above all he is the musician of language. He flatters our senses with tender strains as if from shepherds' pipes, but he also rattles the cornerstones of our thought with trumpet blasts, until they tumble. And then again there are prayer-dithyrambs[58] as if from archangels' tubas, which bear us to transcendental peaks. But the archangels change into demons, the transcendental sounds of heaven into shrill, lunatic laughs from the abyss— thoughts like fiery swords that burn the mark of Cain into our foreheads.[59] And, finally, there is a parting full of immeasurable woe and trembling bliss, a song as if from dying wild swans: "that delights you while it tears you apart." Friedrich Nietzsche! You, my greatest poet of the century, why did you write about women so far beyond what is good? A deep, deep heartbreak for me. It makes me lonelier, older, more remote. Ah, but I know the answer: "Even great spirits have only their five-fingers' breadth of *experience*; just beyond it their thinking ceases and their endless empty space and stupidity begins."[60]

Thus spoke Zarathustra.

---

[58] [In ancient Greece, the dithyramb was a kind of hymn sung in worship of Dionysus, the god of wine, fertility, and divine ecstasy. In his first book, *The Birth of Tragedy*, Nietzsche argued that the dithyramb allowed the ancient Greeks to glimpse this world in an ecstatic experience as part of their orgiastic Dionysian ceremonies. The 1891 edition of Nietzsche's later work *Thus Spoke Zarathustra* included several poems written by Nietzsche in 1888 which he called "Dionysian Dithyrambs."]

[59] [In Genesis 4:15, having subjected Cain to exile as punishment for having killed his brother, Abel, God places a "mark" of an unspecified kind on him, so that nobody should kill him. The term "mark of Cain" thus refers to a sign of ostracism.]

[60] [Nietzsche, *Daybreak*, 226. Emphasis omitted by Dohm.]

The New Mother

It is still not that long ago that custom and habit defined the destiny of daughters. That destiny was called: house, husband, child. Whatever was beyond that was evil and overturned some kind of altar: religion, nature, the world order. If a daughter did not find a husband to manage her intellectual and material existence, then, often enough, over the years she succumbed to hysteria or to a dull resignation, as Gabriele Reuter so masterfully portrays in her book *From a Good Family*.[61] This era is fading. Slowly, slowly one of the greatest upheavals of world history is taking place before our eyes, so gently and gradually that the majority hardly perceive it, or think this "storm in a teacup" is a temporary phenomenon.

The relationship between mother and child, their reciprocal rights and duties, is also involved in this evolutionary process, and is heading toward a re-evaluation.[62] Mothers of today, with a few exceptions, still have the views of earlier times, and these are views that are not fair to adult children. The art of parenting, even of pedagogically inclined mothers, which is brilliant for young and very young children, almost always fails with adolescents and adults. To be sure, fathers no longer sacrifice their daughters at God's command, curses and violations are no longer the order of the day (although they still occur). But in many ways, daughters are still sacrificed to established customs and prejudices, to their parents' decisions.

In her daughter, a mother wants to experience a second edition of her self; the grown girl should adapt herself to the mother's attitudes to life, her value judgments. And if she is not willing to do so, then the mother uses the force of maternal authority, an educating intrusiveness that almost amounts to hypnotism and against which the daughter rebels in her wakeful state, admittedly only if she thinks for herself, wills for herself—if she is an individual. Run-of-the-mill people or people with subservient natures follow the herd instinct (to use Nietzsche's words) and fit themselves to the template without a struggle.

The mother enforces her intentions effortlessly where the nature and type of her daughter is on her side (via heredity). But if mother and daughter do

---

[61] [Gabriele Reuter, *Aus guter Familie. Leidensgeschichte eines Mädchens* (Berlin: Fischer, 1895).]

[62] The theme of this essay is the relationship of mothers of the educated classes to their adult children, particularly their daughters (proletarian mothers are not considered). Male writers may consider the rights of sons—if that is required.

not agree in taste, thoughts, feelings, and temperament, then the ground is laid for covert and open conflicts, for little quarrels and big disputes, which mean a pointless waste of strength for both parties that wears down their minds. The group portrait of mother and daughter, which could be so close to God's heart, is distorted.

If mothers were to be sincere—they aren't, because they are afraid of losing the halo of mother-love—then they would admit that in by far the most cases they wish their daughters out of the house once they have become independent in their internal lives. This is not due to insufficient mother-love; it is, rather, the daughter's fault—if one can call it a "fault" when something comes about with a person's natural development. Thus, around her twentieth year (the point in time of course varies according to the specific character of the person) dissatisfaction becomes noticeable in the girl. She no longer rightly knows what she should do with her life. In the first years of her adulthood the novelties of social activity, flirtation, makeup, theater, dabbling in artistic exercises, are enough to occupy a young person's mind and mood. But the more gifted a girl is, the more quickly the reaction sets in, the tedium of the banal aimlessness of her existence. She becomes nervous, demanding, sullen, inclined to opposition, recalcitrant. She no longer fits in the house, which bears her mother's imprint, not hers. The house is the realm of the mother. She does not like a co-ruler. And secretly she holds it against her daughter that she has still not found "a man." For her daughter, the man is the axis around which—rightly—all motherly thoughts turn, and not only motherly ones; the man (particularly the one who won't come) affects the whole house: brothers, aunts, grandmothers, and, if a great-grandmother is there, her too.

A young man belongs to himself as soon as he goes to university or begins a career in a studio, a workshop, a business; he shapes his life according to his own will. How strong the need for freedom is in young people is shown by the fact that, even if their parents' home offers incomparable comfort, they prefer to begin their studies in a strange city rather than in their hometown. And if circumstances compel a young man to remain in the parental home, then he at least receives—as a symbol of freedom—the house key. The world lies open to him, as far as his finances stretch. But a daughter remains strictly dependent upon her parents. She may not—at least in the higher strata of society—even go across the street alone. Earlier, this close confinement to the parental home and to parental authority was tolerated by young girls. The conception of the inescapability of woman's destiny was oil poured on the waves: it soothed the inner turmoil and outer rebellion.

This belief in natural necessity has crumbled.

A basic error of parents is that they regard their children as their property, their own body and soul, whom it is their right to draw on and wear out.

Any domineering, prejudiced, narrow-minded mother can—despite all mother-love—place obstacles on the life path of her children. And the more strong-minded and principled this woman is, the more disastrous her intervention in the lives of her children—despite all mother-love—will prove to be. If I bend a pipe a little and drop it from my hand, then it springs back into its natural form; but if I have buckled it by too much pressure, then it remains buckled forever, without being able to right itself again.

[...]

But should parents let their daughter do what seems to them erroneous, wrong, without protest? Without protest? No. They should put their advice, their eloquence, their knowledge, their experience at the service of their daughter. But they should keep their protest, their counteractions, within the limits that a friend sets for themselves with friends. And if they are more intelligent than their daughter, then they will understand how to guide their daughter with quiet, clever actions, far removed from authority and command. But pushing their daughter into self-alienation, saying she's making nails for her own coffin, if she resists the categorical maternal "You shall!" with an "I want!": That is not mother-love.

For many centuries a wife was the property of her husband. He could drive her out, sell her, etc. And for many centuries she kept quiet, and the thought of rising up against the yoke only came to her very late. Now we stand at the point of time where the adult daughter no longer wants to recognize her mother's right to ownership of her person. Earlier, sons may have struggled with their parents to assert their personhood. Not daughters, apart from exceptional cases. But now daughters revolt too. Temperamental, strong natures often do so in severe forms. With more sensitive, weaker natures we see a gradual growing apart of mother and daughter.

What daughters of the present want is not release from the family (a youth who goes to university does not want that either), but only release from forced childhood. Internal independence longs for external independence. A person who realizes that they do not need to bear a yoke does not bear it. This urge for freedom and creativity in the young female generation of the present is deep and mighty and one of the characteristic traits of the time.

In Russia young girls (like Sophie Kowalevski)[63] sometimes enter into some kind of sham marriage just to escape the authority of their parents, and not— and this should be noted—in order to lead a footloose, lazy life, but in order to create a self-imposed circle of duties and activities through artistic or scientific studies.

[...]

But mothers want the best for their children? Certainly. Only they tend to think that what is best for them is best for their children. Mothers who are really mothers in spirit and in truth will not only not demand sacrifices from their children (for instance in the choice of a profession or a spouse); they would even be ashamed to accept such sacrifices. The mother gives; she does not take: for this is mother-love.

The times need the "new mother" like the bread of life—the mother who gives up her authority voluntarily and in a timely way. With the emergence of the "new mother," an event apparently contrary to nature emerges. It is the "new daughters," those borne aloft by their times, who create the "new mother," often so that clever and good "old mothers" (by that I don't mean in years) become new in their daughters.

But what will contribute most to the education and conversion of the "old mother," more than insight, justice, and the shedding of prejudices and deep-rooted habits, may be mother-love itself, joined with necessity. Until now, mother-love found little leeway where it applied to forming a daughter's future, for only myrtles or thorns lay in the urns of destiny for all female creatures.[64] That means: a woman would become either a wife or a starving vagrant with no occupation. Before, nothing about that could be changed. But now it can be changed. And a mother would have to be really pig-headed and cold-hearted who, for the sake of her principles, cut off the possibility of a satisfying existence for her daughters. Such a way of acting would correspond quite well with the view of the doctor who opined: "The patient may die as long as my method survives."

In the next generation, authoritarian mothers may be exceptions. The liberated daughters of today (even if their number is still limited) will retain in their minds what they have lost in strength and meaning for their

---

[63] [Sophie Kowalevski (1850–1891), also spelled Sofia Kovalevskaya, was the first woman to hold a PhD in mathematics from a European university and the first woman to hold a full professorship in northern Europe. At the age of eighteen, she married in order to travel outside Russia to study—she needed the permission of her husband or father to do so.]

[64] [In the classical tradition, myrtles are associated with love, while thorns indicate hardship.]

lives through their encapsulation in the narrow circle of the family and by the fact that they had to win their rights only through heavy struggle. And in self-restraint, with intelligent insight, they will recognize the right to self-determination not only for strangers, but also for their own children, when they have matured to individuals. They will smooth the way to the temples for their daughters, where they want to serve the god that they bear in their breasts, even if their mothers pray at other altars. For this is mother-love.

But if the different worlds in which mother and daughter feel at home are never linked by the love of mother and child, as if by high-arched bridges, well, then nature has released the bonds that tied them, and resignation—the melancholy of reason—befits both parties.

There is no love by a higher command, even from the highest.

The right of children is the same as the right of the mother: the right to live one's life as one's own individual, not another's.

But it is still said that a woman should be absorbed in her child and her husband. So strange, so absurd, that I, with my own individuality, should be absorbed in my children! But my children, my husband, they are totally different from what I am! My I is not at all in them. Where is it then, if not in me?

Yes, when I perceive the rights of children, I also perceive the rights and happiness of mothers. They harm themselves when they cling to their adult children who no longer need them, seek refuge in the lives of these children to escape loneliness and the spiritual wasteland of age. Many women of mental and spiritual poverty (as a result of their upbringing) have nothing else in the world that is attached to them or to which they are attached. And because they themselves have not become their own, have no life purpose of their own, they make their children into their self. It has always been the same, until now. If a woman had no luck, no guiding star, in her life, then she set her hopes upon her children, her gifted sons, her beautiful daughters. And the children became people. A son turned out badly, a daughter lived in an unhappy marriage. Others settled far from home, a favorite died. And their mother lived all their tribulations with them; but not their joys. And even if only cheerful lots in life fell in her children's laps, they still gradually moved farther from her, for ascending and descending lines do not meet. The daughter who has become a mother stops being a daughter. And now the young mother again hopes for the future in her children; and her mother, now a grandmother, sees that children promise nothing. This eternally melancholic cycle: that was the lot of the mother.

To restore motherhood to its sensible level is a task for the future.

The women of the next generation will have, besides the obligations that motherhood brings with it, other practical or intellectual areas of work, areas that—when their children are out of their care—tie a bond between them and their colleagues, produce a social community whose duration is assured because it rests on the same interests and goals, while the paths and goals of mother and daughter often diverge. The love of children, forced to become passive, is joined by the love of work, which only runs dry with the ebbing of one's life force.

Indeed, from the instinctive love of mother and child, a higher, purer love can develop on a spiritual basis, free from authority and compulsion. The mother, friend of the daughter; the daughter, friend of the mother! That would be the most beautiful bloom to sprout from the relationship between mother and daughter. The present sows the seeds for that. May sun and air be favorable to it, so that it may blossom magnificently.

Incidentally: the people who adhere doggedly and vehemently to the idea that maternity and family life are the sole purpose of the existence of women may be calm. If they are right, they will be proven right. In the long run, no one can live in an element that is beyond or outside their nature. I once saw a man who wrote with his feet; but he had no hands. If what the women's movement wants fails, if it bears no fruit or sour fruit, then those who are infatuated with it will soon enough climb down again from the pulpits and platforms, they will vacate studios, universities, and workshops and humbly and penitently return to the nurseries and marriage apartments which alone make blessed, where the calf of reconciliation will be slaughtered for the penitent sinner.

We still await the first who will tread this road to Canossa.[65]

---

[65] [A reference to the Holy Roman Emperor (King of the Germans) Henry IV's journey of penitence to Canossa, in Italy, in 1077 CE to ask the pope to revoke his excommunication from the Catholic Church.]

The Old Woman

I have often fought for the rights of women, for the rights of the young girl, the wife, the mother. I have barely touched on the old woman. Now I want to speak about her; about the poor old woman, who is like a shadow cast by creation—to the displeasure of humanity. If woman in general is or was—until recently—the pariah of the human race, the old woman was so three-fold; and she still is today. The young and younger generations—born under happier stars—have not yet had time to grow old.

I want to speak about the old woman's suffering and say how it is to be remedied.

That until the most recent times women were conceded only a sexual value has been said and bemoaned often enough. I say it again, because from this evaluation emerges the disregard that ruins the old woman. If a woman had become unfit as a childbearer, child-carer, and lover, then the justification for her existence had ended. All further claims that she intended to make on society seemed more or less ridiculous; by those with gentler and more be-nevolent dispositions they were at least ignored.

Sexual attractiveness and use for the species—a woman's measure of worth! An animal conception of her being, a naive shamelessness that might have suited an earlier age, but that makes a mockery of the maturity and ele-vation of the current time, for it dehumanizes women. It goes without saying that the condemnation of this kind of outlook does not apply to sensual and aesthetic joy in youth and beauty, to delight in enjoying love.

There are crypts for the living: long illness, unhealable grief. The old age of woman is also such a crypt. She is entombed there during her lifetime.

Poor old woman! Everything is gradually leaving you. At first, your longing gazes follow those hurrying away from you: children, friends, society; but they move farther and farther away—they disappear. Loneliness drapes you like a shroud, oblivion is the inscription over your house, the ravensong of hopelessness croaks over your dwelling. Silence is all around you; and you also fall silent, because no one wants to hear you. Poor old woman! You feel you should be ashamed that you, now so useless and already so old, are still alive. Age weighs upon you like a debt, as if you are usurping a place that belongs to others. You feel an attitude around you that pushes you from life.

A famous artist once said to me (while I sat for him for a painting, and I was over forty years old), that women who have exceeded their fortieth year are a burden on society and would do best to be gathered to their forebears.

The earlier custom of barbaric peoples, who eradicated superfluous female children immediately after birth, seems gentler to me, for newborns, not yet familiar with the pleasant habit of existing, may be less sensitive than full adults to a hastened dispatch into the beyond.

From good and well-meaning people I have heard it expressed that old women are "something horrible." I even heard this saying from the mouth of a young woman who had a mother.

I will not recall here the terrible tragedy—it is not as rare as we think—that emerges when the old live too long for their families. In the educated classes such cruel impulses are locked in the breast's deepest depths. By contrast, among the common people the pious wish that God might retrieve the old is, often enough, openly expressed. The old woman—or even the old man—in retirement is tragic material that has been adapted many times in literature. Recall *King Lear*, Zola's *La Terre*, Turgenev's *Lear of the Steppes*, Balzac's *Père Goriot*.

Woe to the old woman who reads such a wish on someone's brow! The offender, around whose neck they slung a wet towel at the execution site, died from thinking it was the executioner's axe.

Nothing seems more crippling, more deadening for the old woman than the awareness forced upon her by society: you were; you are no longer. She shudders under this, as if she hears the tolling bell that announces death.

I know old women—sensitive natures—who prefer to live far from their families, in foreign cities, foreign countries, in the instinctive fear of being a burden to their own, like a sick animal that crawls away into the thickets of the forest.

But I: I love you, old women. Gladly I knock on the already half-locked doors of your souls, and if they open to me, I often experience lively hours which sound out like evening prayers under silent stars. Some among you understand the voices that come from the grave; with others one has the feeling (that is, if one is a theosophist) that their ethereal, astral body has already half freed itself from the prison in which the crude, material body traps it; it is as if, released from their old home, they seek a new one, shrouded in dark secrets. Only imperfectly do they see and hear what goes on closest to them. They see and hear into the distance, out into the breadths or deep into themselves. The mystical clings to them. The gardens of the old border on the beyond.

One would think that, when a woman has stopped appealing through her sexual charms, society would have to evaluate and appreciate her simply as a human being, according to her individual value. That does not happen. The term "old woman" includes a prejudice and excludes fair appreciation. If a hunter meets an old woman first thing in the morning, then it means bad luck. Even small children learn to shudder before the witch, who is always an old, old witch. The devil is evil. But the peak of evil is scaled by his grandmother. Hah! The devil's grandmother! History is silent about the devil's mother.

The common feeling of society is against the old.

I hear angry calls! Aha! That does not apply to all!

No, there are exceptions. I have known some. They belonged to the stage or the high aristocracy. They were women who collected treasures of experience in rich, eventful lives, original women gifted with humor who preserved intellectual freshness and the gift of being amusing until a great age. To these exceptions also belong the old women of inexpressible good-heartedness who create a lovely gentle atmosphere around us, which we breathe like the perfume of violets. Fame, wealth, and nobility are also mitigating circumstances for "the old woman." But these properties must be present in a high degree of potency to atone for the offense of age; their evening sun must light their whole surroundings. Apart from these exceptions, until now old women have had significance and influence only as wives or mothers of famous or high-ranking men. For example, would a word of Frau Rat have reached posterity, despite her unspoiled, scintillating humor, if she had not been Goethe's mother?

The old woman casts her shadow ahead of her in the aging woman. One dates the aging woman from something like the end of her forties to her sixtieth year; the old woman from her sixtieth year until she departs this life. One tends to think of the aging woman in the image of the mother-in-law, the old woman in the image of the grandmother, although there are very young grandmothers.

[...]

I know an old, very lively, and fun-loving lady who loves going into society to an extraordinary degree. But she declines every invitation. When asked the reason for declining, she answered, in her Silesian way of speaking: "One is so leftover."

Yes, she is right. The old woman is so "leftover." If a woman is no longer considered a sexual being, her conversation is also no longer interesting. What she thinks, feels, judges, is "leftover."

For the old man society is not ruled out at all. Even if he is no longer productive in his advanced old age, he is always, through his knowledge, experience, his social or political relations with the world, still rich enough to be able to take pleasure in himself and bestow it on others. And apart from that, he has the tremendous advantage of not being an "old woman."

And has this disregard for and interment of the old woman no justification whatsoever?

It has a justification, even if no reasonable person will agree with the brutal remarks of the well-known Leipzig doctor who depicts the old woman as a zombie. The justification lies in her superfluity. This is indisputable, if one lets the contemporary social order regarding old women count as normal for all eternity. If the purpose of women's existence—as the majority accepts—is bearing children and raising children, then, when the children are grown, women have fulfilled their destiny. [...]

Age destroys the beauty of forms and lines. The effects of this destruction can be mitigated, in not rare cases canceled out. Old women tend to neglect their outer appearance, because they believe that how they look is entirely indifferent. They no longer count. Who pays attention to them? So they at least make themselves comfortable.

They are wrong.

I would like old women to dress in white. I think this color, which is related to light, befits them. I would like to see in them something priestly, otherworldly, light-seeking. But not just modern symbolism, also aesthetic reasons speak in favor of a white dress. No one should observe the rules of aesthetics more than old women. The most scrupulous cleanliness and diligence in caring for the body, in clothing, should be their law. Every kind of hygienic precaution, everything that serves to maintain strength and suppleness, to avoid sluggishness and corpulence, is part of caring for the body.

It will be objected that old women court mockery if they do things that are not appropriate to their age. That are not appropriate, or that are not seen as appropriate? This difference is important. Of those things that are seen as inappropriate, most are based on habit and the prejudices of the times. Evidence of this is that activities that make old women laughable are applauded, often most vigorously, in men of the same age. An old woman with ice skates on her feet, on a bicycle, on a horse—ridiculous; the eighty-year-old Moltke on a horse was admired as a marvelous phenomenon;[66] only benevolent gazes follow the white-bearded ice-skater.

---

[66] [German Field Marshal Helmuth von Moltke the Elder (1800–1891), who was known for having remained very active to a great age.]

[...]

Hear, old women, what another old woman says to you: Get to it! Have the courage to live! Don't think for a moment of your age. You are sixty years old. You may live to seventy, eighty, even ninety. The youngest people could go to the grave before you. To think ahead to death, feel it in advance, means to hurry toward it, means to disenfranchise the present. If you live only one single day more, you have a future before you. Life is a struggle. Everyone says so. One struggles against enemies. Age is an enemy. Fight!

Do what brings you joy, as far as your mental and physical strength suffices. Precisely because you no longer have a long time before you, live out every minute. The theosophical idea that the richer in brain and heart we go to the grave, the more glorious will be our return, is solemn and noble.

Mock the mockeries with which they want to intimidate you and close the doors to joy. The child and the old woman alike have the right to live. Become old for others: but not for yourself.

[...]

On the Agitators of Anti-feminism

The arguments with which people counted by the public among the intellectual elite summarily dismiss the women's movement are often remarkably naive.

Thus a brilliant writer—at the same time an agitator among antifeminists—advocates the position that, if their nature had always been violated, women would at some point have resisted, would at some point have sought to throw off the yoke under which they sigh.

Slavery lasted for millennia. Proof of its being willed by God? Through endless eras bonded peasants performed serf labor, and a Marx, a Lassalle did not emerge overnight for the proletariat. Sparks kindle no fire if there is nothing flammable nearby. A voice does not need to be loud to awaken an echo. The caller must only stand in the right place.

If for centuries women's capacity for cultural work was disallowed, their contribution to it denied, then eventually they themselves would believe in their incapacity, and it would take strong stimuli to develop the wings to carry them upward from their larval state. Women have often been like little worms that play dead so no one harms them. And if the little worms repeat this maneuver countless times, then they remain—perhaps, at least— apparently dead. A member of the Reichstag[67] recently said: "One cannot talk corpses into living," but one can make the living believe that they in fact have no right to live—at least not for themselves, but only for others. Women who were tortured and burned as witches had hammered into their brains for so long that they were witches such that—by the power of suggestion— they believed in their own witchcraft.

And have women really never resisted, never sought to slip from their enslavement into freedom?

Oh, dear sir, individuals or groups of women have sought this in all times. We learned in school that in antiquity, with the Greeks, Romans, Hebrews, women were unconditionally subjugated to men, entirely confined to the home, and obedience and thrift were the only qualities that earned them recognition. But even from this half-vegetative existence cries for help emerged from women's mental and bodily distress.

It is the greatest writers of the ancient world who provide the most unmistakable evidence of female efforts for emancipation in their time.

---

[67] [The German Parliament.]

Euripides—a despiser of women—cannot do otherwise, in his *Medea*—like Goethe in *Iphigenie*—than lament the lot of women in harrowing verses. And later, in a choral song, he prophesies the coming triumph of woman: "*We will see justice and virtue reconfigured. . . . The time is coming when woman will be honored, and then the voices of the old singers, which once registered woman's lack of reason, will fall silent. . . .*"[68]

Already several thousand years ago women must have become conscious of the unjust treatment that was meted out to them.

And would Aristophanes have been able to write his *Lysistrata* and a number of other comedies if a women's movement had not provided him with the material? In *Women at the Thesmophoria* he has the women hold a gathering in which Euripides is to be condemned as a detractor of women. A friend of Euripides, disguised as a woman, undertakes his defense. In another of his comedies the women convene a public meeting to discuss Plato's ideas about women. It seems to me that more valid evidence for an uprising of women in antiquity cannot be imagined.

In the early Middle Ages, under the pressure of barbaric wars, the complaining and demanding voices of women seem to have been silent for a period. But already in the fourteenth century salvific calls came from Italy regarding the Renaissance for women. Burckhardt, in *The Civilization of the Renaissance*, speaks of the heroic vein in the women of the Renaissance. "There was no question of a separate, conscious emancipation," he writes, "because the matter was self-evident."[69] The women of high standing strove just like men for self-contained personhood complete in every respect. The most glorious thing that was said of the great Italian women was that they had a manly spirit, a manly disposition. The title "virago" was in those days pure praise. We would translate "virago" today with "manwoman." (May the modern anti-feminist not miss this opportunity to learn to tremble.) And Burckhardt adds: "*We can no longer imagine the powerful personality of the ruling women of Italy at that time.*"[70]

At the time of peasant bondage women played a notable role—even if it was behind the scenes—in the politics of France.

---

[68] [Translated from Dohm's German.]

[69] [Translated from Jacob Burckhardt, *Die Kultur der Renaissance in Italien* (Vienna: Phaidon, 1934 [1860]), 225. Dohm reorganizes the sentence slightly and omits the word "separate" (*aparten*).]

[70] [Burckhardt, *Die Kultur*, 226. Dohm reorganizes the sentence slightly and adds the word "today" (*Heute*), giving "Today, we can no longer imagine . . ."]

I assume the bold attempts of the romantics at emancipation are well known. A time in which Schleiermacher could write in his catechism for women, without fear of losing his position: "*Let yourself long for men's education, art, wisdom*[71] *and honor*[. . . .] *I believe in the infinite humanity that was there before it adopted the shell of masculinity and femininity. [. . .] I believe that I do not live to obey or to amuse myself, but to be and to become, and I believe in the power of the will and of education . . . to release me from the fetters of malformation and to make me independent of the limits of sex.*"[72]

Dorothea Veit, Rahel Levin, Caroline Schlegel are living illustrations of purposeful emancipation. "What hindered women," our anti-feminist agitator asks, "from living in art, from revealing themselves completely in artwork?"

Sir forgets something: that the customs of a country are always more powerful than its laws. It takes intellectual courage, often enough the blood of martyrs, to kick against the pricks of custom, for they hold old and even older traditions firmly in an iron grasp.

Certainly, no one cuts off women's outrageous hands, eager for art. But— one reads [in] the memoirs of the painter Seidel (in the time of Goethe)[73] [about] an artist who only owed it to her deafness that, after endless supplications, she finally opened a studio. One reads the lecture that the aged sculptor Elisabet Ney held ten years ago at the great women's congress.[74] With trembling voice, with tears in her eyes, she reported on the difficulties that had confronted her training. The same barriers exist in other areas too. Shortly before her death, the dentist Henriette Tiburtius,[75] who died a few years ago, wrote of the labors she had to expend to acquire a dental practice. In Europe all possibilities for training were cut off to her. But in America, too, in Philadelphia, the faculty behaved very hostilely toward her application.

---

[71] [Dohm writes "science" (*Wissenschaft*) instead of "wisdom" (*Weisheit*).]

[72] [Friedrich Schleiermacher, *Idee zu einem Katechismus der Vernunft für edle Frauen* [1798], in *Kritische Gesamtausgabe*, ed. Hans-Joachim Birkner (Berlin: De Gruyter, 1980-), Section 1, Vol. 2, 153–154.]

[73] [Dohm is probably referring to Louise Seidler (1786–1866), court painter of the dukes of Weimar. According to Dohm's account in chapter 1 of *Die wissenschaftliche Emanzipation der Frau* (1874), Seidler describes in her memoirs the difficulties of opening a studio that were encountered by her friend, the deaf painter Marie Ellenrieder (1791–1863).]

[74] [It is not clear which lecture Dohm is referring to here. Elisabet Ney (1833–1907) was a German artist who emigrated to the United States in 1870. In the 1890s, she toured the United States, giving a lecture titled "The Mission of Art." In 1897 and again in 1903, Ney returned to Germany for short periods, during which she may have also given lectures.]

[75] [Henriette Hirschfeld-Tiburtius (*née* Pagelsen; 1834–1911) was the first female dentist in Germany.]

And only when one of the most prominent professors became a warm advocate for her and eventually proposed a vote of confidence did a dental academy open its doors to her.

Even today, the affordable state painting schools are still closed to women; only expensive private tutors are at their disposal. In the Berlin Industrial Museum they are not admitted to the architecture and painting classes.

And also, in times where the principle "Women belong in the house" was seen as incontrovertible, who paid attention to female artistic or scientific gifts, which, furthermore, do not always reveal themselves with thunder and lightning? Fanny Hensel had to publish her beautiful songs under the name of her brother Felix Mendelssohn. They pelted stones at the first female doctor in America when she conducted her indecent profession. They refused her habitation, like a prostitute.

And if woman had lain asleep for centuries, longer than Sleeping Beauty, if the thorn hedge around her place of slumber had grown as thick as a wall of stone, the prince still would have come eventually to awaken her with the kiss of spirit. The prince—that is, time, wrapped in the purple of divine omnipotence, which has iron feet with which it tramples down whatever opposes it. Ever new forms of being storm from this spiritual childbearer. What do we know of natural laws, which should be unchangeable, eternal? New people reveal new natural laws. Riddles that seemed insoluble are deciphered. "We wander among secrets."[76]

Women's souls resembled and today still partly resemble a coach horn with its melodies frozen. They are thawing in the sun of freedom, and they are beginning to sing and to ring. In the Quran it says: "*Woman is a camel, given to us by God, to traverse the desert of life.*"[77] But even the camel senses—the oasis.

Only speak, speak and write, you anti-feminists! Spring breezes waft even over Chinese walls, penetrate through jail bars. No athlete of anti-feminism impedes women's intellectualization anymore. The time has come. The sparks have become flames, and for miles they blaze over all the lands.

---

[76] [A saying attributed to Goethe, often cited in the wording used by Dohm but originally recorded as "We all wander among secrets" (*Wir wandeln alle in Geheimnissen*) in Johann Peter Eckermann, ed., *Gespräche mit Goethe in den letzten Jahren seines Lebens*, Vol. 1, *1823–1827* (Leipzig: Philip Reclam Jr., 1836), 141.]

[77] [We have not been able to locate this passage in the Quran.]

5

Clara Zetkin (1857–1933)

Introduction

Clara Zetkin (née Eißner, 1857–1933) was one of the leading socialist feminists in Europe in the nineteenth century. A founder of International Women's Day (which takes place annually on March 8), Zetkin stands out among her contemporaries for her parallel commitment to the women's movement and the workers' movement. As Zetkin saw it, any effort to separate the two was not only misguided but also problematic: the success of one was inextricably connected to the success of the other.

Zetkin was born into a socially progressive household in Wiederau, rural Saxony. In the 1850s, with the rise of industrialization, the small town of Wiederau, which was home to textile workers and small farmers, suffered from increasing financial insecurity and eventually poverty. Zetkin's early encounter with poverty left a lifelong mark on her—one that proved to be decisive both for her own development and for the budding socialist movement.

In 1872, the Eißner family moved to Leipzig, and Zetkin was enrolled in the Von Steyber Institute, a teachers' college connected to the bourgeois feminist movement and run by feminists Louise Otto-Peters and Auguste Schmidt. A key aim of bourgeois feminism was to provide women with educational opportunities that would help them gain employment, with the long-term goal of achieving wage equality with men. During her time at the Institute (1875–1878), Zetkin enrolled in classes on history and literature, read social-democratic newspapers and journals, and attended the meetings of the Leipzig Women's Education Society and the General German Women's Association (Allgemeiner Deutscher Frauenverein, ADF). She also began to attend the lectures of Wilhelm Liebknecht and August Bebel, the cofounders of the German Socialist Democratic Workers' Party (Sozialdemokratische Arbeiterpartei Deutschlands, SDAP), which became the Socialist Workers' Party of Germany (Sozialistische Arbeiterpartei Deutschlands, SAP) in 1875. These parties are the historical forerunners of

Women Philosophers in the Long Nineteenth Century. Dalia Nassar and Kristin Gjesdal, Oxford University Press.
© Oxford University Press 2021. DOI: 10.1093/oso/9780190868031.003.0007

the current German Social Democratic Party (Sozialdemokratische Partei Deutschlands, SPD).[1]

However, it was not until Zetkin met Ossip Zetkin from Odessa at one of these lectures that she became committed to the nascent socialist movement. Ossip, who had fled Russia on account of his political activity, introduced Clara to the writings of Marx and Engels, inspired her to live a working-class life, and encouraged her to attend lectures at the Leipzig Workers' Education Society. These experiences sealed her fate, and from then on, she became committed to both socialism and feminism.

In 1881, when the Bismarck government instituted anti-socialist laws, Ossip was forced to leave Germany and convinced Clara to leave with him. He moved to Paris that year, with Clara joining him in late 1882 (following a tour through Austria, Italy, and Switzerland). In Paris, the Zetkins lived in common-law marriage, had two sons, supported themselves through free-lance writing and tutoring, and led an active political life. However, the hardship of immigrant life alongside the financial pressure to overwork resulted in both Zetkins falling ill with tuberculosis, Ossip fatally.

In 1886, Clara Zetkin traveled to Leipzig to convalesce. In Leipzig, she reconnected with her old socialist friends, met with Liebknecht, and gave her first public lecture. She soon won the respect and admiration of a number of Socialist Party leaders, and the Party began to distribute Zetkin's writings to women workers, with the hope of educating them in socialism. After Ossip's death in 1889, Zetkin moved back permanently to Germany, settling in Stuttgart. By 1890, socialism was no longer illegal, and the SAP began to hold regular congresses and publish party-affiliated journals, including the feminist journal *Die Gleichheit*, which Zetkin edited from 1891 until 1917. Under Zetkin's editorship, the journal's subscriptions went from 4,000 in 1902 to more than 124,000 in 1914.[2]

Over the next three decades, Zetkin became the most visible and outspoken member of the German socialist women's movement and of the international socialist women's movement, which was itself led by the female

[1] The SDAP merged with the General German Workers' Association (Allgemeiner Deutscher Arbeiterverein, ADAV) in 1875 to become SAP, and it was not until after World War II that the party took on the current SPD name.

[2] Similarly, with Zetkin leading the women's wing of the SAP, the number of SAP women went from 4,000 in 1905 to more than 174,000 in 1914. The biggest increase in membership happened in 1908, when it became legal for women to join political parties: the number of SAP women went from 29,458 in 1908 to 62,259 in 1909. See Daniel Gaido and Cintia Frencia, "'A Clean Break': Clara Zetkin, the Socialist Women's Movement, and Feminism," *International Critical Thought* 8, no. 2 (2018): 277–303.

section of the SAP. Her theoretical writings were decisive for the direction that German socialism (and European socialism more generally) took on the question of women's emancipation.

For this volume, we have selected three essays by Zetkin, two of which exemplify her arguments on behalf of socialist feminism, while the third concerns race relations in the United States. Titled "Save the Scottsboro Boys!" this third essay illustrates Zetkin's concern with all forms of oppression. The essay was written as an immediate response to the decision by an Alabama court to put eight young African-American men on death row. As Zetkin explains, the eight men, along with a ninth man who was too young to be put on death row, were wrongly accused of the rape of two white sex workers. Despite ample evidence of their innocence, the Alabama court found the men guilty. Zetkin's essay, which was written in 1932, appealed to progressive people everywhere to put pressure on the Unites States to overturn the fraudulent conviction and to stand by the nine youths. As such, it demonstrates her view that people across the world must unite in the struggle against oppression. Specifically, Zetkin calls upon the international communist movement, which was represented in the United States by the American Communist Party (CP).

Zetkin's appeal seems to have been effective: the CP began working closely with the National Association for the Advancement of Colored People (NAACP), and the case was argued before the US Supreme Court in October, 1932. On November 7, the court reversed all convictions on the grounds that the defendants had not received adequate legal counsel. The men were, however, repeatedly put on trial until 1937, when the Alabama court—under severe external pressure—dropped the case against four of the young men, and two others were released on account of their age. The others remained imprisoned, though they were eventually either granted parole or escaped (the last escaping in 1948). All nine men were officially pardoned by the Alabama governor in 2013.[3] As Angela Davis remarks, Zetkin's appeal played a crucial role not only in the Supreme Court's decision but also "in the extension of international solidarity to the struggle for Black equality in the United States."[4]

---

[3] For a comprehensive timeline and account of the trials, convictions, paroles, and pardons, see Valerie R. Stackman, "Scottsboro Boys, 1931–1948," in *50 Events that Shaped African American History: An Encyclopedia of the American Mosaic*, vols. 1 and 2, ed. Jamie J. Wilson (Santa Barbara, CA: Greenwood: 2019), 282–299.

[4] Angela Davis, "Foreword," in *Clara Zetkin: Selected Writings*, ed. Philip S. Foner (New York: International Publishers, 1984), 9–16, here 15.

For this reason, Davis argues, its significance is not only historical; the essay also "holds important lessons" for progressive movements everywhere.[5]

The first two essays included in this volume were originally delivered as speeches at socialist conferences. "For the Liberation of Women!" which Zetkin delivered at the 1889 International Workers' Meeting in Paris, sets out Zetkin's understanding of the women's movement and its relation to the socialist movement and outlines the stakes of women's emancipation. Prefiguring Simone de Beauvoir's claim in *The Second Sex* that the right to vote is abstract and is thus not sufficient to transform the (concrete) situation of women, Zetkin argues that women's emancipation, part of which includes suffrage, cannot be separated from women's work. However, unlike Beauvoir, who only mentions the exploitative nature of labor under capitalism, Zetkin devotes the majority of her analysis to thinking through the relationship between women's emancipation and the emancipation of the worker.

To begin with, Zetkin argues that independence necessarily means economic independence. This is because it is, in her view, only through economic independence that women will no longer be subjugated to men. The struggle, however, does not simply end with women finding employment. For—contra bourgeois feminists—Zetkin contends that employment itself can be a form of slavery. As she puts it, "Freed from their economic dependence on men, women are subjected to economic domination by the capitalists; from the slaves of men they have become the slaves of their employers: they have only changed their master." Accordingly, women's emancipation cannot only be about suffrage, gaining employment, or even achieving wage equality with men. Rather, women's emancipation is inextricably connected to the emancipation of the worker.

Zetkin then goes on to develop her most important argument against the bourgeois feminist movement, which revolves around the notion of "rights." According to the bourgeois feminists, women's right to vote is an "inalienable" or "natural" right that has to do with the fact that women are "persons." Such a conception of rights, Zetkin argues, is based on an ahistorical account of what it means to be human, i.e., on some kind of essence that underlies and makes women persons. However, she elaborates, the notion of women's rights—and the demand that we grant these rights—is wholly historical: "a child of modernity, born from the machine." Without mass industrialization women would not have needed to leave the home and enter the workforce,

---

[5] Davis, "Foreword," 16.

and thus would not have begun thinking about and demanding modern rights. Machines can create the products women had made at home far more efficiently and cheaply. And machines led to a decrease in men's wages. To ensure the family's survival, women were required to participate in the workforce. Zetkin's claim, then, is that it is within this historical situation that the need to press for women's rights emerged. Accordingly, Zetkin concludes that women's rights are connected to the fact that women became workers, and it is therefore as workers that they must be politically emancipated. For this reason, she makes the (perhaps surprising) claim that socialist women "recognize no special rights of women workers!" As Zetkin sees it, precisely because it is the woman as worker who must be emancipated, it follows that women's emancipation *is* the emancipation of the worker.

Given that Zetkin identifies the emancipation of women with that of the worker, she must counter the view, held by some (male) socialists, that women's emancipation results in outright disadvantages to male workers. In other words, she must convince her fellow socialists that workers' emancipation is inextricably tied to women's emancipation.

A look at the historical situation, Zetkin begins, reveals that the reason behind men's lower income has little to do with women entering the labor force and everything to do with capitalism and capitalist ideology, which require workers to work ever longer hours and to produce ever more efficiently. There is, in other words, nothing in principle about women's work that would decrease the wages of men. Rather, women's entry into the workforce has the potential to positively impact all workers. For instance, Zetkin notes that an increase in workers could result in shorter workdays and more time for leisure and education, rather than a decrease in wages. It is thus the capitalist interpretation of work that results in decreased wages. This means, Zetkin continues, that instead of fighting women, male workers should fight capitalism. After all, she concludes with a point that is as relevant today as it was in 1889, if men were concerned with wage decrease, then they should be demanding the elimination of the machine—not women—from the workforce.

Zetkin's speech "Women's Suffrage" was delivered in Stuttgart in 1907 at the first conference dedicated to socialist women. Zetkin, who was largely responsible for organizing the conference, intentionally arranged for it to take place in the same month and in the same city as the congress of the Socialist International, so as to allow the women to attend both. The women's conference was widely regarded as a major success for women socialists in general and for Zetkin in particular. In strong support of Zetkin's organizational and leadership skills, Rosa Luxemburg, who had become a close friend and ally of Zetkin's, argued in her own address at the women's conference that if the socialist women made the city of Stuttgart, and indeed the offices of Zetkin's journal, *Die Gleichheit,* their headquarters, they would become the "moral center" of the international socialist movement.[6] Luxemburg's suggestions were adopted, with Zetkin becoming the leader of the Socialist Women's Office in Stuttgart and *Die Gleichheit* its official organ. Furthermore, several important resolutions, including one in favor of universal suffrage, were adopted at the conference.

In her speech to the women, Zetkin's focus appears to shift: she is, after all, not addressing male socialists and trying to convince them of women's rights. Accordingly, her concern in this later speech is with the situation of women workers and their case for universal suffrage.

As in her 1889 speech, Zetkin's argument is based on the view that suffrage must be understood in relation to women's current historical situation—a situation she describes as a "revolution." She writes: "a revolution . . . is taking place. Women are released from the household as the source of their livelihood, they can exist economically outside the family, they gain their economic independence from the family, from men." It is in the context of this revolution, Zetkin goes on, that suffrage has become relevant. For once women became workers, and began to live financially independently of their families, it became necessary for them to represent themselves (and their needs) in the political sphere.

Zetkin begins the speech by disputing the notion of partial suffrage, to which some bourgeois feminists subscribed. Partial suffrage is based on the idea that only women with property should be granted the right to vote. Such a conception of suffrage, Zetkin argues, is only concerned with those women who are bearers of assets. Thus, partial suffrage means that a woman is granted the vote *despite* the fact that she is a woman, rather than because of it. Partial suffrage is, in other words, not concerned with the emancipation of women.

Once again prefiguring Beauvoir's analysis of the distinctive situation of woman as "the second sex," Zetkin takes note of the differences between women of various social classes and how these differences might result in different struggles. This does not mean, Zetkin emphasizes, that proletarian

---

[6] Rosa Luxemburg, *The Rosa Luxemburg Reader,* ed. Peter Hudis and Kevin B. Anderson (New York: Monthly Review Press, 2004), 237.

women should "reject bourgeois advocates of women's rights if they stand behind and beside them in the struggle for universal suffrage." It does, however, mean that the proletarian women's struggle is not (as is the case with the bourgeois women) against men but against capitalism and capitalist ideology: "proletarian women must be clear that they cannot attain the right to vote in a struggle of the female sex, without distinction of class, against the male sex; but only in the class struggle of all the exploited, without distinction of sex, against all exploiters."

Zetkin's arguments for universal suffrage were endorsed by the SAP, which by 1912 had become the largest political party in Germany. In 1918, Germany granted women universal suffrage—a bittersweet victory for Zetkin. Along with Luxemburg and others, Zetkin, on account of the party's refusal to take a clear antiwar stance, had left the SAP at the beginning of World War I. Zetkin and Luxemburg argued for pacifism on socialist grounds. By pitting worker against worker, war undermines worker solidarity and the international workers' movement. Only if workers are united across national borders, they argued, can the workers' movement achieve success and capitalism be overcome.

With Luxemburg, Zetkin went on to cofound the Independent Social Democratic Party of Germany (Unabhängige Sozialdemokratische Partei Deutschlands, USPD), which she represented in the German Parliament from 1920 until she joined the Communist Party of Germany (Kommunistische Partei Deutschlands, KPD), of which she was a member until 1933, when the National Socialists banned the Communist Party. By that point, Zetkin had developed strong connections to the Soviet Union and decided to move to Moscow, which had become an interim home for her over the last decade.[7] She died near Moscow in June of that year.

While many socialists supported women's rights and women's emancipation, not all of them agreed with Zetkin's understanding of the relation between socialism and feminism or her view that women's struggles varied depending on class. Bebel, for instance, argued that women should unite *across* class differences.[8] Lily Braun, in turn, disagreed with Zetkin's claim

---

[7] On Zetkin's connections to and involvement with the Bolshevik Revolution and the USSR, see John S. Partington, "Clara Zetkin on the Soviet Experiment, 1917–1934," in *1917: The Russian Revolution, Reactions and Impact*, ed. David Morgan (London: Socialist History Society, 2017): 56–82.

[8] See Quataert, *Reluctant Feminists*, 69–70. On the differences between bourgeois and socialist feminists (and the different forms of socialist feminism) during this period, see Marie Kennedy and Chris Tilly, "Socialism, Feminism and the Stillbirth of Socialist Feminism in Europe, 1890–1920," *Science & Society* 51, no. 1 (1987): 6–42, here 21–22.

that women socialists must work with men socialists. Instead, Braun argued that women must struggle *against* man because "the bourgeois philistine morality was so deeply ingrained in him."[9] Men, in other words, are so deeply (and unconsciously) connected to the oppression of women that the feminist movement cannot fruitfully work with, or even alongside, them. Though the debate between Braun and Zetkin took place some one hundred years ago, both of their perspectives remain alive today. Braun's claim resonates with feminist arguments that women's distinctive struggle cannot be understood by non-women and that achieving justice for women can only occur from within a specifically feminist framework. Zetkin's view that the oppression of women workers differs from the oppression of bourgeois women, and that the true enemy of the working woman is not the working man but capitalism and capitalist ideology, reverberates with feminists who argue that the structure of women's oppression cannot be understood in isolation from economic, racial, and social questions. In her attempt to join the women's movement with the socialist movement, Zetkin's thoughts, and those of her critics, remain relevant for us today, as we, too, attempt to understand the connections between different forms of oppression and the struggles that they demand.

---

[9] Cited in Quataert, *Reluctant Feminists*, 104. Braun's brand of socialism, moreover, differed from Zetkin's. While Zetkin subscribed to historical materialism, Braun did not. See Lily Braun, "Left and Right," in *Selected Writings on Feminism and Socialism*, ed. and trans. Alfred G. Meyer (Bloomington: Indiana University Press, 1987), 443–454.

For the Liberation of Women!

[Speech at the International Workers' Congress in Paris, July 19, 1889 (transcription)]

Citizen Zetkin, representative of the female workers of Berlin, rises amid lively applause to speak about the question of women's labor. She explains that she does not want to report on the situation of female workers, because it is the same as that of male workers. Instead, by agreement with her sponsors she will examine the question of women's labor on the basis of principle. Since there is no clarity on this question, it is absolutely necessary that an International Workers' Congress speak out clearly about this subject, by dealing with the question of principle.

It is—the speaker explains—not to be wondered at that reactionary elements have a reactionary view of women's labor. But it is highly surprising that a mistaken view is also found among socialists, in the call for the abolition of women's labor. The question of women's emancipation—that is, ultimately, the question of women's labor—is an economic question, and one rightly expects a better understanding of economic questions among socialists than the one that is revealed in the demand just mentioned.

Socialists must know that, in the current state of economic development, women's labor is a necessity. They must also know that the natural tendency of women's labor leads either to reducing the work time that each individual has to devote to society or to the growth of the wealth of society. And they must know that it is not women's labor in itself which, by competition with male labor power, depresses wages, but the exploitation of women's labor by capitalists, who appropriate this wealth for themselves.

Socialists must know, above all, that social slavery or freedom rests upon economic dependence or independence.

Those who wave the banner of liberation for all human beings may not condemn fully half of the human race to political and social slavery through economic dependency. Just like workers are subjugated by capitalists, women are subjugated by men; and they will remain subjugated as long as they are not economically independent. The indispensable condition for their economic independence is work. If one wants to make women into free human beings, into members of society with equal rights to men, well, then one must neither abolish nor restrict women's labor, except in certain, very isolated, exceptional cases.

The female workers who strive for social equality expect nothing for their emancipation from the bourgeois women's movement, which supposedly struggles for women's rights. That building is built on sand and has no real foundation. Female workers are thoroughly convinced that the question of women's emancipation does not exist in isolation, but is part of the larger social question. They very clearly take account of the fact that this question will not now or ever be solved in today's society, but only after a thorough transformation of society. The question of women's emancipation is a child of modernity, born from the machine.

The emancipation of women means completely changing their social position from the ground up, a revolution of their role in economic life. The old form of production, with its imperfect means of work, chained women to the family and restricted their sphere of activity to the inside of their homes. In the lap of the family, women represented an extraordinarily productive labor force. They generated almost all of the family's items for daily use. In the state of production and commerce of former days it would have been very difficult, if not impossible, to produce these articles outside the family. As long as these older relations of production were in force, women were economically productive.

Mechanical production killed off women's economic activity in the family. Large-scale industry generates all articles more cheaply, quickly, and plentifully than individual industry, which only used the imperfect tools of small-scale production. Women often had to pay more for raw materials, which they bought on a small scale, than for the finished products of large-scale mechanical industry. In addition to the purchase price (of the raw materials), they also had to invest their time and their work. As a result, productive activity within the family became an economic folly, a waste of time and energy. Although women who are productive in the lap of the family may admittedly be useful to particular individuals, this kind of activity nonetheless signifies a loss for society.

That is the reason why the good housekeeper of the good old days has almost completely disappeared. Large-scale industry has made it unnecessary to generate commodities in the home and for the family; it has swept the ground out from under women's domestic activity. At the same time, it has also created the ground for women's activity in society. Mechanical production, which can dispense with muscle power and skilled labor, makes it possible to employ women in many areas of work. Women entered industry wishing to increase their family income. With the development of modern industry, women's labor in industry became a necessity. And with each improvement of modern times, men's labor became superfluous, thousands of workers were thrown onto the street, a reserve army of the poor was created, and wages constantly sank.

Previously, a man's earnings, combined with the simultaneous productive activity of his wife in the home, sufficed to ensure a family's existence; now it is hardly enough to see an unmarried worker through. The married worker must, by necessity, also count on the paid work of his wife.

By this fact, women have been freed from economic dependence on men. A woman employed in industry, who cannot possibly exist in the family as a mere economic appendage to her husband, learns to be self-sufficient as an economic force independently from men. But if women are no longer economically dependent on men, then there is no reasonable basis for their social dependence on them. However, at the moment this economic independence does not benefit women themselves, but the capitalists. By virtue of their monopoly on the means of production, capitalists have seized this new economic factor and made it operate for their exclusive advantage. Freed from their economic dependence on men, women are subjected to economic domination by the capitalists; from the slaves of men they have become the slaves of their employers: they have only changed their master. Even so, they have benefited from this change: they are no longer economically inferior to men and subordinate to them, but their equal. But the capitalists are not content with just exploiting women; on top of this, they use them to exploit male workers more thoroughly.

From the outset, women's labor has been cheaper than men's labor. A man's wage was originally calculated on the basis of covering the upkeep of a whole family; whereas from the start a woman's wage represented only the costs for the upkeep of a single person, and even this only partially, because it was assumed that women would continue working at home in addition to working in the factory. Furthermore, the products manufactured by women in the home with primitive tools, compared with the products of large-scale industry, were equivalent to only a small quantity of moderate social labor. A smaller capacity for work was therefore inferred for women, and this consideration allowed a woman to receive a smaller payment for her labor power. Added to these reasons for women's cheap payment is the view that, on the whole, women have fewer needs than men.

But what makes female labor power especially valuable to capitalists is not only the low price, but also the greater subservience of women. The capitalists speculate on these two moments: remunerating female workers as badly as possible and depressing the wages of men as much as possible through this competition. Similarly, they use child labor to depress the wages of women, and the work of machines to depress human labor power in general. The capitalist system alone is the cause of the fact that women's labor has results directly opposed to its natural tendency: that it leads to a longer workday instead of shortening it substantially; and that it is not synonymous with an increase in the wealth of society—that is, with greater affluence for every individual member of society—but only with an increase in the profit of a handful of capitalists and at the same time with ever greater impoverishment of the masses. The disastrous consequences of women's labor, which are felt so painfully today, will only disappear when the capitalist system of production does.

In order to not be defeated by competition, capitalists must exert themselves to make the difference between the purchase (production) price and the selling price of their commodities as large as possible. They therefore try to produce things as cheaply as possible and sell them as expensively as possible. Capitalists, consequently, have a strong interest in endlessly lengthening the workday and paying workers as ridiculously insignificant a wage as possible. This endeavor stands in direct contradiction to the interests of female workers just as much as to those of male workers. There is therefore no real contradiction between the interests of male and female workers. By contrast, there is an irreconcilable contradiction between the interests of capital and those of labor.

Economic reasons speak against demanding the prohibition of women's labor. The present economic situation is such that neither capitalists nor men can give up women's labor. Capitalists must maintain it in order to remain competitive, and men must count on it if they want to establish a family. Even if we were to eliminate women's labor through legislation, men's wages would not be improved. The capitalists would very soon cover the deficit of cheap female labor power by using better machines more extensively—and in a short time everything would be as before.

After major walkouts, the outcomes of which were favorable for the workers, we have seen that, with the help of better machines, the capitalists undid the workers' achievements.

If one demands the prohibition or restriction of women's labor on the basis of the competition that arises from it, then it is just as logically justified to demand the abolition of machines and the restoration of medieval guild law, which stipulated the number of workers to be employed in each business establishment.

However, apart from these economic reasons, it is principled reasons above all that speak against prohibiting women's labor. Precisely on the basis of the principled side of the question, women must be ready to protest with all their strength against any attempt of that kind; they must oppose it with the most energetic and most justified resistance, because they know that their social and political equality with men depends only and alone on their economic independence, enabled by their work in society, that is, outside the family.

On the basis of principle, we women protest most emphatically against restricting women's labor. Since we absolutely do not want to separate our cause from the workers' cause in general, we will not formulate any special demands; we request no other protection than that which labor generally demands against capital.

We admit only a single exception for the benefit of pregnant women, whose condition demands special protective measures in the interest of the woman herself and her offspring. We recognize no special women's rights at all—we recognize no special rights of women workers! We expect full emancipation neither from admitting women to what is called free industry and to education equal to men's—although the demand for these two rights is only natural and just—nor from the granting of political rights. The countries in which supposedly universal, free, and direct suffrage exists show us how small the real worth of this is. The right to vote without economic freedom is no more and no less than a bill of exchange with no market value. If social emancipation depended on political rights, there would be no social question in countries with the universal right to vote. The emancipation of women, like the emancipation of the whole human race, will be exclusively the work of the emancipation of labor from capital. Only in a socialist society will women, like workers, gain full possession of their rights.

In view of these facts, there remains nothing else for women who are serious in wishing for their liberation than to affiliate themselves with the Socialist Workers' Party, the only party that strives for the emancipation of workers.

Without the assistance of men, yes, often even against the will of men, women have come under the socialist banner; it must even be conceded that in certain cases they have been driven there irresistibly against their own intentions, simply by a clear assessment of the economic situation.

But now they stand under this banner, and they will stay under it! They will fight under it for their emancipation, for their recognition as human beings with equal rights.

Insofar as they go hand in hand with the Socialist Workers' Party, they are ready to participate in all the efforts and sacrifices of the struggle, but they are also firmly resolved, quite rightly, to demand all the rights owed to them after the victory. With regard to sacrifices and duties, as well as to rights, they want to be no more and no less than companions in arms, who are accepted under the same conditions into the ranks of the combatants.

Women's Suffrage

[Delivered in Stuttgart at the International Socialist Congress
on August 22, 1907]

[…]

Socialist women do not consider women's right to vote as the question of all questions, the solving of which will eliminate all the existing social impediments to the free, harmonious development and pursuit of life of the female sex. For it does not affect the deepest cause of these impediments: private property, which is the root of the exploitation and oppression of one person by another. A glance at the situation of the politically emancipated, but socially unfree and exploited, male proletarians shows that. Conferring suffrage on the female sex does not abolish the class contradiction between exploiters and exploited, from which arise the most serious social obstacles for the free development and harmonious advancement of proletarian women. It also does not eliminate the conflicts that emerge for women, as members of their sex, out of the social contradictions between men and women in the capitalist order. On the contrary: the full political equality of the female sex prepares the ground upon which these conflicts can grow to their full severity—conflicts of various kinds, the most extensive and painful of which is that between professional work and motherhood.

For us socialists, therefore, women's suffrage cannot be the "end goal," as it is for bourgeois women. However, we value its attainment as a stage, to be desired most deeply in the struggle for our end goal. The right to vote helps bourgeois women dismantle the barriers that, in the shape of the prerogatives of the male sex, constrain their possibilities for education and occupation. It arms proletarian women in the struggle they are conducting to achieve full humanity against class exploitation and class domination. It enables them, to a higher degree than before, to participate in the struggle for the attainment of political power by the proletariat for the purpose of overcoming the capitalist order and establishing the socialist order, in which alone the question of women's rights can be solved.

We socialists demand women's suffrage not as a natural right with which women are born. We demand it as a social right founded on women's revolutionized economic activity, in their revolutionized social being and personal consciousness. The subsistence economy housewife of the good old days has been relegated to the old folks' parlor by capitalist production. In her place, the professionally employed woman, but above all the woman working for a wage, who stands in the midst of society's economic life and production, has become the type that represents the most socially important form of female economic activity. The occupational and trade statistics of all capitalist countries reflect this change. What women previously created productively within the four walls of the home was for the consumption, the good, of the family. What flows from their busy hands today, the useful, convenient, and beautiful things their brains devise, appear as commodities on the social commodities market, and women join millions of others as sellers of labor power, the most important social commodity, on the social labor market.

Thus a revolution of women's position in the family and society is taking place. Women are released from the household as the source of their livelihood, they can exist economically outside the family, they gain their economic independence from the family, from men. In many cases, the family also no longer offers them a satisfying life purpose. Like men, under the same conditions—often under even harder ones—women must take up the struggle with hostile life, whether impelled by external or internal needs. In this struggle they require full political rights like men, for such rights are weapons, means by which a woman can and must defend her interests.

Together with their social existence, women's worlds of feeling and thought are also revolutionized. They feel their lack of political rights as a crying injustice, which for long centuries the female sex bore as a matter of course. In a slow, painful course of development women are rising from the confines of the old family life to the forum of public life. They demand their full political equality—as expressed in the right to vote—as a social necessity of life and as a social declaration of maturity. The right to vote is the necessary political correlate of the economic independence of women.

One would think that, considering this state of affairs, the whole disenfranchised female sex would struggle in one phalanx for universal women's suffrage. However, that is not so. Bourgeois women do not stand unified and united behind the principle of the full political equality of the female sex, let alone struggle, as a firmly cemented power, with all their energy for universal women's suffrage. That is ultimately not due to the lack of insight and shortsighted tactics of the leaders in the women's rights camp, although these may have some things to answer for. It is the unavoidable consequence of the different social stratifications within the world of women.

Not only the purpose for which the right to vote is introduced, but also the value of this right itself differs according to the social stratum to which women belong. The value of suffrage stands in inverse relation to the amount of property. This value is the least for the wealthiest women; it is the greatest for proletarian women. Thus the contest for women's suffrage is also dominated by class contradiction and class struggle. It cannot be a unified contest of the whole sex, especially not when it does not relate to a bloodless principle but to its single concrete, vital content: universal women's suffrage.

We cannot expect bourgeois women to change their spots. Proletarian women cannot, therefore, count on the support of bourgeois women in the struggle for their civil rights: the class contradictions preclude including the bourgeois women's rights movement in their struggle. That is not to say that they reject bourgeois advocates of women's rights if they stand behind and beside them in the struggle for universal women's suffrage, in order to strike together while marching separately.[10] But proletarian women must be clear that they cannot attain the right to vote in a struggle of the female sex, without distinction of class, against the male sex; but only in the class struggle of all the exploited, without distinction of sex, against all exploiters, likewise without distinction of sex.

In their struggle for universal women's suffrage, proletarian women find strong allies in the socialist parties of all countries. The socialist parties' advocacy for women's suffrage is not founded on ideological and ethical considerations. It is dictated by historical knowledge and, above all, by the understanding of class position, of the proletariat's practical preparations for struggle. The proletariat cannot fight its economic and political battles without the participation of its women, awoken to class-consciousness, gathered and trained and equipped with the social rights to struggle. Thanks to the increasing application of women's labor in industry, in many trades, movements for a better wage can only be executed if women workers also participate in them as trained and organized class fighters. Also the political work, the political struggle of the proletariat, must be shared by women.

---

[10] [The expression "march separately but strike together" is common in Marxist and other leftist discourse, used, for example, by Vladimir Ilyich Lenin in "Social-Democracy and the Provisional Revolutionary Government" [1905], in *Collected Works*, Vol. 8, *January–July 1905*, ed. J. Jerome, trans. Bernard Isaacs and Isidor Lasker (Moscow: Progress Publishers, 1962), 290.]

The intensification of the class struggle between the exploiters and the exploited increases the significance of women's awakening to class-consciousness and their involvement in the proletarian emancipation movement. The strengthening of trade union organizations has not—as bourgeois fools had optimistically expected—brought social peace, but an era of huge lockouts and strikes. The purposeful collaboration of the proletariat in political life leads to the sharpest intensification of political struggles, an intensification that leads to new methods and means of struggle. In Belgium and Holland, the proletariat had to supplement its parliamentary struggle with political mass strikes. In Russia, the same weapon was tested in the revolution with the greatest success.[11] In order to wrest electoral reform in Austria from their opponents, the Austrian proletariat had to stand ready for battle, to hold ready the revolutionary weapon of the mass strike.

Huge strikes and huge lockouts, but above all revolutionary mass strikes, lay the highest sacrifices upon the proletariat. And the proletariat cannot, like the propertied classes, pass these sacrifices on to hirelings, it cannot finance them from a well-filled bag of money. They are sacrifices that every single struggling member of the class must bear personally. Therefore they can only be made if the women of the proletariat have acquired historical insight into the necessity and significance of the sacrifices. The glorious Austrian struggle for suffrage has shown how significant, indeed imperative, it is to saturate the female proletariat with a socialist mindset, from which flows willingness to sacrifice and heroism. This would not have been victorious without the active cooperation of proletarian women. It must be especially emphasized that the success of our Austrian brothers is a consequence of the loyalty, willingness to work and sacrifice, and courage, as much as it is of the martial virtues, that our female Austrian comrades demonstrated in struggle. ("Bravo!")

It follows from this briefly sketched state of affairs that the proletariat has a vital practical interest in the political equality of the female sex, and is urged to join the struggle for the full civil liberty of woman. This struggle galvanizes the masses of women and helps educate them to class-consciousness. The conferring of suffrage on women is the precondition for the purposeful participation of proletarian women in the proletarian class struggle. At the same time, it creates the strongest incentive to pursue the awakening, gathering,

---

[11] [Zetkin is here referring to the First Russian Revolution of 1905, a wave of mass social and political unrest, which led to constitutional reform, including the establishment of a multi-party system.]

and training of the female proletariat with the same zeal as the enlighten-ment and organization of the male proletariat.

As long as women are without political rights, they are also often thought to be without power, and the influence they are nevertheless able to exer-cise on political life is underestimated. On the stock exchange of parliamen-tary life, only the ballot has market value. The shortsighted, who only count mandates and ballots in political struggle, consider efforts to awaken the fe-male proletariat to class-conscious life as a kind of diversion, as a luxury, that social democracy might only allow if it had an abundance of time, strength, and means. They overlook the compelling class interest that the proletariat has in developing the class struggle in the women's world, and in proletarian women contending purposefully beside their brothers.

From the moment women are emancipated and have votes to grant a mandate, this interest will become clear to even the most shortsighted in our ranks. That moment begins the race of all parties for the votes of prole-tarian women, for they form the majority of the female sex. Socialist parties must make sure they drive all bourgeois parties from the field through their work of enlightenment. Their struggle for the civil rights of women works toward this. This has been shown by the history of the struggle for suffrage in Finland and the first campaign for suffrage there, which was conducted as universal suffrage for men and women. Women's suffrage is an ideal means of breaching the last and perhaps the firmest stronghold of the ignorance of the masses: in the political indifference and backwardness of broad masses of the female proletariat. And we must tear down precisely this stronghold, be-cause it hampers and makes more difficult the present proletarian struggle, and threatens the future of the class. ("Bravo!")

But in our days of intensified class struggle the question arises: For which women's suffrage should socialist parties fight? Years ago this would have seemed irrelevant. The answer would have been: for universal women's suffrage. For at that time, partial women's suffrage would have been seen as merely a half measure, as insufficient progress, but still as a first stage toward the political emancipation of the female sex. Today this harm-less notion is no longer possible. Today, the socialist parties must declare emphatically that they can only struggle for universal women's suffrage, that they point-blank reject partial women's suffrage as a distortion and mockery of the principle of political equality. What was previously done instinctively—strengthening the position of power of property by intro-ducing partial women's suffrage—now occurs consciously. Two tendencies in bourgeois parties work to break the inherent resistance to women's suffrage: the increasing external and internal distress of large circles of bourgeois women, who must struggle for their civil rights, and the growing fear of the political advance of the fighting proletariat. The introduction of partial women's suffrage appears in this situation as a saving way out. The proletariat must pay the cost of peace between the men and women of the propertied classes. The propertied classes are eyeing the introduction of partial women's suffrage, for they see this as a wall to protect them against the swelling political power of the fighting proletariat. Events in Norway have proven this: When the storming proletariat, which fought under the leadership of social democracy, could no longer be denied universal suffrage in the local councils, the reform was ruined by the introduction of partial women's suffrage. It was declared outright by bourgeois politicians that census suffrage for women should be a counterweight against the universal suffrage of men.

In partial women's suffrage we behold less the first stage of the political emancipation of the female sex than, rather, the last stage of the political emancipation of property. It is a privilege of property, not a universal right. It does not emancipate a woman because she is a woman, but *although* she is a woman; it does not raise her to full citizenship as a person, but as a bearer of assets and income. It therefore leaves the great mass of the female sex politically unfree, and just chalks up their unfreedom to a different account.

But beyond the proletarian women who are left without rights, partial women's suffrage attacks their class. It works as a plural vote of those with property and strengthens their political power. It is therefore also inappropriate to see partial women's suffrage in practical terms as a step toward the political emancipation of proletarian women by universal suffrage. On the contrary: because partial women's suffrage increases the political power of those with property, it strengthens the reactionary forces that throw themselves against the further democratization of the right to vote to the benefit of the proletariat, without distinction of sex.

One more thing: partial women's suffrage lets bourgeois women exclude themselves, satisfied, from the struggle for the political equality of the whole female sex. In no country where partial women's suffrage exists in administrative or legislative bodies do politically emancipated women struggle with all their strength for the civil rights of their poorer sisters, for universal women's suffrage. The more the reactive propensity grows to erect a bulwark against the increasing power of the proletariat by introducing partial women's suffrage, the more necessary it is to enlighten proletarian women about this interrelationship of things. That prevents them from letting themselves be misused as fetchers and carriers for an injustice against themselves and their class under the slogan: justice for the female sex.

Our demand for women's suffrage is not a women's rights claim, but rather a mass claim and class claim of the proletariat. It is fundamentally and practically an equally important organic part of the entire social democratic suffrage program. The demand must therefore not just be agitated for at all times, but above all also be contested in conjunction with all struggles for suffrage that socialist parties conduct for political democracy. In line with this notion, the majority of the Commission has resolved that every struggle for suffrage must also be conducted as a struggle for women's suffrage. The rights of proletarian women, like those of proletarian men, must win through common struggle. [...]

Save the Scottsboro Boys!

Appeal, April 1932

MOPR[12] comrades, MOPR friends, and all of you whose conscience still speaks like a human being's and whose heart still beats like a human being's, unite! Unite to prevent an unimaginable, a particularly terrible crime of justice, which, without your swift, decisive action, will be inscribed into the history of crimes of justice in the United States, which is already too rich in abominations and atrocities.

The outrage and horror have still not fully ebbed away after the burning of Sacco and Vanzetti[13]—two innocents, even according to bourgeois class rights, if these were applied without prejudice—on the modern pyre of the electric chair. But the executioners already stand ready to deliver eight more innocents to this agonizing death, using this tool of torture and murder.

In the state of Alabama, nine young black men, who have hardly grown out of boyhood—the oldest of them is barely twenty years old—have been condemned, one "only" to lifelong penal servitude, but eight to death.

And this is despite the fact that it is certain that they did not commit the crime of which they are accused—namely, having raped two white prostitutes. The accusation is a deliberate lie, concocted for the most sinister purposes of landowners and factory owners. They want to have the black youths burned alive, in order to terrorize the working masses of blacks, who are rebelling against their exploitation and, by doing so, forming a united front with their white brothers and sisters against hunger, imperialist wars, and bloody white terror.

This serious allegation has proven untenable from the beginning and cannot withstand any genuine examination. One of the prostitutes herself later retracted the allegation formally, firmly, and decisively. The judges brushed this fact away, blind and deaf. The basest racial hatred of whites against blacks, this expression of a human and cultural attitude, which is as arrogant as it is base, has incited and goaded on the beast of the lynch mob.

---

[12] [MOPR is the Russian acronym of International Red Aid, an international organization founded in 1922 by the Communist International, with the aim of helping political prisoners of class war.]

[13] [Nicola Sacco and Bartolomeo Vanzetti, two American anarchists, originally from Italy, accused of murder during a robbery in Massachusetts in 1920 and executed using the electric chair in 1927. The trial and sentencing were suspected of being influenced by anti-Italian and anti-leftist prejudices, and international riots followed the execution.]

The beast rages in the state of Alabama and will have its sacrifices. For its de-lectation, eight black boys shall be burned upon the modern pyre.

The supreme court of Alabama has still not spoken, which means the Supreme Court of the United States cannot be called on against the shameful judgment of the worst racial hatred. The atmosphere of racial hatred and lynch brutality in which the trial was conducted and the sentence pro-nounced raises the fear that the confirmation of the death sentence by the su-preme court of Alabama will happen so late, and will be enforced so quickly and immediately afterward, that appeal to the United States Supreme Court will be impossible.

Faced with this obvious, appalling possibility, it is necessary to act quickly, immediately, with the most extreme exercise of force, to lose no time, to use every minute, so that eight young human lives may be spared the grisly fate of being burned on the electric chair.

MOPR comrades, MOPR friends from all countries! It is, of course, self-evident that, as you have until now, you will continue to deploy your whole strength and dedication toward the demand: "Take the eight black boys down from the electric chair, let them out of the prisons, just like with the brave, in-nocent, condemned labor leaders Tom Mooney and Warren Billings,[14] just like with the Harlan miners[15] and all political prisoners." Yes, you will make possible what seemed impossible, increasing your selfless, vigorous exertion to rescue the eight black boys. Thus you remain the firm, unswerving elite troops in the struggle against the impending crime of racial hatred, of lynch justice and the lust for exploitation. To prevent the judicial murder of eight black boys, the strongest, most invincible forces of the masses must be force-fully deployed everywhere toward this goal.

All of you whose conscience still speaks like a human being's, whose heart still beats like a human being's! Rise up to rescue these eight young individ-uals, who shall be dragged by the executioner onto the pyre of the electric chair, and whose only fault is to have been born with black skin! Speak! Act! Your foremost ranks will not lack countless unprejudiced human thinkers from the United States. They have not forgotten that in the United States

---

[14] [Two labor leaders convicted of a bombing in San Francisco in 1916, who each served more than twenty years in prison before being released and pardoned. Serious irregularities affected the trial, which initially resulted in death sentences. These were commuted after widespread international agitation.]

[15] [In 1931, wage cuts to miners in Harlan County, Kentucky, who were already struggling due to the Great Depression, resulted in strikes and skirmishes between business owners and union members. These struggles were still ongoing when Zetkin wrote this appeal for the black youths.]

women and men of the most highly developed minds, dispositions, and characters have, by deploying their name, their social position, their health, and not seldom their lives, deployed their whole personhood toward ending black slavery, toward the liberation and equality of their black brothers and sisters. The great example of these great dead should not—*cannot* be—just academic learning; it must operate again as a living force. Recorded indelibly in the history of the United States are the most glorious, heroic women and men who, undaunted in mass struggle for human rights and humanity against deep-rooted prejudice, hatred, and incitement, have unfurled and carried forth the banner of full liberation and equality for all those without social rights, the scorned and the downtrodden. It cannot happen that, beside this brilliant side of history, the dark, blood-dripping chronicle of lynching and judicial crimes will be increased by the agonizing murder of these eight black boys. Think of the unspeakable agonies and torments, the long custody with the piercing daily, hourly question whether tomorrow or the day after tomorrow the executioner will stand at the threshold of the cell to lay the eight chosen sacrifices down on the blazing altar of racial hatred.

MOPR comrades, MOPR friends, all of you, whose conscience still speaks like a human being's, whose heart still beats like a human being's, raise your voice! Act! The strong, irresistible call of the immense, uncountable masses must drown out the judges' judgment, prejudiced by racial hatred, the raucous cry of the lynch mob. The hands of the immense, uncountable masses must clench themselves into a giant fist, which shreds the verdict and overturns the electric chair. Anyone, everyone, each person who is silent, who steps aside dully, resigned or even indifferent to the struggle to save these eight blacks, makes themselves complicit in an inexpiable crime, which would be an indelible dark spot in the history of the United States, of humanity.

The struggle to save these eight young lives from torture and murder in the electric chair is part of the great, far-reaching historical lawsuit between unprejudiced, cultured humanity and bigoted, narrow-minded, brutal, bloodthirsty racial hatred, whose roots reach back to savageness and barbarity. In this struggle, in this lawsuit, humanity must win. Its victory is certain if everyone consciously, bravely does their full duty. To the work, to the struggle to perform our duty! And thus also to the work and to the struggle for a strong MOPR, steeled in the struggle against white terror and for the international solidarity of all working people of all races and nations!

6

Lou Salomé (1861–1937)

Introduction

More often than not, Lou Andreas-Salomé (1861–1937) has been remembered
for her friendship with famous poets and intellectuals. Friedrich Nietzsche,
Rainer Maria Rilke, and Sigmund Freud were some figures with whom she, for
longer or shorter periods of time, was close. An English-language biography
of Salomé bears the subtitle *Nietzsche's Wayward Disciple*.[1] The English translation of her memoir, *Lebensrückblick*, has the subtitle *The Intimate Story of her
Friendships with Nietzsche, Rilke, and Freud*. Salomé, however, was more than
a muse, mentor, and collector of male geniuses. She was the author of a significant oeuvre that includes both literature and groundbreaking philosophical
work. Her philosophy developed in dialogue with contemporary intellectuals
as well as historical figures, including Baruch Spinoza (1632–1677).[2] Salomé's
contribution spans the philosophy of religion, philosophy of life, philosophy
of art and literature, and psychoanalysis.

Louise von Salomé was born into a German-speaking family in imperial
St. Petersburg, a cosmopolitan city that she characterized as a mix of Paris
and Stockholm.[3] She was the youngest of six children and the only girl. In
her memoirs—which combine intellectual autobiography and freestanding
reflections on her childhood, youth, and adult life—she retrieves her coming
of age. Opening with the melancholy observation that "our first experience,
remarkably enough, is that of loss," Salomé describes, in sobering language,
how academic endeavors fail to fill this void and thus, for her, represent
a work of mourning.[4] In her teenage years, her religious and philosophical

---

[1] See Rudolph Binion, *Frau Lou: Nietzsche's Wayward Disciple* (Princeton, NJ: Princeton University
Press, 1968).

[2] See Binion, *Frau Lou*, 15–16, 294, 337, 401, 496. See also Sandra A. Wawrytko, "Lou Salomé
(1861–1937)," in *A History of Women Philosophers*, Vol. 4, *Contemporary Women Philosophers, 1900-
Today*, ed. Mary Ellen Waithe (Dordrecht: Kluwer, 1995), 69–102.

[3] Lou Andreas–Salomé, *Looking Back: Memoirs. The Intimate Story of her Friendship with Nietzsche,
Rilke, and Freud.*, ed. Ernst Pfeiffer, trans. Breon Mitchell (New York: Marlowe, 1995), 1.

[4] Salomé, *Looking Back*, 34.

interests led her to Pastor Hendrik Gillot, who tutored her through a formidable reading list. She read literature and the Bible but also works by Spinoza, Leibniz, Rousseau, Voltaire, Kant, Fichte, Kierkegaard, Schopenhauer, and others.[5] But Gillot, who was twice her age, had invested romantically in their relationship. Salomé needed distance. After her father died in 1879, Salomé and her mother left Russia.

Like many other intellectual women, Salomé set out for Zurich, where the university was open to women. She attended classes in theology, philosophy, art history, and other subjects as a *Hörerin*, i.e., she attended lectures but did not sign up for the exams.[6] However, illness soon forced her to leave Zurich, and she embarked on a tour of Europe. During this period, she met the philosopher Paul Rée. Rée's friend Malwida von Meysenbug (herself no less than an intellectual powerhouse) introduced Salomé to Nietzsche. Soon a friendship was forged between Salomé, Nietzsche, and Rée. A famous portrait photograph was taken of the three of them: Salomé, whip in hand, in a cart being pulled by Nietzsche. Rée is leisurely posing next to them. In her memoirs, Salomé describes the taking of this photograph and how Nietzsche had given instructions about the details.[7] She could not, though, have anticipated how her name would forever be associated with this picture and how it would shape the image of her as a femme fatale. Salomé's life and person have been the subject of systematic mythologizing but also artistic appraisals such as Frank Wedekind's two Lulu plays, Irvin D. Yalom's 2011 novel, and a 2018 biographical film.[8]

Salomé's first book, the novel *The Struggle Over God* (*Im Kampf um Gott*), was published in 1885 under the pseudonym Henry Lou. In her autobiography, she remarks that no other work of hers enjoyed such a favorable reception. In 1887, Salomé married the philologist and Persia scholar Friedrich Carl Andreas. They had an open relationship, and it was also understood that Salomé would continue her publishing, now under her married name of Lou Andreas-Salomé (today the hyphenated last name is used less in the scholarly literature). Salomé socialized with Georg Simmel, Ferdinand Tönnies, Hedwig Dohm, and other nineteenth-century luminaries.

---

[5] See H. F. Peters, *My Sister, My Spouse: A Biography of Lou Andreas-Salomé* (New York: Norton, 1962), 53–54.

[6] Wawrytko, "Lou Salomé," 70. This chapter offers a solid survey of Salomé's philosophy.

[7] Salomé, *Looking Back*, 42.

[8] Wedekind's Lulu plays are *Earth Spirit* (1895) and *Pandora* (1904). The film is Cordula Kablitz-Post's *Lou Salomé: The Audacity to Be Free*. Yalom's *When Nietzsche Wept* offers a semi-fictional account of Salomé's life and plays on the image of her as a *femme fatale*.

Nietzsche acknowledges Salomé's importance for his *Thus Spoke Zarathustra* (1883–1885).[9] Salomé, in turn, authored the first German-language study of Nietzsche's work, a study in which she pioneers a mix of biographical and philosophical methodologies. She places Nietzsche within his philosophical context and culture but also discusses his arguments and the development of his thought. Although she has been criticized for presenting Nietzsche's work as a "system," Salomé offers a clear, hermeneutically rich account that places individual works within the context of a larger philosophical and cultural vision.

Salomé, however, was not the only woman philosopher who took an interest in Nietzsche's writing. In the 1890s, Nietzsche's work was hotly debated. In spite of his outspoken misogyny—so forcefully documented by Dohm (see chapter 4)—many women took inspiration from his work. What attracted, and sometimes provoked, these women philosophers was Nietzsche's attempt to critique and overturn traditional, petit bourgeois values and his will, in his early writings, to investigate the idea of a deeper unity between human life and the larger metaphysical context into which it is born.

After the turn of the century, Salomé became increasingly interested in psychoanalysis and started working in this area. She met Freud in 1911 at the International Congress in Weimar and soon began to spend longer periods of time in Vienna, where she became a member of the Wednesday meetings of the Psychoanalytic Society. She also practiced psychoanalysis at her home in Göttingen. Freud and Salomé remained friends until her death. Salomé's contributions to the psychoanalytic literature include essays on bisexuality and narcissism (which she views as potentially positive rather than simply regressive or destructive), as well as pathbreaking observations on women's sexuality.[10]

Salomé's works in literature, criticism, and philosophy include *Ibsen's Heroines* (1892), *Friedrich Nietzsche* (1894), *Rainer Maria Rilke* (1928), *The Freud Journal* (1958), and many essays on Russian art and culture. She is also the author of a significant body of correspondence, the most famous of which is with Rilke. Upon Salomé's death, her library was quickly confiscated

---

[9] For Nietzsche's letters to and thoughts on Salomé, especially in 1882, see http://www.nietzschesource.org/#eKGWB.

[10] For an English translation of the narcissism essay, see "The Dual Orientation of Narcissism," *Psychoanalytic Quarterly* 31 (1962): 1–30. See also Wawrytko, "Lou Salomé," 75–77. Salomé, though, had developed these thoughts before she turned to psychoanalysis.

by the National Socialists, who accused her, on account of her psychoanalytic work, of engaging in "Jewish Science."

For this volume, we have included a section of Salomé's 1910 work *The Erotic*. The book was written in response to an invitation from the philosopher Martin Buber, who characterized it as a "pure, powerful, essential piece of work."[11]

The erotic, for Salomé, is a broad and comprehensive category. It fluctuates indeterminately between the corporeal and the mental. As she puts it, the problem of the erotic "must be regarded as a special case within physical, psychic, and social relations in general . . . it *relates* all three of these kinds of relations *to each other*, and thus merges them into a single problem—*its* problem." Salomé's claim, then, is that the erotic cannot be reduced to romantic longings or to sexual relationships. It marks, instead, a central point of connection between mind and body, self and other, the individual human being and the totality of nature. In this sense, the erotic is key to our understanding of the human being.[12]

At the outset of her study, Salomé identifies two methodological challenges presented by the subject of the erotic. First, she points out that the erotic is often objectified; it is studied at a distance, drained of life, and thus mischaracterized from the get-go. As a result, we only reach a definition of the erotic at the price of losing the object under investigation. Second, she worries that traditional philosophical methods, for example, a logical-analytical approach, can only see the subject of the erotic from the outside, from within a medium that constitutively fails to grasp its full complexity.

Salomé also turns to critical cultural theory. She seeks to identify a third alternative to the Hellenistic celebration of eroticism (broadly conceived) and

---

[11] Angela Livingston, *Lou Andreas-Salomé: Her Life and Work* (London: Gordon Fraser, 1984), 104. The book appeared in a series that Buber edited, and it was probably Buber who gave the book its title. According to Binion, Salomé's title most likely included the term *Erotic Affects*. Binion, *Frau Lou*, 327n.

[12] Another philosopher of this era, Helene Stöcker (1869–1943), developed her own philosophy of love. Stöcker, who had studied romantic thought (and worked with the young Wilhelm Dilthey on his biography of Friedrich Schleiermacher), is often presented as a Nietzschean. Like Salomé, though, her thoughts are rooted in Spinozism, as well as her background in romantic philosophy. For a discussion of Stöcker's philosophy, feminism, and pacifism, including her relationship to Salomé, see Tracie Matysik, *Reforming the Moral Subject: Ethics and Sexuality in Central Europe, 1890–1930* (Ithaca, NY: Cornell University Press, 2008), esp. 55–95. Stöcker's dissertation is published as *Zur Kunstanschauung des XVIII Jahrhunderts* (Berlin: Mayer and Müller, 1902). In 1941, during the National Socialist era, she emigrated to the United States, where she continued to work for the peace movement.

the puritan, Christian approach—two ways of thinking that, she suggests, have come to dominate our discourse of the erotic. In Salomé's account, human beings share a sexual drive with other animals—with "everything that breathes," as she puts it. What distinguishes human eroticism is, among other things, the way it is centered around individuality. While eroticism is a natural drive, it still applies that in (the rest of) nature, the importance of the individual is downplayed vis-à-vis the species. However, for us humans, the erotic takes the form of love. We treat loved ones as irreplaceable; we see them as ends in themselves rather than as mere means to satisfying a desire. Whereas a philosopher like Schopenhauer regards individuation as the root of deeply felt metaphysical isolation, Salomé views it as a condition of possibility for the loving encounters that distinguish human beings from other animals. Yet Salomé's analysis of the erotic does not end with the idea of love. She sees the human being as driven by a need (stemming from the erotic) for change and new impulses. It is as such that the human being lives in and contributes to culture. In Salomé's view, the erotic can be identified neither with the purely natural drives nor with individuation or social life. Rather, it exists in and through the mutual relationships between them.

Salomé views the erotic as deeply manifested in our psychical-emotional lives. It is rooted in a primal dream, a desire for a full merging of individuals and a unity that leads, as it were, to immortality through reproduction. This means, she argues, that even in a hyperspecialized modern society, the erotic has the power to bring us back to a fundamental natural origin. At the end of the day, Salomé links this to a feeling of wholeness, a sense of an existence that is one and undivided.

For Schopenhauer, whom Salomé quotes in her work, the erotic is, as she renders it, a "devilish trap." Salomé, by contrast, seeks to bring out the productivity of the erotic and its importance for unifying the bodily and the intellectual aspects of the human being. In and through the (erotic) encounter with an other, the other becomes "a meeting point for us with life, with this outside of things that could otherwise never be entirely integrated." Gesturing back to a set of arch-romantic tropes, Salomé describes how love can open us to nature. It is as if "the beloved were not only itself at all, but also the leaf that trembles on the tree, the beam that gleams on the water—transformed into all things and transformer of things: an image scattered in the infinity of the universe, so that we are at home wherever we may wander."

In Salomé's view, there is a relationship between the erotic and art. As she argues, art is at the center of human life. Both the erotic and art unify the natural, the intellectual, and the social. Our erotic being makes us creative, but, at an even deeper level, it discloses the deepest unity of the human being, that between intellect and body.

Salomé also postulates a link between the erotic and religious longing. Needless to say, this was a provocative gesture at the time—and perhaps still is. For her, however, religion is associated with what she describes in her memoirs as "the most positive aspect of [her] life: the feeling of a deeply shared destiny with all things." This, one must assume, is what makes her suggest that "any type of belief, even the most absurd, would be preferable to seeing humankind lose its sense of reverence entirely."[13]

Salomé published *The Erotic* the year before she met Freud. Freud quickly recognized the importance of her work. She was one of the first women to take on a career as a psychoanalyst.[14] Freud even trusted his daughter Anna to be analyzed by Salomé. Salomé, in turn, reflects on her encounter with psychoanalysis in her Freud study. Her correspondence with Freud, which began in 1912 and ended in 1936, is published in a separate volume.[15] It provides interesting insights into the practical and philosophical dimensions of psychoanalysis, sometimes touching on individual cases (should patient X divorce her husband?), other times on large-scale, philosophical concerns, including issues related to life, death, faith, and love. Whereas Freud, as Salomé puts it, had a hard time forgiving common man his religion, she studied religion with interest and fascination.

Salomé's contributions to psychoanalysis, however, should not be separated from her larger philosophical work, including *The Erotic*. There is, for example, a continuity between her insistence on a mind-body unity in *The Erotic* and her later work in psychoanalysis.

While Salomé cultivated friendships with feminists such as Meysenbug and Helene Stöcker, she was accused, by Dohm and others, of focusing more on women's psychology than on their rights and societal status. With respect and admiration but also a critical edge, Dohm discusses Salomé's seemingly uncritical attitude toward Nietzsche (for this criticism, see Dohm's "Nietzsche and Women" and our introduction to chapter 4). However, as is clear from Salomé's study of Henrik Ibsen's independent-minded heroines, Salomé's approach to the "woman's question" cannot be disentangled from

---

[13] Salomé, *Looking Back*, 10–11.
[14] Wawrytko, "Lou Salomé," 76.
[15] Sigmund Freud and Lou Andreas-Salomé, *Letters*, ed. Ernst Pfeiffer, trans. William Robson-Scott and Elaine Robson-Scott (New York: Harcourt Brace Jovanovich, 1972).

a larger awareness of repressive social forms. As some scholars argue, in fin-de-siècle European culture, intellectuals like Salomé were interested in women's psychology precisely because it puts into relief the kinds of social pressure under which, ultimately, we all suffer.[16] However, we should note that for Salomé, the term *woman* is not understood as an essentialist or biological concept. In her study of Nietzsche, for example, she not only connects womanhood with productivity and pregnancy (widely conceived) but also repeatedly describes Nietzsche as a feminine spirit.[17] Here, as in other areas, Salomé is ready to question the governing consensus, break social taboos, and pose new philosophical questions.

Salomé's study of the erotic is a major philosophical contribution. It is original in its argument, provocative in its conclusions, and offers a deep-going discussion of human embodiment and the way in which we, culturally and socially, have taken care of—or failed to take care of—this aspect of our existence. The work is at times technical and densely argued, yet it is worthy of the full attention of the reader. As a philosopher of embodiment, critic of social forms, and author of a groundbreaking contribution to psychoanalysis, Salomé's importance as a philosopher is still being uncovered.

---

[16] See Matysik, *Reforming the Moral Subject*, 250–257.

[17] E.g., Lou Andreas-Salomé, *Nietzsche*, ed. and trans. Siegfried Mandel (Urbana: University of Illinois Press, 2001), 30, 49.

Selections from *The Erotic*

Introduction

You can tackle the problem of the erotic however you want, but you will always feel that you have done so very one-sidedly, especially if you tackle it by means of logic—that is, from the outside.

That means: by subtracting the immediate liveliness of impressions so much and for so long that you find yourself in the most comfortable consensus with the largest possible group. Or, put another way: by representing things unsubjectively enough, as foreign enough to ourselves, that we obtain—instead of the whole, unfragmented expression of life—a disassembled patchwork, which, as a result, may be fixed firmly in words, handled safely for practical purposes, surveyed completely from one side.

But this method of presenting things, which necessarily makes everything material and disenchants it, is now supposed to be applied to things that can only be known subjectively, experienced individually—to what we usually call "mental [*geistig*]" or "psychological [*seelisch*]" impressions of things. Put simply, in other words: this method is supposed to be applied to impressions precisely insofar as they—in principle—escape it. Furthermore, for the sake of the consensus that this is supposed to achieve, we can only ever explain these different kinds of effects on the basis of this one effect, while everything else that could be said about them is only a supplement, a description. But, however logically consistent this supplement is, it can only persuade people subjectively, even with this formal help.

This self-contradictory half measure, or halving, is especially typical for the problem of the erotic, because the erotic itself seems to fluctuate indeterminately between the bodily [*leiblich*] and the mental [*geistig*].

This contradiction is not mitigated by blurring or blending various methods with each other, but, on the contrary, only by working them out more sharply, handling them more rigorously. One could say: only by taking something fully into our hands, placing upon it increasingly more reliable limitations, as matter and material, do we confirm and verify that the scope of our self extends beyond it. In this way, we survey the one-sidedness of both the thing considered and the method: we survey the road in two directions, as it were. Life is revealed to us only on this road, which only an optical illusion seems to bring together to one point. For the further we go into something, the deeper it opens up for us in both directions, as the line of the horizon rises with every step toward it.

But a little further along the way, this precise way of regarding things begins to seem one-sided itself. That is, where its own material withdraws from the senses and understanding, into the uncontrollable, although this material can still be observed as existing in the mind or gauged in practical terms. From beyond the short stretch of surveillance that is solely accessible to our minds, an altered standard of "truth" and "reality" arises for what lies within this stretch. Measured by this standard, even what is most materially tangible, most logically comprehensible, becomes a convention sanctioned by human beings, a signpost for purposes of practical orientation. Beyond that, it evaporates into the same merely symbolic value as the things we grasp as "mental" or "psychological." And with that, at *both* ends of our road the commandment: "You *shall* make for yourself an image and a likeness!"[18] arises so inviolably that the allegorical—which is eloquent only in signs and comparisons, on which all mental description depends—is incorporated into the basic value of human ways of knowing. As in that horizon line, receding before us step by step, "heaven and earth" always merge into *one* image for us: the primordial optical illusion—and at the same time the ultimate symbol.

Foundation

This ultimate equivalence, far from undervaluing the external character of things, re-emphasizes their independence from the additional things that are often assigned to them. It first fully teaches us unprejudiced insight into all the conditions of what is "most material," including what is most bodily: objective reverence for them. Reverence in a meaning for which we have, by far, still not become simple and devoted enough: without any sidelong glances at ethical, aesthetic, religious, or other secondary meanings—but focused only on the sense of the physical itself. Focused on this sense as if [focused] on the side that has become clear to us of inconceivably long experiences: like explorations in the realm of what exists for us, the traces of these things are

---

[18] [This phrase is most likely a reference to the prohibition against idol worship in Exodus 20:4 in the Old Testament (repeated with almost identical wording in Deuteronomy 5:8): "Thou shalt not make unto thee any graven image or any likeness *of any thing*" (King James Bible Online, https://www.kingjamesbibleonline.org/Exodus-20-4/).]

still legible everywhere, like battle scars or trophies. As if, holding still before such an ancient thing, wise in practical matters, which resists our scrutiny in a completely different way from the mental, the movement of life seemed to solidify to firmer traits and forms. And as if this meant that our intellect itself, this descendant born late into the world of the physical, could climb about on it with probing fingers like a small, delicate, and still foolish little boy in his grandfather's lap.

With regard to the foundation of the erotic, namely sexuality, a more thorough determination would have to proceed physiologically. As a form of need like hunger, thirst, or other expressions of our bodily life, sexuality first becomes accessible on such a basis, including for further insight into its nature and function. And, just as only careful individual research and testing of facts can inform us about our needs for nourishment or other bodily needs, here, too, the only valid guideline is the one that, in the area of ethics, we often celebrate as the highest. That is, that what is smallest, least, or found in the lowest things is no less worthy of attention than what is endowed with all human dignity.

The assessment, biased by absolutely no unobjective considerations of both sexual activity and abstinence, seems crucial for this. If, after some consideration, this still remains an open question, it may be connected (among other things) to the fact that the internal secretions of the glands and their relationship to each other (which may be able to substitute for each other more than we realize) are not known at all as precisely as the external sexual secretions. As a result, we cannot really see which of their influences we are subject to, even when outward sexual activity does not occur. (Like, for instance—to take the most common example—when only the uterus or male member is removed, but not the ovaries or scrota, the secondary [sexual] characteristics are not affected.)

Of course, it would be possible to draw conclusions from this point (or any similar point about sexual abstinence) that make sexual abstinence not just admissible for health, but valuable—in the sense of increasing strength by reabsorbing and replacing it. And many women would then feel, with a secret smile, that they have long known something about this. That is, those in whom the coercive sexual discipline of all the centuries of Christianity, at least in some social classes, has become a natural independence from the naked need of the instinctive. Today these women should therefore think twice—no: ten thousand times—before, in the name of modern, free love, they give up the fruit of long, hard cultural struggle, which for them personally fell almost effortlessly in their laps. For it takes far fewer genera-tions to lose something than to acquire it.

However, in the same unbiased way, we should consider other possibil-ities that could warn us against devaluing the sexual too casually—such as the cases that reveal sexual attraction as the natural substitute for the tre-mendous stimulants given to a growing child's body by the strong external stimuli, still so new to it, in the rest of its sensual life. The cases of young sick people, who, even without any impetus of their own, recovered through sexual experiences. Or cases of anemic girls who, even in marriages they did not desire, thrived and gained strength under the influence of the altered tissue tone and metabolism. All the cases where there is evidently a danger that, because it is dammed up, the deepest source of vitality [Lebenskraft] in the time between youth and maturity would not be realized productively, but concentrated to a kind of toxic effect that inhibits and impedes life. And even if these kinds of indications can be opposed by others, we must still state how often bodily inhibition damages a person's mental capacity, indeed their most individual human value.

For these reasons, anything that can contribute to the levelheaded exam-ination of such questions should be welcome. Also, these questions must be treated *as a problem entirely of their own*, without interference, whether from a preexisting idealization of bodily contingencies (such as sometimes emerges in a modernized "Hellenism") or from the claims of the erotic in the narrower sense. For it should also be emphasized how little today's striving to refine and individualize the feelings of love can solve these kinds of questions by itself. However, it is no less commendable for that, and every pure force that it helps foster remains a great gain. Of course, the increasing subtlety of choices in love at first only makes love harder to fulfill. Our physiological ma-turity only very rarely coincides with such exceptional mental states—and, incidentally, both of these also coincide almost as rarely with the maturity of mind and character of a person who should make a permanent commitment.

Generally, it works out badly to mix together all possible practical perspectives—hygienic, romantic, pedagogical, utilitarian—because in the process whatever is purely factual always seems to be passed from one thing to another in order to be expressed. So, for instance, physiological concerns are expressed prematurely due to ideals of robust physical body culture [Körperkultur], or, conversely, discredited by ideals of delicateness. The latter, then (out of fear of being confused with their more robust peers) are quickly pressed into expedited marriages, which are arranged with so many facilitating concessions that, eventually, one suspects that these proceedings are physiologically grounded—with which we have happily reached our starting point again. And so, in order not to lapse into either a frivolous or traditional tone, a free and an enthusiastic and a somewhat stuffy-philistine tone are used alternatingly. This is roughly similar to how, long ago, deposed gods were degraded to demons, and now no one can imagine that people once believed in them as gods—until more skeptical research discovers that it is these gods who live again in their successors.— For this reason, perhaps, some disregard for their former rank, as well as for all reforming outlooks and past struggles, is beneficial to the unbiased contemplation of things.

Theme

The problem of the erotic is characterized by two things:

For a start, it must be regarded as a special case within physical, psychic, and social relations in general, and not just, as often happens, as autocratically isolated. Rather, it *relates* all three of these kinds of relations *to each other*, and thus merges them into a single problem—*its* problem.

Rooted in the deepest foundation of all existence, the erotic always grows from the same rich, strong soil—to whatever height it may extend, to however powerful and massive a tree it may unfold. Even where its soil is completely built over, it always persists underneath with the dark, earthy power of its roots. And its vast value for life is that, however capable it may be of attaining broad sole legitimacy or embodying high ideals, it is not dependent on this, but can draw strength from any soil, and adapts itself to serve life under any conditions.

Thus, we find the erotic already associated with the almost purely vegetative processes of our physical body [*Körperlichkeit*], closely united with them. Even if it is not, like these functions, absolutely necessary for existence, it still has a very strong influence on them. Therefore, even in the higher stages and forms of the erotic, even at the peak of the most complex delights of love, it always retains something of this deep, simple origin. It always retains something of that beneficial happiness that the physical body [*Körperliche*] feels in the immediate sense of its satisfaction as ever new, young experience, as life in its primal sense. Just like every healthy person always enjoys waking up, or their daily meals, or a walk through the fresh air, with new pleasure, as if reborn every day, and just like one rightly sometimes recognizes the beginnings of nervous degeneration when suddenly the concepts of "boring" and "monotonous" bring tedium into this everydayness and basic necessity, so too, behind and beneath the usual delights of one's love life there is always something unsensational and unmeasurable that the human being shares with everything that breathes.

Even in animals, the erotic is not limited only to this, since the sexual activity of higher animals is accompanied by an effect in the brain, which excites its nervous material. In these cases, the sexual intersects with sensation, eventually with the romantic, up to their most finely branched tips and peaks in the realm of what is most individual in humans. But, from the start, this increasing development of love takes place on an increasingly unsteady foundation. It takes place, not on the basis of what is always consistent and equally applicable, but on the basis of that law of all things animal, according to which the intensity of a stimulus decreases with repetition. Greater selectivity in the object and the moment—which are evidence of higher love—is paid for with weariness in what was so fiercely coveted. It is paid for with the desire for what has not yet been repeated, for the still unweakened intensity of stimulus: for *change*. It could be said that natural love life—in all its developments, and in the most individualized perhaps most of all—is built on the principle of infidelity. For, at least in its coarse sense, habituation—to the extent that it represents an opposite, counteracting power—still falls under the effects of the more vegetatively conditioned needs of our physical body, which are hostile to change.

However, it is the more intellectual principle—that is, the principle of more complex life—that urges change and the selective exhaustion of stimuli. It is the behavior that has been enhanced with meaning, which, precisely for this reason, is ignorant of the ancient steadiness and stability of the more primitive processes. And, in some respects, it is this steadiness and stability that make these processes a secure foundation for us, almost like the inorganic—almost like solid earth or rock. So it is neither weakness nor inferiority if the erotic by nature has a strained relationship with fidelity; rather, this signifies its ascent to new contexts for life. And, therefore, even where the erotic is already involved in these contexts, it retains much of this insatiable sensibility, precisely because it is based on the most primordial processes of the life of the organs. Yes, if even this, the "most bodily [*Allerleiblichste*]" in us, should be considered with reverent impartiality, then the erotic truly deserves similar respect, even in its reckless swaggering. It deserves this even though we are only used to seeing it as what it has been made into, namely the scapegoat for every love tragedy.

The circumstance in which the erotic discards its worst habits, at least in the most favorable cases, is given in our mental behavior. When we absorb something into knowledge and consciousness, instead of only into physical or psychological desire, then we experience it not only in the decreasing intensity of the stimulus of the satiation of this desire, but also in the increasing interest of the understanding, and therefore as unique, human, and irreplaceable. From this emerges the full meaning of that which, in love, urges one person to another, as if to a second, another irreplaceable I, in order to be fulfilled in reciprocal interaction with this other as an end in themselves, not as a means for love.

Although love only gains its social significance with this step, this clearly does not apply to the physical side of the erotic. The reconciliation of this physical side with its external consequences, its unavoidable connection to the circle of general interests, means it has a social side even in its earlier stages. But here its deepest meaning for life is exposed: its degree of mental vitality, compared to which even the drive for change seems to be a lack of inner mobility, because it needs impulses from the outside to get going, which in this case would only disrupt and impede. In this way, fidelity and consistency acquire an altered background: in this preeminence of what is liveliest, of what develops life the most, new organizational possibilities are clearly present. An enduring world becomes realizable again, a renewed, more secure ground for all becoming of life, analogous to our physical foundation and to what our organism produces in the child as the ultimate corporeal goal of love.

However, the essence of the erotic is not completely described by these three stages, but only by their *interrelationship*. For this reason, it is difficult to describe a hierarchy in this area. The erotic does not appear as the clear hierarchical structure that can be established theoretically, but as a living, indivisible whole, always complete in itself. We may estimate the erotic to be greater or smaller, but we never know from case to case whether it encompasses its full content, including where it is unaware of this content. For example, the child corresponds physiologically to the full purpose of love even when the dull unconsciousness of primitive times attributes its creation to strange demonic causes.

For this reason, it is necessary to add to the discussion up to this point, since the physical moment in the erotic, which influences everything to the end, is in turn influenced from the start by broader moments, which escape precise description. The problem can only be characterized by the *total emotional excitation* [*Totalergriffenheit*] of the creature.

The Sexual Process

In the world of the (relatively) most undifferentiated living beings, the act of copulation takes place through a small, spherical whole, in itself so unarticulated that it could almost be a symbol for the whole situation. In the fusion of single cells (which also sometimes seems to underlie their reproduction), the two cells' nuclei totally merge with each other, forming the new creature, and only what is inessential, at the periphery of the old cell, disintegrates, dying off. Procreation, child, death, and immortality collapse into one. The child is still interchangeable with its parent, the successor interchangeable with its predecessor, roughly in the same way that pieces are interchangeable in the realm of so-called inanimate things.

As soon as, with the progress of the articulation of organs, conjugation [zygosis] stops involving the total organism and can only occur partially, the following contradiction becomes very clear: what preserves life also necessitates death. Often so immediately that both processes appear to be the same, even if they take place in two beings, in two generations. When the differentiation of individual beings finally goes so far that these individuals are irreplaceable, and therefore the progenitors cannot actually survive in the product of their procreation, death withdraws from the immediate union. The animal, with its developed corporeality, only participates indirectly in the sexual process, i.e., by giving up only what it acquired through heredity and not what it acquired in its development as an individual. The species is passed on under the table, so to speak.

With that, the process would have reached the opposite of its starting point. The whole survival instinct, which originally made the cell nucleus so ingeniously creative, would have emancipated itself—almost perversely— from that which, originally so irrelevant, died off at the periphery of the cell. But all these great upheavals have, from primeval times until now, simply been ignored by the sex cells themselves, as if they still ruled the whole realm of life as before, and not just a single small and ever smaller province within it. This is because, insofar as they contain everything from which even a very differentiated individual can be built, they not only carry unchanged within themselves the same character of totality, but also imprint their temporary influence on the body that houses them.

It may well stem from such influences that precisely the most primitive type of connection between living beings, the total fusion of single-celled organisms, corresponds allegorically to what, in the highest dreams of love, the mind imagines as the full joy of love. That is arguably why love is so easily associated with longing and trepidation about death, which are not even clearly differentiated from each other; with something like a primal dream in which oneself, one's lover, and their child could still be one, and just three names for the same immortality.

On the other hand, this is also the reason for the contrast between the crudest and the most transfigured things related to love, which can stand out comically even in animals, when they connect their sexual needs with a kind of sentimental hypnosis. In the human world these fluctuations between coarseness and oversensitivity are not always humorous. A murky apprehension of this also induces the spontaneous, deeply instinctive shame that very young, innocent people can feel regarding sexual union. This shame is due neither to their inexperience nor to well-intentioned moralizing, but to the fact that they feel that the urge to love each other applies to their whole selves, and the transition from that to a bodily sub-activity baffles them. It is almost as if they were in the clandestine presence of a third person, a stranger: the body, like a partial person in itself. As if, just beforehand, in the helpless language of their longing, they had been almost more intimately, more totally, more immediately close.

Meanwhile, the sexual itself strives, as much as possible, to dissolve the contrasts and contradictions by which it is led astray due to the division of labor of the bodily functions. It restlessly associates with all the drives it can get hold of. Perhaps initially most closely related to the instinct to feed, which, as one of the earliest to evolve, also relates to everything, it soon puts this behind it as already too specialized. If lovers today still say that they would like to devour each other for love, or if terrible female spiders really do so with their pitiful little mates, such a frightening incursion of eating into loving does not really occur. On the contrary, it is sexual desire as *total declaration* [*Totalkundgebung*] that drags all the separate organs along with it in its excitement. It manages this very easily. After all, since all these organs came (so to speak) from the same nursery as the contents of the sexual organs, any of them could have played the role of "sex cells," if pride had not entangled them in such extensive differentiation. For that reason, the memory with which the sexual obtrudes upon them echoes strongly in them. They forget how tremendously much they have achieved in the meantime, and, more than is appropriate for proper, civilized organs of the higher animal species, indulge in unexpected longing for the good old days of first forms and divisions in the ovum.

The unlimited, general excitement of the creature that the sexual process triggers is based on such a (in the human realm one would say "sentimental") mood of backwardness. And the more it is squeezed into a corner in the course of evolution, made into a special process, the stronger the significance of its total influence over the rest becomes. For what occurs in this process— the merging of two beings in erotic intoxication—is not the only union, and perhaps not even the actual one. It is, above all, within us [as individuals] that all the specialized lives of the body and the mind once again ignite each other in a shared longing, instead of each living for itself, indifferent, hardly noticing the other, like members of a large family who only remember that they are "one flesh and blood" on major holidays [*Gedenktagen*]. The more complex the kinds of organisms that we ascend to, the greater will be the festivals and jubilees that are natural to such experiences. Under the influence and effort of the germ plasm, these, like a great-uncle from America, suddenly alert everything, including the most hidden outer corners of our being, to a splendid celebration of origin and sex [*Herkunfts- und Geschlechterfeier*].

Thus, it is said with certain justification that love, even unhappy love, always makes us happy—if you understand this sentence unsentimentally enough, that is, without considering the partner. For although we seem to be fulfilled by our partner, we are in fact fulfilled by our own condition, which makes us, like a typical drunk, totally incapable of dealing objectively with anything. The beloved object is only the stimulating cause, in the same way that a sound or scent from outside can get tangled in a nighttime dream, affecting whole worlds. Lovers even instinctively gauge their common bond by their joint internal mental-bodily productivity [*geistig-leiblichen Produktivwerden*], in which they are focused on and relieved by each other in the same way as bodies focus on and relieve each other in the act of love. If, instead, they engage too literally with the suspect extolments of the other, then we soon see the well known fall from the clouds of glorification that every more experienced person, shaking their heads, tends to predict for all those in love. When this happens, the poor folly of love, having been decked out as a princess with gold tinsel, turns back into Cinderella. In bespangled dress she forgot that it was only the other's gratitude for their own happiness that dressed her like that. Yes, perhaps it was even the case that, unconsciously, something about doing so was based on a wish to overcompensate for the erotic selfishness that only celebrated itself in her, and which therefore placed an intangible mental figment, like a golden shadow, between her and the other to mediate her to him.

The Phantasm of the Erotic

Now, it is interesting to see how, precisely at this point, the theme of the erotic is treated the most poorly. Indeed, this mental involvement in the intoxication of love contains so much—intoxication, such clear symptoms of drunkenness, that there seems to be no alternative other than to shunt it into the realm of the romantic or to mistrust it as somewhat pathological. This sore point in the story is usually barely touched upon, as if the dunce's cap that our understanding temporarily puts on here discourages us from taking its condition seriously. In general, we content ourselves with putting sexuality under the microscope where it is localized in the lower parts of the brain and then adding unerotic emotional material to it (for instance, goodwill, kindness, friendship, sense of duty, and the like), so that, thank God, it is gradually combined with them. All this is not at all promoted by intoxicated overestimation run wild; on the contrary, at first this only obstructs the idea of love as socially beneficial.

But something very human in sexual experience is left out when the human folly in it is dismissed as a *quantité négligeable* [negligible factor]. Only the most foolish outpourings of lovers from all times and peoples provide to the full extent of what human beings, thanks to their feverish intellect, have made out of sexuality. And they only do so when we consider sexuality neither romantically nor with a half-medical interest.

For sexuality contains the mental language of that which, since primeval times, sex has striven to express, with physical [*körperlicher*] distinctness, as its only meaning: that it takes and gives the whole. In this way, the mind learns of the revolution of the sex cells, which these—as the only full participants in the remaining natural processes [*Physis*]—gradually bring about, the uprising of these underdeveloped, freeborn things—our original nobility, as it were—in the well-ordered state of the body. In the mind, as the supreme, aggregating organ over the diversity of the other organs, their high-handed will finds an echo. Yes, the mere existence of the mind already realizes their most demanding wishes to an extent, insofar as it reflects them back upon everything as a uniform power, even if, for now, only as a trick of smoke and mirrors, as an illusion.

It is understandable why even Schopenhauer reached deep into his metaphysical sack in order to proscribe this illusion of love as one of the most devilish traps of the "will to life," along with its dazzling bait: you can literally feel the rage of someone who has been duped. For indeed, from the moment the sexual is ranked as just a single process among the many others in the highly organized body, the burning, eager emotional excitation of the whole [*Gesamtergriffenheit*] must, in a way, die off into nothingness. It can only be a luxury on top of the sexual facts, a work of enticement and seduction, that clothes and adorns what is necessary and real with a lavish overabundance that reality never repays. And yet this excitation is not merely a product of self-deception, however many others it may deceive. Rather, it seeks, for the first time by purely intellectual means, to pioneer its own way, an intellectual way, through physical [*körperlichen*] hardships to some lost paradise. That is why we experience this excitation all the more surely the truer our love is, and if our brainpower helpfully intervenes, then even more insanely.

It is not unusual for the behavior of lovers toward each other to express a little of this notion of appearing to the other only as transfigured, veiled, and—without posing or intending to—entering, spellbound, into their fantasy image. Certain things, the most beautiful, can only be experienced in their full being as stylized, not as purely realistic. It is as if tremendous poetic fullness can only be incorporated into these things with the help of a more controlled form, after being arranged by reverent longing for beauty, in which one gives oneself with both more restraint and more unreservedness than ever, and therefore in an entirely new mingling of beings. And it is as if in this effect, mediated by delusion, they have more binding influence on each other than any actual dependence would ever bring about. For even if the other remains "outside" for us, external to us—just touching, fruitfully, the perimeter of our being—the whole of the rest of the world still first arises for us from this point. The other becomes a meeting point for us with life, with this outside of things that could otherwise never be entirely integrated. The other becomes the medium through which life becomes eloquent for us, finds tones and accents that strike our soul. Loving, in the most serious sense, means knowing someone whose coloration things must adopt if they want to reach us fully, so that they stop being indifferent or frightening, cold or hollow, and even the most threatening of them stretch themselves out tamely at our feet, like vicious animals at the entrance to the garden of Eden. Something of this powerful sentiment lives in the most beautiful love songs, as if the beloved were not only itself at all, but also the leaf that trembles on the tree, the beam that gleams on the water—transformed into all things and transformer of things: an image scattered in the infinity of the universe, so that, wherever we may wander, we are at home.

That is why we justifiably fear the end of the intoxication of love due to getting to know each other too thoroughly. That is why every true intoxication begins with something like a creative jolt, which sets senses and mind vibrating. That is why, despite being totally preoccupied with the other, we only have limited curiosity about what they actually "are," and even when they have far exceeded our expectations, which has strengthened and deepened our union in all respects, under some circumstances we are strongly disappointed just because there is no longer leeway to relate to the other creatively, poetically, "playfully." Often, small irritations then get attached to the same little traits that once particularly encouraged that kind of relationship and therefore delighted us. That they can subsequently not just leave us indifferent, but irritate us, reminds us of the fact that a strange world once trembled against our nerves—and remained strange.

Eroticism and Art

We recognize the ultimate, actual drives of the erotic best when we compare it with other very imaginative productions, especially artistic creativity. There is certainly a deep relationship here—one might almost say a blood relationship, in that in artistic behavior, too, older forces become co-effective and assert themselves with passionate excitement along with those that have been acquired by individuals. Both cases include mysterious syntheses of past and present as the basic experience, and the intoxication of their secret interaction. In these dark border regions, the role that the germ plasm itself may play in the case of art has hardly been researched, almost not at all. However, the fact that the artistic drive and the sex drive provide such extensive analogies, that aesthetic delight so easily slides into the erotic, and erotic longing so instinctively grasps for the aesthetic, for decoration (the erotic longing of animality perhaps directly and creatively procures animal decoration), seems to be a sign that they have grown from the same root. It seems to signify the same ascent of unspent primal life to what is most personal, and, to an extent, the same homecoming of the dispersed, particularized forces back into the warm depths of the earth, upon which everything creative rests and through which what is created may be born as a living whole. And if the sexual may be called a reawakening of what is most ancient, of its embodied memory, then it is just as true that, within the artistic creator, inherited wisdom becomes the most personal memory, associated with what is most present, most particular to them, a kind of wake-up call from the sleep of the past by the turmoil of the hour.

But in the artistic process, in this turmoil, the physical arousal of the emotional excitation of the whole is only an accompanying moment, while the result itself emerges as a very individual mental product. In the sexual process, by contrast, the physical processes set the mental exaltation in motion only as an aside—for the sake of no other "work" than a child's bodily existence. For this reason, the erotic expresses its intoxication in mere delusions, in "untruths," much more than the artistic. In the artist, too, the artist's particular state breaks through the norm, like an anomaly, a violation of the present, of what is given and firmly fixed, by the exciting interplay of the demands of past and future within them. But the "internal comportment of love [*inwendige Liebesverhalten*]," which is *the artist's* most valuable thing, finds both its final explanation and its eventual fulfillment on intellectual ground, and gathers and resolves itself more or less completely in the artist's work. On the other hand, the erotic state of mind, because it lacks this justifying closure, is filed away with the business of the rest of life, as a particular kind of eccentricity, or at least as non-normal.

Thus while the artist can fantasize much more freely than the lover, not constrained by their life circumstances to a reality that obtrudes on the beloved in practical ways, in fact only they, as creator, inscribe their fantasies onto such a thing. That is, only they create new reality from what is present at hand, while the lover only powerlessly endows it with their inventions. Instead of being able to stop with the harmony achieved in the work that is produced, like artistic imagination can, the poetry of love therefore remains uncompleted throughout life, seeking and giving, and tragic in its outer works insofar as it can neither disengage its thinking from the physical givenness of its object nor limit it to it. As a result, love becomes the most bodily thing that haunts us, as well as, seemingly, the most spiritual, believing the most in spirits. It lives wholly and completely in the body, but wholly and completely in it as a symbol, as a corporeal cypher for everything that might sneak into our minds, through the gates of the senses, to awaken them to their most presumptuous dreams. As a result, love always adds to possession the notion of the unattainable; it twins fulfillment and renunciation as only different in degree. The fact that love makes us creative beyond our capabilities makes it such an incarnation of longing, not only for us and what we long for erotically, but also for all the heights it causes us to dream of.

But whereas in artistic creation the bodily co-excitation in mental creation subsides as an irrelevant side effect without anything more, in the erotic, in bodily creativity, it does not behave like that. The mental excess vibrating alongside it collapses, as it were, into a newly struck undertone, in which it speaks for what is unclear, inexpressible. It is as if, simply by becoming individualized to the point of spirituality, something—instead of being discounted as a mere auxiliary tool or accompanying means—gained the characteristic of proceeding spontaneously, always reorganizing, even enlivening, the most invisible, most unreal world with its breath.

Idealization

Here we can ask what the best explanation is for this whole urge to idealization, which seems to be so deeply embedded in creative processes. And whether, in fact, this urge forms an essential moment in the realization of these processes, insofar as these processes can be seen as a synthesis of outer and inner, of what is furthest with what is nearest, of the content of the world and the contents of the self, of primal ground [Urgrund] and apex [Gipfelung].

Even if we do not consider such exceptional processes, but our everyday existence, the mere human fact of our consciousness rests on a similar basis: the same need to consolidate a juxtaposition of world and self, of outer and inner, that is already co-given within it. Only the scope of this consolidation differentiates what humans, in contrast to animals, can attain. As long as the consciousness of life increases, so does this process: encompassing deeper-lying, further-reaching things, and thereby approximating the behavior we have called creative, in the narrower sense of the word. Until, that is, an opposition of such resounding significance is overcome, until it is discharged in such fruitful unity, as if, in a sense, the becoming of a world and the birth of an I were once more experienced, lived through. And this alone infuses an independent living core into what we create, instead of it being a merely derivative apparent being [Scheindasein] and superficiality.

To the extent that things like this occur, we see idealizing activity in full flow. The lover and the creator, creative in the child and in the work of the mind, are recognizable in their naive, objectively completely unmeasurable ecstasies. The opposition mentioned above—and the more so the more significant it is—can obviously only find common ground as a consequence of such mutual elevation, only settle its claims and differences on such a heightened level. The inducement, the elevated feeling of life itself, immediately determines this course of action. It is as if, in this way, a kind of consecration takes place, in which both parties come together in union, so that, unified, they seem to stand on "sacred ground." As if what we call "idealizing" were, so to speak, a primary act of creation performed by creatures, something from their very first independent repetition and continuation of all life. And also, therefore, something that appeared early, already in the drive to physical [körperlichen] pairing, anticipated in the first traces of cerebral activity. And as if this were the source of the great jubilation of being, like jubilant birdsong in the morning when the sun is about to rise over a new day of creation. For there are no three things on earth that are more deeply connected than these three: creating, adoration, and joy.

When one gropes one's way into the dark of human origins and human prehistory, then one stumbles, as if on the last recognizable point, upon religious pronouncements. That in which newly awoken consciousness, suddenly confronted with an outside world, merges with the latter, is always God, in some form. It is God who guarantees the unity from which the diverse aspirations of burgeoning culture can first emerge. Compared to poorly awakened, merely animal self-reflection [Selbstbesinnung], becoming conscious [Bewußtwerden] in itself is such a high enhancement of life that it is conceivable how—out of all the sudden difficulties and the helplessness that emerged with it—consciousness raised the divine as the first human primal creation [Urschöpfung]. This signifies nothing less than that the decisive weapon in the battle for life was no longer just purely material animality, though many times superior in power, but *an act of imagination*. Not, to be clear, as a disarming underestimation of the factually given enmity of the other, but rather as its overestimation in the intangibility of magically strong effects—but only insofar as human power simultaneously feels itself becoming more deeply conscious: feels that it is not the same as the mere materiality of the visible. And, therefore, despite all the compulsiveness of enmity, the battle is no longer only the momentary search for prey but, at the same time, a grasping of one's unity with those living around one, a unity in which the animal is rooted without anything further;—an attempt to experience this unity in the divine, in what is elevated to magic. Yes, even in the spilled blood, the devoured flesh, the human being, exchanging forces with its enemy, forges something of this kind of covenant, of a religious union. Insofar as human beings presuppose facts as existing, but in doing so posit them as their future, they celebrate the communion of their spiritual salvation in advance, for the first time hungering and thirsting in a new way.

Only because this inner compulsion to enhance, to idealize things, even in the most primitive sense, means "to behave creatively," only for this reason do we find it everywhere, including on the summits of human activity, eventually terminating in the finest peaks of human experience. For this reason, our highest productivity has the peculiar character of almost feeling more like conception than the ultimate intensification of our self-activity [*Selbsttätigkeit*], and as if in our most extreme achievements there dwells a surrender to values beyond ourselves. It is where we are fully rulers of life like never before that we are closest to a mood of consecration and devotion: for these are not so much special kinds of experience as ultimate emphases of its intensity. As if, on the way to ever more fruitful discharge, ever more creative being, our self would be sterile if it did not, at its summits, feel itself mysteriously redivided into the original duality of its foundation, which alone guaranteed its unity. As if, under a thousand changing disguises and refinements, something of the symbols of the primordial divinity passed through everything, a traveling companion to all persons and times. As if the creative power itself were only the reverse side of worship—and the ultimate image for all events were a unifying fertilization and conception.

Eroticism and Religion

Religion is one of the things that is defined in the most various ways, the essence of which has always been explained in the most contradictory ways. This may well be due to the degree to which, in its basic affect, religion is one with our most intimate vital affects [*Lebensaffekten*] in general—with the inner facts [*innern Tatsachen*] by which we ourselves stand and fall, and which, precisely for this reason, do not seem to allow the distance that makes theoretical assessment possible.

Thus the erotic, too, is initially incorporated directly into the religious, and vice versa, on the basis of that enhancement of life which, fruitfully stimulating inside and outside, becomes conscious. In this way, this unifying power, this enhanced joy in living and volition, specializes into narrower bodily or mental desire. The connection between these would therefore be the same as with all other human activities, in which the recoloration of the religious only allows the original basic color to show at its base or its peak. But the sexual seems particularly closely linked to religious phenomena insofar as the creativity of its process asserts itself so early, in what is bodily generative [Leiblichzeugerische], and thus already gives its character of general exaltation to the purely physical [körperlichen] frenzy: a sort of spirituality granted in advance. And if the mind lends its cerebral stimuli [Gehirnreize] to sexual affect in this way, then, on the other hand, in religious fervor, as in any strong psychic activity, the tonic stimuli of the body are co-effective. All human development lies between the two, without gaps—its multiplicity joins unity to unity, and beginning and end encompass each other within it. For even religious fervor would not exist without the intuition that bears it: that the highest things we dream of can germinate in our most earthly soil. That is why the religious cults of antiquity were intertwined with sexual life so much longer and more deeply than with other expressions of life, and even in the so-called spiritual religions ("founder religions") this connection always survives somewhere.

Moreover, religious and erotic fervor run parallel in a particular way, i.e., regarding their conceptual omissions, which clarifies both of their natures quite well.

Just as it is only one step from the sublime to the ridiculous, one could, with all due respect and wonder before the intellectual achievements of the great religions, find that, through sober observation of reality, the mental world [Denkwelt] of those affected by religion exhibits a fatal similarity to the exuberant ideas in the fantasies of lovers—in both their method of creation and their wishful content. Admittedly there is a tremendous difference in the valuation they claim is appropriate to their object: for even the most fiery love does not demand or expect the disinterested view of everyone else to see with its own clairvoyant-blind eyes, while religious faith fully emphasizes the overpowering truth of its divine image for everyone. Not, as one often hears, out of pure narrow-minded intolerance, but out of deep compulsion and the sole meaning of its essence itself. And this is the case despite the second difference: despite the fact that religious faith sketches the contours of its image out of even more unrestrained subjectivity. The drive to love always remains shackled to an object of reality, even in forming illusions, and in artistic creation the most freely invented constructs must at the same time provide a standard for their own realization. But the religious person projects their ideas out of themselves, without having to positively "verify" them in either their origin or their goal, with unimpeded strength of mind [*Seelengewalt*], and for this reason affects the heavens so monumentally.

As a result, in this person suffused with feeling, in whom it seems least appropriate, it is precisely the theoretical aspect of the assumptions of their faith that comes so strongly to the fore, especially visible, especially demanding. Their various assumptions, less correctable than any others, because less capable of being associated with other things, must expand ever more rigidly into a world completely outside all other things.

But this is only an apparent contradiction. In order to express itself so authoritatively, religion must of course isolate its world of thought from everything.—However, this authority is itself only a reflection of the universality and originality of its practical significance for everything, according to which nothing exists without it, and it is, as it were, co-effective in everything, grounding everything in the depths, crowning it on the heights of anything that is achieved. This apparent contradiction reveals nothing except how little life can be caught in its own theorizing, how it must emerge precisely as what is most lopsided, most distorted in the image for which it sat as a model in its supreme liveliness. Faith has the profound formula for this in the claim that God can only be known in his immediate experience of himself. Any degree of truth that could otherwise be attributed to him could not make him any "truer" for us. If, essentially, anything that holds still so that the mind can scan it is already associated with lifelessness (most completely in the scientifically dissectable object), then the life that is closest to the source is the most intangible, running through the smallest-meshed nets of the mind. Whatever is always new, newly there, must always leave everything fixed behind it, separating it from itself—not only because it only partially corresponds to it, but [also] because from the outset it is a sloughed-off husk, an out-of-date dross, a fossil in the making, as it were.

For this reason, the delusional character of the ideas regarding the erotic, as well as the religious, is not in itself a flaw that should be eradicated, but rather proof of the true living character of these ideas. Except that the lover's physically conditioned exuberance projects, to an extent, his or her images ahead of the full mental experience: bizarre, whimsical, touching, uplifting, a hazy fleeting reflection. By contrast, the pious person, wanting to give form to the ultimate spiritual experience, must draw on what is less spiritual, and thereby always grasps what is eternally in the past. Truly a vast granite world, projected onto dead, persisting things by the tremendous vitality of inner events! And therefore also such an enduring shelter for those who seek a shield and protection amid the hardships of being. For all religion retains this double character: that it is something different in the blaze of those experiencing it from in the neediness of those who hold it to be true, something different as wings than as crutch.

Religion and love are as little able to avoid the moment of thought in the course of their processes as anything in the realm of our human experience can dispense with it, for nothing occurs that is not both inner event and outer symbol at the same time. Yet the forms of these symbols mean something precisely to the same degree as they pretend to be less. Therefore, they most of all mean something not when they claim to embody the most spontaneous ecstasies or inviolable universality, but, on the contrary, when they enter into as many multiple, verifiable relationships with each other as possible, so mutually sustaining and conditioning that they can continually confirm each other—or, as we like to call it: represent external reality—almost without noticeable inner involvement on our side.

This, however, is the great teaching that follows from this for both religious and erotic experience: that the way here has to turn back to life itself. That for what is most living, the other way, the way into mental verifications and confirmations, is obstructed after a short stretch, hopelessly blocked, because only life can fully reflect life. For religious behavior, this means boundless entering into everything that is—for what could there be that was not a throne and footstool for its feet, as the cosmos is for God! For love, this means its fulfillment in the social.

Erotic and Social

The erotic occupies an intermediate position within the two great emotional groups of the egoistic and the altruistic. Or, less ambiguously: the shrinking, contracting of our individual will from indifference to alienation, hostility; or, on the other hand, its widening to involve the other, the one who faces it, as part of oneself. Over the course of time, both groups continually change their stance toward each other and their human valuation, and the way their conflict is balanced determines the character of an epoch. Each group always needs the other to supplement it, and everyone has a stake in both and would endanger themselves most extremely by too much one-sidedness. For in order to give oneself, one must be able to possess oneself, and in order to possess, one must first be able to take from things and people that which cannot be stolen, that which can only be bestowed with an open soul. The two opposites, on the surface growing irreconcilably apart, are at root connected in the deepest reciprocal way [*wechselwirkender Zusammengehörigkeit*], and if the self-dissipating: "I want to be everything!" and the miserly, lusting: "I want to have everything!" are brought to a highest encompassing desire, they have the same meaning.

From this, their common parentage, the third group of emotional relations, that of the erotic, seems to split off as a middle form, perhaps the original form [*Urform*], between the individual animal and its brother creatures: strangely, and unconcerned by their contradictions, binding both components in itself, whereby they mutually enhance each other to increasingly seething force [*gärenderer Triebkraft*]. Thus in all of nature it is precisely the *different* protoplasm corpuscles that generatively seek each other, that gradually develop the sex differences that enable ever more manifold specialization. And so, among human beings as much as animals, the old commonplace is proved right, according to which the love of the sexes is a battle of the sexes, and nothing so easily crosses over into the other as love and hate. For if selfishness expands in sexuality, at the same time it also intensifies to its fiercest desire. And if it proceeds in selfish assault, it only does so to set everything it conquers on a throne, yes, high above itself. It is always hindered by its physical determinateness from a one-sided, clear elaboration of its mental purposes—and yet, more deeply than anything else, this indicates the universal One that we are in ourselves.

We may not, therefore, conclude from this limitation that the more intellectual human egoism, or even just the intellectual fraternization of everything with everything else, must in itself be superior to sexuality, and present the latter as basically not much more than a preliminary step toward clearer stages of development. On the contrary, within its realm sexuality traverses all the stages, from the most primitive to the most complex, from the most bodily limited to the most mentally free, on its own ground. Sexuality is not further ennobled where the accidents of life graft relationships onto it that have matured elsewhere, even if they are of a friendly or kindhearted nature. Rather, these relations just as often endanger the driving forces of its essence, which flow to it from much deeper. In itself full of creative elements of egoistic as well as altruistic kinds, it [i.e., sexuality] also extends independently in both directions. Above, we considered it deliberately one-sidedly, according to its own joyful intoxication, its union of all forces, which first became a full truth without illusion only for itself, that is, according to its egoism. In the same way, one can also view it as altruistic-productive: one can see the other, the partner, until now only the occasion for its effusiveness, arouser of gratifying illusions, become truth and life event for it.

However, this "egoism of two" also seems suspiciously egoistic, and only overcome in the relationship to the child—thus only in the point where sexual and social love meet and are reconciled, mutually completing each other.

But it is characteristic of sexual love, which accomplishes its "social" work in the bodily sense that this physical activity already contains everything that it develops further mentally. Indeed, it can rightly be said that all love creates two people—besides the one bodily conceived in the union, also a fictional one. However, it is precisely this bodily created person that tends to first lead the way out of love as a mere daze. At least insofar as it occurs in natural life, primitively and in itself, rutting is socialized in the brood, love in the child.

7

Rosa Luxemburg (1871–1919)

Introduction

The tragic death of Rosa Luxemburg (in Polish, Róża Luksemburg, also Rozalia Luxenburg, 1871–1919) is well known. She was the flaming revolutionary whose life was prematurely cut off when she, as an antiwar activist, socialist, and leader of the Spartakusbund (Spartacus League, the precursor of the German Communist Party), was savagely beaten and shot in the head by members of the German Freikorps. Less well known are the details of her intellectual life and work. It is for good reason that Hannah Arendt called her "the most controversial and least understood figure in the German Left movement."[1]

Luxemburg's writing spans an impressive range of topics and genres—from academic treatises to popular pamphlets. She writes on political economy, international politics, imperialism, art, and culture. She is also the author of a formidable correspondence (with friends and fellow socialists), a substantial part of which is of direct political and philosophical relevance.

Luxemburg was born in a small town in Poland, which at the time was still occupied by the Russian (Tsarist) empire. Her family was Jewish, spoke German at home, and cultivated a cosmopolitan outlook that would remain important throughout Luxemburg's life. Luxemburg was politicized at a young age and educated herself in the classics of socialist thought. From early on, she sought to develop spontaneous, grassroots politics (rather than a centralized or party-led program). For her, a top-down revolution could not be a revolution proper. With her emphasis on the people over the party, Luxemburg is seen as a champion of a humanitarian Marxism. She was a pacifist and a committed anti-nationalist—positions that placed her in opposition to both the German government and the German Socialist Party.

---

[1] Hannah Arendt, "Rosa Luxemburg: 1871–1919," in *Men in Dark Times* (New York: Harcourt Brace, 1983), 33–56, here 34.

Luxemburg left Poland for Zurich in 1887. In the aftermath of a series of strikes in the 1880s, the Polish police had stamped down on political activity. As a teenager engaged in underground political activity, Luxemburg was no longer safe. At the time, the University of Zurich was open to women students, including women from other countries. In Zurich, Luxemburg encountered an enclave of political thinkers and activists who had been attracted by the liberal safe haven the city offered. It was there that she met Leo Jogiches, another socialist who had fled the Tsar's police. Jogiches became Luxemburg's lover, but also an important collaborator.

At the university, Luxemburg first studied zoology but then turned to economics and philosophy (including lectures on modern philosophy up to Kant).[2] She was one of the first women in Europe to obtain a PhD in economics. Her doctoral dissertation, defended in 1898, was titled "The Industrial Development of Poland." Her work was both evidence-based and theoretically sophisticated. It drew on empirically meticulous studies undertaken during a stay in Paris, and it developed cutting-edge analyses of the Polish economy as it entered an increasingly globalized economy. Luxemburg's dissertation was published as a book in the same year it was defended. This was a rare honor at the time.

In the same year she defended her dissertation, Luxemburg married Gustav Lübeck. The marriage allowed Luxemburg, as a Polish citizen, to move to Berlin. By this point, Luxemburg was already well connected with the German socialist network. Although women could not yet vote (or stand for office or be part of the official, political decision-making process), Luxemburg soon became involved in the Socialist Party. She made her voice heard through her activism, writing, and public speeches. Leading up to and during World War I, she became increasingly frustrated with the Socialist Party. Her criticism of the party's revisionist politics but also its official endorsement of the war led to imprisonment. This, however, did not stop her engagement. As a reaction to what they saw as docile party politics, Luxemburg and Karl Liebknecht initiated the radical Spartacus League. Shortly after, Liebknecht and Luxemburg were brutally murdered.

Luxemburg had a long-lasting friendship with Clara Zetkin, whom she first met at the Social Democratic Party's Stuttgart Congress in 1898. While the two disagreed on central issues such as the status of women's rights over

[2] For Luxemburg's classes at the University of Zurich, see Verena Stadler-Labhart, *Rosa Luxemburg an der Universität Zürich, 1889–1897* (Zurich: Verlag Hans Rohr, 1978).

and against the rights of workers, they both criticized the party's stance on war and militarization, which pit worker against worker and placed nationalist concerns above the concerns of humanity.[3]

From 1907 onward, Luxemburg taught for six months of the year at the Social Democratic Party School in Berlin. *Introduction to Political Economy (Einführung in die Nationalökonomie)*, from which the present excerpt is drawn, was conceived in this period. The text, initially intended for a series of booklets, is based on her lectures on political economy. However, while working on the manuscript, Luxemburg decided to add material relating to pre-capitalist societies. Moreover (and somewhat relatedly), she became increasingly concerned about the standard Marxist conception of the expansion of capital. She saw imperialism—the forceful appropriation of non-capitalist economies—as a sign of capitalism's inherent need for expansion. Such an expansion is necessary, she argued, because the surplus value produced in capitalist societies is greater than what can be consumed or put into circulation so as to create further value. Capitalism, in other words, remains dependent on non-capitalist pockets and ever-increasing expansion into new territories. For this reason, Luxemburg understood imperialism to be an intrinsic part of capitalism. Accordingly, a study of the working patterns of capitalism must include reflection on its annexation of new territories. Wishing to develop this argument into a book-length study, she broke off writing *Introduction to Political Economy* so as to concentrate on what is often seen as her major work, *The Accumulation of Capital* (1913).[4]

Luxemburg returned to *Introduction to Political Economy* while in prison during World War I. She was allowed to write, and her work from the prison includes her famous letters, in which she discusses politics, philosophy, art, and existential and personal questions.[5]

Introduction to Political Economy was first published in 1925 (edited by Paul Levi), six years after Luxemburg's death. Luxemburg had planned ten chapters, but after her death, only five were found. Because Luxemburg herself did not get to finish her work, the text needs to be read with vigilance and, for scholarly purposes, accompanied by other material from the period. Yet *Introduction to Political Economy* presents many of Luxemburg's key ideas in

---

[3] For a discussion of the friendship and of the question of feminism, see Stephen Eric Bronner, *Rosa Luxemburg: A Revolutionary for Our Times* (University Park: Penn State University Press, 1981), 70–72.

[4] See editor's introduction to *The Complete Work of Rosa Luxemburg*, vol. 1, ed. Peter Hudis, trans. David Fernbach, Joseph Fracchia, and George Shriver (London: Verso, 2014).

[5] Georg Adler, Peter Hudis, and Annelies Laschitza, eds., *The Letters of Rosa Luxemburg*, trans. George Shriver (London: Verso, 2013).

an accessible, energetic, and energizing form. The existing chapters address topics such as economic history, production of commodities, and wage labor. The present selection is from her discussion of wage labor, a topic that she only takes up in this form in *Introduction to Political Economy*.

When Luxemburg was working on *Introduction to Political Economy*, Marx's theory of labor (especially his claim about the value of labor power) was coming under attack for, among other things, having isolated labor power from the market in which the worker must purchase goods and services.[6] Luxemburg does not discuss this debate in detail, but it clearly informs her text. Her analysis, though, is rooted in Marxist principles. While some people bring objects to sell in the marketplace, others have nothing to sell except their labor. As Luxemburg puts it, "in order to be able to live, each person must supply and sell commodities. Producing and selling commodities has become a condition of existence for human beings. Anyone who does not bring commodities to the market does not receive any means of existence." However, unlike other commodities, labor is indistinguishable from the (activity of the) person who is offering it for sale. At stake, in other words, is both a commodity and a human life. But even this commodity is sold in a market where workers must sustain themselves and pay for food, accommodation, and services.

The value of a commodity is determined by its production costs. When human beings offer their labor for sale, these costs include food, clothing, housing, and so on. In short, the worker needs to survive in order to be able to work. Workers must, therefore, work x number of hours simply to cover the costs that the employer extracts in order to keep them alive. However, because workers can work beyond what is needed to maintain their existence, they can also sustain the life of others. Whatever exceeds their costs of living will count as the surplus value of the work and, in a capitalist economy, be appropriated by the employer. This opens up the possibility of one person systematically taking advantage of other people's work. In a capitalist economy, selling one's labor power means accepting that the value of surplus labor can be withheld by the buyer. Thus, Luxemburg points out, in traditional Marxist fashion, there is a conflict of interest between the buyer

[6] For a helpful account of these debates, the perceived weaknesses of Marx's contribution, Luxemburg's response, and her critics, see Michael R. Krätke, "A Very Political Economist: Rosa Luxemburg's Theory of Wages," in *Rosa Luxemburg and the Critique of Political Economy*, ed. Riccardo Bellofiore (London: Routledge, 2009), 159–174.

and seller of labor: whoever gets to keep the value of surplus labor will grow in wealth and prosperity.

In her work, Luxemburg carefully analyzes the internal relationship between wage labor and the logic of surplus value. From a capitalist employer's point of view, surplus value—the difference between the value produced, on the one hand, and the costs of production, on the other—can be maximized in a number of ways. One way is simply to reduce pay and thereby reduce the costs that are spent on each individual worker. As Marx had already pointed out, this is the rationale behind early-nineteenth-century household manuals and cookbooks for workers. They give advice for frugal living—not so much in order to help the worker but to legitimize low wages. This is also the ideological motivation behind the idea of workers as spendthrifts whose problem is not that they are underpaid but rather that they overspend or do not carefully plan for the future.

Profit can be increased by imposing longer hours on the worker and/or reducing the hourly pay. As Luxemburg points out, an employer will rarely take responsibility for this but will instead blame external factors. This, she argues, explains why periods of recession do not necessarily lead to losses for private companies, even though individual workers face job insecurity, reduced pay, and other hardships. In both cases, the bottom line, to follow Luxemburg, is that the demand for labor is less than what is being offered (i.e., the number of workers). It is, in other words, in the interest of the employer that there exists a pool of unemployed, a reserve army of potential workers that can press the wages down *and* serve as a living example of the destitution of the unemployed. Luxemburg here follows Marx, who sees official poverty, the so-called Lazarus stratum of the working class, as a necessary part of a capitalist economy. Yet she also goes beyond Marx, especially in her emphasis on the importance of trade unions for the determination of the value of labor. Furthermore, Luxemburg's methodology, in *Introduction to Political Economy* and other works, is characterized by a willingness to move from a theory-driven account of economic laws to an account that is also informed by lived experiences and concrete historical studies.

For Luxemburg, economic exploitation can and must be understood historically, and not simply in light of the scientific laws of capital (as elaborated by Marx and Engels). For instance, in *Introduction to Political Economy* and other works from this period, Luxemburg argues that slavery is the oldest form of class domination and economic exploitation. Accordingly, she resists Engels's argument that slavery emerges with private property. As she points out, slavery reaches back to ancient societies, though the problem is drastically exacerbated with the introduction of private property.

Unlike premodern forms of slavery and serfdom (writing in a European context, Luxemburg primarily focuses on an analysis of ancient slavery and modern wage labor), a modern worker does not produce objects for shared consumption (e.g., the produce from a farmstead). Instead, the workers are often set repetitively to produce objects for which they have no need (e.g., a small part of a train). As Luxemburg puts it: "everything the worker produces [now] belongs to the entrepreneur." And with the modern money economy, the amount produced is not limited to the amount the entrepreneurs and their families can possibly consume (which, on Luxemburg's analysis, was the case in premodern economy). The production—and the possibility of financial gain—has no end. Again, in Luxemburg's words, capital "is the means to unlimited accumulation of wealth. In the form of money, wealth loses nothing in value even through the longest storage; on the contrary . . . wealth in the form of money seems to grow simply through storage." And with this grows the temptation, in the system of wage labor, for the capitalist to lengthen workers' hours, reduce pay, and find other ways to minimize production costs, often at the expense of the worker's living conditions and safety.

From a perspective like Luxemburg's, the entrepreneurs' accumulation of wealth is an act of theft—it is a theft of value but also, at the end of the day, of hours, days, and weeks of the worker's life. Classes are distinguished by different interests, and the conflict of interest is, ultimately, a question of power. Power works on multiple levels: as brute force, as economic manipulation, *and* as ideologically saturated images of what counts as a good life and what it takes to be a productive citizen. Luxemburg's analysis is as follows: "There is a crusade by capital against every trace of luxury, comfort, and ease in the life of the workers. . . . There is a striving to reduce the consumption of workers to a simple, barren act of intake of a minimum of food to feed the body, like livestock is fed or machines oiled."

According to Luxemburg, exploitation has not always been the rule. She assumes the existence of a primitive economy in which goods were shared equally among working people and there were hardly any non-workers. In this state, be it a historical fact or a utopian point of contrast, there was no exploitation of workers by nonworkers. There was, furthermore, no unpaid work or surplus value. However, in the present essay, what Luxemburg is most interested in is the transition from simple production to a capitalist economy. In her view, it is not exploitation that creates the possibility of capitalism. Rather, capital and proletariat must already be in place for systemic inequality to come about. Hence, as she argues, a modern capitalist system can only emerge when laborers appear as wage workers, when they have, as it were, achieved "personal freedom" and "freely" bring their labor as a commodity to sell. At this point, wage labor fully enters the logic of the marketplace.

Luxemburg contends that only a radical societal change—that is, a revolution—can overthrow the systemic economic oppression we find in modern, capitalist societies. Revisionist politics, by contrast, can only offer temporary relief. Yet she does not call for a top-down organization of political activity. Political activity, in her view, needs to be activism that comes from below, from the people whose world is in need of change. Hence, Luxemburg, in her work and through her teaching, emphasizes the necessity of educating workers. Theory, however, is a tool to facilitate action but cannot predict or determine it. In this spirit, Luxemburg opens her reflections on political economy with a series of critical points on the theory of economy, academia, and the existing relationship between political theory and practice. Luxemburg's bottom-up politics—and her insistence on the need for a spiritual-educational transformation that can drive political change—is another point that distinguishes her contribution from Marx.

In her work and political activism, Luxemburg focuses on the questions of imperialism, militarism, and the relationship between them. She remains opposed to nationalism, regarding it as a way to prevent international worker solidarity and to bolster false bourgeois interests and loyalties.[7] Opposing Marx as well as Lenin, she argues that imperialism does not simply signify the internal crisis of late capitalism but was present in earlier forms of capitalist economies (i.e., it was part of this economy from the very beginning). Moreover, she pays attention to the ways in which global capitalism levels cultural differences and dissolves particular life forms. Luxemburg also offers detailed, anthropological descriptions of changing cultures—a part of her work that, in its focus on local conditions rather than a universal, communist goal, Lenin judged as a senseless and unproductive deviation from Marxist orthodoxy.

---

[7] For a discussion of this point, see Joan Cocks, *Passion and Paradox: Intellectuals Confront the National Question* (Princeton, NJ: Princeton University Press, 2002), esp. 45–71. Cocks sketches interesting parallels and contrasts between Luxemburg and Franz Fanon and also discusses Luxemburg's failure to consider strategic, anti-imperialist nationalisms.

Luxemburg further deviates from Marxist orthodoxy in that she argues that capitalism is not a system that simply feeds on (and will therefore be overcome by) internal dialectical movements. As she sees it, it is not given that its collapse will ensue from internal weariness. Capitalism, instead, thrives by gradually accumulating parts of the world that have been left out of the capitalist economy, in a process of international as well as domestic exploitation.[8] Luxemburg's critique of capitalism and imperialism goes hand in hand with her anti-nationalism.

While Luxemburg's work was not immediately recognized by official Marxists, her analysis of capital, wage, war, oppression, and imperialism now plays a crucial role in critical theory more broadly. This applies both to Luxemburg's analysis of capital *and* to her important conception of the relationship between theory and practical political work.

---

[8] For Luxemburg's account of imperialism, see, for example, Paul Frölich, *Rosa Luxemburg: Ideas in Action*, trans. Johanna Hoornweg (Chicago: Haymarket Books, 2010), chap. 9.

Wage Labor
Selections from *Introduction to Political Economy*

1.

All commodities are exchanged according to their value, which means according to the socially necessary work they contain. Although money acts as a mediator, that does not change this basis for the exchange of commodities; money is only the naked expression of social labor. The amount of value placed in each commodity is expressed by the amount of money for which the commodity is sold.

On the basis of this law of value, perfect equivalence prevails between commodities on the market. And full equivalence would also prevail among the sellers of commodities if, among the millions of different kinds of commodities that come onto the market everywhere for exchange, one single commodity did not have an entirely special nature: labor power [*Arbeitskraft*]. This commodity is brought to the market by those who do not own any means of production by which to produce other commodities.

As we know, in a society based exclusively on the exchange of commodities, a person receives nothing except through exchange. We have seen that the commodity a person brings to the market is the only claim this person has to a share in the mass of social products, and at the same time the measure of this share. Each person gets, in the form of the desired commodities they freely choose as much of the amount of work achieved in society as they themselves deliver in socially necessary work, in the form of some sort of commodity. Thus, in order to be able to live, each person must supply and sell commodities. Producing and selling commodities has become a condition of existence for human beings. Anyone who does not bring commodities to the market does not receive any means of existence [*Existenzmittel*].

However, the production of any commodity requires the means for work—tools and the like, plus raw materials and auxiliary materials, and similarly a workplace, a workshop with the required working conditions such as lighting etc., and finally a certain quota of means of subsistence [*Lebensmittel*], in order to be able to survive during the period of production and until the sale of the commodity. Only a few insignificant commodities are produced without any outlay on means of production: for example, mushrooms or berries gathered in the forest, or shells gathered on the beach by inhabitants of the seashore. But even for these, some means of production, like baskets and so on, are still necessary, and in all cases, some means of subsistence, which enable existence during this work, are needed. But in any society with developed commodity production, most kinds of commodities require very significant, sometimes enormous, outlays on means of production. Anyone who does not have these means of production, and therefore is not in a position to produce commodities, has nothing left to do but to bring themselves—that is, their own labor power—to the market as a commodity.

Like every other commodity, the commodity of labor power has a specific value. The value of any commodity is, as we know, determined by the amount of work required for its production. Likewise, in order to produce the commodity labor power, a specific amount of work is necessary, namely the work that produces sustenance, food, clothing, etc., for the worker. Therefore, the amount of work that is required to keep a person capable of work, to maintain their labor power, is the amount that their labor power is worth. The value of the commodity labor power is thus represented by the amount of work that is necessary to produce the means of subsistence for the worker.

Furthermore, as with every other commodity, the value of labor power is appraised on the market by *price*, that is, by money. The monetary expression—that is, the price—of the commodity labor power is called its "wage." With every other commodity, the price rises when demand grows faster than supply and sinks when, conversely, the influx of the commodity is greater than demand. The same also proves to be the case with respect to the commodity labor power: with rising demand for workers, wages in general have a tendency to rise; if demand decreases or if the job market is overcrowded with fresh commodities, wages tend to fall. Finally, as with any other commodity, the value of labor power, and therefore also ultimately its price, increases if the amount of work necessary to produce it increases—in this case, if producing the means of subsistence for the worker requires more work. Conversely, every saving in the work necessary to produce the means of subsistence for the worker leads to the depression of the value of labor power, and therefore also of its price, that is, of the workers' wages. "Diminish the cost of production of hats," wrote David Ricardo in the year 1817, "and their price will ultimately fall to their new natural price, although the demand should be doubled, trebled, or quadrupled. Diminish the cost of the subsistence of men,[9] by diminishing

---

[9] [In her translation of this passage from English into German, Luxemburg replaces Ricardo's term "men" with "workers" (*Arbeiter*).]

the natural price of the food and clothing, by which life is sustained, and wages will ultimately fall, notwithstanding that the demand for labourers may very greatly increase."[10]

Thus the commodity labor power is distinguished from other commodities on the market by almost nothing except that it is inseparable from its seller—the worker—and that it therefore cannot tolerate a long wait for its buyer. Otherwise, it perishes, along with its bearer (the worker), due to a lack of means of subsistence, while most other commodities can easily tolerate a more or less lengthy waiting time until sale. The peculiarity of the commodity of labor power is therefore not expressed on the market, where only its exchange value plays a role. It lies elsewhere—in the use value of this commodity.

Every commodity is bought because of the benefit it can bring when it is used. Boots are bought to serve as footwear; a cup is bought to drink tea from. What can labor power serve for when it is bought? Obviously for work. But that doesn't tell us anything. People always could—and had to—work, for as long as human society has existed, and yet whole millennia went by in which labor power as a purchasable commodity was entirely unknown. On the other hand, if we imagine that a person could only provide sustenance for themselves with all their labor power, then buying such labor power— i.e., labor power as a commodity—would be pointless. For if someone buys and pays for labor power, then puts it to work with their own means of production and eventually obtains, as a result, only sustenance for the bearer of the commodity they purchased—the worker—then it would be the same as if the worker, by selling their labor power, just acquired someone else's means of production in order to use them to work for themselves. From the standpoint of commodities exchange this would be just as pointless a business as if someone bought boots in order to give them back to the cobbler as a present.

If human labor power could not be used in any other way, then it would have no benefit for its buyer and therefore could not appear as a commodity on the market. For only products with specific benefits can feature as commodities. Therefore, for labor power to appear as a commodity at all, it is not enough that a person can work if they are given the means of production; rather, they must be able to work more than is

---

[10] [Original English from David Ricardo, *On the Principles of Political Economy and Taxation* (London: John Murray, 1817), 542–543.]

necessary to produce their own means of existence. They must be able to work not only to maintain themselves, but also for the buyer of their labor power. In being used, that is, in work, the commodity labor power must therefore be able not only to replace its own price, which means its wage, but beyond that also to deliver surplus labor [*Mehrarbeit*] for the buyer.

The commodity labor power does in fact have this agreeable property. But what does that mean? Is being able to perform surplus labor something like a natural property of human beings or of workers? In times when people took years to make an axe out of stone or made fire by rubbing two pieces of wood together for hours, when they needed many months to make a single bow, even the shrewdest and most ruthless entrepreneur could not have squeezed surplus labor out of a person. A certain level of productivity of human work is therefore necessary for human beings to be able to deliver surplus labor at all. That means that human tools, skill, knowledge, and mastery of the forces of nature must already have reached a sufficient level for a person's strength to be able to produce not only the means of subsistence for themselves, but beyond that potentially also for others. But this perfecting of tools and knowledge and sure mastery of nature is gained only by long millennia of agonizing experience by human society. The distance from the first crude stone instruments and the discovery of fire to today's steam and electrical machines signifies the entire course of the social development of humanity, a development that was only possible within society, through social coexistence and collaboration. Thus the productivity of work, which gives the labor power of contemporary wage workers [*Lohnarbeiter*] the agreeable property of performing surplus labor, is not a naturally given physiological peculiarity of human beings, but a *social phenomenon*, the fruit of a long history of development. The surplus labor of the commodity of labor power is only another expression for the productivity of social labor, by which one person's work may sustain many people.

However, this productivity of work—especially where, due to fortunate natural conditions, it is already possible in primitive levels of culture—does not always and everywhere lead to the sale of labor power and its capitalist exploitation. Let us transport ourselves for a moment to those blessed tropical regions of Central and South America, which were Spanish colonies from the discovery of America until the beginning of the nineteenth century, those regions with a hot climate and fruitful soil, where bananas are the main nourishment of the population.

"I do not believe," Humboldt wrote, "that there is another plant on the globe that, on such a small speck of soil, can produce such a considerable mass of nourishing material."[11]

"According to this principle," Humboldt calculates, "one finds the very curious fact that, in an especially fertile country, a half hectare of soil cultivated with bananas of the large species (*Platano arton*) can feed over fifty individuals; whereas by contrast the same speck of land in Europe (assuming the eighth grain)[12] would give a mere 576 kilograms of wheat flour, i.e., not enough for two persons."[13]

Furthermore, the banana requires the least effort from people—it only needs the earth around its roots to be turned lightly once or twice. "At the foot of the Cordillera, in the humid valleys of the Directorates of Veracruz, Valladolid or Guadalajara," Humboldt says further, "a man only needs to busy himself with hard work for two days per week to feed a whole family."[14]

It is clear that the productivity of work in itself easily allows exploitation here, and a scholar with a real capitalist soul like Malthus even cries out tearfully at the description of this earthly paradise: "What immense powers of production are here described! What resources for unbounded wealth[.]"[15] That means, in other words: How wonderfully gold could be struck from the work of these banana-eaters for busy entrepreneurs, if one could only harness these layabouts and make them work. But what did we see in reality? The inhabitants of these blessed regions did not think of grubbing about to accumulate money, but only looked after the trees a bit here and there, enjoyed their bananas, and, in their large amounts of free time, lay in the sun and enjoyed life. Humboldt, also very distinctively, says: "In the Spanish colonies one often hears the claim that the inhabitants of the hot region (*tierra caliente*) could not emerge from the state of *apathy* in which they had been plunged for centuries until a *royal order* ordered the destruction of the banana plantations (*platanares*)."[16] From the European capitalist standpoint, this so-called apathy is the mental state of all peoples who still live

---

[11] Alexander von Humboldt, *Versuch über den politischen Zustand des Königreiches Neu-Spanien*, Vol. 3 (Tübingen: Cotta, 1812), 17–18.

[12] [An old-fashioned measure of the yield of a crop, meaning a harvest of eight times the amount of the crop originally planted.]

[13] Humboldt, *Versuch*, 22.

[14] Humboldt, *Versuch*, 24.

[15] Thomas Robert Malthus, *Principles of Political Economy Considered with a View to Their Practical Application* (London: John Murray, 1820), 383. [Luxemburg here paraphrases Malthus's exclamation as "what enormous means for the production of infinite riches! (Welch enorme Mittel zur Produktion unendlicher Reichtümer!)."]

[16] Humboldt, *Versuch*, 23–24. [Emphasis added by Luxemburg.]

in circumstances of primitive communism, in which the purpose of human work is just satisfying the natural needs of human beings and not accumulating wealth. As long as these circumstances prevail, the exploitation of one person by others by using human labor power to produce surplus labor is unthinkable, even with the greatest productivity of work.

Modern entrepreneurs were not the first to discover this agreeable property of human labor power. In fact, we already see the exploitation of surplus labor by nonworkers in ancient times. Slavery in antiquity, as well as serfdom and bondage in the Middle Ages, are based on the level of productivity that had already been attained at the time, that is, the capacity of human work to sustain more than one person. These are different forms in which one class of society made use of this productivity, through being sustained by another class. In this sense, ancient slaves and medieval bondsmen are direct forebears of today's wage workers.

However, despite its productivity and despite its exploitation, neither in antiquity nor in the Middle Ages did labor power become a commodity. The peculiarity of the contemporary relation of wage workers to entrepreneurs, which differentiates it from slavery and bondage, is, above all, the personal freedom of the worker. The sale of commodities is the private business of each person, based on full individual freedom. An unfree person cannot sell their labor power. But, as a further condition, it is necessary that the workers own no means of production. If they did have means of production, then they would produce commodities themselves and not alienate their labor power as a commodity. The disentanglement, the separation of labor power from the means of production is, therefore, alongside personal freedom, what makes labor power into a commodity today.

In the slave-based economy, labor power is not separated from the means of production. On the contrary, this power itself forms a means of production and belongs, alongside tools, raw materials, etc., to its master as private property. Slaves themselves are only one part of the undifferentiable mass of the slave owner's means of production. In serfdom, labor power is legally chained directly to the means of production, to the soil: it is only an accessory to the means of production. The payments and levies of serfdom are not made by persons at all, but by pieces of land; if the piece of land passes into the hands of other workers as inheritance or the like, then its levies pass over with it.

Nowadays, the worker is personally free, and not someone's property, nor chained to the means of production. On the contrary, the means of production are in one set of hands, labor power in another, and the two owners face each other as independent and free, as buyer and seller—the capitalist as buyer, the worker as seller of labor power.

But in the end, personal freedom and the separation of labor power from the means of production, even when work productivity is high, do not always lead to wage labor [*Lohnarbeit*], to the sale of labor power. We see an example of this in ancient Rome, after the great mass of free smallholders were displaced from their pieces of land through the emergence of great noble estates with a slave economy. They remained personally free people, but because they no longer had land and soil, and thus no means of production, they went in masses from the country to Rome as free proletarians. However, they could not sell their labor power there, for they found no buyers for it; the rich landowners and capitalists did not need to buy free labor power, because they were maintained by slave hands. In those days, slave labor sufficed completely for the satisfaction of all the necessities of life of the landowners, who had everything possible done for them by slave hands. But they could not use labor power for more than their own lives and luxury, because the purpose of slave production was only one's own consumption, and not the exchange of commodities. The Roman proletariat were thus barred from all livelihood based on their own work, and there was nothing left for them to do but to live from begging—begging from the state, living off periodic distributions of means of subsistence. Thus, in ancient Rome, instead of wage labor, there emerged mass feeding of propertyless free people at public expense, which is why the French economist Sismondi said: In ancient Rome society maintained its proletariat; today the proletariat maintain society.[17]

But if today the work of the proletariat for both their own and others' maintenance, the sale of their labor power, is possible, that is because today free work is the *only* and exclusive form of production, and because, as the production of commodities, it is not aimed at direct consumption, but at the production of products for sale. Slave owners bought slaves for their own comfort and for luxury, and feudal lords extorted payments and levies from the serfs for the same purpose: in order to live high on the land with their kind. Modern entrepreneurs do not have workers produce food, clothing, and luxury for

---

[17] [Luxemburg is probably paraphrasing Marx here, who himself paraphrases Sismondi in his preface to the second edition of *The Eighteenth Brumaire*. See Karl Marx, *Der achtzehnte Brumaire des Louis Bonaparte*, in Karl Marx and Friedrich Engels, *Werke* (Berlin: Dietz, 1962–) (hereafter abbreviated MEW), Vol. 16, 359. The original can be found in Jean Charles Léonard de Sismondi, *Études sur l'économie politique*, Vol. 1 (Paris: Treuttel et Würtz, 1837), 35.]

their own use, but commodities for sale in order to make money from them. And this business makes them capitalists, like it makes workers wage workers.

Thus we see that the simple fact of the sale of labor power as a commodity indicates a whole array of specific social and historical relations. The appearance of labor power as a commodity on the market indicates: (1) the personal freedom of the workers; (2) their separation from the means of production and the collecting of the means of the production in the hands of nonworkers; (3) a high degree of productivity of work, i.e., the possibility of performing surplus labor; (4) the general dominance of a commodities economy, i.e., the creation of surplus labor in the form of commodities for sale as the purpose of buying labor power.

Externally, from the standpoint of the market, the buying and selling of the commodity of labor power is a completely ordinary business, which goes on in thousands of instances each moment, like buying boots or onions. The value of the commodity and the changes in value, its price and its fluctuations, the equality and independence of the buyer and seller on the market, the voluntary nature of the business—everything is exactly like any other sales business. But, through the particular use value of this commodity, through the particular circumstances that first create this use value, this everyday market trade of the world of commodities becomes a new, entirely particular set of social relations.

Let us see further what develops out of this market trade.

2.

An entrepreneur buys labor power and, like any buyer, pays its value—that is, its costs of production—by paying the workers, in wages, a price that covers the workers' upkeep. But, with the average means of production used in society, the purchased labor power can produce more than its own costs of upkeep. As we know, this is a precondition of the whole business, which would otherwise be pointless; the use value of the commodity labor power consists in this. Because, as with any other commodity, the value of the upkeep of labor power is determined by the amount of work that is required for its production, we can assume that the nourishment, clothing, etc., that are necessary for the daily maintenance of a worker in an employable condition require, for example, six hours of work. The price of the commodity labor power, that is, its wage, must normally amount to six hours' work in monetary form. But the workers do not work six hours for the entrepreneur, but longer, say, for example, eleven hours. In these eleven hours, each worker first, in six hours, reimburses the entrepreneur for their wage, and then on top of that gives another five hours of work for free, donated to the entrepreneur. The workday of each worker therefore necessarily and normally consists of two parts: one paid, in which the worker only pays back the value of their own upkeep, where they work for themselves, so to speak, and an unpaid part, in which they do donated work [*geschenkte Arbeit*] or surplus labor for the capitalists.

The situation was similar in earlier forms of social exploitation. At the time of serfdom, the serfs' work for themselves and their work for their lords were separated both temporally and spatially. The peasants knew exactly when and how much they worked for themselves and when and how much for the maintenance of their gracious lords, whether these were aristocratic or religious lords. They first worked a few days on their own fields, then a few days on the lords', or they worked mornings on their own and afternoons on the lords', or they worked consistently for a few weeks only on their own and then a few weeks on the lords'. So, for example, around the middle of the twelfth century, serf labor in one village of Marmoutier Abbey in Alsace was specified in the following way: From mid-April until mid-May each farmstead provided one man's work for three full days per week; from May until St. John's Day one afternoon per week; from St. John's Day until haymaking two days per week; at harvest time three afternoons per week; and from Martinmas until Christmas three full days per week. Admittedly, in the late Middle Ages the work for the lords grew so persistently with the progress of serfdom that soon almost all the days in the week and all the weeks in the year belonged to bonded service and the peasants hardly had any time left to cultivate their own fields. But even then, they knew very precisely that they did not work for themselves but for others. It was not possible to be deceived about that, even for the stupidest peasant.

With modern wage labor the matter is completely different. Workers do not create objects in the first part of their workday that they need themselves: their food, clothing, etc., so they can produce other things for the entrepreneur later. On the contrary, a worker in a factory or at a plant produces the same object all day, and indeed mostly an object that they only need for their private consumption in the smallest way or not at all: something like steel nibs or rubber bands or silk fabric or cast-iron pipes. In the undifferentiated heap of steel nibs or rubber bands or fabric that they have created all day, each piece looks exactly—to a hair—like another; you cannot perceive the smallest difference among them according to whether one part is paid or unpaid work, whether one part is for the worker, another for the entrepreneur. On the contrary, the product on which a worker works has no use for them at all, and not one little piece of it belongs to them; everything the worker produces belongs to the entrepreneur.

In this, there is a great external difference between wage labor and serfdom. In normal circumstances, serfs must absolutely have some time to work on their own fields, and whatever they work on for themselves belongs to them. With modern wage workers their whole product belongs to the entrepreneur, and so it looks as if their work in the factory has nothing at all to do with their own maintenance. They receive their wage and can do what they want with it. For that, they have to work on what the entrepreneur assigns, and everything they produce belongs to the entrepreneur. But the difference that is invisible to the workers shows up very well later in the entrepreneurs' accounts, when they calculate the proceeds of the production of the workers' work. For capitalists, this is the difference between the sum of money that they take in after the sale of the product and their outlay for the means of production and the wages of their workers. That which remains as profit is precisely the value that is created from the unpaid work, that is, the surplus labor, that the workers did. Each worker, therefore, whether they produce rubber bands or silk fabric or cast-iron pipes, produces first their own wages and then donates surplus value [*Mehrwert*] for the capitalists. If, for example, they weave eleven meters of silk fabric in eleven hours, then six meters of that contain the value of their wage and five are surplus value for the entrepreneur.

But the difference between wage labor and slave or serf labor has even more important consequences. Slaves and serfs performed their work mainly for private use, for the lords' consumption. They created objects of food and clothing, furniture, luxury items, etc., for their lord. However, this was the normal situation, before slavery and serf relationships degenerated under the influence of commerce and headed toward collapse. But in each age, the human capacity for consumption and luxury in private life has specific limits. Full stores, full stables, rich clothes, a sumptuous life for oneself and one's whole court, richly outfitted rooms—the ancient slave owners or medieval nobles could not use more than that. These kinds of objects, which serve for daily use, cannot be preserved in too large stockpiles, because they would be destroyed: grain easily goes bad or is eaten by rats and mice; stocks of hay and straw easily catch fire; clothing material is damaged etc.; dairy products, fruit, and vegetables in general cannot be preserved well. Consumption in the slave economy, as in the serf economy, therefore had natural boundaries even in the most sumptuous life, and therefore the normal exploitation of slaves and peasants also had limits.

It is different with modern entrepreneurs, who buy labor power to produce commodities. What workers produce in the factory or at the plant is mostly totally useless for themselves, but just as useless for the entrepreneurs. The latter have the purchased labor power produce, not clothes and food for themselves, but some sort of commodity that they themselves do not need at all. They have silk material or pipes or coffins produced only in order to let them go again as quickly as possible, to sell them. They have them produced in order to get money from selling them. And their outlays are reimbursed, like the donated surplus labor of their workers, in the form of money. It is for this purpose, to turn the unpaid work of the workers into money, that they do the whole business and buy labor power. But money, as we know, is the means to unlimited accumulation of wealth. In the form of money, wealth loses nothing in value even through the longest storage; on the contrary, as we will see later, wealth in the form of money seems to grow simply through storage. And in the form of money wealth knows no boundaries at all; it can grow infinitely. For that reason, the hunger of modern capitalists for surplus labor also has no boundaries. The more unpaid work that can be obtained from the workers, the better. To squeeze out surplus labor and, indeed, to squeeze it out boundlessly—that is the actual purpose and the task of buying labor power.

The natural drive of capitalists to increase the surplus labor squeezed from the workers finds, above all, two simple routes, which emerge by themselves, so to speak, if we observe the composition of the workday. We saw that the workday of each wage worker normally consists of two parts: the part where the worker reimburses their own wage, and the other, where they deliver unpaid work, surplus value. Thus, in order to increase the second part as much as possible, the entrepreneur can proceed in two directions: either lengthen the whole workday or shorten the first, paid part of the workday, which means depressing the wage of the workers. In fact, capitalists use both methods simultaneously, and, therefore, in the system of wage labor there is a constant double tendency: to lengthen work times and to reduce wages.

When capitalists buy the commodity labor power, they buy it, like every commodity, in order to derive benefit from it. Every buyer of commodities seeks to derive the most possible use from their commodities. If we buy boots, for example, then we want to wear them for as long as possible. The full use, the whole benefit of the commodity, belongs to the buyer of the commodity. Therefore, from the standpoint of purchasing commodities, a capitalist who has bought labor power is perfectly right to demand that the purchased commodity serve them as long as possible and as much as possible. If they paid for the labor power for a week, then the week's use belongs to them, and from their standpoint as purchaser they have the right, if possible, to have the worker work twenty-four hours seven days a week.

But on the other hand, a worker, as seller of the commodity, has a totally opposite standpoint. Admittedly, the use of the labor power belongs to the capitalist, but this has a limit in the physical and mental efficiency of the worker. A horse can only work eight hours, day after day, without being ruined. A human being must also have a certain time for food, clothing, rest, etc., in order to recover their strength, which is used up in working. If they do not have that, then their labor power is not only used up, but also destroyed. Through excessive work it is weakened, and the life of the worker shortened. So, if every week, by limitless use of labor power, a capitalist shortens the life of a worker by two weeks, then it is as if they acquired three weeks for one week's wage. From the same standpoint of trade in commodities, therefore, this means that the capitalist steals from the worker. Thus capitalists and workers champion two exactly opposed standpoints with respect to the length of the workday, both on the basis of the commodities market, and the actual length of the workday, which is only decided as a *question of power* in the course of the struggle between the capitalist class and the working class.

In itself, the workday is therefore bound to no specific limits; depending on the time and place we find an eight-hour, ten-, twelve-, fourteen-, sixteen-, eighteen-hour workday. And on the whole, there exists a centuries-long struggle over the length of the workday. In this struggle we see two important stages. The first begins at the end of the Middle Ages, in the fourteenth century, where capitalism took its first shy steps and began to shake the firm carapace of guild rule. At the time of the blossoming of handicrafts, the normal customary work time amounted to about ten hours, in which mealtimes, sleeping time, time for rest, the Sunday and festival day rests were observed with all comfort and fuss. The old handicrafts, with their slow methods of work, were not sufficient for the incipient factory enterprises. And so, the first thing that capitalists won from the governments is compulsory laws for the lengthening of workdays. From the fourteenth to the end of the seventeenth century we see in England, as well as in France and Germany, crude laws about the *minimum workday*, which means prohibitions on workers and journeymen working less than a specified work time—mostly twelve hours per day. The struggle with the laziness of the worker: that is the great call from the Middle Ages until the eighteenth century.

But once the power of the old guilds was broken and the masses of proletariat, without any means of work, were thrown upon the sale of their labor power, and on the other hand the great manufacturing facilities emerged with feverish mass production—since the eighteenth century the page has turned. There begins a sudden, and so unrestrained, draining of workers across all ages and sexes, that whole worker populations were mowed down in a few years, as if by a plague. In the year 1863 a representative in the British Parliament declared: "The cotton trade has existed for ninety years. . . . It has existed for three generations of the English race, [. . .] during that period it has destroyed nine generations of factory operatives."[18] And a bourgeois English writer, John Wade, writes in his work on the "History of the Middle and Working Classes" about: "The cupidity of mill-owners, whose cruelties in the pursuit of gain have hardly been exceeded by those perpetrated by the Spaniards in the conquest of America, in the pursuit for gold."[19] In England in the 1860s, in certain branches of industry such as lace production, small children of nine to ten years old were still employed from two, three, and four o'clock in the morning until ten, eleven, twelve o'clock at night. In Germany, the conditions that predominated until recently, for example in quicksilver mirror making and in baking, and as they still uniformly predominate today in dressmaking and cottage industry, are well known.

Modern capitalist industry first brought about the previously wholly unknown invention of night work. In all earlier social conditions, the night was seen as a time determined by nature itself for people to rest. Capitalist business discovered that the surplus value that was squeezed from workers at night was not in any way distinguishable from that which was squeezed out by day, and introduced the day and night shift. Similarly, Sunday, which in the Middle Ages was upheld by the guilds in the strictest way, was sacrificed

[18] [MEW, Vol. 23, 282. Original English cited from Member of Parliament W. Busfeild Ferrand's speech to the House of Commons (Ferrand, HC Deb, April 27, 1863, Vol. 170 cc 782–783).]

[19] [MEW, Vol. 23, 258n64. Original English cited from John Wade, *History of the Middle and Working Classes; with a Popular Exposition of the Economical and Political Principles Which Have Influenced the Past and Present Condition of the Industrious Orders* (London: Effingham Wilson, 1833), 114. Luxemburg's translation replaces Wade's phrase "in the conquest of America" with "against the Redskins of America" (*dem Grausamkeiten der Spanier gegen die Rothäute Amerikas*).]

to the hunger of the capitalists for surplus value and added to the other workdays. Dozens of small inventions also contributed to the lengthening of work time: taking meals during work without any pause, cleaning machines not during the workday but after its end, which means during the recovery time of the workers, etc.

This practice of the capitalists, which in the first centuries prevailed entirely freely and limitlessly, soon made a new series of laws about the workday necessary, this time not for the compulsory lengthening, but for the shortening, of the workday. And indeed, the first legal determinations on the maximum workday were not compelled so much by the pressure of the workers as by the simple survival instinct of capitalist society. Right away, the first couple of decades of unlimited large-scale industrial economy had exerted such a destructive effect on the health and living conditions of the working mass of people, engendered such monstrous mortality, illness, physical crippling, mental dilapidation, epidemic illnesses, and military incapacity, that the existence of society itself seemed deeply threatened.[20] It was clear that, if the natural drive of capital for surplus value were not reined in by the state, it would sooner or later turn whole states into gigantic graveyards, upon which only the bones of the workers would be seen. And without workers, no exploitation of workers.

Therefore, in its own interest, in order to enable exploitation in the future, capital had to set some limits for exploitation in the present. The people's strength had to be somewhat spared in order to ensure their further exploitation. The uneconomical robbery economy had to transition into rational exploitation. From that, the first laws about the maximum workday emerged, and the whole of bourgeois social reform. We have a counterpart to this in hunting laws. Just like precious game is ensured a certain closed season by law so that it can propagate efficiently and serve reliably as the object of the hunt, social reform ensures a certain closed season for the labor power of the

---

[20] Since the introduction of general military service, the average height of grown men, and with it the legally stipulated height for conscription, has shrunk more and more. Before the great revolution [i.e., the French Revolution of 1789], the minimum height for infantry in France was 165 cm; according to the law of 1818 it was 157 cm; after 1832 it was 156 cm; on average in France over half are decommissioned due to insufficient height and infirmity. The military standard for height in Saxony in 1780 was 178 cm, only 155 cm in the [eighteen-]sixties; in Prussia 157 cm. In 1858 Berlin could not provide its contingent of recruits—it was short of 156 men. [In this footnote, Luxemburg is paraphrasing Marx, who is himself paraphrasing claims by Justus von Liebig; see MEW, Vol. 23, 253n46; Justus von Liebig, *Die Organische Chemie in ihrer Anwendung auf Agricultur und Physiologie*, Part 1, *Der chemische Proceß der Ernährung der Vegetabilien*, 7th ed. (Braunschweig: Friedrich Vieweg, 1862), 117–118n.]

proletariat, so that it can serve efficiently for exploitation by capital. Or, as Marx says: The limiting of factory labor was dictated by the same necessity that compels the farmer to spread manure over the fields.[21]

Factory legislation was born step by step in hard, decades-long struggle against the resistance of individual capitalists, at first for children and women and in individual industries. Then followed France where, under the first pressure of the victorious Parisian proletariat, the February revolution of 1848 proclaimed the twelve-hour workday, which was the first general law about the work time of all workers, including grown men, in all branches of work. In the United States, right after the Civil War of 1861, which abolished slavery, a general movement of workers began for the eight-hour day, which swept across to the European continent. In Russia, the first protection act for women and minors emerged from the great factory unrest in Moscow's industrial district in the year 1882,[22] and the eleven-and-a-half-hour workday for grown men [emerged] from the first general strike of 60,000 textile workers from St. Petersburg in the years 1896 and 1897.[23] Germany now lags behind all other modern great states, with protection acts only for women and children.

Until now we have only spoken about a single dimension of wage labor: work time, and already we see how much the simple transaction of commodities, the buying and selling of labor power, involves particular phenomena. But here it is necessary to speak with the words of Marx: "It must be acknowledged that our worker emerges from the process of production looking different from when he entered it. In the market, as owner of the commodity 'labour power,' he stood face to face with other owners of commodities, one owner against another owner. The contract by which he sold his labour power to the capitalist proved in black and white, so to speak, that he was free to dispose of himself. But when the transaction was concluded, it was discovered that he was no 'free agent,' that the period of time for which

---

[21] [Luxemburg is paraphrasing Marx, whose actual words are "the limiting of factory labor was dictated by the same necessity as forced the manuring of English fields with guano." See MEW, Vol. 23, 253; English translation adapted from Karl Marx, *Capital: A Critique of Political Economy, Das Kapital* Series 1, trans. Ben Fowkes (New York: Penguin, 1976), 369.]

[22] On June 1, 1882, a protection act for minors was issued, which prohibited work by children under twelve years old in factories and manufacturing facilities and limited the work time of twelve-to fifteen-year-olds to eight hours. On June 3, 1885, a further law followed, which prohibited night work for women and adolescents under seventeen years old in cotton, linen, and wool factories.

[23] On June 2, 1897, the Tsarist government had to issue a law that reduced the workday in plants to eleven and a half hours and stipulated holidays for rest from work. It came into force on January 1, 1898.

he is *free* to sell his labour power is the period of time for which he is *forced* to sell it, that in fact the vampire will not let go, 'while there remains a single muscle, sinew, or drop of blood to be exploited.' For 'protection' against the serpent of their agonies, the workers have to put their heads together and, *as a class*, compel the passing of a law, an all-powerful *social barrier*, by which they can be prevented from selling themselves and their families into slavery and death *by voluntary contract with capital*."[24]

Worker protection laws are in fact the first official recognition by contemporary society that the formal equality and freedom that underlie the production of commodities and the exchange of commodities is already fracturing, capsizing in inequality and unfreedom, ever since labor power appeared on the market as a commodity.

3.

The second method of capitalists to increase surplus value is depressing workers' wages. Wages, like the workday, are in themselves bound by no specific limits. In particular, when we speak of workers' wages, we must distinguish between the money that a worker receives from the entrepreneur and the amount of means of subsistence that they gain for it. If we only know that the wage of a worker amounts to, for example, two marks per day, then we know basically nothing.[25] This is because, for the same two marks, one can buy much less means of subsistence in times of high prices than in times of low prices; and in one country—in fact almost in every region of a country— the same two-mark piece means a different standard of living from that in another. The worker can even get more money as their wage than earlier and at the same time live, not better, but just as badly or even worse. The actual, real wage is therefore the sum of the means of subsistence that the worker gets, while the monetary wage is only the nominal wage. If, therefore, the wage is only the monetary expression of the value of labor power, then this value is represented in reality by the amount of work that is used to produce the necessary means of subsistence of the worker.

But what are "necessary means of subsistence"? Apart from individual differences between one worker and another, which are irrelevant, the

---

[24] [MEW, Vol. 23, 319–320. Cited from Marx, *Capital*, 415–416. Emphasis added by Luxemburg.]
[25] [The mark is the German currency that existed before the introduction of the euro in 2002.]

various standards of living of the working class in various countries and times prove that the concept "necessary means of subsistence" is very changeable and malleable. A better-off contemporary English worker considers the daily consumption of steaks to be necessary to life, while a Chinese coolie lives on a handful of rice.

Due to the malleability of the concept of "necessary means of subsistence," a struggle develops between capitalists and workers over the size of the workers' wages that is similar to the struggle over the length of the workday. Capitalists state their standpoint as purchasers of commodities by declaring: "It is entirely right that, like any honest buyer, I must pay for the commodity of labor power according to its value, but what is the value of labor power? Its necessary means of subsistence? Now, I do indeed give my workers exactly as much as is necessary for life; but what is absolutely necessary in order to keep a person alive is given first by science, by physiology, and second by general experience. And of course I give, exactly to a hair, this minimum; for if I were to give a penny more, then I would not be an honest buyer, but a fool, a philanthropist, who makes a gift out of their own pocket to the person from whom they bought a commodity. I don't give an extra penny to my cobbler or cigar seller; I try to buy their commodities as cheaply as possible. Likewise, I try to buy labor power as cheaply as possible, and we are perfectly quits if I give my workers the barest minimum with which they can keep themselves alive."

The capitalists are perfectly within their rights here, from the standpoint of commodity production. But the workers are no less in the right, who, as sellers of commodities, counter: "Admittedly, I can claim nothing more than the actual value of my commodity, labor power. But I demand that you really pay me this full value. So I do not want more than the necessary means of subsistence. But what are the necessary means of subsistence? You say the science of physiology and experience answer this, which show what a person needs at a minimum in order to be kept alive. You therefore slip absolute, *physiological* necessity into the concept 'necessary means of subsistence.' But this is against the law of the exchange of commodities. For you know as well as I do that what is decisive for the value of any commodity on the market is the work that is *socially* necessary for its production. If your cobbler brings you a pair of boots and demands twenty marks for them, because they worked on them for four days, you will say: 'I can get boots like that from the factory for twelve marks, for there the pair is made in one day by a machine. Your four-day work was therefore not necessary, speaking socially, because it is now customary to produce boots by machine—even if it was necessary for *you*, because you don't work with machines. But I can't do anything about that and will pay you only for the socially necessary work, say twelve marks.' If you would proceed like that when buying boots, then in buying my commodity labor power you must also pay me the socially necessary cost of maintaining it. And everything is socially necessary to my life that, in our country and in the current age, is considered the usual upkeep of a person of my class. In a word, you must give me not the physiologically necessary minimum that barely keeps me alive, like an animal, but the socially customary minimum, which ensures my accustomed standard of living. Only then will you have paid the value of the commodity as an honest buyer; otherwise you buy it under its value."

We can see that, from the pure standpoint of commodities, the workers are just as right as the capitalists. But the workers only assert this standpoint over time, for they can only assert it as a social class, that means as a whole, as an organization. Only with the emergence of trade unions and the workers' party do workers begin to enforce the sale of their labor power at its value, i.e., the maintenance of their lives as a social and cultural necessity. However, before the emergence of trade unions in a country, and before their establishment in each individual branch of industry, the tendency of capitalists to reduce means of subsistence to the physiological, animal (so to speak) minimum, that means to routinely pay for labor power under its value, is decisive for the composition of wages. The times of the uncurbed reign of capital, unopposed by any resistance by worker coalitions and organizations, led to the same barbaric degradation of the working class in respect to wages as it did in respect to work time before the introduction of factory laws. There is a crusade by capital against every trace of luxury, comfort, and ease in the life of workers, which they were accustomed to from the early times of handicrafts and the peasant economy. There is a striving to reduce workers' consumption to a simple, barren act of taking in a minimum of feed to the body, like livestock is fed or machines oiled.

[...]

4.

In ratcheting up workload and depressing the living standard of the working people to the level possible for animals, and sometimes considerably below this, modern capitalist exploitation resembles exploitation in the slave economy and in serf bondage during the worst exploitation of the two latter forms of economy, that is, as they neared their collapse. But what the capitalist production of commodities alone has yielded, and what was wholly unknown to all earlier times, is the partial non-employment and hence non-consumption of the working people as a perpetual phenomenon—that is, the so-called reserve army of workers.

Capitalist production depends on the market and must follow its demand. But this changes constantly, and engenders changing, so-called good and bad business years, seasons, and months. Capital must constantly adapt itself to this change of the economic situation, and consequently employ now more, now fewer workers. In order to have the necessary amount of labor power, even for the highest demands of the market, to hand at each moment, capital must therefore, in addition to the number of employed workers, perpetually hold in reserve a considerable number of unemployed at its disposal. The non-employed workers, as such, get no wage. Their labor power is not bought; it only lies in storage.

The non-consumption of part of the working class is, therefore, an essential component of the wage law [*Lohngesetz*] of capitalist production. How these unemployed eke out their lives does not concern capital; however, capital repels every attempt to abolish the reserve army as a danger to its own survival interests. The English cotton crisis of the year 1863 provides a glaring example of this kind. When the spinning factories and weaving mills of England suddenly had to interrupt their production due to the lack of American raw cotton, and nearly one million members of the working population became destitute, some of these unemployed decided, in order to stave off imminent starvation, to emigrate to Australia. They requested a grant of two million pounds sterling from the British Parliament in order to enable the emigration of 50,000 unemployed workers. The cotton manufacturers raised a cry of indignation against this request by the workers. The industry could not manage without machines, and the workers were like machines—they must therefore be available. "The country" would suffer a loss of four million pounds sterling if the starving unemployed suddenly left. Parliament accordingly refused the emigration fund, and the unemployed remained chained to their hunger in order to form the necessary reserve for capital.

The French capitalists provided another drastic example in the year 1871. After the fall of the Commune, the slaughtering of Parisian workers with and without judicial form was conducted on such an enormous scale that ten thousand proletariat (and indeed the best and most able, the elite of the workforce) were massacred. In the middle of the satisfying feeling of revenge, the unease emerged among entrepreneurs that the lack of available "hands" could soon become harmful to capital; that is, at exactly the time that industry was heading for a lively upswing in business after the end of the war. For that reason, many Parisian entrepreneurs applied to the courts in order to moderate the persecution of the Commune fighters and save the workhands of the arm of capital from the butchery of the sword.

The reserve army has a double function for capital: first, to provide labor power for any sudden upswing in business, and second, to exert constant pressure on the employed through competition with the unemployed, and to bring their wages down to a minimum.

Marx differentiated four different strata in the reserve army, whose function for capital and whose conditions of life take different forms. The highest stratum is the periodically unemployed industrial workers who are always present, in all—even the best placed—occupations. Their personnel changes constantly, because each worker is unemployed at certain times, employed at others. Their number also fluctuates strongly with the course of business: it becomes very large at times of crisis and small in good economic situations; but it never dries up, and in general grows with the advance of industrial development.

The second stratum is the proletariat that streams from the countryside to the city: unskilled workers, who appear on the market with the lowest demands and, as simple workers, are not chained to a specific branch of work, but wait for employment as a reservoir for all.

The third category is the low proletariat, who have no regular employment and are constantly searching for casual work of one form or another. Here we find the longest workdays and the lowest wages, and therefore this stratum is not only just as useful to capital, but also just as indispensable, as the former higher strata. This level is constantly recruited from the excess numbers in industry and agriculture, but especially from the failing small handicrafts and menial occupations, which are dying out. It forms the broad basis of cottage industry and works behind the curtains everywhere, so to speak, behind the official stage of industry. This stratum not only does not tend to disappear, but, on the contrary, it grows—as much due to the increasing effects of industry in the city and on the country as to its members having children.

Lastly, the fourth stratum of the proletariat reserve army are the straightforward paupers, the poor. Some of them are capable of work—and, in times of good business, are partly employed by industry or trade, and in times of crisis are the first to be cast out—and some of them are incapable of work: aged workers whom industry can no longer use, proletarian widows, orphans and children of paupers, crippled and maimed victims of large-scale industry, of the mines, etc.; and lastly there are those unaccustomed to work: vagabonds and the like. This stratum flows directly into the lumpenproletariat:[26] criminals, prostitutes. Pauperism, says Marx, is the hospital of the working class and the dead weight of its reserve army. Its existence follows just as necessarily and inevitably from the reserve army as the reserve army follows from the development of industry. Poverty and the lumpenproletariat belong to the conditions of existence of capitalism and grow together with it: the greater the social wealth, functioning capital, and mass of workers employed by capital, the greater the available stratum of the unemployed, the reserve army; the greater the reserve army in relation to the employed mass of workers, the greater the lowest stratum of poverty, of pauperism, of crime. The size of the unemployed and unwaged therefore inevitably grows with capital and wealth, and with it the Lazarus stratum [*Lazarusschicht*] of the working class—official poverty. "*This*," says Marx, "*is the absolute general law of capitalist accumulation.*"[27]

The formation of a constant and growing stratum of the unemployed was, as we have said, unknown in all earlier forms of society. In the primitive communist community everyone works, of course, because this is necessary for sustenance—partly out of immediate need, and partly under the pressure of the moral and legal authority of the tribe, the community. But *all* members of society are provided with whatever means for life are available. The standard of living of primitive communist groups is admittedly quite low and simple, the comforts of life are primitive. But to the extent that the means for life are there, they are there for all, equally, and poverty in today's sense, the exclusion from the means available to society, is entirely unknown in these times. A primitive tribe sometimes or often starved, if nature was unfavorable to it, but its lack was the lack of society as such; one section of the members of society suffering lack while another section had excess was unthinkable; for to the extent that the means of subsistence of society as a whole were ensured, the existence of each individual member was ensured.

[...]

---

[26] [The German term *Lumpenproletariat*, coined by Marx and Engels, has entered into English with this specific meaning, i.e., as the lowest level of the poor, as described here by Luxemburg. The term is sometimes given instead as "rabble proletariat" or "ragged proletariat."]

[27] [MEW, Vol. 23, 674. Cited from Marx, *Capital*, 841–842. In addition to this short quotation, Luxemburg is paraphrasing Marx throughout the second half of this paragraph.]

Capitalist production of commodities is therefore the first economic form in the history of humanity in which the lack of employment and lack of means of a large and growing stratum of the population, and the direct, hopeless poverty of another, equally growing stratum, are not only a consequence, but also a necessity—a condition of life—of this economy. The uncertainty of existence of the whole working mass and the chronic lack, and in part the direct poverty, of certain broad strata are, for the first time, a normal phenomenon of society. And the scholars of the bourgeoisie, who cannot imagine any other form of society than today's, are so steeped in this natural necessity of the stratum of the unemployed and destitute that they explain it as a natural law willed by God. [...]

5.

So far, we have investigated what standard of living the capitalist commodities economy ensures for the working class and its various strata. But we still know nothing precise about the relationship of this standard of living of the workers to social wealth as a whole. Because, for example, the workers could in one case have more means of subsistence, richer food, better clothing, than before, but if the wealth of the other classes has grown much faster, then the *share* of the workers in social products has become smaller. Consequently, workers' standard of living in itself, taken absolutely, can rise while their share, taken as relative to other classes, can sink. But the living standard of any person and any class can only be rightly judged if one evaluates it relative to the conditions of the time and the other strata of the same society. The prince of a primitive, half-wild, or barbaric tribe in Africa has a lower standard of living—that is, simpler habitation, worse clothing, rougher food—than an average factory worker in Germany. But this prince lives "princely" in comparison to the means and demands of his tribe, while the factory worker in Germany, compared with the luxury of the rich bourgeoisie and the needs of the current time, lives really poorly.

Thus, in order to rightly judge the position of the worker in today's society, it is necessary to investigate not only the absolute wage (that means the size of the worker's wage in itself), but also the relative wage: that is, the share of the whole product of a worker's work that is constituted by their wage. We assumed in our earlier example that, with an eleven-hour workday, a worker must work off their wage, that means their means of subsistence, in the first six hours, and then must create surplus value for capitalists for another five hours. In this example we also presupposed that the production of the worker's means of subsistence would take six hours of work. We also saw that capitalists seek by all means to depress workers' standards of living in order to increase the unpaid work, the surplus value, as much as possible. But let us assume that the workers' standard of living does not change, that is, they always have to procure the same amount of food, clothing, linens, furniture, etc. Thus we assume that their wage, taken absolutely, does not fall. If, however, the production of all these means of subsistence has become cheaper through advances in production and now, for example, requires less time, then workers will now need a shorter time to work off their wage. We assume that the amount of food, clothing, furniture, etc., that a worker needs per day now no longer requires six hours of work, but only five. Then, in an eleven-hour workday, a worker will work to replace their wage not for six hours but only for five, and has a whole six hours left for unpaid work, for creating surplus value for capitalists. The worker's share in the product has become one-sixth smaller; the share of the capitalists has grown by one-fifth. But the absolute wage did not fall.

The living standard of workers can even increase, i.e., absolute wages can rise, say by ten percent—and not just monetary wages but the workers' real means of subsistence. But if in the same, or nearly the same, time the productivity of work rises by fifteen percent, then the workers' share in their product, that is, their relative wage, has in fact sunk, although the absolute wage has risen.

The share of a worker in their product therefore depends on the productivity of work. The less work is needed to produce their means of subsistence, the smaller their relative wage. If the shirts they wear, the boots, the caps, are produced with less work than before due to advances in manufacturing, then a worker may be able to procure the same amount of shirts, boots, and caps with their wage, but still acquires a smaller share of the social wealth, the total social labor.

But certain amounts of all sorts of products and materials are involved in a worker's daily practice. The price of the workers' living standard is reduced not only by the manufacturing of shirts, but also by the manufacturing of cotton, which provides the material for the shirts, and machine industry, which provides the sewing machines, and the yarn industry, which creates the yarn. Likewise, the workers' means of subsistence are reduced in price not only by advances in baking but also by American agriculture, which provides masses of grain, and advances in railway and steamship transport, which deliver grain from America to Europe, etc. Thus each advance of industry, each increase in the productivity of human work, leads to the workers' sustenance costing ever less work. Workers must therefore employ an ever smaller part of their workday in replacing their wage, and the part in which they do unpaid work, surplus labor for the capitalists, becomes ever larger.

But the constant, unceasing progress of technology is a necessity, a condition of life for capitalists. The competition between individual entrepreneurs compels each of them to produce their products as cheaply as possible, which means with the greatest possible savings in human work. And if one capitalist has introduced a new, improved process in their factory, this competition forces all other entrepreneurs in the same sector to immediately improve technology in order to not let themselves be knocked out of the field, that is, from the commodities market. This is expressed visibly on the surface in the general introduction of machine industry in place of manual industry and the ever-faster introduction of newer, improved machines in place of the old. Technical inventions in all areas of production have become daily fare. Thus the technical transformation of the whole of industry, as much in actual production as in means of transport, is an unremitting phenomenon, a law of life of capitalist commodities production. And each advance in the productivity of work is expressed in the reduction of the amount of work that is necessary to maintain a worker. That means: capitalist production cannot take a step forward without reducing the workers' share of the social product. With each new invention of technology, with each improvement in machines, with each new application of steam and electricity to production and transportation, the workers' share of the product becomes smaller and the capitalists' share greater. The relative wage falls ever lower and lower, unstoppably and without interruption; and the surplus value, i.e., the wealth of the capitalists that is squeezed, unpaid, from the workers, grows higher and higher just as unstoppably and constantly.

We see here, again, a striking difference between the capitalist production of commodities and all earlier economic forms of society. As we know, in primitive communist society, straight after production the product is shared equally among all working people, that is all members, for there are basically no nonworkers. Under conditions of serfdom, equality is not the norm, but rather exploitation of workers by nonworkers. But the share of the workers, the serfs, in the fruits of their labor is not specified; on the contrary, it is the share of the exploiters, the lords, that is fixed precisely as the specified bonds and dues that they are to get from the peasants. What is left after that, in work time and product, is the peasants' share, so that in normal conditions, before the most extreme degeneration of bondage, it is possible for peasants, within a certain scope, to increase their own share by extending their powers of labor. Admittedly, this peasants' share becomes ever smaller with the advance of the Middle Ages, due to the growing demands of the nobles and the clergy for dues and bonds. But these norms are always specified, if arbitrarily fixed, and visible to people—even if these people are brutes. They are fixed norms that specify the serfs' share in the product, as they fix the share of the feudal bloodsuckers.

As a result, medieval serfs and bondsmen see and feel very exactly when greater burdens are laid upon them and their own share is shrunk. And therefore a struggle against this reduction of their share is possible, and actually breaks out, even where it is only barely possible, as an open struggle of the exploited peasants against the reduction of their share in their work product. Under certain conditions, this struggle is even crowned with success: the freedom of the town citizenry emerged by the originally bonded craftsmen gradually divesting themselves of the manifold bonds, inheritance taxes, death fees, sumptuary rights, and whatever else the thousand means of fleecing of feudal times were called, until they seized the rest—political rights—in open struggle.

In the wage system there exist no legal or customary rights or even only forcible, arbitrary specifications of the share of workers in their product. This share is determined by the prevailing level of productivity of work, by the status of technology, and not by some caprice of the exploiters but by the advance of technology, which unceasingly, mercilessly depresses the share of the workers. It is this, an entirely invisible power, a simple mechanical effect of competition and commodities production, that wrests from workers an ever greater portion of their product and leaves an ever smaller one, a power that carries out its effect silently, unnoticeably, behind the workers' backs, and against which struggle is, therefore, entirely impossible.

The personal role of the exploiters is, admittedly, visible where it concerns the absolute wage, that is, the real standard of living. A reduction in wages, which causes a depression in the real standard of living of the workers, is a visible attack by the capitalists against the workers and is usually answered by the latter, where trade unions exist, with immediate struggle, and in successful cases is even resisted. By contrast, the lowering of the relative wage apparently occurs without the least personal participation of the capitalists, and against that the workers have no possibility at all for struggle and resistance within the wage system, i.e., on the basis of commodity production. The workers cannot fight back against the technical advances of production, against inventions, introductions of machines, against steam and electricity, against improvements in means of transportation. The effect of all these advances on the relative wage of the workers comes about entirely mechanically from the production of commodities and from the character of labor power as a commodity. The most powerful trade unions are therefore entirely powerless against this tendency of the relative wage to sink rapidly. Struggling against the lowering of the relative wage therefore also means struggling against the character of labor power as a commodity, which means against capitalist production as a whole. The struggle against the dropping of the relative wage is therefore no longer a struggle on the basis of the commodities economy, but a revolutionary, subversive attempt against the existence of this economy; it is the socialist movement of the proletariat.

[...]

6.

Only if we consolidate all the consequences of the wage relations presented above can we picture the capitalist wage law that determines the material life circumstances of the worker. For that, above all, the absolute wage must be distinguished from the relative wage. The absolute wage, again, appears in a double form: once as a sum of money, that is, as the nominal wage; second as a sum of the means of existence that workers can obtain with this money, that is, as real wage. The monetary wage of the workers can remain constant or even rise, and the standard of living—that is, the real wage—can still fall.

Now, the real wage has the constant tendency to fall to the absolute minimum, to the minimum for physical existence, which means capital has a constant tendency to pay for labor power *under* its value. A counterweight to this tendency of capital is only created by labor organization. The main function of trade unions is that, by increasing the needs of the workers, by their moral elevation, they create in place of the minimum for physical existence, the minimum for cultural social existence. That means a certain cultural standard of living for the worker, below which wages cannot fall without immediately calling forth a struggle of the coalition, a resistance. Therein also lies the great economic significance of social democracy, which, by intellectually and politically shaking up the broad masses of workers, raises their cultural level and thereby their economic needs. When, for example, subscribing to a newspaper or purchasing brochures becomes part of the workers' lifestyle, their economic standard of living rises accordingly and, as a consequence, so do wages.

[...]

8

Edith Stein (1891–1942)

Introduction

"The goal of phenomenology," writes Edith Stein (1891–1942), "is to clarify
and thereby find the ultimate basis of all knowledge."[1] In *On the Problem of
Empathy* (1917), her doctoral dissertation and first published book, Stein
seeks to trace this basis back to the lived body and the empathy we have with
other human beings, two phenomena that she takes to be closely connected.

The first generation of phenomenologists—some would even say phenomenology as such[2]—sought to uncover the universal basis of the human
experience of the world. Phenomenology, on this understanding, does not
so much seek direct first-level scientific knowledge (this is the job of the sciences). Instead it asks, in a Kantian vein, about the conditions of the possibility for knowledge and experience. In the early phenomenological
tradition, these conditions are traced back to the first-person perspective of
consciousness. For the phenomenologists who gathered around Alexander
Pfänder (in Munich) and Edmund Husserl (in Göttingen and later Freiburg),
the affective and emotive dimensions of consciousness were seen as particularly significant, yet understudied, aspects of human experience.[3] While crucial for our understanding of human values, this facet of experience, they
argued, cannot be reduced to perception or belief but begs its own line of
investigation. Stein's work significantly contributes to this line of research.[4]

Stein was born in Breslau (now Wrocław, Poland). While her family
was Jewish, Stein went through a secular period before she converted to
Catholicism in 1922. Stein initially studied at the University of Breslau

---

[1] Edith Stein, *On the Problem of Empathy*, trans. Waltraut Stein (Washington, DC: Institute of
Carmelite Studies, 1989), 3.

[2] See Dan Zahavi, "Editor's Introduction," in *Oxford Handbook of Contemporary Phenomenology*,
ed. Dan Zahavi (Oxford: Oxford University Press, 2012), 1–4.

[3] For a helpful overview of the different approaches to emotions developed in early phenomenology,
see Dermot Moran and Rodney K. B. Parker, "Editors' Introduction," *Studia Phaenomenologica* 15
(2015): 11–27.

[4] See Ferran, "The Emotions." See also Íngrid Vendrell Ferran, "Empathy, Emotional Sharing and
Feelings in Stein's Early Work," *Human Studies* 38 (2015): 481–502.

Women Philosophers in the Long Nineteenth Century. Dalia Nassar and Kristin Gjesdal, Oxford University Press.
© Oxford University Press 2021. DOI: 10.1093/oso/9780190868031.003.0010

(1911–1913). She started with language and literature, history, and philosophy, but when she discovered Husserl's *Logical Investigations* (1900–1901), her studies became more focused. Around this time, she saw a newspaper report that a woman, Hedwig Conrad-Martius, had won a prize for a philosophical thesis.[5] Inspired by this, Stein went to study with Husserl in Göttingen. In spite of his suggestion that she should continue with literature or history—subjects more fitting for a woman—she stuck to philosophy. Her studies were interrupted by World War I, when she tended to sick soldiers at a lazaretto in Austria. In 1916, she returned to her philosophy studies, now as Husserl's assistant in Freiburg. Stein was not the only woman in Husserl's circles. Along with Conrad-Martius, other women phenomenologists included Erica Goethe, Betty Heimann, Anna Hoffa, Gerda Walther, and Margarete Ortmann. In her unfinished autobiography, *Life in a Jewish Family: An Autobiography, 1891–1916*, Stein describes her friendships with many of these women, as well as the challenges they faced as women (philosophy) students.[6]

In 1916, Stein submitted her dissertation, *On the Problem of Empathy (Das Einfühlungsproblem in seiner historischen Entwicklung und in phänomenologischer Betrachtung)*, and graduated *summa cum laude*. An abbreviated version of the dissertation was published the following year. She started working toward a habilitation, the second dissertation that is typically required for academic positions in Germany. Husserl, however, was unwilling to support a woman for a habilitation.[7] Following a period of frustration over, among other things, their philosophical differences, Stein resigned from her position as Husserl's assistant.[8] She returned to Göttingen in the fall of 1919, with the hope of pursuing a habilitation there. Göttingen, too, let her down; her habilitation, entitled "Individual and Community," was not even sent out for review. Stein, however, appealed this decision to the Prussian Ministry of Culture, and in 1920, a milestone ruling was issued that "membership in the female sex" was no obstacle to habilitating at German universities. At this point, Stein did not

[5] See Edith Stein, *Life in a Jewish Family: An Autobiography, 1891–1916*, trans. Josephine Koeppel (Washington, DC: Institute of Carmelite Studies, 1986), chap. 5. The main body of this work was written in 1933; the latest additions are from 1939. An abridged version of the work was posthumously published in German in 1965.

[6] Stein, *Life*, 240.

[7] See Mary Catharine Baseheart and Linda Lopez McAlister, with Waltraut Stein, "Edith Stein (1891–1942)," in *A History of Women Philosophers*, Vol. 4, *Contemporary Women Philosophers: 1900–Today*, ed. Mary Ellen Waithe (Dordrecht: Kluwer, 1995), 157–189, esp. 158–159.

[8] Alasdair MacIntyre, *Edith Stein: A Philosophical Prologue, 1913–1922* (Lanham, MD: Rowman & Littlefield, 2005), 105.

attempt to return to habilitate at Göttingen. Indeed, it would be another thirty years before the first woman habilitated in philosophy in Germany.[9]

On account of the hardships she faced with her habilitation, Stein decided to take a teaching position at an all-girls school. In 1932, she obtained a position as *Dozent* at the German Institute of Scientific Pedagogy in Münster. However, just one year later, in 1933, she was forced to resign due to anti-Semitic legislation; the same legislation would also make it impossible for her to publish her work. Later that year, she was admitted to the Carmelite convent in Cologne. As the political situation grew worse, Stein and her sister were sent to safety in a convent in Echt, Netherlands. During the National Socialist occupation of the Netherlands, the two were arrested by the National Socialists and deported. During the deportation, Stein is said to have rejected an offer to flee and leave others behind. She was murdered in Auschwitz in 1942.

Stein was beatified as a martyr in 1987 and, eleven years later, canonized by the Catholic Church. Her work is published in a multi-volume English translation by the Institute of Carmelite Studies. The collected works include *Essays on Women*, a series of shorter texts from the 1920s and early 1930s that investigate issues of gender, education (reflecting insights Stein gained as a teacher), and related topics from a phenomenological position. Stein's reflections on gender are sometimes essentializing but also thought-provoking and philosophically acute (this especially goes for her views on education). Another significant contribution is her work on the philosophy of psychology and the humanities.[10] Further, her philosophy includes discussions of psychologism, volition, the relationship between the sentient and the mental aspects of human beings, political philosophy, ethics, and aesthetics. In the wake of Martin Heidegger's *Being and Time* (1927), Stein authored a series of objections to his position, including his philosophy of death and dying. With her background as a nurse during World War I, Stein approached this field with personal experience as well as analytic rigor. She criticized what she viewed as Heidegger's individualist, almost solipsistic

---

[9] Katharina Kanthack habilitated at the Free University in Berlin in 1950 (she had been delayed because of the war). See Baseheart and McAlister, "Edith Stein," 158–159. Anna Tumarkin, a Russian who gained her PhD in Switzerland in 1895, was the first professor of philosophy in Europe (she became an extraordinary professor at the University of Bern in Switzerland in 1909). Tumarkin's doctoral work was on Herder and Kant.

[10] This work is based on the manuscript for her planned habilitation, which was first published in a 1922 volume celebrating Husserl's sixtieth birthday (the volume was delayed because of financial hardships). See Edith Stein, *Philosophy of Psychology and the Humanities*, ed. Marianne Sawicki, trans. Mary Catharine Baseheart and Marianne Sawicki (Washington, DC: Institute of Carmelite Studies, 2000).

position, as well as what she took to be a too simplistic conception of the anxiety we feel in the face of death. For Stein, this anxiety is not simple but bifurcated into a fear of nothingness as well as a fear of one's own nonbeing.[11]

On the Problem of Empathy, from which the following excerpts are taken, marks the transition of women philosophers into a more traditional academic system and more traditional academic styles of writing. Stein's text is technically demanding yet worthwhile in terms of its systematic contribution to phenomenology as well as the history of this movement.

In *On the Problem of Empathy*, Stein enters into dialogue with Husserl's philosophy, especially his *Ideas I* (1913). Following Husserl's advice, she also discusses the work of the Munich phenomenologist Theodor Lipps. As Stein later recalls, she turned to empathy in order to account for a lacuna in Husserl's work: his failure to explain fully the experience of intersubjectivity.[12] By emphasizing the importance of the lived body and our direct, empathic relationships to others, Stein extends the phenomenological project beyond Husserl's published contributions at the time.

In its published version, *On the Problem of Empathy* is divided into three chapters. The rest of the work was not published, and the typescript is lost. The published chapters are "The Essence of Acts of Empathy" (chapter 2), "The Constitution of the Psychophysical Individual" (chapter 3), and "Empathy as the Understanding of Spiritual Persons" (chapter 4). The following excerpt is from chapter 3, which focuses on the living body and the relationship between self and other.

Stein distinguishes between sympathy and empathy. While sympathy designates a feeling *with*, empathy denotes a feeling *in* (*Einfühlung*).[13] Stein is primarily interested in empathy. Previous phenomenologists, such as Lipps, had viewed empathy as a feeling of oneness, as, so to speak, a losing oneself in another. Stein challenges this account. In her view, empathy is not an experience of oneness with the other but rather the condition of possibility for such an experience. It is crucial to Stein's argument that empathy is a feeling into *an other*. Only in this way, she argues, can we see that the distinction between

[11] See Edith Stein, *Werke*, Vol. 6, ed. Lucy Gelber and Romaeus Leuven (Freiburg: Herder, 1962), 69–135.

[12] Stein's account of her decision (*Life*, 269) complicates the common assumption that "it was Husserl who suggested that she should work on the topic of empathy." For this assumption, see, for instance, Dan Zahavi, *Self and Other: Exploring Subjectivity, Empathy, and Shame* (Oxford: Oxford University Press, 2014), 123–124.

[13] In *On Empathy*, Stein sometimes talks about empathy with others' beliefs, expectations, etc. She also designates empathy in the literal sense as the comprehension of an act of feeling. See Stein, *Werke*, Vol. 6, 92.

myself and the other is, indeed, an inherent part of empathy. Empathy allows me to connect with the experiences of an other (e.g., her pain, joy, sorrow, etc.) without dissolving the other into myself. As this is not *my* pain, joy, or sorrow, the experience with which I empathize is not primordial for me but only for the other. Stein thus speaks of a non-primordial experience (e.g., empathy with an other's sorrow) that announces a primordial one (the sorrow as experienced by the other). This is something empathy and memory share. In both cases we bring to life a primordial experience that is no longer primordial. Yet memory targets my own feelings or experiences, whereas empathy is directed toward others.

While psychologists take an interest in empathy and its various manifestations, phenomenology focuses on its essence. With reference to the psychological currents in the Munich phenomenology circles, Stein notes that phenomenology is prior to psychology—both methodologically and in terms of the topics studied (i.e., the conditions of possibility of experience). Moreover, she takes issue with some of the psychologically oriented accounts of our relationship with others. She argues, for example, that the physical expressions of an other (e.g., her brows are furrowed in frustration, she cries if she is sad) should not be seen as a *sign* of her inner life, because that would imply that the inner and outer were somehow separated or mechanically connected (in the way smoke signifies fire). Rather, the outer, Stein contends, *manifests* or *expresses* the inner: sadness is in and through the sorrowful face and the tears, not mechanically causing it. The other is a psychophysical entity that presents itself as a totality. When it comes to other human beings, the inner and the outer are not two distinct entities that are causally related. Outer expressions can symbolize inner ones but do not *signify* them, as an effect would signify a cause (Stein ascribes such a view to the early Lipps but acknowledges that he later changes his perspective). Stein exemplifies her point by way of the difference between blushing and reddening in the face: reddening is *caused* by physical exercise (e.g., running a particularly strenuous lap), while blushing is an *expression* of the body as minded (such as when the I is made aware of the presence of another human being).

As Stein sees it, the I relates to the other as a psychophysical entity. My body *is* emphatically me: it is the point zero of my orientation in the world, that which enables experience. I am in the world as embodied, and the world presents itself to me, as the phenomenologists would say, as a mind embodied. In the same way, the other I is a minded body and an embodied mind—and it is as such that I relate to the other. In this way, Stein rejects the view of the human being as split between mind and body. She also rejects the psychologist and intellectualist trends within phenomenology. As she argues, the body is not given as a mere object (such a notion of the body would be an abstraction and thus presupposes a more fundamental bodily givenness). Furthermore, from a phenomenological point of view, my own embodied space and outer (objectivized) space are constitutively different— that is, my experience of my body is different from my experience of, say, my desk and the book I am reading. It is impossible to get to the experience of the lived body from an external, objectivized point of view. Phenomenology thus aims to describe the body as living and, at the same time, as mine.

In relating empathically to others, I relate *as* a living body to another living body. When, for instance, I see somebody's hand resting on the table, I recognize that this hand is not my own. It is, in this sense, an "object." Yet in relating to it, I see it as *somebody's* hand. I do not *first* see it as an object and then, *secondarily*, ascribe it to another human being. The hand is given to me *as* somebody's hand, *as* part of a living body.

How, then, do I relate to the other as a living body? At stake is not an intellectualizing move or an inference. Rather, it is that the other is given (presented) to me in such a way that I see her—primordially and at a phenomenologically fundamental level—*as* another human being. That is, I do not see another human being as an object that is *also* a human being or a human being who is *also*, say, happy or sad. Instead, the other is disclosed to me as an other who is happy or sad—and demands my response as such. For Stein, empathy is the basic bond through which the I relates to an other.

Empathy allows me to transcend my individuality. It is, Stein argues, the condition of possibility for intersubjectivity. Stronger still, as she puts it, "empathy, as the foundation of intersubjective experience, becomes *the condition of possibility for the cognition of the existing external world*" (emphasis added). The world is given to us as embodied subjects relating to other embodied subjects and acknowledging that they, too, present a perspective on the world, an experiential point zero to which phenomena are disclosed. The relationship with others is therefore not secondary. Furthermore, by relating to an other, the I also sees itself as an I—as living with and among others toward whom it is open yet from whom it is constitutively different.

Given her emphasis on embodiment, Stein expands her notion of empathy beyond the domain of the human. Like Max Scheler, Else Voigtländer, Gerda Walther, and other phenomenologists, Stein is influenced by vitalist philosophy. She sees the human body in continuity with nature at large. Just as Stein is able to distinguish the expressive, living, and moving body, on the one hand, and mere mechanical movement, on the other, she argues, by way of expansion, that we can see *all living* bodies in this way—as, say, tired, sluggish, buoyant, and so on. Just as I can see an other's laugh as an expression of happiness, I can also see a dog wagging its tail as an expression that carries meaning. According to Stein, we can even have empathetic fulfillment with plants, i.e., we can see them thrive and so on.[14] The degree to which the empathy is fulfilled will, however, vary in each case.

The emphasis on the other's expressions as meaningful does not imply that we cannot be deceived or misled. Others can fake pain or be stoic when in pain such that I do not realize that they are in agony. However, it would be wrong, Stein argues, to take these derived cases as normal cases. According to Stein, this is precisely what Scheler did. In taking the derived cases as his basis, he overlooked how the world is given to an I as a psychic-physiological being (her definition of an individual) with a capacity for empathy. As a pure I, the I could have all kinds of objects given, but it could not perceive animated, living bodies—that is, living individuals. And in Stein's view, the constitution of other individuals is, and remains, related to our experience of ourselves *as selves*. In this way, empathy serves to explain not only how we relate to and understand others but also how we experience ourselves. Furthermore, others can sometimes understand us better than we understand ourselves. While, in her example, I can think that I am simply checking up on others, others can make me aware that in reality I seek approval after, say, an act of kindness. As a psychic-physiological individual, the I does not have a full comprehension of itself. For that, it needs others. For Stein, inner perception and empathy thus work jointly to give myself to myself.

There is today a growing interest in Stein's contribution to the phenomenological movement. New light has been shed on her work as Husserl's assistant (her editing of his manuscripts and the exchanges they had in the period up to 1918): she was not simply taking on practical, secretarial tasks for him but also contributed intellectually to the formation of his thought. Moreover, increasing attention has been paid to Stein's independent, systematic position and her role as a key phenomenologist. It is safe to say that Stein is now recognized as a twentieth-century philosopher of the first rank.

---

[14] We find the phenomenological interest in plants and animals further pursued in Conrad-Martius's work, especially after World War II. For an early treatment of the issue, see Hedwig Conrad-Martius, "Pflanze und Tier," in *Metaphysische Gespräche* (Halle: Max Niemeyer, 1921), 1–26.

Selections from *On Empathy*

The I and the Living Body

In order to gain greater clarity, we must take a step that we have hesitated to take until the course of the investigation demanded it: the step from the psychic to the psychophysical. This separation is an artificial one, for the mind is given to us as a mind in a living body. What is the living body? How and as what is it given to us?[15]

a. The Givenness of the Living Body

Again, we start out from the sphere that forms the foundation of all our investigations: the sphere of pure consciousness. How is my body constituted for consciousness?

For a start, my physical body is given to me in acts of external perception. But if we were to pretend that our body were given to us only in this way, we would construct a very peculiar object. That is, a real thing, a physical body, whose motivated series of appearances exhibit strange gaps. A thing that withholds its reverse side from me even more stubbornly than the moon, which makes a fool of me by inviting me to consider it from new sides and, when I try to respond to its invitation, hides these sides from me. Of course, what eludes my gaze is accessible to my touching hand; but even this relationship of seeing and touching is different for my body from how it is for all other things. Every other thing that I see says to me: touch me, I am really what I give myself out to be, I am tangible, not a phantom. And everything that I touch calls to me: open your eyes and you will see me. Sense of touch and sense of sight (to the extent that one can speak of senses in the pure sphere) call each other as witnesses, without passing off responsibility onto each other.

In addition to this unique lack in the externally perceived body, it has another peculiar characteristic. I can approach and move away from every other

---

[15] [Stein uses two German words for "body"—*Leib* and *Körper*—with different connotations. In this text, *Körper* refers to a body as a physical object, basically an inert physical object, while *Leib* conveys the idea of a living, animated body. To distinguish between these terms in English, in this text *Leib* has been translated consistently as "living body" and *Körper* as "physical body," with occasional exceptions when the more general term "body" is used. This occurs near the start of the section "The Givenness of the Living Body," where Stein occasionally uses *Leib* in a general sense while she is explaining the distinction between "living body" and "physical body"; and when *Leib* or *Körper* appears as part of a longer word, for example, *leibgebunden* ("body-bound" or "bound to the body") and *Körperteil* ("body part" or "part of the body").]

thing, can turn toward or away from it, at which point it disappears from my gaze. This approaching and moving away, the movement of my physical body and other things, is marked by changes in the series of appearances of each thing. It is not at all easy to see how to distinguish between the two cases (the movement of other things and the movement of my physical body), or in general how to grasp the movement of one's own physical body, if we stick to our pretense that our physical body is only constituted in external perception and not uniquely as a living body.

Therefore, in order to speak more precisely, we must say: all other objects are given to me in many, infinitely variable appearances and changing postures, and sometimes they are not given to me at all. But this one object is given to me in series of appearances that only vary within very narrow boundaries. And it is continually there, with constant obtrusiveness, as long as I have my eyes open, and always in tangible proximity to me in a way that no other object is. It is always "here," while all other objects are always "there."

But here we have already reached the limits of our pretense and must get rid of it. For even if we close our eyes tightly and stretch our hands out away from us, even if we do not let any body part touch another, so that we can neither take hold of nor see our body, even then we are not free of it. Even then, the body is inescapably there in full "bodiliness" (hence the name), and we find ourselves inescapably bound to it. This confinement, its belonging to me, could never be constituted in external perception. A living body perceived only externally would always only be a physical body of a special kind, even a unique kind, but never "my living body."

Now, let us see how this new way of being given [Gegebenheit] comes about. Among the real components of consciousness, of this region of ineradicable being, are the sensations—as a particular form of the highest category "lived experience." We must differentiate between "sensings" [Empfindnissen] that are localized in the body (which will be considered below) and other sensations [Empfindungen].

The sensation of pressure or pain or cold is given just as absolutely as the lived experience of judging, willing, perceiving, etc. But, in contrast to all these acts, sensation has a unique character. It does not, like these, spring from the pure I; it never adopts the form of the *cogito*, in which the I directs itself toward an object. Therefore, when I reflect upon sensation, I can never find the I within it. Rather, sensation is always "somewhere," spatially localized, at a distance from the I, perhaps very close to it but never in it. And this "some-where" is not an empty place in space, but something that fills space. And all these somethings where my sensations occur combine into a unity: the unity of my living body. They themselves are sites of the living body. Within this unified givenness, through which the living body as a whole is always there for me, differences emerge. The various parts of the living body, constituted for me in sensation, are at various distances from me. Thus my torso is closer to me than my extremities, and I can say meaningfully that I move my hands closer or farther away. When I speak of distance from "me," therefore, it is an imprecise way of speaking: I cannot really establish a distance from the "I," which is non-spatial and cannot be localized.

Instead, I relate the parts of my living body, as well as everything spatial outside it, to a "zero point of orientation" which my living body encompasses. This zero point is not localized geometrically in exactly one place in my phys-ical body. Moreover, it is not the same for all data, but for visual data it is located in my head, for tactile data in the center of my living body. Thus the I has no distance from the zero point, and everything that is given at a dis-tance from the zero point is also given at a distance from the I.

However, this distance of the parts of the physical body from me is fun-damentally different from the distance of other things from each other and from me. Two things in space are a certain distance from each other; they can approach each other and eventually touch each other: then the distance disappears. They can even, perhaps, fill the same part of space—if they are not impenetrable material things but, for example, objects of hal-lucination. . . . Likewise, a thing can approach me, its distance from me can decrease, and it can eventually touch . . . not me, but my physical body. In that case, the distance from my physical body (but not from me) has be-come zero. It is not the same size as the distance of the part of the body that is touched from the zero point.

I could not say that a stone that I hold in my hand is just as far or "only a little bit farther" from the zero point as my hand itself. The distance of the parts of my living body from me is not at all comparable to the distance of other phys-ical bodies from me. The living body as a whole is at the zero point of orien-tation, whereas all physical bodies are outside it. The "space of the body" and "external space" are completely different from each other. I would not get at the former just by perceiving externally, or at the latter just by "perceiving bodily." But, since my living body is constituted in two ways—as a sensing (bodily perceiving) living body and as an externally perceived physical body of the external world—and since it is experienced in this double givenness as the same thing, it gains a place in external space, it fills part of this space.

There is still a little more to be said about the relationship between sensations and "bodily perception." The analysis of sensations tends to be different in other contexts. People tend to see sensation as what "gives" us the external world, and therefore they tend to separate "sensation" and "what is sensed," or the "content of sensation" and "sensation as function" (in Stumpf's sense). For example, they tend to separate a red that is seen and the having of this red.[16] I cannot agree with this. The red of an object is "perceived," and I must distinguish between the act of perception and the thing that is perceived. Analyzing perceptions leads me to "sensory data," I can therefore view the perception of qualities as the "objectification of sensory data." But the qualities do not become sensations because of this, and the sensations do not become qualities; nor do they become acts of giving. As components of external perception, they are elements that cannot be further analyzed.

If we consider sensation from the side of the living body, then we find analogous phenomenological factual material [*Tatbestand*]. I can speak about a "sensed" living body as little as I can speak of a "sensed" object of the external world. Instead, here, too, we need to take an objectifying view.

If my fingertip touches the table I must distinguish: first, the sensation of touch, the tactile datum, which cannot be broken down any further; second, the hardness of the table and the correlative act of external perception; third, the touching fingertip and the correlative act of "bodily perception."

What makes the connection of sensation and bodily perception particularly intimate is the fact that the living body is given *as* sensing, and the sensations are given as *in* the living body. It would be beyond the scope of this work to investigate the significance of all the types of sensation for bodily perception.[17] However, we must raise one point. We said the "external" and "bodily perceived" living body are given as the same. This requires a more detailed explanation.

---

[16] Cf. Österreich, *Phenomenology of the I*, 122f. contra Husserl, *Logische Untersuchungen II*, 359ff. [The full references are: Traugott Konstantin Oesterreich, *Die Phänomenologie des Ich in ihren Grundproblemen*, Vol. 1, *Das Ich und Selbstbewußtsein. Die scheinbare Spaltung des Ich* (Leipzig: Leipzig: Johann Ambrosius Barth, 1910), 122f.; and Edmund Husserl, *Logische Untersuchungen II*, part 2 (Halle: Max Niemeyer, 1901), 359ff. In the critical edition of Husserl's works, the latter can be found in *Husserliana: Gesammelte Werke* (The Hague: Martinus Nijhoff, 1950–2014) (hereafter abbreviated as Hua.), Vol. 19, ed. Ursula Panzer (The Hague: Martinus Nijhoff, 1984), 372ff.]

[17] The data of the various "senses" are not localized in the same way and therefore do not contribute to the composition of the living body in the same way.

I do not only see my hand and (bodily) perceive the same hand as sensing, but I also "see" the fields of sensation of the hand, which are constituted for me in bodily perception. And, on the other hand, when I highlight a part of my living body by observing it, I simultaneously have an "image" of the relevant body part. One is given, though not perceived, with the other. We have an exact analogue in the realm of external perception.

We do not only see the table and touch its hardness, but we also "see" its hardness. The garments in van Dyck's paintings are not only as *shiny* as silk, but also silky *smooth* and silky *soft*.

Psychologists call this phenomenon *fusion* [*Verschmelzung*] (italics in original) and usually reduce it to "mere" association. This "mere" reveals the psychologistic tendency to view explaining as explaining away—the tendency to position the explained phenomenon as a "subjectively produced formation" without "objective significance."

We cannot accept this opinion. A phenomenon remains a phenomenon. It is all very well if you can explain it, but the explanation adds nothing to it and takes nothing away from it. The visibility of tactile qualities would remain, and would lose nothing in value, if it could be explained by association. In any case, we do not think such an explanation is possible, because it contradicts the "phenomenon" of association. The typical form of association that we experience is "something reminds me of something."

Thus, for example, the sight of a table edge is associated with the memory that I once bumped into it. However, I do not remember the sharpness of this edge, but see it. To give a more instructive example: I *see* the hardness of sugar and know or remember that it is sweet; I do not remember (or I only remember incidentally) that it is hard, and I do not see that it is sweet. By contrast, the scent of a flower really is sweet and does not remind us of a sweet flavor.

This suggests possibilities for a phenomenology of the senses and sense perception, which, however, we cannot pursue here.

At this point, we are only interested in how the above applies to our case. The living body that we see does not remind us that it can be the site of multiple sensations. Nor is it just a physical body occupying the same space as the living body that is given as sensing in bodily perception. Rather, it is given as a sensing living body.

So far, we have only considered the living body at rest. We can now go a step further.

Let us imagine that I (i.e., my living body as a whole) move through space. As long as we disregarded the constitution of the living body, this phenomenon was not characterized in any particular way, and not distinguished from a kaleidoscopic shifting of the surrounding external world. Now we add, as something completely new, the lived experience of "I move"—the apperception of self-movement [*Eigenbewegung*]. This apperception is built on multiple sensations and is completely different from externally perceived movement of the physical body. The grasping of self-movement and the changes of the external world combine in the form of "if . . . then": "If I move, then the image of my surroundings shifts." This applies to the perception of individual spatial things just as much as it applies to the spatial world more broadly. It also applies just as much to movements of parts of the living body as it does to the whole living body.

If my hand rests on a rotating ball, then this ball and its movement are given to me in a series of changing tactile data. These merge into *one* intention running through it all, which can be consolidated in an "apperceptive grasp": a unified act of external perception. I have the same sequence of data if my hand glides over the resting ball, but the lived experience of "I move" is added to these data, and, with the apperception of the ball, enters that form of "if . . . then." Something analogous occurs with visual data. While standing still, I can become aware of the changing appearances of a rolling ball, and I can have the same sequence of "adumbrations of the ball" if the ball stands still and I move my head or even only my eyes (which, again, comes to givenness for me in "bodily perception"). That is how the parts of the living body are constituted as movable organs, and how perception of the spatial world is constituted as dependent on the behavior of these organs.

But that does not yet resolve how we get to conceiving of the movement of the living body as the movement of the physical body. If I move part of my living body, then besides the bodily awareness of self-movement, I have an external (visual or tactile) perception of a movement of the physical body, documented in changed appearances of the body part. And, since I conceive of the bodily perceived and the externally perceived body part as the same, an identifying correspondence between the movement of the living body and the movement of the physical body arises: the self-moving living body becomes the moved physical body. And, furthermore, the "I move" is "seen with [*mitgesehen*]" the movement of part of my physical body. The unseen movement of the physical body is grasped with [*miterfaßt*] the lived experience of "I move."

The confinement of the I to the sensing living body needs a little more clarification. The impossibility of shedding this living body points to its special givenness. This attachment cannot be shaken; the bonds that tie us to it cannot be dissolved. All the same, we have some freedom. All objects of the external world are given to me at a certain distance: they are always "there," while I am always "here"; they are grouped around me, around my "here." This grouping is not rigid or unalterable; the objects move closer to and farther away from me and from each other. I can also regroup them by shifting them closer or farther away or exchanging their places—or, instead, by altering my "here" instead of their "there," choosing another "standpoint." With each step forward a new little piece of the world is disclosed to me or manifests the old one to me from a new side. In the process I always take my living body with me. Not only I, but also it, is always "here," and the various "distances" of its parts from me are only variations within this *here*.

However, I can undertake, imagine, the "regrouping" of my surroundings "merely in thought" instead of in reality. For example, I can let the pieces of furniture of my room wander in my imagination and "imagine" how it would look.

Just as easily, I can wander through the world in my imagination. I can stand up from the desk "in thought," go into a corner of the room and observe from there. And when I do that, I do not take my living body with me. The I that stands there in the corner perhaps has a fantasy body, i.e., one—if I may say so—that is seen in "bodily fantasy [*Leibphantasie*]." Furthermore, it can look back at the living physical body at the desk, which it left, just like it can look at the other things in the room. That living physical body is also an object that has been made present [*vergegenwärtigt*], i.e., an object given in presenting [*vergegenwärtigender*] outer intuition.

And, finally, the real living body has not disappeared, but in fact I continue to sit at the desk, unseparated from my living body. Thus my I has been doubled,[18] and although the real I has not been separated from the living body, this still demonstrates the possibility of "going out of one's skin," at least in fantasy. There exists the possibility of an I without a living body.[19]

---

[18] I believe that the lived experience of the "doppelganger" can be understood on this basis. For example, in the famous poem by Heine, the poet wanders through the streets to his lover's house and sees himself standing in front of the house. This is a way of being given to oneself as doubled in memory or imagination. To what extent one has "oneself" in each case—more on that later. [The reference is to Heinrich Heine, "Die Heimkehr 1823–1824 XX," in *Historisch-kritische Gesamtausgabe der Werke*, Vol. 1, *Buch der Lieder*, ed. Manfred Windfuhr, with Pierre Grappin (Hamburg: Hoffmann und Campe, 1975), 230.

[19] Of course, it should be investigated what kind of I that could be, and whether a world could be given to it, and, if so, what sort of world.

By contrast, a living body without an I is simply impossible. To imagine my living body abandoned by the I means to imagine, not my living body, but a physical body resembling it trait by trait: my corpse. (When I leave my living body, it becomes a physical body for me like any other [physical object]. And if I think of it as leaving me—instead of my leaving it—then this leaving is not "moving oneself," but a simple movement of a physical body.) This can be shown in other ways. A "dead" limb, a limb without sensations, is not part of my living body. A foot that has "fallen asleep" hangs off me like a foreign body that I cannot dislodge, and lies outside the spatial zone of my living body, in which it is included again as soon as it "wakes up." Every movement that I perform with it in that state has the character "I move an object" (i.e., by my living movement I call forth a mechanical movement), and is not itself given as living bodily movement.

The living body is essentially constituted by sensations. Sensations are real components of consciousness and, as such, belong to the I. So how could a living body be possible that was not the living body of an I?[20] Another question is whether we could conceive of a sensing I without a living body, i.e., whether there could be sensations that did not constitute a living body. To me, the question cannot be quickly answered, because—as I already suggested—the sensations of the various sensory spheres are not involved in the composition of the living body in the same way.

We must therefore consider whether, in the case of sensations that are clearly experienced in particular parts of the living body (sensations of touch, temperature, pain), this localization belongs to them necessarily and inseparably. In that case, they would only be possible for a living bodily I. For sensations of sight and hearing etc., a further special analysis seems to be necessary. We do not need to decide these questions here. To do so, we would need a phenomenology of external perception. In any case, the unity of the I and the living body—if not the full scope of their reciprocal relationships—has already been established in our consideration of the sensations. We also encounter the causal relationship of the psychic and the physical in the realm of sensations. A purely physical process—a foreign body penetrating my skin, something bearing a certain amount of heat touching the surface of my physical body—becomes the phenomenal cause of sensations (sensations of pain, temperature), and proves to be a "stimulus." We will frequently encounter such phenomenal

[20] We should consider whether a consciousness that only exhibited sensory data and no acts of the I should be seen as lacking an I. In that case, we could speak of an "animated" living body, but one without an I. But I do not believe such an opinion is tenable.

causal relationships ("conditional" relationships, in Husserl's terms) as we further pursue the connections between the mind and the living body.

[...]

c. Mind and Living Body, Psychophysical Causality

This dependence of lived experience on the influences of the living body is an essential characteristic of the mental realm. Everything psychic is consciousness bound to the body. Within this realm, lived experiences that are essentially psychic (sensations that are bound to the body, etc.) are distinct from those that have a psychic character only inessentially: the "realizations" of mental life.[21] The mind, as the substantial unity that is manifested in individual psychic lived experiences—as shown by the phenomenon of "psychophysical causality" described above and by the essence of sensations—is based on the living body, and forms with this living body the "psychophysical individual."

Now we must consider the character of the so-called "intellectual feelings." This label already tells us that these are seen as inessentially psychic, as not bound to the body (even if certain psychologists may not like to acknowledge this corollary). And no one who brings the pure essence of these feelings to givenness would claim that a bodiless subject would be unable to experience joy, sorrow, or aesthetic values.

In contrast to this, many prestigious psychologists see "complexes of organ sensations" in feelings. As absurd as this definition seems if one considers feelings in their pure essence, in a concrete psychic context we do find phenomena that, although they do not justify this definition, do make it comprehensible.

"Our heart stands still" for joy, it "tenses up" with pain, it pounds from fearful anticipation, and our breath falters. We can pile up the examples, but they all deal with cases of psychophysical causality, i.e., with effects that the psychic realization of lived experience exerts on bodily functions. If one imagines away the living body, these phenomena disappear, but the mental acts remain. For example, you have to admit that God rejoices over a sinner's repentance without having heartbeats or other "organ sensations." (This reflection is possible whether or not you believe in the existence of God.) You can be convinced that in reality no feeling is possible without such sensations, and that no being exists that experiences feelings purely.

---

[21] The deliberations below will provide greater clarity on this point.

However, these feelings are *comprehensible* as pure, and their accompanying [physical] effects are experienced as such, and not as feelings or components of feelings.

The same thing can be shown in cases of pure psychic causality. My "wits stand still" from shock (i.e., I sense a paralyzing effect on my thinking), or I am "distracted" with joy, do not know what I am doing, perform pointless actions. A pure spirit can also be frightened, but its wits do not stand still. It feels joy and suffering in all their depth, but they exert no effects.

I can take these reflections further. "Observing" myself, I also discover causal relationships between my lived experiences and the capacities and properties of my mind that are manifested in them. These capacities can be cultivated and sharpened by activity or depleted and blunted.

Thus my "power of observation" grows if I work in natural science. My "faculty of discrimination," for example for colors, grows if I busy myself with sorting threads of finely graded shades of color. My "capacity for pleasure" grows if I focus my life on pleasure. Every capacity can be increased by "training." On the other hand, there is a certain degree of "habituation," where things move in the opposite direction. For example, an "object of pleasure" which is served to me again and again will be "done" for me; eventually it will arouse aversion and disgust and so on.

In all these cases, the psychic realm has an effect on physical matters, in phenomenal terms. But the question is what kind of "effect" is present here, and whether it is possible to derive an exact scientific concept of causality and general causal lawfulness from this phenomenon of causality. Rigorous natural science is based on this concept, while descriptive science only deals with the phenomenal concept of causality. But a rigorous concept of causality and uninterrupted causal determination is also a presupposition of rigorous causal-genetic psychology, which attempts to follow the model of the modern science of physical nature. In our context, we must content ourselves with pointing out these problems, without being able to work toward solving them.

d. The Phenomenon of Expression

Our consideration of the causal effects of feelings has taken us further than we anticipated. However, we have not exhausted what we can learn from the study of feelings. In addition to the accompanying effects of feelings, which we have already considered, a new phenomenon emerges: the expression of feelings.

I blush with shame, I angrily clench my fist, I furrow my brow in frustration, I moan with pain, I cheer for joy.

The relationship between feeling and expression is completely different from the relationship between feeling and the accompanying physical effects. I do not notice physical lived experiences following causally from psychic ones; far less do I notice the two merely occurring simultaneously. Instead, when I live through a feeling, I feel that it ends in an expression, or releases this expression from itself.[22]

In its pure essence, feeling is not closed off in itself; instead, it is, as it were, loaded with energy that must be discharged. This discharging is possible in various ways. One way of discharging is well known to us: feelings release or motivate acts of will and actions. Exactly the same relationship exists between feeling and the appearance of an expression [Ausdruckserscheinung]. The same feeling that motivates an act of will can also motivate the appearance of an expression. And, depending on its meaning, the feeling dictates which expression and which act of will it can motivate.[23] By nature the feeling must always motivate something, it must always be "expressed;" but various forms of expression are possible.

Here one may object that very often in life feelings occur without motivating an act of the will or a bodily expression.

We "civilized people" must famously "control" ourselves to restrain the bodily expression of our feelings. We are similarly constricted in our actions

---

[22] To prevent misunderstandings, I emphasize that I take "expression" in the sense used above to be fundamentally different from verbal expressions. I cannot explain the distinction at this point. However, in order to avoid confusion due to the equivocation, I would like to call attention to it from the outset.

[23] We do not need to discuss here the question if expressive movements [should be seen] as actions, whether originally purposive—as Darwin thinks—or involuntary and purposeless—as [Ludwig] Klages suggests ("Die Ausdrucksbewegung und ihre diagnostische Verwertung," [Zeitschrift für Pathopsychologie (1914):] 293 [Reprinted in Ludwig Klages, Sämtliche Werke, 2nd ed. (hereafter abbreviated as SW), Vol. 6, ed. Ernst Frauchinger, Gerhard Funke, Karl J. Groffmann, Robert Heiss, and Hans Eggert Schröder (Bonn: Bouvier, 2000), 57–137]). In any case, Klages also emphasizes the close connection between phenomena of expression and action. According to Klages, all naive doing and accomplishing proceeds just as easily and involuntarily from lived experience as expressive movements do, and he thinks this compulsive form of action is the original one, which is only gradually supplanted by voluntary actions (336; SW, Vol. 6, 126f). In his famous treatise The Expression of the Emotions, Darwin gives a description, based on careful observation, of bodily phenomena corresponding to certain affects, and attempts to expose the psychophysical mechanism by which these bodily processes come about. He neither considers the descriptive difference between expressions and their accompanying effects nor seriously questions what makes these processes an expression of the affect that elicits them.

and our acts of will. Now, there is certainly the option of "letting off steam" in a wish. An employee who does not dare show their superior that they think he is a jerk or an idiot by giving him scornful glances, and who cannot get rid of him, can still secretly wish him to the devil.

Or one can carry out actions in fantasy that one is prevented from in reality. The thirst for action of someone born in restricted circumstances, which cannot be fulfilled in reality, is lived out by surviving battles and accomplishing miracles of bravery in their imagination. The creation of another world in which I can do what is forbidden to me here is itself a form of expression.

Thus—as Gebsattel relates[24]—someone dying of thirst in the desert sees oases with bubbling springs or lakes, which revive them. When joy fills us, it does not linger in tranquil devotion to the gratifying object, but is expressed, among other things, in the fact that we completely surround ourselves with what gratifies us. We seek it in our real environment or obtain it by making it present in memory or our free imagination, ignoring everything that does not fit with it, until our state of mind perfectly harmonizes with our environment.

This unique kind of expression requires a full explanation. It is not enough—as usually occurs in psychology—to say that feelings influence the "reproduction of representations" and how frequently that occurs. Another kind of expression exists, or a surrogate for expression, and this is what a "self-controlled" person falls back on, someone who adopts a smooth facial expression due to social or aesthetic or ethical considerations. A feeling can release an act of reflection which makes itself into its own object. The lived experience "ends" in this act of reflection, just like it ends in an act of will or a bodily expression. It is often said that reflection weakens feeling and that a reflective person is not capable of intense feelings. This inference is completely unjustified. Feeling can "end" in a "passionate" expression of feeling as well as in "cool" reflection; the kind of expression says nothing about the intensity of the feeling that is expressed.

The outcome of our considerations up to this point is: by nature, feeling needs to be expressed, and the various kinds of expression are various essential possibilities for this.[25] Feeling and expression are connected by essence

---

[24] [Viktor Emil Klemens Franz Freiherr von Gebsattel, *Zur Psychologie der Gefühlsirradiation* (Leipzig: Engelmann, 1907),] 57f.

[25] Jonas Cohn uses the term "expression" in another, broader sense (*Ästhetik*, 56), namely, for everything "external" in which we glimpse an inner life. But this lacks the thing that we think is

and meaning [*Sinn*], not causality. And, like the other possible forms of expression, bodily expression emerges from feeling, and is experienced as determined by it according to its meanings [*Sinne*]. However, I not only feel how feeling pours into expression and is discharged in it, but at the same time this expression is also given to me in bodily perception.

The smile by which I express my joy experientially is given to me at the same time as a distortion of my lips. In experiencing [*leben*] joy, the expression of joy in the mode of actuality is also experienced. The simultaneous bodily perception occurs in the mode of inactuality: I am not conscious of it. But if I direct my attention to the perceived change in my living body, then it seems to be caused by feeling.

Therefore, in addition to the experienced unity of meaning [*Sinneseinheit*], there is a causal connection between feeling and expression. The expression uses psychophysical causality to realize itself in a psychophysical individual. In bodily perception, the experienced unity of lived experience and expression is broken up, the expression separated off as a relatively independent phenomenon.

As a result, the expression can be generated on its own. I can cause a distortion of my mouth that is similar to a smile, to the point of "being confused with" it, but which is not a smile.

Similar perceptual phenomena can also emerge as different phenomena of expression independently of the will. I blush from anger, from shame, and from exertion; in all these cases I have the same perception that my "blood rises to my face." But I experience the same process in one case as an expression of anger, in one case as an expression of shame, and in one case not as an expression at all, but as a causal consequence of exertion.

We said an attentive gaze would be needed in order to make an intentional object (in the full sense) out of a bodily perceived expression. Even a felt expression, although experienced in the mode of actuality, still needs a special shifting of the gaze in order to become a grasped object—a shifting of the gaze that is not a transition from inactuality to actuality. This is a peculiarity of all non-theoretical acts and their correlates.[26]

---

specific to expression: its motivatedness. [The full reference is: Jonas Cohn, *Allgemeine Ästhetik* (Leipzig: Engelmann, 1901), 56.]

[26] Cf. Husserl, *Ideen*, 66. [The full reference is Edmund Husserl, "Ideen zu einer reinen Phänomenologie und phänomenologischen Philosophie," *Jahrbuch für Philosophie und phänomenologische Forschung* 1, no. 1 (1913): 66. In the critical edition, this reference is to Hua., Vol. 3, ed. Marly Biemel, Walter Biemel, and Karl Schuhmann (The Hague: Martinus Nijhoff, 1950), 82).]

Being able to objectify the phenomena of expression that are experienced and grasp them *as expressions* is a further condition of possibility for producing these expressions voluntarily. However, a bodily change that resembles an expression is not given in the same way as an expression. Furrowing the brow from anger and furrowing the brow to feign anger are clearly distinguishable, even if I move from bodily perception to external perception. When phenomena of expression appear as outpourings of feelings, they are simultaneously expressions of the mental properties manifested in them. For example, a furious gaze betrays a fierce temper.

[...]

The Transition to the Other Individual

We have given an account, at least in outline, of how we should understand an individual I, or an individual: it is a unified object in which the conscious unity of an I and a physical body are inseparably joined, so that each of them adopts a new character. The physical body emerges as a living body; consciousness emerges as the mind of the unified individual. This unity is shown by the fact that certain processes (sensations, general feelings) are given as belonging simultaneously to the mind and to the living body. It is also shown in the causal connection of physical and psychic processes and the causal relationship this mediates between the mind and the real external world. The psychophysical individual as a whole is a part of the nexus of nature.

The living body, as opposed to the physical body, is characterized by the fact that it is the bearer of fields of sensation. It is located at the zero point of orientation of the spatial world, is freely mobile and composed of mobile organs, and is the field of expression of the lived experiences of the I that belongs to it and the instrument of its will.[27] We have gleaned all these

---

[27] It may seem noteworthy that we have not mentioned the concept that tends to be foremost in other definitions of the individual or the organism: the concept of *purpose*. This is not in order to avoid burdening my account with the discussion of the concept of purpose, but for material reasons: I do not believe that one can speak of an *immediately experienced* subordination of a psychophysical event to a unified purpose. The concept of purpose is also not at issue in the empathic grasping of another individual.

characteristics from observing our own individuality. Now we must show how the other's[28] individuality is composed for us.

a. The Fields of Sensation of the Other's Living Body

Let us begin by considering what allows the other's living body to be conceived as a living body, what singles it out from other physical bodies. First, therefore: how are fields of sensation given to us? As we have seen, our own fields of sensation are given to us originarily [*originäre Gegebenheit*] in "bodily perception." Furthermore, they are "co-given" to us in our external perception of our physical body, in that entirely unique way in which things that are not perceived can be there with the things that are perceived. The fields of sensation of others are there for me in the same way: the other's living body is "seen" as a living body. We are faced by this kind of givenness, which we will call *con-originarity* [*Konoriginarität*] in the way that we perceive things.

The averted sides and the inside of a spatial thing are co-given with the sides that are seen. In short: the whole thing is "seen." But (as we have seen) each givenness from one side includes tendencies to move on to new givennesses. If I fulfill these tendencies, then I perceive the previously averted sides in a full sense: what was previously given con-originarily is now given originarily. Such a fulfillment of what is intended or anticipated is also possible in "co-seeing" one's own fields of sensation, except this occurs, not in progressive external perception, but in the transition from external perception to bodily perception.

The co-seeing of others' fields of sensation also includes these kinds of tendencies, but, in principle, they cannot be fulfilled originarily. I cannot bring them to originary givenness, either in progressive external perception or in the transition to bodily perception. The only fulfillment possible is an empathic making-present. I can bring those fields of sensation to givenness, make them visible to myself, in another way apart from empty representations, that is, in con-originarity—not with the character of perception, but by making present [. . .]. These fields of sensation owe their

---

[28] [The German term *fremd* means "foreign," "alien," "strange," or "other," and can refer to another person or to anything that is not one's own. The term is often translated as "foreign" in the context in which Stein is using it here, i.e., to refer to another person and their experience. For this volume, *fremd* is generally translated as "other" (and occasionally "other person"), despite the fact that this loses the distinction with the word *andere* ("other"), which Stein also uses to refer to other individuals.]

character of being "there themselves" to the physical body with which they are given in person. This will become clearer when we observe actual sensations themselves, instead of fields of sensation.

A hand resting on a table does not just lie there like the book beside it. It "presses" against the table (more or less strongly), it lies there limply or stretched out, and I "see" this sensation of pressure and tension in a con-originary way. If I fulfill the tendencies that lie in this "co-grasping," then my hand (not really, but only "so to speak") slides into the place of the other's hand. It slides into this hand, occupies its place and posture, and senses its sensations—not originarily and not as its own, but "with it." This occurs in exactly the same way as empathy, the essence of which we defined earlier in contrast to one's own lived experience and every other kind of making-present. During this projecting of oneself, the other's hand is constantly perceived as part of the other's physical body, while my own hand is given as part of my own living body, so that the empathized sensations constantly contrast, as other, with my own (even if I am not paying attention to this contrast).

b. The Conditions of Possibility of Sensory Empathy

The possibility of sensory empathy (or, more precisely, "sensing-in" [*Einempfindung*]) is ensured by: the conception of one's own living body as a physical body and of one's own physical body as a living body; the fusion of external and bodily perception;[29] the possible change of position of this physical body in space; and, finally, the possibility of modifying the real attributes of this body in the imagination while retaining its type.

If the size (length, breadth, span, etc.) of my hand were given to me as immutably fixed, then attempting to empathize with a hand that had other attributes would fail due to their differences. However, in fact empathy succeeds very well even with men's and children's hands, which are very different from mine. My physical body and its limbs are not given as a fixed type, but as an accidental realization of a type that can vary within firm boundaries. On the other hand, the type must be retained. I can only empathize with physical bodies of this type, only grasp these as living bodies. However, this does not delimit things unambiguously.

There are types that have various levels of generality, and various levels of possibility for empathy correspond to these. The type "physical human

---

[29] It would perhaps be possible to arrive at a genetic explanation of empathy from the phenomenon of fusion. But you must draw on your own lived experience, and not simply talk about fusing the other's exterior with your own lived experience.

body" does not delimit the realm of possible objects of my empathy (more precisely speaking: of what can be given to me as a living body), but rather a realm within which a certain degree of empathic fulfillment is possible.

In the case of empathy with another person's hand [*Einfühlung in die fremde Hand*], there exists the possibility of extensive, if not "adequate," fulfillment: what I sense non-originarily can correspond trait by trait with the other person's originary sensing. If, by comparison, I consider a dog's paw, for instance, then I also have something that is not just a physical thing but a sensing part of a living body. Here, too, a certain sort of projection is possible, for example a sensing-in [*Einempfinden*] of pain, if the animal is injured. But other things—certain postures and movements, for instance—are given to us only as empty representations, without the possibility of fulfillment.

The further we go from the type "human," the smaller are the number of possibilities for fulfillment. The conception of other living bodies as belonging to the same type as mine makes good sense of the language of "analogizing" that is present in grasping someone else. This analogizing has nothing to do with "analogical conclusions."

There are topics here that should be investigated. But we must content ourselves with what we have said above as an indication of the "transcendental" questions that arise, without being able to get into a more detailed discussion.

c. The Outcome of Sensory Empathy and Its Absence in the Available Literature on Empathy

At the end of the process of empathy, in our case and in general, there is a new objectivation. As a result, just like at the beginning, we are confronted by the "sensing hand." (It is present the whole time, in contrast to progression in external perception, but we are not always paying attention to it.) But what we are confronted with now has a new dignity, because what was previously represented as empty is now filled. An other I is already given to us with the constitution of the stratum of sensation of the other's physical body (which, strictly speaking, we may no longer call a "physical body"). This is the case even if it is not necessarily an "awake" I that can be conscious of itself, because sensations essentially belong to an I. Until now, this basic stratum of the constitution [of the individual] has always been neglected (as we already noted).

Volkelt occasionally deals with "sensing-in," but he characterizes it cursorily as the reproduction of sensation, without investigating its unique essence, and does not consider its significance for constituting the individual.

Rather, he only considers it as a means for bringing about the only thing that he calls empathy, i.e., empathy for feelings and especially for moods. He does not want to call sensing-in empathy, because if empathy stopped with sensations it would be "something downright miserable and lamentable."[30] We do not think that about empathy at all; but on the other hand, after our discussion above, we also cannot value sensations as little as Volkelt does. And, finally, emotional motives should not cause us to separate things that essentially belong together. The grasping of others' lived experiences—whether these are sensations, feelings, or whatever—is a unified, typical (if also multifariously differentiated) modification of consciousness and requires a unified name. We have chosen the term "empathy," which is already commonly used for part of the phenomenon in question. If someone wants to reserve this term for this more limited area, then they must coin a new expression for the broader area.

Lipps contrasts sensations with feelings when he says: When I see a person who is freezing, I do not see the sensation of cold, but the discomfort they feel. The realization that this discomfort is aroused by sensations is only the outcome of reflection. We understand how Lipps arrives at this claim: it is the consequence of his one-sided attitude toward the "symbol," the phenomenon of "expression." To Lipps, only lived experiences expressed by a facial expression, gesture, or suchlike are given "visibly," or intuitively. And, in fact, sensations are not expressed. But to say that they are therefore not given to us directly at all, but only as foundational substrata of emotional states, is a strong claim.

Anyone who does not see in someone else's "goose-flesh" or their blue-frozen nose that they are freezing, but must first think that the discomfort this person feels must be a "chill," must be suffering from strange conceptual anomalies. After all, uncomfortable shivering does not need to be based on sensations of cold at all, but can also emerge, for example, as the accompanying physical effect of a state of excitement. On the other hand, I can very well "freeze without freezing," i.e., have sensations of cold without feeling in the least uncomfortable. Our knowledge of others' sensations would therefore be in bad shape if we could only arrive at them by a detour via the emotional states that are based on them.

---

[30] [Johannes Volkelt, "Die Bedeutung der niederen Empfindungen für die ästhetische Einfühlung," *Zeitschrift für Psychologie und Physiologie der Sinnesorgane* 25 (1901): 10.]

d. The Other's Living Body as a Center of Orientation for the Spatial World

We come to the second constituent of the living body: its position at the zero point of orientation. This constituent cannot be separated from the givenness of the external spatial world. As a merely physical body, the physical body of another individual is given as a spatial thing like other spatial things. It is also given at a specific place in space, at a specific distance from me (the center of spatial orientation), and in specific spatial relationships to the rest of the spatial world. Now, when I conceive of the other's body as a living body of sensation and transfer myself empathically into it, I gain a new image[31] of the spatial world and a new zero point of orientation. It is not that I relocate my zero point there, for I retain my "originary" zero point and my "originary" orientation, while I gain the other empathically, non-originarily. On the other hand, I am not gaining a fantasy-orientation, a fantasy-image of the spatial world. Instead, it has con-originariness, like empathized sensations. This is because the living body that it relates to is simultaneously a perceived physical body, and also because this orientation is given as originary for the other I, although not originarily for me.

With this orientation we have moved a vast step forward in constituting the other individual. This is because, by doing so, the whole fullness of external perceptions in which the spatial world is essentially constituted is empathized in the I that belongs to the sensing living body. A subject that has sensations has become one that carries out actions. And, with that, all the determinations are applied to it that arise from immanently considering the essence of the consciousness of perception.[32] We can also apply to this orientation claims about the various essential possible modalities of implementing actions, about the actuality and inactuality of acts of perception and of what is perceived. The externally perceiving I can, in principle, perceive in the way the *cogito* does, i.e., in the mode of "being directed" specifically at an object. With that, the possibility is given of reflecting upon the completed act. Which form of implementation is present each time is, of course, not preordained by the empathy of a perceiving consciousness in general; rather, specific indications are needed on a case-by-case basis. But the essential possibilities present in individual cases are determined a priori.

---

[31] The term "image" gives a poor image of the conception of the spatial world, for what we have is not an image that presents the world to us, but this world itself, seen from one side.

[32] Cf. the analyses in Husserl, *Ideen*, 48f., 60ff. [Hua., Vol. 3, 57f., 74ff.].

e. The Other's Worldview as a Modification of One's Own

The worldview that I empathize in the other is not only a modification of mine on the basis of the other's different orientation, but also varies with how I conceive of the attributes of their living body. For a person without eyes, the world's entire optical givenness is lost. Of course, there is a [visual] view of the world that corresponds to this person's orientation, but if I ascribed it to them I would be suffering from a crude deception of empathy. The world is constituted for this person only by their other senses, and, due to my lifelong habits of visual perception and thought, it may be impossible for me to obtain an empathic fulfillment of their world as it is given in empty representations. But these empty representations and the lack of visual fulfillment are given to me. This applies even more to the empathy of those who do not have all of their senses than to those who do have all of their senses.

This shows the possibility of enriching one's own worldview through another's; it shows the significance of empathy for experiencing the real external world. This significance is also noticeable in another respect.

f. Empathy as Condition of Possibility for Constituting One's Own Individuality

From the zero point of orientation that is gained through empathy, I must consider my own zero point as one spatial point among many, no longer as the zero point. And by this—and only by this—I learn to see my living body as a physical body like others. In originary experience, by contrast, it is only given to me as a living body and, in addition, (in external perception) as an incomplete physical body that is different from all other physical bodies.

In "iterated empathy" I again conceive of that physical body as a living body. In this way I am first given to myself as a psychophysical individual in the full sense, for which being based on a physical body is constitutive. This iterated empathy is also the condition of possibility for that mirror-image-like givenness of myself in memory and imagination (and presumably also for the conception of a mirror image itself, which we will not get into here), which we have often run into. As long as only one zero point is given to me, and my physical body [is] in this zero point, the possibility certainly exists of displacing my zero point, together with my physical body. There also exists the possibility of displacing the zero point in my imagination, which then conflicts with the real zero point and the orientation that belongs to it (as we saw, this possibility is the condition of possibility for empathy). But it is not possible to freely look at myself like I look at another physical body. If I glimpse myself in a childhood memory on the top of a tree or, fantasizing, on the banks of the Bosphorus, then I see myself as another [person], or as another [person] sees me. And that makes empathy possible for me.

But its significance extends further.

g. The Constitution of the Real External World
in Intersubjective Experience

Due to its conflict with my originary orientation, the world I glimpse in imagination is a world of nonbeing (although I do not have to bring this not-existence to givenness for myself while I am living in my imagination). [By contrast,] the world I glimpse empathically is an existing world that is posited as being, like the originarily perceived world. The perceived world and the world given by empathy are the same world, seen differently. But not just the same world seen from different sides, as when in originary perception I run through continuous manifolds of appearance, passing from one standpoint to the other, of which every earlier one motivates a later one, every subsequent one supersedes the preceding one.

The transition from my standpoint to the other's is, admittedly, carried out in the same way, but the new standpoint does not replace the old one; rather, I hold onto both simultaneously. The same world is not presented now in one way and then in another, but simultaneously in both ways. And it is not only presented differently depending on the respective standpoints, but also depending on the attributes of the observer. As a result, the *appearance* of the world proves to be dependent on individual consciousness, but the *world* that is appearing—which remains the same however and to whomever it appears—is independent of consciousness. [If I were] confined within the limits of my individuality, I could never get beyond "the world as it appears to me." It would then be conceivable that the possibility of the independent existence of the world (which could still be given as a possibility) would always remain unproven. But as soon as I step outside these limits with the help of empathy and arrive at a second and third appearance of the same world that is independent of my perception, that possibility is proven. Thus empathy, as the foundation of intersubjective experience, becomes the condition of possibility for the cognition of the existing external world, as Husserl[33] and, similarly, Royce[34] claim.

[...]

h. The Other's Living Body as the Bearer of Free Movement

We have come to know the other's living body as a bearer of fields of sensation and as an orientation center of the spatial world, and now we find a further constituent in its free mobility. The movements of an individual are not given to us as mere mechanical movements. There are certainly cases of this sort—just as there are with one's own movements. If I take hold of one hand with the other and lift it up, then the movement of the raised hand is given to me as mechanical, just as much as the movement of a physical body that I lift. The concurrent sensations constitute the consciousness of the change of position of a part of my body, but not the lived experience of "I move."

By contrast, I have this lived experience in the moving hand, of both its self-movement and its communication with the other hand. When this self-movement is externally perceived at the same time and both movements are conceived as the same (as we stated earlier), it is "seen" as self-movement.

The difference between "living" and "mechanical" movement intersects here with that of "self-movement" and "co-movement." The one cannot somehow be reduced to the other. This is shown, for a start, by the fact that each "living" movement is, at the same time, also a mechanical movement.

On the other hand, self-movement is not given *as* living self-movement, because there is also mechanical self-movement. If a rolling ball hits another during its movement and "takes it along with it," then we have the phenomenon of mechanical self-movement and co-movement.

Now, the question is whether there is also such a thing as living co-movement. I believe that this must be denied.

If I travel through a landscape on a train or am pushed along on an ice rink without myself performing sliding movements, the movement seems to me (if we disregard everything that is not co-movement) only to be given in the change of appearances of my spatial surroundings. It can be conceived just

---

[33] Cf. *Ideen*, 279 and 317 [Hua., Vol. 3, 329, 372f.].

[34] Cf. [Josiah Royce,] "Self-consciousness, Social Consciousness and Nature," [*Philosophical Review* 4, no. 5 (1895): 465–485; and 4, no. 6 (1895): 577–602].

as easily as movement of the landscape as it can be conceived as movement of my physical body. Hence the famous "optical illusion": the trees and telegraph poles flying past; the stage trick that simulates traveling along a path by moving the curtains, etc.

Co-movement can therefore only be conceived as mechanical, not as living. Every living movement thus seems to be self-movement. However, "communicated" movement must be distinguished from co-movement.

If a rolling ball does not "take" a resting one "with" it, but by its impact "confers" its own movement on it (perhaps coming to a standstill itself), then we have the phenomenon of communicated mechanical movement. Now, such a communicated movement cannot only be perceived as mechanical, but also experienced as living. However, it is experienced not as "I move" but as "being moved." If I am pushed and fall over or if I am hurled down a slope, then I experience the movement as living, only not as "active" (that is, as proceeding from an "impulse") but as communicated, as "passive."

In relation to others' movements [*fremden Bewegungen*], we find differences analogous to those we find in one's own movements. If I see someone travel past in a car, then their movement seems to me not to be different in principle from the "resting" parts of the car. It is mechanical co-movement, which I perceive externally, and with which I do not empathize. We should absolutely distinguish that, of course, from this person's conception of this movement, which I make present empathically when I transfer myself into their orientation. It is totally different with movement that a person performs, for example if they get up inside the car. I "see" a movement of the same type as my own self-movement; I conceive it as self-movement; I follow the tendency of the "co-perceived" self-movement to be fulfilled when I participate in it empathically, in the way we have already learned about; and, finally, I carry out the objectification in which it confronts me as a movement of the other individual.

In this way, the other's living body with its organs is given to me as movable. And free mobility is closely linked with the other constituents of the individual. We must *conceive* this physical body *as an already living body in order to empathize living movement in it*; we will never conceive of the self-movement of a physical body as living movement. (Even if, perhaps, we illustrate its difference from communicated movement or co-movement through quasi-empathy, for example when we "inwardly participate" in the movement of balls that are struck and striking each other.) The other aspects of the balls' character prohibit us from attributing to them living movements that are made present.[35] By contrast, rigid immobility conflicts with the phenomenon of the sensing living body and the living organism in general.[36]

The idea of a completely immobile living being cannot be realized; being held fast, motionless, in one place means "turning to stone." Spatial orientation is completely inseparable from free mobility. For a start, with the cessation of self-movement the varieties of perception would become so limited that the constitution of a spatial world (even an individual one) would be put in question. Then the possibility of transference into the other's living body, and with that a fulfilled empathy and acquisition of their orientation, would end. Free movement is therefore completely, irremovably part of the composition of the individual.

i. Phenomena of Life

We must now consider a group of phenomena that participate in the composition of the individual in a particular way, insofar as they appear in the living body and also as mental lived experiences. I might call them the specific phenomena of life. [These include] growth, development and aging, health and illness, freshness and dullness (general feelings, as we said, or the manner and way "of feeling in one's body [Leibe]," as Scheler often says), living and dying.

[...]

In considering general feelings in one's own lived experience, we saw how they "fill" the living body and mind, and lend a certain coloration to every mental act as well as to every bodily process. And we saw how they are then—in the same way as fields of sensation—"co-seen" in the living body. We also "see" in a person's gait and posture, in their every movement, their "way of feeling," their freshness, dullness, and so on, and we fulfill this co-intended lived experience of the other when we empathically carry it out with them.

We see such freshness and dullness not only in people and animals, but also in plants. And here, too, we have the possibility of empathic fulfillment. Admittedly, in this case I am grasping a considerable modification of my own life. The general feeling of a plant does not appear as a coloration of its acts, for there is no indication that such acts are present. I therefore have no

---

[35] Because every living body is at the same time a physical body, and every living movement at the same time mechanical, it is possible to consider physical bodies and their movements "as if" they were living bodies. Empathizing movement in physical bodies plays a large role in the literature on aesthetic empathy.

[36] Even if plants do not have the free movement of animals, the phenomenon of growth is still essential to them, and that includes movement that is not mere mechanical movement. In this we can include turning toward the light and other living movements that they perform.

right to ascribe to the plant an "awake" I and a reflective consciousness of its feelings of life [*Lebensgefühle*]. Furthermore, the other constituents of animal being that are known to us are missing. It is at least doubtful whether a plant has sensations,[37] and empathy is therefore unwarranted if we think we are inflicting pain on a tree that we are cutting down with an axe. A plant is also not an orientation center of the spatial world and is also not freely mobile, although—in contrast to everything inorganic—it is capable of living movement. On the other hand, the lack of these constituents does not justify us in also reinterpreting those constituents that are present and distinguishing botanical life-phenomena from our own. I will leave aside the question of whether we should view phenomena of life as essentially psychic or only as an essential foundation for psychic existence.[38] That they have the character of lived experience in a psychic context can hardly be contested. [...]

[37] Certain phenomena almost indicate sensitivity to light and possibly a certain sensitivity to touch, but I do not want to make a decision about this.

[38] Then these phenomena would also be conceivable as non-psychological, and plants would be conceivable as mindless living beings.

9

Gerda Walther (1897–1977)

Introduction

Gerda Walther (1897–1977) draws on social theory and socialist thought in order to investigate phenomenological questions and concerns. This interdisciplinary focus and approach distinguishes Walther from other early phenomenologists, and sheds important light on the (underexplored) bridge between socialist philosophers and the phenomenological movement. As such, Walther's contributions invite new philosophical insights and a more balanced understanding of the intellectual history of the long nineteenth century.

Walther was born in the Black Forest in a tuberculosis sanatorium founded and directed by her father, Otto Walther.[1] Otto Walther was a well-known social democrat, who was forced out of Frankfurt in the 1880s due to his political activities. This, however, did not prevent him from giving his daughter a political education. From early on, she read the works of Hegel, Marx, and Engels. In 1914, while still attending gymnasium (high school), she became an active member of the youth group of the Munich Social Democratic Party. Two years later, when she enrolled at the University of Munich, Walther's goal was to study economics, politics, and sociology with Max Weber and Walther Lotz. She was, however, quickly dissatisfied with the courses on offer: none, she complained to her father, engaged with Marxist political thought or historical materialism. Still, she did not drop out but followed the advice of her father, who convinced her that it was necessary for a socialist to become familiar with other perspectives.

Her attitude toward the University of Munich shifted after she enrolled in a course titled "Introduction to Psychology," taught by the philosopher Alexander Pfänder (1870–1941). Pfänder was a founder of the Munich Phenomenological Circle and the author of one of the first books of the

---

[1] Linda Lopez McAlister, "Gerda Walter," in *A History of Women Philosophers,* Vol. 4, *Contemporary Women Philosophers, 1900-Today*, ed. Mary Ellen Waithe (Dordrecht: Kluwer, 1995), 189–206.

emerging phenomenological movement (*Phänomenologie des Wollens. Eine psychologische Analyse* [1900]). In his works, Pfänder sought to provide detailed analyses of sentiments (*Gesinnungen*), such as love, friendship, and the feeling of "inner union." Over the next few semesters, Walther attended other courses offered by Pfänder, such as logic, epistemology, and the history of philosophy. She also participated in the meetings of the Munich Phenomenological Circle. Other participants included Max Scheler, Moritz Geiger, Theodor Conrad, and Hedwig Conrad-Martius.[2] In this period, Walther became familiar with the work of Edmund Husserl, including his *Logical Investigations* (1900–1901) and *Ideas I* (1913). This prompted her to transfer to Freiburg in 1917 to study with Husserl.

Husserl was at first hesitant to take Walther as a student—in part because of her political interests. For this reason, he asked his assistant, Edith Stein, to appraise her. Stein's impression of Walther was positive, and Walther was admitted in her first semester at Freiburg to both Stein's introductory course in philosophy (which was known as the "philosophy kindergarten") and Husserl's courses. Walther chose, however, not to write her dissertation with Husserl, and she returned to Munich to work with Pfänder. There were at least two reasons for this. The first is that Husserl did not give his students much freedom in terms of their dissertation topic; Walther, however, was determined to write about social communities.[3] The second reason has to do with her philosophical disagreements with Husserl, some of which she had already expressed in a keynote address in 1918.[4] In that context, Walther argued that Husserl's methodology, which involves bracketing everything that is empirical, can only offer an empty, general, and formal conception of the self. Martin Heidegger, who attended Walther's lecture, regarded this as a crucial critique of Husserl.[5]

---

[2] Alessandro Salice, "The Phenomenology of the Munich and Göttingen Circles," *Stanford Encyclopedia of Philosophy* (Winter 2019), ed. Edward N. Zalta, https://plato.stanford.edu/archives/win2019/entries/phenomenology-mg/.

[3] In her autobiography, Walther also expresses her disagreement with the way Husserl treated his students. As she recounts, Husserl's first impression of her was that, given her political interests, she would not be of any "use" to him. She immediately challenges his view, saying that she should not be of use to him, but he—as her teacher—of use to her. See Gerda Walther, *Zum anderen Ufer. Vom Marxismus und Atheismus zum Christentum* (St. Goar: Reichl Verlag, 1960), 203; see also McAlister, "Gerda Walther."

[4] Walther gave this lecture at the inaugural meeting of the Freiburg Society of Phenomenology. See Rodney Parker, "Gerda Walther and the Phenomenological Community," *Acta Mexicana de Fenomenología* 2 (2017): 45–66, here 49. In her autobiography, Walther provides a detailed discussion of her education in phenomenology, first with Pfänder, then with Stein and Husserl, and then again with Pfänder. See Walther, *Zum anderen Ufer*, 196–220.

[5] Parker, "Gerda Walther and the Phenomenological Community," 50.

In 1922, Walther moved to Heidelberg to work on a habilitation (the degree necessary for an academic position in Germany) with Karl Jaspers.[6] However, due to economic hardships, she was forced to leave Heidelberg at the end of 1923. After a short stint with relatives in Copenhagen, Walther returned to Germany and supported herself with occasional work while pursuing her scholarship on the side. In the end, she did not complete her habilitation.

In 1923, Walther published *The Phenomenology of Mysticism*, where she offers a phenomenological analysis of the lived mystical experience, distinguishes mystical experience from other similar experiences, and investigates the limits of phenomenology in relation to mystical experience (i.e., what phenomenology can and cannot say about mystical experience).[7] Her lifelong interest in mysticism was, in part, inspired by a spiritual experience that took place in November 1919. Walther's final major work was an autobiography published in 1960. Titled *On the Other Bank: From Marxism and Atheism to Christianity (Zum anderen Ufer. Vom Marxismus und Atheismus zum Christentum)*, Walther's autobiography details not only her childhood and early education but also her introduction to phenomenology, her place in the movement, and her personal experiences with key thinkers, including Husserl, Stein, Heidegger, and her longtime friend Conrad-Martius. In addition, it traces her intellectual transformations—from socialism to phenomenology to Christianity—as well as her daily life and experiences during the Third Reich. On account of her interest in mysticism, Walther was pursued by the Gestapo. She refused, however, to cooperate. Walther also published an essay on Hitler's reliance on occultism.[8]

Walther's dissertation was titled "A Contribution to the Ontology of Social Communities." In it, she offers an illuminating investigation of the history of phenomenology, the phenomenological method, and the differences between phenomenology and ontology, as well as a detailed analysis of the nature of social community. Walther graduated *summa cum laude*, and the dissertation was published with only slight alterations in the 1922 *Jahrbuch*

[6] By this stage, Stein's appeal to the Prussian Ministry of Culture had been successful, and from 1920 onward, women were permitted to habilitate in Germany. See our introduction to chapter 8.

[7] A partial English translation of this book is available in Rodney Parker, ed. and trans., "Gerda Walther, *Phenomenology of Mysticism*, Introduction and Chapter 1," in *Gerda Walther's Phenomenology of Sociality, Psychology, and Religion*, ed. Antonio Calcagno (Berlin: Springer, 2018), 115–133.

[8] This essay was published in English as "Hitler's Black Magicians," *Tomorrow* 4, no. 2 (1956): 7–23.

für Philosophie und phänomenologische Forschung. The selections in this volume come from the published version of Walther's dissertation.

Walther begins her account by outlining the differences between ontology and phenomenology (by which she means Husserl's form of phenomenology). She traces the presuppositions of phenomenology back to Augustine and Descartes.[9] Whereas ontology aims to investigate the essence of real objects, phenomenology is concerned not with the essence of objects but only with their appearance. At the center of phenomenology is the study of objects in their "givenness" to the *cogito* or the "pure I." This means, Walther elaborates, that although phenomenology can ascertain that there are real and independent things in the world—by inferring from what is given to the pure I—it cannot (and does not aim to) move beyond what is thought. According to Walther, (Husserlian) phenomenology is limited in its investigations to the circle of the pure I's consciousness and can only shed light on the experiences of consciousness, in which something must be given, i.e., it can explore what these experiences are, and why things are given in this particular way to consciousness. Thus, she contends that phenomenology does *not* investigate reality—being and the essence of objects. Such an investigation would require ontology—i.e., the realist phenomenology that was being carried out in Munich.

At the heart of the phenomenological method is the idea of a "reduction," the bracketing of the inessential aspects of experience so as to get at its pure structures. Walther goes on to distinguish two forms of reduction: the phenomenological and the ontological.[10] The *phenomenological* reduction reduces the object to its appearance in consciousness and to the state of consciousness in which it appears. The question of whether the object actually exists (is real) is "bracketed" from consideration and left undecided. By contrast, the *ontological* reduction does not aim to determine the specific correlates of the consciousness of the phenomena. It is concerned instead with grasping the pure "what" of the object—its essence—by excluding everything that is contingent or inessential. The ontological reduction thus takes

---

[9] By emphasizing ontology, Walther also places herself in opposition to Husserl. As she notes in her autobiography, in her first meeting with Husserl, he expressed disagreement with the Munich phenomenologists who had "remained" with ontology and did not follow his "transcendental turn." Walther, *Zum anderen Ufer*, 202.

[10] Though Heidegger does not speak of reduction, recent work in phenomenology has described Heidegger's work as an ontological reduction, or a "reduction to being," in contrast to Husserl's reduction, which is described as a "reduction to objectness." See Jean-Luc Marion, *Reduction and Givenness: Investigations of Husserl, Heidegger, and Phenomenology*, trans. Thomas A. Carlson (Evanston, IL: Northwestern University Press, 1998).

objects "as pure essences in their own sense, as belonging to themselves," rather than as "mere counterparts of all experiences of pure consciousness." This means that an ontological reduction is concerned with the reality of the object, with its specific and concrete appearance. Accordingly, Walther draws a distinction between the "pure I" of the phenomenological attitude (which she defines as a merely formal and abstracted moment of "viewing and making actual *pure* current experiences") and the "real I," which is a concrete, real subject.[11]

Having established these important (and sometimes polemical) differences, Walther turns her attention to determining the ontology of social communities. The text included in this volume comes from this second part of Walther's work. Drawing on Marx, Weber, and Pfänder's analysis of the sentiments, especially Pfänder's understanding of "inner union," Walther addresses classical phenomenological questions such as knowledge of others and other minds. She disagrees with Husserl and Stein on the role that empathy plays in bringing us to awareness of others (see the introduction to chapter 8). As Walther argues, Husserl and Stein take empathy to be the essential means by which the self becomes aware of other minds.[12] By taking notice of the ways in which others express themselves—through their body language, their gestures, their speech—the self is able to grasp the other. According to Husserl and Stein, empathy is essential for the formation of community. Walther, by contrast, argues that community is based on a different way of being with others—a way that is more original and fundamental than empathy.

In this context, she asks, what is the ontological structure of a community? To address this question, Walther poses a series of more precise questions and then assesses the coherence and meaningfulness of their possible responses. The questions she poses include: Does a social community require its members to share an external characteristic (such as dressing in a certain way), or does it require its members to share physical features (such as height or a tattoo)? Must the members of a social community know one another, or at least know *of* one another? What kind of interaction is necessary for

---

[11] As noted above (note 4), this critique of Freiburg phenomenology goes back to Walther's keynote address in 1918, and is elaborated in the introduction in *Ein Beitrag zur Ontologie der sozialen Gemeinschafte* (Halle: Max Niemeyer, 1922), 1–17.

[12] While this is the more common way of interpreting both Husserl and Stein, other interpretations have been put forth. See, for instance, Dan Zahavi, "Empathy and Other-Directed Intentionality," *Topoi* 33, no. 1 (2014): 129–142.

members of a social community to form such a community (i.e., is it physiological, chemical, or spiritual)?

Walther responds to these questions by examining various forms of
community. For example, she investigates the family community, which
reveals to her that a community need not be based on external signs or
physical features, given that members of a family do not necessarily share
these. Through this form of analysis and description, Walther arrives at the
conclusion that the essence of social community involves a specific kind
of interaction between the members of the community, which she calls
intentional.

Walther proceeds to explicate what "intentional" means by (again) crit-
icizing false assumptions. For instance, she explains that a community
cannot be intentional if its intention simply revolves around the products
that the community creates. In focusing on the products of the community,
Walther argues, one might "lose sight" of the community itself, and thereby
"take these products to be the only real thing in the community." Drawing
on Marx's critique of fetishism, she adds that "community life itself seems
to us to be the primary and more important thing. We also do not believe
that a community is only present when such objective formations [*objektive
Gebilde*] have proceeded from the community life of the members as community products."

This leads Walther to consider the difference between community and
society—a difference that, she argues, is often overlooked by sociologists,
such as Weber, who claim that the essential feature of a community is to
be located in an "agreement" reached by the members of a community (an
agreement can be a tradition, a custom, or a fixed statute, etc.). This view
mistakenly regards individuals as somehow capable of existing prior to the
community (after all, they must exist prior to the community if they are to
reach an agreement to form a community). Moreover, it misses the fact that
there are many societies that *are* governed by an agreement of some sort but
that cannot be described as *communities*.

To clarify this point, Walther offers the example of workers at a construction site, who work under a certain kind of agreement. Each of the workers
has a specific role to play, and they all follow the same rhythm and tempo of
work to keep the construction going. Furthermore, they are all directed by a
sense of unity, i.e., the construction. But, she asks, does this make them into
a community? Walther's answer is no, because although each of the workers
has the same goal (construction), and they understand one another through

this shared goal, they lack what she calls an "inner connectedness," a "feeling of belonging together," or an "inner oneness."

By emphasizing the inner bond or oneness, Walther draws attention to the *experience* of the persons involved. From the outside, the workers appear to be involved in a community. But, she asks, do they themselves *experience* a bond, a unity, with the others? If they do not, then this is not a community. In this way, Walther challenges a sociological perspective that does not take into account the subjective experience of the individuals involved, and thus fails to distinguish community from society. Her contention is that community emerges only if the *subjective experience* of unity is present.[13]

This provides the basis for Walther's examination of the relation between the individual and the community. In this context, Walther's goal is to determine the point in which the individual senses herself as an individual—as the center of her own thinking, acting, and willing—and feels herself as a member of a community. Walther does this, first, by emphasizing that community is based not on sameness but on the feeling of "unity" that the members individually experience. She then analyzes what this feeling of unity involves. On the one hand, it is a feeling that I experience for myself and regard as *my* feeling. On the other hand, the feeling of unity does not only concern myself; others are always part of it. Walther writes, "in this embeddedness, in this background, from which these lived experiences emerge, I am not only alone as 'my self' but I have incorporated others in this background . . . and I feel that I am one with them (unconsciously, automatically, or on the basis of an explicit oneness)." In other words, although my lived experiences are lived *in and through* myself, my self *already* involves others. I take others with me as I go about making decisions and acting in the world. Others are implied (whether consciously or unconsciously) in these decisions and actions. For this reason, Walther continues, " 'My' lived experiences, insofar as and *only* insofar as they are communal lived experiences, do not spring only from myself, from my isolated self. . . . Rather, they originate simultaneously from others *in me*, from the we, the 'people who also,' in whom I rest."

Walther's emphasis on community, and her contention—contra Husserl and Stein—that empathy is a later concept, one that comes after community— has significant implications. In the experience of empathy, I imagine my way

---

[13] For a discussion of Walther's understanding of the inner experience of community, see Alessandro Salice and Genki Uemura, "Social Acts and Communities: Walther between Husserl and Reinach," in *Gerda Walther's Phenomenology of Sociality, Psychology and Religion*, ed. Antonio Calcagno (Dordrecht: Springer, 2018), 27–46.

into another's experience—into her joy or her suffering—but in so doing, I do not experience the joy or suffering *as my own*. Rather, I regard the joy as the experience *of the other*. This means that I am never able to fully identify with the other, or to fully experience myself *as* the community.[14] In a community, by contrast, where self is both self and more than self, the other's pain or joy are *also my pain and joy*. I experience them as my own. This gives me an entirely different form of access to the other, one that is missed if we believe that the experience of the other first emerges through empathy.

With the recent revival of interest in early phenomenology, Walther's thought has received new attention. Her dissertation and her work on the phenomenology of mysticism have become significant sources for understanding not only the history of the movement but also its systematic range and potential.

---

[14] On the differences between Stein's and Walther's accounts of community, see Antonio Calcagno, "On the Vulnerability of a Community: Edith Stein and Gerda Walther," *Journal of the British Society for Phenomenology* 49, no. 3 (2018): 255–266.

Selections from *A Contribution to the Ontology of Social Communities*

The Sense of the Term "Social Community" and a Preliminary Determination of Its Essential Features

We will now deal with communities, and specifically with *social* communities. What sort of communities are those? There are all sorts of communities, and therefore, in the first place, all sorts of connections between objects in a unity that overarches the individual parts and yet contains them. One could perhaps speak of a community of carbon and hydrogen atoms in a benzene molecule and other connections of this kind. But usually one only speaks of communities in relation to this kind of connection between living creatures. But is that, by itself, a *social* community? Apart from human beings, plants and animals are also living creatures; all kinds of imaginary figures and their like also fall under this term. Is a community of plants, like, say, the spherical volvox algae, a *social* community? Or is an ant- or beehive, a pack of predators, or the famous symbiosis of the hermit crab with the sea anemone a social community? We might perhaps call these formations communities in a certain sense, but never *social* communities. Even a community of angels, fairies, dwarves, mermaids, centaurs, etc., would not be a *social* community.

A social community, rather, always seems to need to have *humans* among its members. But must *all* its members be humans, or only one or several of them? A community between God and humans, angels and humans, fairies etc. and humans, even a friendship of a human being with their dog or horse, would no doubt be a kind of community—but would it be a *social* community? Certainly not! We must therefore understand a social community as a connection of humans *with each other*, of humans *only* with humans; and further, on a higher level (if necessary), as a connection, a community, of such communities with each other. But what is a community? What must be present for humans to form a *community*, specifically?

The word "community" suggests something *in common*. Therefore, in investigating the essence of social communities, we must direct our attention to what this thing in common may be. At first, one might think that such a community exists when there is a similar external feature. And, in fact, we do often notice that sort of thing in the members of the social formations that we call communities. Thus we find with many associations that their members wear the sign of the association. The members of a tribe and similar formations of this kind often wear the same costumes; the members of a totem group have tattoos of the same totem animal; the members of a family bear the same names. You might therefore think that some common external hallmark of this sort is what is essential for a community. However, if we look more closely this does not hold up. There are communities whose members do not have any such external feature in common. For example, often the closest bonds of friendship do not show such an outer feature—even if such a feature may be a *symbol* or *sign* of belonging to a community. But the community, not that feature, is the primary thing. The shared feature is therefore not an essential constituent of community "in general."

You might think that a purely external, physical, common feature might well not suffice for establishing a community; such a feature must instead have to do with similar physical traits, for instance a similar facial structure, similar physique, etc. Certainly in many communities there may be such similarities among the members, especially with members of families, racial communities, and the like. But there are also many people who exhibit the same [physical] similarities and likenesses without forming a community. Equally, in many communities the members do not show likenesses of this kind at all. Therefore shared physical features also do not constitute community "in general," even if they may be—perhaps even have to be—found among members of certain kinds of communities.

But if it is not the body that must be the same or similar for the members of a community, perhaps it is their *life*, understood *physically*, that must, under all circumstances, proceed in the same way or similarly. This might mean the whole course of their life or only part of it. However, even people who have the same physical lives do not always seem to form a community, while, conversely, people with very different physical lives (e.g., the seriously ill and the healthy) are often united in a community. Therefore physical life, even if it is the same, also does not suffice as the foundation of community "in general."

For a social community to exist, then, there must be an entirely or partly similar *mental-spiritual life*, with at least partly *similar intentional contents* or directions of intentions. No doubt this is a necessary condition for social communities; but is it also sufficient?

Let us imagine that someone in China, someone in Argentina, and someone in Norway all dedicated their lives to solving the same scientific problem, and that they also used the same methods and materials to do so. Their mental-spiritual life would thus have the same intentional contents and would take place in the same way, certainly for much of their lives. However, as long as they do not know about each other, these people do not form a community.

"As long as they do not know about each other," we said—so perhaps, in order for a social community to exist, *knowing-about-each-other* must simply be added to a similarity (in whole or in part) of mental-spiritual life and its intentional contents. At first glance this might almost seem to be the case. However, in our opinion this would not be sufficient either. No doubt it is absolutely necessary that the members of a community know about each other for a formation of this sort to exist. But if we imagine that each of the three people knew something about the others purely intellectually—for example, that they investigated the same problem in the same way as the others— would a community be given just by that? Certainly not!

But what if they were to connect with each other, if they exchanged and compared the results of their research in order to come to grips with the solution to the problem "together"? In short, what if, in addition to knowing-of-each-other, we added an *interaction* with each other. Would a community not be given in this case?[15]

In fact, many sociologists see what is essential to *society*, as well as to *community*, in such an interaction of its members, and they try to derive social types from the forms of this interaction. This applies especially to Simmel,[16] Max Weber[17] (in part of his "Categories")[18]—and, to an extent, Husserl.[19] Yet does such mere interaction suffice for the presence of a community?

[15] [The word translated here as "interacting" or "interaction" (*Wechselwirken* or *Wechselwirkung*) is an important term in phenomenology (as well as in early German romanticism) and is more often, and more precisely, translated as "reciprocal action" or "reciprocity." The term describes a reciprocated effect of one party on another, and perhaps has less of a connotation of closeness and community than "interaction." However, the word appears so frequently in Walther's text that the translation here is to the more readable "interaction." To avoid confusion, no other German term has been translated as "interaction" in this text. For a more technical translation, it would therefore be possible to substitute "reciprocal action" for every instance of "interaction" in this translation of Walther.]

[16] Especially Simmel in his *Soziologie*. [Georg Simmel, *Soziologie. Untersuchungen über die Formen der Vergesellschaftung* (1908); reprinted in *Georg Simmel Gesamtausgabe*, Vol. 11, ed. Otthein Rammstedt (Frankfurt am Main: Suhrkamp, 1992).]

[17] Max Weber defines as "communal action" all action that is oriented toward the behavior of other subjects—and in fact even if it does not relate to the same contents as the behavior of these other subjects does. Cf. Weber, "Über einige Kategorien der verstehenden Soziologie," 265ff. For Weber, this same content is not added even by "agreement" (279ff.), whereas to us it seems really essential. [This reference is to Max Weber, "Über einige Kategorien der verstehenden Soziologie," *Logos* 4 (1913). This essay can also be found in *Max Weber Gesamtausgabe* (hereafter abbreviated as MGW) (Tübingen: Mohr & Siebeck, 1983–), Section I, Vol. 12, 389–440).]

[18] Weber, "Über einige Kategorien der verstehenden Soziologie."

[19] In his (unpublished) lecture "Natur und Geist." [Husserl's lecture "Natur und Geist. Vorlesungen Sommersemester 1919" can be found in Hua., *Edmund Husserl Materialien*, Vol. 4, ed. Michael Weiler (Leuven: Husserl Archives, 2002).]

Most importantly, of course, we ask what sort of interaction this must be: physical, physiological, psychological, consciously intentional—or something else? A purely physical interaction is present when two fishermen collide their boats in impenetrable fog—because they can neither see nor hear each other—and both boats capsize, and they drown. It is clear that a purely mechanical-physical interaction of this sort has nothing at all to do with a community being formed by the two fishermen—although they also lead partly similar lives with partly similar life purposes.

The situation is similar with a purely physiological interaction. Let us imagine that two students who study the same subject—for instance medicine—but in different countries, and who do not know each other at all, meet on holiday in the same train carriage. They do not speak to each other, but perhaps each sees from the other's outfit, and the books they are reading, that the other also studies medicine; thus they know of their partly similar life purposes. One has a cold; the other has typhus. The one sick with typhus infects the one with the cold and the other way around, without this being known to them either before or after it happens. After they have traveled a short distance together, they part and never hear from each other again. Here, too, a community of the two certainly does not exist, despite their purely physiological interaction in infecting each other.

Because community is a psychological-spiritual formation, all purely physical, chemical, physiological, etc., ways of interacting do not apply, unless they are necessary accompanying phenomena of intentional lived experiences or trigger certain lived experiences of this sort. (But even then, it would be the intentional lived experiences induced by them that would be decisive [for the formation of community].) For us, therefore, an interaction of people of any sort that is not (or does not mediate) an interaction of psyche to psyche, of mental life to mental life, of consciousness to consciousness, of spirit to spirit, is out of the question. It can therefore only involve an *intentional interaction* (not to be confused with an intended/deliberate interaction!), or a psychological interaction with intentional components.

What do we mean by that? We understand by [an intentional interaction] (in the broadest sense) that the mental-spiritual being and behavior (in the broadest sense) of a (human) subject has, through any intentional lived experiences (in the broadest sense) of another human subject, some influence on the mental-spiritual being and behavior *of this other subject*. And, furthermore, that the mental-spiritual being and behavior of this second subject in turn somehow influences the mental-spiritual being and behavior of the first subject through *its* intentional lived experiences (in itself and from the outset, or only because it is itself influenced by the first subject).[20]

But does such an intentional interaction between the inner life of two or more human beings, combined with the other moments mentioned above, suffice for a community to come about and be present? Two people who mutually berate and hit each other are certainly in an intentional interaction, among other things, and, furthermore, show partially similar contents and external forms of their mental lives. However, we cannot claim that they form a community, even if, with Simmel, we may designate them as *socialized* in the broadest sense. But a *community* is not *formed*, despite the presence of an intentional interaction and the two other moments. What is still missing?

Above, we mentioned that the mental lives of those who form a community must proceed entirely or partly along the same or a similar course and have the same or similar intentional contents, in order for a community to be present. Well, what about that? In order to be incorporated into a community, to "form a community," the members of a social formation must obviously not only be in some kind of general intentional interaction, but in their interaction with each other they must also lead the same mental-spiritual life in relation to the same intentional contents *in the same sense* and in the same way.[21]

Besides the interaction, they must lead the same mental-spiritual life in relation to the same *intentional* contents. Is that right? In any community, do we have, in addition to the members' knowledge of each other and their interaction, the same contents of consciousness, to which all the members relate intentionally in exactly *the same way*? In many communities this is no doubt the case, such as in research communities and all communities where the same goal is striven for without a division of labor. But such communities are only a certain subspecies of community "in general." We would therefore confuse the definition of a *special* essence of community with that of its *general* essence if we were to regard this determination as decisive for the essence of community "in general." It seems this definition would be too narrow. As soon as a division of labor is introduced into the interactions of the members of a community, they all relate intentionally to something in

[20] [Walther writes "second" again here, probably in error, and it has been translated as "first" to make better sense of the sentence.]
[21] Cf. [Adolf] Reinach, "Die apriorischen Grundlagen des bürgerlichen Rechtes," [*Jahrbuch für Philosophie und phänomenologische Forschung* 1, no. 2 (1913): 685–847, here] 707ff.

common, but not in the same way, and then their mental-spiritual lived experience also does not proceed in exactly the same way.

We can already see this within the family—in which, as is well known, the first division of labor historically occurred. Certainly in the most primitive family a man and a woman form a community and their lives relate to something in common: subsistence for themselves and their relatives. But they do not relate to it in the same way. For instance, the woman serves this purpose through agriculture, producing baskets and mats, and preparing food, while the man pursues the same purpose in hunting, in defending against enemies, etc.

Does this mean that we must drop the same intentional contents, and possibly also similar life purposes and partly similar mental and spiritual lives, as essential constituents for community? Nonetheless, we saw above that, although individuals just knowing of each other and interacting may suffice for socialization in the broadest sense, it does not suffice for community formation. For the latter, there must also be present an interaction in relation to a similar content in the same sense.

How can we get out of this dilemma? We seem to have reached a dead end—or have we perhaps only let some equivocations escape our attention, and if we differentiate them, then these contradictions would dissipate? Let us investigate our terms thoroughly again.

The formation of community, it seems, includes a "common" (similar) mental-spiritual life, along with the same intentional life purpose of the members of the community, who know of each other and are interacting intentionally. Yet, as we saw, especially with a division of labor (in the broadest sense) within the community, the lives of its members proceed in thoroughly different ways.

Let us first investigate more precisely what it means that the members of a community must have a common intentional life purpose. Does it mean, for instance, that some *real* object, such as a house or the like, belongs to them in common, to which they all relate consciously? Certainly, people who form a community *can* have some sort of common possession of this kind; community *can* really rest on an intention toward a common possession or another common real relationship (like, for instance, a common ancestry or a common situation of servitude etc.). However, it does not *need* to. A real relationship of that kind (or of any kind) to some real object can be completely lacking without a community ceasing to exist. The common intention need not be directed at either an external *real* object or an external *real* relation of the members as its content; it does not need to be a physically, physiologically, or psychologically real object. By that, of course, we do not mean that the content of the common intention could or must be fully detached from all past, present, and future reality. Because the communities we are dealing with here are *social* communities, i.e., communities of *real* people, that sort of full detachment of content from all relation to reality is essentially impossible for a meaningful community.

The object of the common intention does not need to be real, but it must have some relation to reality. It could be that it deals with an ideal demand that is elevated by the people who form a community to a guiding star of their *real* behavior (possibly only within the community), or that it deals with the *real* working out of a scientific system, the real *realization* of an artistic ideal, etc. This sort of relationship to reality, of whatever kind it is, must of course always be present in the common content of community life. However, despite that, the content that is thought, the object of the common intention, need not itself always be something real. Let us make this clear with an example.

For instance, let us imagine that, in a well-organized game, a number of children playfully invent a benevolent fairy and build her a temple in which they worship her. They would form a "community of servants of this fairy." Here, the intentional object of this communal life (i.e., life "in service to the fairy") is absolutely not a real object and is also not thought as such, for at root the children know very well that their fairy does not exist in reality, and they are only acting as if it did. Here what is real is only the behavior of the children "in service to the fairy." Nonetheless, the children can form a community "in service to the fairy," even though they are not in a real relationship with her. It would certainly be a community of a peculiar sort, but still a community. The question is: what lies at the basis of this community?

First and decisively, we have here a common (i.e., present in everyone) *intentional relationship to a specific object*,[22] in this case the fairy. The thought object of this relationship is the same, and each member means it to be the same as what the others think—but it does not need to be real.[23] Here what is real are only the intentional lived experiences of the children, in which they "mean" the fairy, and the behavior of the (real) children, which proceeds from these real lived experiences and their intention. But the intended object

---

[22] Cf. e.g., Aristotle, *Nikomachische Ethik*, trans. Eugen Rolfes, 2nd ed. (Leipzig: F. Meiner, 1911), 195–196.

[23] We are grateful for valuable suggestions on this from private docent Dr. M. Heidegger in Freiburg.

itself (the fairy) is not real as a result, and just as little does this object (the fairy) thereby stand in any other real relationship to the children, apart from being thought in a real lived experience. Therefore there is present here neither a real object nor a real relationship of real objects to the members (except the real intentions).

The content of this same intention is the same: namely, the same fairy. However, this does not mean that the various members' intentions toward the same object, i.e., the way in which they intend (mean, think, imagine, etc.) it, must be exactly the same. The noema (the representation, signification, meaning, etc.) through which *the same* intended object (i.e., the common "content" of the mental life of the members) is thought does not need to be the same or identical for everyone. Only the object itself, which the noema aims at, must be the same, even if it is thought differently (within certain boundaries; see below). Only in an ideal case would the noema also be fully the same among all members, but that is not necessary for forming a community. To return once more to our above example, the emphasis of feeling and the vividness of imagination in representing the fairy can be profoundly different among the different children.

Thus, on the "objective" side (in the broadest sense), only the same intention to an identical object (in the broadest sense) is necessary for community; but this says nothing about the way of representing and the way of being of this object. (It can be a real, unreal, or fictive formation of some sort.) The intending lived experiences, like their subjects, are real, of course. To that *can* (but need not) be added the same real relation (in addition to the real intention) to this object (for instance a common possession, common ancestry, etc.) or to a symbol of this object (idolatry, tattooing of a totem animal, etc.). But there only *always* needs to be present a (real) *intentional* relationship to the object. The other real relationships can be added to this, but do not need to be. Similarly, the noema in which this object is thought can also vary.

Now, what is the situation with the "same" mental life of the members? No doubt it must be thoroughly ruled by a more or less actual or habitual, direct or indirect intentional relationship to the same intended object, insofar—and only insofar—as the formation of community extends into the whole mental life of the individuals. In fact, this intentional relationship, in the broadest sense of the life of that object, must have the same sense despite the variety in the way that it is represented etc. [...] We must deliberately express ourselves somewhat vaguely here, since a more precise definition of what is meant by this "same sense" could easily be too narrow, and would only apply to a specific type of community but not to community "in general."

But the matter could perhaps be clarified in the following way. It must be possible to connect all the mental-spiritual expressions of the lives of the members of the community, *insofar* as they are motivated by this common intentional object, so that they never conflict or mutually frustrate or neutralize each other. Indeed, where there seem to be such conflicts within a community, either it is not a true community or these conflicts are "outgrowths" and "symptoms of illness," which must disappear again if they are not to lead to the dissolution of the community. Instead, the mental-spiritual life of the various members must be connected in a unified whole, within the same context of meaning, even if perhaps only very indirectly.

Let us make this clear with an example. For instance, let us imagine, on the one hand, an old, completely uneducated peasant woman who has never left her remote village. This old woman hears that Germany is at war and that it must win—and she knits stockings for the soldiers, in order to contribute in *her way* to the "victory of Germany." This victory of Germany is thus the intentional object toward which her action is directed. On the other hand, let us imagine, for instance, the German kaiser as supreme commander of the imperial army, and his activity toward a victorious advance of the German troops. His intentional object, which motivates his action, is therefore also the victory of Germany. Certainly a sheer unbridgeable difference yawns between the representation the kaiser has of Germany's victory—and his activity toward it—and the representation the little old woman has of Germany's victory and her contribution to it. Nevertheless, the kaiser and the little old woman relate intentionally to the same object: the victory of Germany. And despite all their differences, their actions motivated by this object can combine into a *concordant* unified collective action with a unified relation of motivation, even if this only happens thanks to many intervening links. (We have a similar example in the various partial contributions of individual workers to the production of a pin, as presented in Adam Smith's classic example of the division of labor in manufacturing.)

Conversely, in the above example the enemy commanders may perhaps imagine the German troops and their victory in a way that is much closer to how the kaiser imagines them than the way the little old woman does. However, a community is not formed between them and the kaiser, because, in relation to the same intentional object (Germany's victory), their entire acting and striving goes toward thwarting everything the kaiser undertakes.

290 WOMEN PHILOSOPHERS IN THE LONG NINETEENTH CENTURY

Their action therefore does not form a unified context of meaning with the *same orientation* as his.

Having said that, we can now clarify the significance of the unified context of meaning that must exist among the members of a community, in relation to the same intentional object, in their community life and community action. It is like a supreme leitmotif that permeates mental-spiritual life within the community, among all its members, even if they play different variations of the tune and with different instruments. Each must, in their own way, play in such a manner that, in the end, despite all deviations, they do not disturb the whole piece and its harmony, but together with the other players let it grow and realize it.

In some circumstances, certain common formations and products grow from the lives of the members of a community that have been determined in this way. These formations and products differ according to the type of community and its members. [They include,] for example, economic, cultural, artistic, legal, ethical, religious, etc., products that, according to their essence as "works" in the broadest sense, point to the "accomplishments" of individuals and communities as their origin.[24] You might think that such common products were also necessarily part of the essential constitution of a community. In fact, many researchers have proceeded primarily from these products of community life in sociological and historical investigation and research into communities. This applies in particular to W. Wundt, who investigates the development of language, morals, religion, etc., in his "folk psychology."[25] These are all certainly very important phenomena of community life, both as products and expressions of its spirit and as having repercussions for the unfolding and development of community life. However, in our opinion, when investigating these products of community life one must be careful not to entirely lose sight of community life and the community itself and take these products to be the only real thing in the community.[26] Rather,

---

[24] We are taking these concepts from E[dmund] Husserl's (unpublished) lecture on "Natur und Geist."

[25] [Wilhelm Wundt (1832–1920) is often regarded as the father of modern psychology. He founded the first psychology lab at the University of Leipzig in 1879.]

[26] An error that W. Wundt does not make to this extreme, but which causes trouble, for example, in many theories of political economy. It is to the eternal credit of Karl Marx and the Marxists that they emphatically pointed this out again and again. Cf. Karl Marx, *Kapital*, Vol. 1, the section about the "fetish character of commodities"; Rudolf Hilferding, "Böhm-Bawerks Marx-Kritik," Sections 1 and 2 in *Wiener Marx-Studien*, Vol. 1; and Max Adler, "Kausalität und Teleologie," Section 15, 369 *ibid*. [The relevant section in Marx's work can be found in MEW, Vol. 23, part 1 ("Ware und Geld"), chapter 1 ("Die Ware"), section 4 ("Der Fetischcharakter der Ware und sein Geheimnis"). The other references are to Rudolf Hilferding, "Böhm-Bawerks Marx-Kritik," *Marx-Studien* 1 (1904): 1–61, esp. 3f.; Max Adler, "Kausalität und Teleologie im Streite um die Wissenschaft," *Marx-Studien* 1 (1904): 195–433.]

community life itself seems to us to be the primary and more important thing. We also do not believe that a community is only present when such objective formations [*objektive Gebilde*] have proceeded from the community life of the members as community products. (It is of course another matter when lost communities and their lives can only be *accessed* from their products. See below.)

In contrast to this, other researchers think a community consists only in the *actual* interaction and the *actual* communal life of its members. So, for example, W. Wundt remarks, using the terminology of his social theory of actuality, that the real essence of the "social organism" consists "in the actuality of its being." He claims that the common traits of the members of the community consist "merely in their activity . . .," and that "all social formations" are "not static being, but processes, actions, and they only possess reality as such."[27] [. . .]

If you think that communities are fully constituted when a number of people, knowing of each other, interact, and in doing so lead a similar mental-spiritual life, which is interwoven by a common unified sense [*Sinneinheit*] as a "leitmotif," then you are certainly close to an opinion like that. But let us test once more the findings we have come up with so far. What was it that we worked out as the essential, ontological constituents of community "in general"? Have we already found the really essential thing for community in general—were the features that we discovered sufficient, or only necessary, for composing a community?

We found a number of people who, in a certain layer of their life, relate to the *same intentional* object (in the broadest sense). *These people had to know about each other and about their relation to the same intentional object.* On the basis of this knowledge, they entered into *direct or indirect interaction with each other,* and from this interaction emerged a *communal life*[28] (possibly with common products), which *was, in a unified sense, immediately or mediately motivated by that intention toward the same object (in the broadest sense).*

Now, does all this suffice for composing a community? It is certainly necessary—but is all the above not also found in the sphere of society? Is

---

[27] Cf. among others Wilhelm Wundt, *Völkerpsychologie*, Vol. 7, "Die Gesellschaft," 19f. [Wilhelm Wundt, *Völkerpsychologie. Eine Untersuchung der Entwicklungsgesetze von Sprache, Mythos und Sitte*, Vol. 7, *Die Gesellschaft* (Leipzig: Alfred Kröner, 1917).]

[28] The social life characterized on the basis of these three determinations corresponds approximately to what Max Weber calls "communal action" (loc. cit., 275f.). [Weber, "Über einige Kategorien der verstehenden Soziologie."]

there no essential difference between community and society? And if there is such a difference—then in what does it consist? Have we already exhibited the ownmost [*ureigenste*] characteristic of community, the essential feature, that must be given wherever a community is present, that is to be found in *every* community and *only* in communities?

The Difference between Community and Society

Above, we spoke not only of the "same" intentional object and a concordant mental-spiritual life of people who were interacting with each other, but also of a *common* intentional object and a *common* mental-spiritual life. But by doing so, did we not include in our definition the thing that we were looking for in the first place? Have we not presupposed what we wanted to explain?

Is a community present anywhere that any people, knowing of each other, relate to each other through interaction, where they direct themselves to each other in their mental life and their actions and thereby relate to the same intentional object (in the broadest sense)? There could be no community if all this were missing—but are there not formations similar to communities that have all this but that are not communities?

For instance, let us take as an example a number of indiscriminately collected workers—Slovaks, Poles, Italians, etc.—who are all employed on a construction site. They do not understand each other's language, do not know each other, have never before had anything to do with each other—they all just want to earn a living and have thus accidentally been employed by the same entrepreneur. Now, for instance, they are putting up something like a wall. Some fetch the bricks, some pass them along to others, who eventually give them to the bricklayers, who spread them with mortar and lay them on top of each other. The work must proceed very precisely in a certain rhythm so that it does not falter—the workers must all orient themselves to the others and take and give the stones in the same tempo, so that the continuity of the work is not interrupted. Perhaps the workers also cook and live together, for as long as they are employed on the construction site.

Do they form a community? Viewed from the outside, it might well seem so. We have a number of people who know of each other and who are interacting and oriented to each other in their behavior. With that, we have what (for example) Max Weber calls "communal action." Furthermore, at one level of their mental lives these people relate to the same intentional object with a unified sense: the bricks, the walls, the whole construction. A partly similar mental-spiritual life results from this, which is permeated by a unity of sense and regulated by the same intentional object (the construction and earning a living by working on this construction). All this is present and, furthermore, the workers know it.—Do we have a community here?

We assumed that the workers did not know each other more than just described; we added that they belonged to different nations with different languages. Let us now assume that they face each other mistrustfully and with enmity, or at best indifferently, as rivals for wages, as members of foreign nations. Can we then speak of a community, despite all their conscious external interaction and the shared meaning of their behavior? In our opinion, you can only speak here of a *societal* connection, even if it is of a specific sort. But how do we move on? How do we get from a formation of this sort to a community, with which, at first glance, this formation has a deceptive similarity?

We could, for instance (following in the footsteps of Max Weber),[29] believe that the most essential feature of community is found in people's relatedness to each other, in their interactions. How would it be if, for example, each interaction was regulated by "agreement," by tradition, by custom, or by some fixed statute, a right in the broadest sense—would we not then have a community before us? Perhaps it is the case that in social formations that are not communities the relationship of the members is looser, the "chances" (to use Max Weber's language) that all members orient their behavior to each other are smaller, than in communities? Accordingly, the difference between communities and other similar social formations would lie in the fact that the "chances" for *concordant* interaction, for an adaptation as exact as possible of the behavior of one person to that of the others, is greatest in communities?

Certainly something like this is present in the formation of communities. In a community with a "community spirit" (we will see later what that is), the orientation of the members to each other and their interaction is certainly greater, their connection firmer, than in a mere society. But does the

---

[29] Cf. Weber, loc. cit. However, in this article Weber does not deal with the essence of community, and in this respect our remarks are *not* criticisms of, or polemic against, Max Weber. We are only attempting to apply his method and classificatory perspective to *our* problems, and *here* they appear to us to be extremely valuable and fruitful, but not sufficient. But we are of course very conscious that Max Weber himself investigated and *wanted* to investigate other problems than us, and also to an extent other sides and aspects of the being of social phenomena. [Weber, "Über einige Kategorien der verstehenden Soziologie."]

essential constitution of community lie in this? Is it this unanimity, and this greatest possible probability of an interaction occurring that expresses the sense of connection, that alone characterizes the essence of community? Or are these [characteristics] only the *consequences* and *accompanying phenomena* of that which makes the community into a community, of that which distinguishes it from other social formations? For instance (to apply some categories from Max Weber), would a community be made from a society if the relations and interactions of the members were unequivocally regulated by tradition, custom, convention, arrangement, a textually fixed statement, or finally—as an ultimate ideal—by this fixed statement being maintained and implemented by members who were employed to do that?[30]

Certainly not!

Let us take our earlier example of the workers on the construction site. Let us imagine that a work order was established that specified exactly at which tempo, rhythm, in which order, etc., the workers were to work, when lunch break was, when the beginning and end of work were, etc. All this is specified in a fixed, written work regulation. In addition, there is an army of foremen, work leaders, overseers, etc., who implement this work regulation. But otherwise everything is as before: the workers do not understand each other's language, they do not know each other, they face each other as rivals with enmity or indifferently. Could we then speak of a community? In our opinion: no!

Some people think that [in order for a community to exist] everyone must only inwardly "rank" all the others "besides" themselves and treat them as equal. But if everyone inwardly placed everyone else besides themselves as equals, yet did not suspend their full enmity or indifference toward them, then, too, in our opinion no community would be present. However, if, instead of inner alienation and indifference, indeed enmity, we added to all the other specifications an *inner connection*, of whatever kind—however loose it might be, however small its scope, even if it only extended to coexistence at work on this construction site and had only the same duration as this— would we not then have a community before us?

Here—and *only* here—it seems to us a real community would be present. Only through its inner connectedness, that feeling of belonging

[30] Thus in the "institution" in Max Weber's sense. Cf. loc. cit., 286ff. [Weber, "Über einige Kategorien der verstehenden Soziologie."]

together—however loose and limited it may be—does a social formation change into a community. By contrast, as long as this feature is lacking, we would group all social formations (including organizations and institutions etc. in Max Weber's sense) together under the collective term *societal formations*. (These also include very diverse subdivisions and subtypes.) We stand on the same ground here as those researchers (e.g., Ferdinand Tönnies[31] and Giddings,[32] to name just two) who see the essential feature of community in "that *feeling of belonging together,*" that *inner oneness*.[33] All social formations that exhibit such inner oneness of their members, and *only* these, are communities, in our opinion. And in our opinion, it is only with these that we can talk, strictly speaking, of *communal* lived experiences, actions, goals, aspirations, volitions, wishes, etc. (in contrast to *same* or *similar* lived experiences, actions, etc., which may perhaps be present with societal affiliations). But not *all social* affiliations present such a feeling of belonging together, such inner connectedness. Of course, we do not think *all* sociology should be reduced to this [factor], as, for instance, Giddings tries to do. Rather, it seems to us that this is the most essential—if not the only—consideration *only* for the sociology (and ontology and phenomenology) of *communities*, but *not* for the sociology of other social formations, i.e., for all types of socialization in the broadest sense.

[...]

"Communal" Life on the Basis of Oneness

We saw above that the essential components of a full-blown community include a "communal" life, which, we can now say, is based on the reciprocal inner oneness of the members, and at the same time is motivated by

[31] Cf. F. Tönnies, *Gemeinschaft und Gesellschaft*. Incidentally, we do not thoroughly agree with all of Tönnies's further remarks. [See Ferdinand Tönnies, *Gemeinschaft und Gesellschaft* (Leipzig: Fues/R. Reisland, 1887). Tönnies (1855–1936) was a German sociologist and author of a number of works on the nature and ideal of social organization.]

[32] Cf. F[ranklin] H[enry] Giddings, [*The*] *Principles of Sociology* [(London: Macmillan, 1896)]. [Walther refers to a German translation, probably *Prinzipien der Soziologie*, trans. Paul Seliger (Leipzig: Klinghardt, 1911). Giddings (1855–1931) was an American sociologist who developed sociology into a statistical and analytical science.]

[33] [The term translated here as "oneness" is *Einigung*, also frequently translated as "unification" or "union" in other translations of Walther. We decided to use the less common English word "oneness" to reflect the specific meaning that Walther gives the term in this context, including its emphasis on the importance of subjective experience—the feeling of belonging, of togetherness—for the constitution of community.]

their common object, in the sense described above. Or perhaps, now that we have introduced the essential feature of the oneness and reciprocal oneness of the members of the community, we no longer need such a common object (in the broadest sense) of community life? No doubt we always have such an object where the oneness of the members with each other is itself based on their oneness with some object lying outside of them. But we saw that this oneness can also stretch immediately from subject to subject, that in many cases the members of a community unite with each other purely as themselves, as these empirical or spiritual persons, without first taking a detour via a shared oneness with some third object. What is going on with the common object in these cases? Is such a common object always necessary in order to standardize the life of the united members in a meaningful way?

In any case, it is clear that there is a close connection between the common object and the intentional foundation of oneness, even if they may not always need to completely coincide. But is a common intentional objectivity absolutely necessary within or alongside the intentional foundation of the oneness and reciprocal oneness of the members of the community, which runs through their communal life as a leitmotif? Is it not the case that an objectivity of this sort only exists in communities with a shared purpose (in the broadest sense)?

a. Reflexive and Iterated Communities

There are certainly also communities where no common real or ideal *external* object seems to dominate and rule communal life, for example in a friendship, in marriage, in the family, etc. At first glance this might really seem to be the case. However, if we observe these communities more closely, then we find that there is no *external* purpose that unites the members (the members apparently live only for the sake of themselves and their oneness, without pursuing any *external* purpose). Here, too, communal life is permeated and regulated by a shared sense [*Sinn*], and this sense is precisely the oneness, the community itself: the community and life in the community are ends in themselves. Here, the goal of communal life is to "live out," to demonstrate, to deepen, to unfold, and to maintain the oneness and community of the members. In our opinion, however, we cannot say that, because the sense of the community turns back on itself, it has no sense in common, no guiding objectivity [*Leitgegenständlichkeit*]; it is just that here, it is not an external object or sense lying outside the community and its members as persons. Such communities—we could call them *reflexive communities*, because of their self-referential nature—simply have a *special kind* of object of this sort.

It is similar in cases where, within the structural context of a larger community, some of its members are connected in a community within the community, which relates to this encompassing community (for example, to its maintenance, domination, organization, promotion, etc.). In this case, we could speak of "*iterated*"[34] *communities*. For example, political parties are communities of this kind (as long as they are really communities, and not just social associations). Similarly, for example, one could count among these kinds of community a community "to care for the German spirit and the German disposition" within the larger community of the German people, as well as many other communities.

Thus it does seem necessary that an intentional object or sense of communal life, shared by all members, should be part of every community, as long as we grasp this definition broadly enough. That is, we should grasp this definition as meaning that, under certain circumstances, instead of an "object" outside the community and its members, the community itself, or the intentional foundation of the reciprocal oneness of the community members, can be this object (in the broadest sense).

But how should we conceive of this "communal life" itself and its relationship to the reciprocal oneness of its members, which is its foundation? We must be careful not to grasp the concept of communal life too narrowly. In particular, we do *not* want to understand by this a necessarily *spatiotemporally* coordinated life, which proceeds in an identical way. In other words, the members of a community who are leading a communal life in our sense do not need to live together spatially. Those of their actual lived experiences that are part of their communal life also do not need to occur simultaneously. These lived experiences only occur simultaneously in ideal cases of communal co-experiencing [*Miterlebens*], and especially in "we-experiences [*Wir-Erlebnissen*]" (see below). But communal life is not at all limited to these ideal cases.

How, then, should we understand communal life? We will start from Max Weber's definition of "communal action." As we saw above, Weber counts as communal action any action (in the broadest sense) in which the subject

---

[34] Cf. Husserl, *Ideen*, 109, 210ff., 219f.; and Stein, *Zum Problem der Einfühlung*, 18f. [Walther is referring to section 3f of Stein's *On the Problem of Empathy*, where Stein discusses "iterated" or "reflexive" empathy.]

298 WOMEN PHILOSOPHERS IN THE LONG NINETEENTH CENTURY

of this action relates to other subjects, orients itself *to* them in its behavior. We added that, in our opinion, this action of the various subjects must, in the end, relate concordantly to the same intentional object (in the broadest sense) and that all the subjects must be in reciprocal oneness with each other. But we want to talk not only about *action* in the broadest sense, but also about any intentional lived experience, internal or external, passive or active; we want to talk about psychophysical, mental-spiritual behavior in general, in the broadest sense.

We said that the main characteristic of communal life, its most essential foundation, is the reciprocal oneness of its subjects—of whatever kind this oneness might be. Communal life in our sense is interwoven with this; it is founded on this.

But what does that mean? Of course, we do not mean that a subject's lived experience or behavior only belongs to communal life if it is always accompanied by an actual lived experience of oneness with one or more other people. That would define it too narrowly. We mean something else. As we have seen, oneness is not only actual uniting oneself with the other, but can also be *habitual*: a unified, habitual resting in another or others. And it does not matter whether this emerges through explicit or actual uniting oneself or through unconscious growing together. *It is habitual oneness in particular that, in our opinion, must found and underpin all community life.*

b. The Category of "People Who Also . . ."

How shall we represent this founding [of community life] by habitual oneness?

Other people are always "given," as a more or less clear and detected "copresence"—even if only in a dark awareness in the background, not in attentive knowing or representing. These are the "people who also . . ."

(This is an essential category for understanding communities. This "also" can be defined completely differently depending on the kind of oneness and its intentional founding: as people who "also" evaluate like that, "also" have goals like that, "also" feel, want, think, etc., like the relevant subject itself. Of course, the "also" does not always relate to *external* goals, ways of behaving, lived experiences, etc. Rather, it can also relate to basic attitudes toward the whole of life, the whole cosmos, totally apart from the differentiation and expression of these attitudes in individual lived experiences, opinions, actions, etc. Certainly, in the case of people who unite immediately on the basis of their essential differences, who supplement each other [as, for example, sometimes happens with men and women], only this sort of "also" is present. However, it is nonetheless an "also" that may, in addition, hint at the higher unity of the two, which is potentially contained in them but which will only be realized if they form a community.[35] [This will only become clear in the following, when we discuss community at the second level.])[36]

These "people who also . . ." are always present somehow, however indeterminately, in the background of the subject. The subject is not only darkly aware of them, but also unified with them, in *those* strata in which the sense of community requires it. It rests in them and belongs to them, however loosely and in however limited a part of its total lived experience—and they "belong to it"—it forms a "we" with them. The subject's life, insofar as it is community life, is not just *its* life, does not only pour out from *itself*, as a single individual, but emanates from its unity with the others *within* itself. In this case, lived experience is characterized for the experiencing subject not as just "I experience like this," but as "*we* experience like this": "I *and the others*"—with whom I am united—"are experiencing *like this in me*" and we are one in this, in our lived experience.

But what does this communal lived experience look like, in which the I lives from itself and the others in it?

c. Communal Lived Experience (We-Experience) "for Itself"

The "we" does not stand "behind" or "above" the individual who experiences. It is not a "we" that is separate from individuals and breathes its lived experiences into them in a kind of emanation, so that these lived experiences enter their selves and from there go on to be actualized in the I-center of these selves. The we is also not a distinct but disembodied subject, which individuals might grasp in a special kind of empathy and make its lived experiences their own on the basis of this empathy. If that were the case, communal lived experiences and we-experiences would just be those lived experiences that individuals borrowed from this kind of mysterious subject in this kind of empathetic act. It is also not that, suddenly, a new, "common" I-center, an independent, real "communal I-center" (whatever one might imagine by that) emerges, which somehow, in a totally mysterious way, absorbs and actualizes the "common" lived experiences of the members of a community as "we."

---

[35] [Brackets are Walther's.]
[36] [Brackets are Walther's.]

All this has nothing to do with what we understand by communal lived experiences and "we-experiences."

These communal lived experiences and we-experiences take place and are actualized completely in the *individual* I—in the I-center—of the individual members of the community. Such lived experiences do not stream into the individual self and its basic essence from a mysterious, special communal-lived-experience-source-point behind them. Even if such a thing existed (perhaps in mystical lived experiences shared by many people, or mass suggestion), it would be, at best, a special case of we-experience. Community life would be too narrowly defined if it were restricted to these kinds of (hypothetical) cases.

Rather, the issue must be represented in something like the following way: *My* lived experiences actually take place in *my* I-center; they stream into it from *my* background of consciousness, *my* self, in which this I-center is embedded. But in communal lived experiences, in this embeddedness, in this background, from which these lived experiences emerge, I am not only alone as "my self," but I have incorporated others in this background. I have absorbed these others intentionally behind my I-center in *my* self (or they grew there by themselves) and I feel that I am one with them (unconsciously, automatically, or on the basis of an explicit oneness).

"My" lived experiences, insofar as and *only* insofar as they are communal lived experiences, do not spring only from myself, from my isolated self, my "only-I-myself" behind the I-point. Rather, they originate simultaneously from others *in me*, from the we, the "people who also . . .," in whom I rest, with whom I am one. I live and experience from myself *and* from *them in me* at the same time: from "us." Thus, even *before* these lived experiences enter the I-point, before they are actualized in it, they are communal lived experiences, because they originate as stirrings from me *and* from the others *in me*.

Let us illustrate this with an analogy. We can compare the psychological subject to a light: energy flows into it from a power source (through wires or in any other way), which it then converts into luminosity. If we hold on to this image, then we could represent communal lived experiences as if electric currents ran from one lamp with a dynamo machine into the wires, and from there into the light of another lamp. These currents could be converted into luminosity by the first lamp at the same time as they radiate from the other lamp as light, or they might only charge the wires of the second lamp with new energy and wait there until they are radiated as light there too, perhaps much later. They could be radiated just as they are or combined with this second lamp's own energy. If we imagine that the energy of one lamp can only be converted into blue light, and the energy of the other lamp only into yellow light, then, through such a combination of energy, the yellow lamp could now also emit blue beams of light, and the blue lamp yellow beams. Or both (or one of the two) lamps could also emit, besides their own yellow or blue light (respectively), green light in the most varied nuances, as the combination of their mutual energies and kinds of light. One could perhaps represent communal lived experience in a similar way (of course taken with a large grain of salt).[37]

Thus I do not first have lived experiences that emerge from me as an *isolated* individual I and individual self, which I then compare with the empathically grasped lived experiences of others, and only then—if by doing that I discern that the others "also" experience the same thing as I do just like I do—unite myself with these others and their lived experiences. I do not just conceive of these lived experiences afterward as communal lived experiences and designate them as such. This sort of thing may *precede* some communal lived experiences, but they are *never* true communal lived experiences in our sense. The latter do not arise in this way.

True communal lived experiences also do not arise by my having previously absorbed someone else's individual lived experience, which I have grasped empathically, and made it my own, so that it has become habitual in me and now emerges in me again as if it were my own. In this case, it could occur to me (for example on the basis of a recollection) that (and how) I previously borrowed this lived experience from another person. I could then, on the basis of this recollection, *call* it a "communal lived experience"—a lived experience in common to me and the other person, to us both.[38]

However great a role such lived experiences may play in the emergence and becoming conscious of community and of communal lived experiences, they are still never in themselves communal lived experiences in our sense. Rather, communal lived experiences in our sense include *only* those lived experiences that, *on the basis of my oneness with others*, emerge from them *in me* and from me *in them*, from *us—in me,* as *in them*—before they enter my (or their) I-center, before they are actualized in it. My I-center (like my pure

---

[37] [Walther uses a Latin phrase here: *cum grano salis*.]

[38] Cf. Stein, op. cit.; and Scheler, "Der Formalismus in der Ethik," 548. [Stein, *Zum Problem der Einfühlung*; Max Scheler, "Der Formalismus in der Ethik und die materiale Wertethik. Neuer versuch der Grundlegung eines ethischen Personalismus," *Jahrbuch für Philosophie und phänomenologische Forschung* 2 (1916): 21–478. Reprinted in Max Scheler, *Gesammelte Werke* (GW), ed. Maria Scheler and M. S. Frings (Bern: Francke; Bonn: Bouvier, 1954–), Vol. 2, 61–100.]

I) is of course always individual and singular; it can *never* be "common" to me and others. But this does not negate the fact that a community has been formed, which exists behind the I-center. This has already taken place in that deep mental stratum from which lived experiences emerge as stirrings before they enter the I-center in general.

However, you might think that these communal lived experiences must at least be limited to other people's previous or simultaneous lived experiences, which I have grasped empathically and absorbed. But this is not the case. Stirrings of lived experience could very well emerge from the communal self (as we will call this stratum) that these "people who also . . ." have never actually had, and perhaps never will have. For what enters me from others is not limited to individual lived experiences. Rather, it can also concern total attitudes in specific areas, or even attitudes toward the whole of life, or toward the totality of being (in worldview-based communities), or else it might only include the others' spiritual person, their basic essence. (In that case, we have before us that which Scheler calls the "collective person [*Gesamtperson*].")[39] In this case, lived experiences emerge from the "common spirit"; they proceed from the "communal self" into my I-center and from there penetrate outward. My total attitudes then arise from the communal self, but they are not individuated, actual communal lived experiences that emerged within me.

Let us analyze the inner structure of these individual communal lived experiences and of all community life more precisely, in order to prevent misunderstandings and reinterpretations. First, it is extremely important to clarify the difference between mere *empathizing*—as grasping any other person's lived experiences—and communal lived experiences.[40] When I empathically grasp the lived experiences, states, person, etc., of another human being, I have a totally different originary lived experience from when I experience the same lived experiences of the other myself, as communal lived experiences.

To begin with, let us clarify this in the case of individual actual lived experiences:

---

[39] Cf. Scheler, "Formalismus in der Ethik," 555ff.

[40] [Walther often uses the German term *fremd*, meaning "foreign," "alien," "strange," or "other," to refer to other people and their experiences. Although this term is often translated as "foreign" in this context, in this text (as well as the text by Stein also included in this volume) *fremd* has been translated as "other," and occasionally as "another person," wherever this is a more natural way to describe other people and their experiences in English. This loses the distinction with *andere* ("other"), another term that is frequently used in the same context, but is easier to read.]

(1) In empathy, I grasp others' lived experiences through words, facial expressions, and other phenomena of expression,[41] but in doing so I am immediately aware that *I do not myself* experience these lived experiences originarily and in person. I am immediately aware that these lived experiences belong to the other, that they emerge from *their* self and are actualized in *their* I-center, and are only given to me through phenomena of expression. They confront my lived experience as not-originary, as objectified lived experiences grasped by me, which are separated from my I, which do not belong to it.

Nothing about that changes if, (2) I happen to have, originarily and in person, the same lived experiences as those that I grasp empathically in the other. Despite this sameness, the lived experiences stand *beside each other* as *non-united*, as *belonging to different subjects*. I experience *like this*—and the other experiences *like this*. The two may happen to be the same, and I may be immediately aware of this sameness in experiencing my own lived experiences and in empathically grasping the other's lived experiences. However, together with my lived experience *for me, closed off* in myself and *separate, I stand beside* this other, who is just as much closed off in themselves and separate. There exists, as it were, an intentional "wall," a mental "opening," an "interstice" between me and the other (of course this interstice is non-spatial; it is only spatial metaphorically).

(3) It is no different with *sympathy* [*Mitfühlen*] (and "re-living" in Reinach's sense).[42] Here, I grasp someone else's lived experience empathically and experience it "with" them. I experience the same as them originarily, but "for their sake." The relationship of my lived experience *to them* in this sense is essential here—this lived experience would *not* occur like that for me myself, just *for me*.[43] I empathically grasp that someone else is (now) happy about something. The object of their happiness is perhaps not pleasant for me, but indifferent, or totally unpleasant. But *because* they are happy (this "because they" is essential), I am also happy with them and *for them*. (Even with a kind of empathizing in which a lived experience of one's own is attached to someone else's lived experience, and is the same kind of lived experience as their lived experience, these [their lived experience and my lived

---

[41] Cf. Stein, op. cit. [Stein, *Zum Problem der Einfühlung.*]

[42] Cf. Reinach, ["Die apriorischen Grundlagen des bürgerlichen Rechtes,"] 784f.

[43] Cf. Scheler, *Sympathiegefühle*, 10f. [The full reference is *Zur Phänomenologie und Theorie der Sympathiegefühle und von Liebe und Haß. Mit einem Anhang über den Grund zur Annahme der Existenz des fremden Ich* (Halle: Niemeyer, 1913). Revised (1923) edition reprinted as *Wesen und Formen der Sympathie* in GW, Vol. 7, 7-258.]

experience] must not be confused. If, for example, someone is happy and I, in empathically grasping their happiness, am happy *about their happiness*, this is completely different from if I am happy *with* them, *for* them, or if I am simultaneously happy about the same thing as they are.) Of course sympathy presupposes a kind of inner unity with the other, but it is a different unity from communal lived experience. In the latter, the participants originarily experience the same thing or a similar thing, in the same or a similar way, at the same time or later, out of the common stratum, with a feeling of their unity. I experience what I experience not only *for the other* and *with* them, but at the same time also for *myself*. For what concerns and pertains to the "we" also concerns *myself for myself, as part of the we*, as part of the community; it does not only concern the others, or myself "for the others."

Communal lived experience is different in principle from sympathy. We will analyze it precisely. First, we empathically grasp an other's lived experience. Now this lived experience changes into a communal lived experience. (It could of course also emerge as a communal lived experience from the beginning, but in order to work out the difference clearly, we will assume that it changes into one.) What changes? For example, I look at a view with another person. While doing so, they announce aloud their enthusiasm about the beautiful view. I grasp their lived experience empathically: it confronts me as an *other's* lived experience, not as a lived experience belonging originarily and in person to me.[44] This is the case even if I am just as enthusiastic about the view as they are—or, instead, even if I give myself up completely to their enthusiasm, experience it with them *for them*. In the first case, I experience the same thing myself. And in the second case I experience the same thing *for* them and *with* them: I thoroughly participate in their enthusiasm, I am also happy—originarily—but *for their sake*; I, for myself, would not—considered only from myself—behave like that. By the same token, if I experience the same thing from myself, in this case, too, their enthusiasm about the view and my enthusiasm about the view stand *separately beside each other*, despite their similarity. Then, suddenly, there occurs a remarkable "leaping into each other" of my lived experiences into their lived experiences and of their lived experiences into my lived experiences: we are suddenly "together"; the intentional "wall," the mental "interstice," has been broken through. It is as if I *myself* experience from myself what they experience, as if they experience it in me and I experience it in them. (If they also *actually simultaneously*

---

[44] Cf. Stein, *Zum Problem der Einfühlung*, 10.

originarily experience *exactly the same* as me, then we would have a "we-experience" in the narrowest sense—it would then be a particularly excellent special case of communal lived experience.) *Now* the other's lived experience also *belongs to me*, although they experience it; I myself am also in this lived experience, almost in the way that I am simultaneously originarily "in" my own identical or similar lived experience.

This peculiar "belonging to me" of the other's lived experiences in we-experiences and communal lived experiences is something with its own specific character. It must not be confused with other determinations of lived experience which, to superficial observation, have a certain similarity with them. They should not be confused, for example, with the consciousness that someone else "has" a lived experience "from me." For instance, I might have been happy about this view earlier, in the presence of another person, and have expressed my happiness about it. They adopted this happiness from me, and now repeat it (at the same time, or later)—perhaps unconsciously—in exactly the same way and with exactly the same expressions. I recognize my happiness in their happiness and say "they got that from me," "that belongs to me (in *this* sense)." This is completely different from "leaping into each other," from "belonging-to-me," from communal lived experience, in which I am *united* with the other and their lived experience. For in the latter case, the other's lived experience belongs completely to themselves; they did not *absorb it externally* from me—or rather, if they did so, then they only did so because it suited them so perfectly that it could have emerged in them just as well without the mediation of one of my lived experiences.

Communal lived experience also has nothing to do with *imitating* others' lived experiences. (Even if imitation can play an empirical-genetic role in the emergence of communal lived experiences.)[45] In imitating the actual (or potential) behavior or lived experience of a (real or fictitious) subject, I grasp their lived experience empathically and "slip into it," so to speak. So, for instance, in our above example I can imitate the other's expressions of enthusiasm, their gestures and tones of voice, like an actor, without *myself* really and truly being enthusiastic like them—perhaps I am in fact totally unmoved, the landscape leaves me totally cold. The lived experience of the other only lies over me like a mental veil that does not belong to me: it did not proceed from my ownmost self.

---

[45] Cf. A[loys] Fischer, "Über Nachahmung und Nachfolge," *Archiv für Religionspsychologie* 1 [(1914): 68–116].

It is the same with *suggestion*. This is not communal lived experience either, and communal lived experience is not at all, like some psychologists claim,[46] just "normal suggestion." In suggestion, the other's empathically grasped lived experience immediately passes over into an identical originary lived experience of one's own, without the experiencing subject knowing it. The subject usually even takes the suggested lived experience immediately as a lived experience of its own and does not experience it as embedded in the more or less clear awareness of "people who also . . ." The other's lived experience that has elicited the subject's own—suggested—lived experience therefore does not confront the subject as the cause of this lived experience or as a similar lived experience of the other. The subject thus cannot feel united in that peculiar way with the other's lived experience and *its* subject. The subject that experiences [*erfahren*] suggestion lives totally in the object of the suggested lived experience, is fully and totally intentionally turned toward this object. This subject generally does not consider and compare its own lived experience with the lived experience of the person who made the suggestion; it can therefore also not feel one with that person in the lived experience of the same thing.

Even if the subject did make the person who gave the suggestion and the latter's lived experience into its intentional object, that lived experience would seem just as foreign as before. [The only difference would be] that [the first subject] would now see that the other subject experiences the same thing as itself and that it "has" its lived experience "from the other subject" (in the above sense), mediated by suggestion. But this would never be inner oneness in the sense that we showed to be the necessary foundation for communal lived experience. No doubt such inner oneness could be based on a suggestion, but then it would be added to this suggested lived experience, just like it would be added to any other lived experience, as a *new* moment with its own specific character—but it would never be given by suggestion alone. Suggestion, therefore, is a special case of similar lived experience, characterized by its genetic origin. This is the case whether it is an individual lived experience that is suggested or a whole attitude, from which further individual lived experiences can emerge that the giver of the suggestion did not have. It

---

[46] Cf. T[heodor] Lipps, "Die soziologische Grundfrage," *Archiv für Rassen- und Gesellschaftsbiologie* 4, no. 5 (1907) [: 652-674. This journal was a racist publication that ran from 1904 to 1944 and promoted eugenics. The journal was the public voice of the Society for Racial Hygiene (Gesellschaft für Rassenhygiene), which was founded by the editor of the journal with the goal of promoting and popularizing eugenics and which was disbanded in 1945].

is similar to living involuntarily in one or several others *without* inner one-ness, which we investigate just below.

Now, you might think that a communal lived experience must always exist wherever one or more subjects live in one human being—where that person is, as it were, "inserted [*steckt*]" in them all. For example, something like this would exist if, at a lecture, all the listeners were totally suffused by the lec-ture and the speaker's lived experiences. Here—at least in an ideal case—all listeners would have exactly the same lived experiences (compared to each other and the lecturer), absorbed from the lecturer. You might think that in this case we are dealing with a particularly full and complete communal lived experience. However, that is not the case at all, because the listeners, or some of them, could be inwardly completely detached from the opinions of the speaker, despite being filled by them. It may happen all too often to people with a sensitive nature that other people invade them, as it were, to such an extent that in their momentary attitudes, or even in their total attitude, they end up "seeing everything with the other's eyes," etc., although this does not correspond to their own attitudes at all. Who has not had it happen to them that, after being with a particular group, for a long time you are not free of its "spirit," its total attitude—even with respect to matters that this group did not refer to while you were with it? Perhaps the group even reverberates in you, lives on in you, although you feel that its attitude is not at all suitable to you, and you bridle against it and seek with all your strength to thrust it away.

But this, too, cannot be called a communal lived experience, although in this case, too, other subjects are taken into, or have invaded, one's own self, so that here, too, my stirrings come "into" me, into my I-center, from them, from the others.

But even if the subject in question did not feel those others as opposed to itself, if it did not strive to "eject them" from itself, if instead it let them and their attitude peacefully reverberate within itself, without taking a position against them, but also *without counting them as its own*, without having that feeling of belongingness and oneness with them—even then there would not exist a communal lived experience in our sense. For in this case, although others would indeed live in this subject while it lived from them, this sub-ject would not feel as if it were living *from itself* at the same time. The subject would not feel as if, in living *with* the others from the unity of itself and the others within itself, it simultaneously lived from itself as part of the com-munity, as part of the we. [Rather,] in this case, it lives *only from the* others in itself, but not from itself and *the others* in itself, as in proper communal lived experience. The latter only arises when each "living-in-the-others" has added to it that peculiar feeling that, although this lived experience occurs "in the others," it belongs at the same time to the experiencing subject itself, as itself, and it belongs to them because it is itself contained in the unity with them. The lived experience does not belong "to the subject" because it is "contained" in the subject and emerged in the subject, or because the subject could experience this in itself in a similar way or exactly the same way (which could go hand in hand with a feeling of indifference or separateness), but because the subject is united with the others.

Likewise, of course, pathological phenomena, such as split personalities, where occasionally a different complex from the usual, "normal" complex in the self (in the "subconscious") of a person is decisive for the meaningful grouping [Sinngruppierung] of their lived experiences, have nothing to do with communal lived experiences. This is because these phenomena lack the relationship to other subjects, they lack oneness with them, and they lack the conscious confrontation of the various split personalities in the relevant subject as *independent* psychophysical subjects, as well as their reciprocal oneness with each other. [...]

Thus the fact that a subject may be able to empathically grasp, re-live, imitate, or otherwise be suffused by a subject of others' lived experiences may be the foundation and precondition of communal lived experience, but it is not sufficient to characterize it. Neither, as we have seen, is communal lived experience already given when a subject manages to transform the empathically grasped lived experiences of others into its own originary lived experience [Eigenerleben],[47] so that the "others'" lived experience becomes "*its*" lived experience. In contrast to Theodor Lipps, as we said, we could never accept that as communal lived experience, although we do not dispute that all this forms an essential *precondition* and *presupposition* of communal lived experience.

Rather, in true communal lived experience we always have, in relation to other subjects and their lived experience, that remarkable "leaping into each other," the "belonging-to-me," that we have already mentioned. Here a "beam" from my lived experience sinks, as it were, into that of the other, becoming linked to and interwoven with it. (Of course, that does not mean that my lived experience may not, under certain circumstances, have first been awoken by that lived experience of the other, which, without the latter, I myself might perhaps not have come to experience—originarily—like *that*.)

---

[47] Cf. Stein, *Zum Problem der Einfühlung*, 12ff.

On the other hand, the characteristic of oneness in communal lived experiences is not always necessarily connected with a subject having previously empathically grasped certain subjects with similar or identical lived experiences in originary experience. This oneness can also concern a mere "empty representation," or even a fiction, of such other subjects. For example, on a journey through a foreign country, a subject could be enchanted by an unusually beautiful landscape. As this happens, perhaps they think of some *possible* other subjects (although they are now totally alone and perhaps do not even know such subjects personally) who would "also" be pleased in this way by this landscape *if* they saw it, or who would have been happy *if* they had seen it earlier, or who would be happy if they were to see it later—even if the relevant subject is long dead. And the first subject can very well feel one with these imagined (potential or merely fictitious) "people who also . . ." and their happiness, although it does not know them and knows nothing about them—not even whether they exist. It only knows that they must have *this* kind of nature, so that they would "also" have this happiness about this landscape, if . . . And in thinking of these people and their happiness, in oneness with them, the subject can experience its own happiness as the happiness of a fictitious we, as happiness that it experiences itself, but which is embedded in that awareness of the (perhaps only potential) "people who also . . .," with whom this subject is united,[48] although, as we said, it is now perfectly alone and perhaps does not even know such people. Only later—if at all—does this subject perhaps get to know such people, when they would fulfill in reality the place that the "empty intention" toward these "people who also . . .," which had been previously—a priori, as it were—assigned to them.[49]

---

[48] Cf. Scheler, *Sympathiegefühle*, 131.

[49] Cf. Scheler, "Der Formalismus in der Ethik," 557f. and 563f.—Unfortunately, Scheler's book *Vom Ewigen im Menschen* (Leipzig: Neue Geist/Peter Reinhold, 1921) [GW, Vol. 5] only came to our attention during the printing of the present work. We can therefore only note briefly here that he also presents this view there (especially 149ff.). Of course, ethical-metaphysical perspectives also play a part in Scheler's work, which we do not want to consider more closely here and which we do not want to take as the basis of our deliberations—at least not *here*.

Bibliography

Cited in Editors' Introductions

Adler, Georg, Peter Hudis, and Annelies Laschitza, eds. *The Letters of Rosa Luxemburg*. Translated by George Shriver. London: Verso, 2013.

Albisetti, James C. *Schooling German Girls and Women*. Princeton, NJ: Princeton University Press, 1988.

Arendt, Hannah. *Rahel Varnhagen: The Life of a Jewess*. Edited by Liliane Weissberg. Translated by Richard Winston and Clara Winston. Baltimore: Johns Hopkins University Press, 1997.

Arendt, Hannah. "Rosa Luxemburg: 1871–1919." In Hannah Arendt, *Men in Dark Times*, 33–56. New York: Harcourt Brace, 1983.

Baseheart, Mary Catharine, and Linda Lopez McAlister, with Waltraut Stein. "Edith Stein (1891–1942)." In *A History of Women Philosophers*, Vol. 4, *Contemporary Women Philosophers: 1900–Today*, edited by Mary Ellen Waithe, 157–189. Dordrecht: Kluwer, 1995.

Bauer, Nancy. *Simone de Beauvoir, Philosophy, and Feminism*. New York: Columbia University Press, 2001.

Bebel, August. *Woman under Socialism*. Translated by Daniel De Leon. New York: Schocken, 1904. Reprint, 1971.

Becker-Cantarino, Barbara. *Schriftstellerinnen der Romantik. Epoche—Werke—Wirkung*. Munich: C. H. Beck, 2000.

Behler, Ernst. "La doctrine de Coppet d'une perfectibilité infinie et la Révolution française." In *Le Groupe de Coppet et la Révolution française. Actes du quatrième Colloque de Coppet, 20–23 juillet 1988*, edited by Etienne Hofmann and Anne-Lise Delacrétaz, 255–274. Lausanne: Institut B. Constant, 1990.

Beiser, Frederick C. *After Hegel: German Philosophy 1840–1900*. Princeton, NJ: Princeton University Press, 2014.

Beiser, Frederick C. *German Idealism: The Struggle against Subjectivism, 1781–1801*. Cambridge, MA: Harvard University Press, 2002.

Beiser, Frederick C. *The Romantic Imperative: The Concept of Early German Romanticism*. Cambridge, MA: Harvard University Press, 2003.

Beiser, Frederick C. *Weltschmerz: Pessimism in German Philosophy, 1860–1900*. Oxford: Oxford University Press, 2016.

Binion, Rudolph. *Frau Lou: Nietzsche's Wayward Disciple*. Princeton, NJ: Princeton University Press, 1968.

Braun, Lily. "Left and Right." In *Selected Writings on Feminism and Socialism*. Edited and translated by Alfred G. Meyer, 443–454. Bloomington: Indiana University Press, 1987.

Broad, Jacqueline, ed. *Women Philosophers of the Seventeenth Century: Selected Correspondence*. Cambridge: Cambridge University Press, 2002.

Bronner, Stephen Eric. *Rosa Luxemburg: A Revolutionary for Our Times.* University Park: Penn State University Press, 1981.

Bruin, Karen de. "Romantic Aesthetics and Abolitionist Activism: African Beauty in Germaine de Staël's *Mirza ou Lettre d'un voyageur.*" *Symposium: A Quarterly Journal in Modern Literatures* 67, no. 3 (2013): 135–147.

Calcagno, Antonio. "On the Vulnerability of a Community: Edith Stein and Gerda Walther." *Journal of the British Society for Phenomenology* 49, no. 3 (2018): 255–266.

Child, Lydia Maria. *The Biography of Madame de Staël and Madame Roland.* Boston: Carter and Hendee, 1832.

Cocks, Joan. *Passion and Paradox: Intellectuals Confront the National Question.* Princeton, NJ: Princeton University Press, 2002.

Conrad-Martinus, Hedwig. "Pflanze und Tier." In *Metaphysische Gespräche,* 1–26. Halle: Max Niemeyer, 1921.

Creuzer, Friedrich, and Karoline von Günderrode. *Friedrich Creuzer und Karoline von Günderode. Briefe und Dichtungen.* Edited by Erwin Rohde. Heidelberg: Winter, 1896.

Dasey, Robin. "Women's Work and the Family: Women Garment Workers in Berlin and Hamburg before the First World War." In *The German Family,* edited by Richard Evans and W. R. Lee, 221–255. London: Routledge, 1981.

Davis, Angela. "Foreword." In *Clara Zetkin: Selected Writings,* edited by Philip S. Foner, 9–16. New York: International Publishers, 1984.

Diethe, Carol. *Nietzsche's Women: Beyond the Whip.* Berlin: De Gruyter, 1996.

Dohm, Hedwig. "Die alte Frau." *Die Zukunft* 14 (January 3, 1903): 22–30.

Dohm, Hedwig. *Die Antifeministen. Ein Buch der Verteidigung.* Berlin: Holzinger, 2015 [original: 1902].

Dohm, Hedwig. "Reaktion in der Frauenbewegung." *Die Zukunft* 29 (November 18, 1899): 279–291.

Dohm, Hedwig. "Sind Berufsthätigkeit und Mutterpflichten vereinbar?" *Die Woche. Moderne illustrierte Zeitschrift* 38 (September 22, 1900): 1667–1669.

Drewitz, Ingeborg. *Bettine von Arnim. Romantick—Revolution—Utopie.* Dusseldorf: Diederichs, 1969.

Engels, Friedrich. *Origin of the Family, Private Property and the State: In Light of the Researches of Lewis H. Morgan.* Edited with an introduction by Eleanor Burke Leacock. Translated by Alec West. New York: International Publishers, 1972.

Erhardt-Siebold, Erika von. "Harmony of the Senses in English, German, and French Romanticism." *PMLA* 47, no. 2 (1932): 577–592.

Extending New Narratives in the History of Philosophy. http://www.newnarrativesinphilosophy.net/.

Ezekiel, Anna C. "Introduction." In Karoline von Günderrode, *Poetic Fragments,* 1–37. Albany: SUNY Press, 2016.

Feilchenfeldt, Konrad. "'Berliner Salon' und Briefkultur um 1800." *Der Deutschunterricht. Beiträge zu seiner Praxis und wissenschaftlichen Grundlegung* 36 (1984): 77–99.

Ferran, Íngrid Vendrell. *Die Emotionen. Gefühle in der realistischen Phänomenologie.* Berlin: De Gruyter, 2008.

Ferran, Íngrid Vendrell. "The Emotions in Early Phenomenology." *Studia Phaenomenologica* 15 (2015): 349–374.

Ferran, Íngrid Vendrell. "Empathy, Emotional Sharing and Feelings in Stein's Early Work." *Human Studies* 38 (2015): 481–502.

Fichte, J. G. *Foundations of Natural Right according to the Principles of the Wissenschaftslehre.* Edited by Frederick Neuhouser. Translated by Michael Baur. Cambridge: Cambridge University Press, 2000.

Fichte, J. G., and F. W. J. Schelling. *The Philosophical Rupture between Fichte and Schelling: Selected Texts and Correspondence (1800–1802).* Translated and edited by Michael G. Vater and David W. Wood. Albany: SUNY Press, 2012.

Fontana, Biancamaria. *Germaine de Staël: A Political Portrait.* Princeton, NJ: Princeton University Press, 2016.

Frank, Manfred. *The Philosophical Foundations of Early German Romanticism.* Translated by Elizabeth Millán-Zaibert. Albany: SUNY Press, 2004.

Frank, Manfred. *"Unendliche Annäherung." Die Anfänge der philosophischen Frühromantik.* Frankfurt: Suhrkamp, 1997.

Frederiksen, Elke and Katherine Goodman. "'Locating' Bettina Brentano-von Arnim, A Nineteenth Century German Woman Writer," in *Bettina Brentano-von Arnim: Gender and Politics,* ed. Elke Frederiksen and Katherine Goodman, 13–34. Detroit: Wayne State University Press, 1995.

French, Lorely. *German Women as Letter Writers: 1750–1850.* London: Associated University Presses, 1996.

Frölich, Paul. *Rosa Luxemburg: Ideas in Action.* Translated by Johanna Hoornweg. Chicago: Haymarket Books, 2010.

Fuchs, Renata. "'*Dann ist und bleibt eine Korrespondenz Lebendig*': Romantic Dialogue in the Letters and Works of Rahel Varnhagen, Bettina Brentano von Arnim, and Karoline von Günderrode." PhD diss., University of Illinois–Urbana Champaign, 2015.

Gaido, Daniel, and Cintia Frencia. "'A Clean Break': Clara Zetkin, the Socialist Women's Movement, and Feminism." *International Critical Thought* 8, no. 2 (2018): 277–303.

Gjesdal, Kristin, and Dalia Nassar, eds. *The Oxford Handbook of Nineteenth-Century Women Philosophers in the German Tradition.* New York: Oxford University Press, forthcoming.

Goldstein, Robert Justin. *Political Repression in 19th Century Europe.* New York: Routledge, 1983.

Goodman, Katherine R., and Edith Waldstein. *In the Shadow of Olympus: German Women Writers around 1800.* Albany: SUNY Press, 1992.

Green, Karen. *A History of Women's Political Thought in Europe, 1700–1800.* Cambridge: Cambridge University Press, 2014.

Günderrode, Karoline. *"Ich Sende Dir ein zärtliches Pfand." Die Briefe der Karoline von Günderrode.* Edited by Birgit Weißenborn. Frankfurt am Main: Insel Verlag, 1992.

Hagengruber, Ruth. "History of Women Philosophers and Scientists." 2019. https://kw.uni-paderborn.de/fach-philosophie/forschung/philosophy-in-the-media/.

Hawkins, Richmond Laurin. *Madame de Staël and the United States.* Cambridge, MA: Harvard University Press, 1930.

Heffernan, George. "Phenomenology, Psychology, and Ideology: A New Look at the Life and Work of Else Voigtländer," *Phenomenological Investigations* 1 (2021): 1–49.

Hegel, G. W. F. *Elements of the Philosophy of Right.* Edited by Allen Wood. Translated by H. B. Nisbet. Cambridge: Cambridge University Press, 1991.

Henrich, Dieter. *Konstellationen. Probleme und Debatten am Ursprung der idealistischen Philosophie (1789–1795).* Stuttgart: Klett-Cotta, 1991.

Herold, J. Christopher. *Mistress to an Age: A Life of Madame de Staël.* Indianapolis: Bobbs-Merrill, 1958.

Hippel, Theodor Gottlieb von. *The Status of Women: Collected Writings*. Edited and translated by Timothy F. Sellner. Bloomington, IN: Xlibris, 2009.

Hölderlin, Friedrich. *Sämtliche Werke*, Vol. 2. Edited by Friedrich von Beißner. Stuttgart: Cotta, 1953.

Holmgren, Janet Besserer. *The Women Writers in Schiller's Horen: Patrons, Petticoats, and the Promotion of Weimar Classicism*. Newark: University of Delaware Press, 2007.

Holst, Amalia. *Über die Bestimmung des Weibes zur höheren Geistesbildung*. Edited by Berta Rahm. Zurich: Ala Verlag, 1984.

Hudis, Peter. "Introduction," in *The Complete Work of Rosa Luxemburg*, Vol. 1. Edited by Peter Hudis. Translated by David Fernbach, Joseph Fracchia, and George Shriver. London: Verso, 2014.

Isbell, John Claiborne. *The Birth of European Romanticism: Truth and Propaganda in Staël's "De l'Allemagne."* Cambridge: Cambridge University Press, 1994.

Jardine, Nicholas. *The Scenes of Inquiry: On the Reality of Questions in the Sciences*. Oxford: Oxford University Press, 1991.

Kasper, Max. *Kepler*. Edited and translated by C. Doris Hellman. London: Dover, 1959.

Kennedy, Marie, and Chris Tilly. "Socialism, Feminism and the Stillbirth of Socialist Feminism in Europe, 1890–1920." *Science & Society* 51, no. 1 (1987): 6–42.

Knapp, Ulla. "Frauenarbeit in Deutschland zwischen 1850 und 1933, Teil I," *Historical Social Research/Historische Sozialforschung* 28 (1983): 42–62.

Kneller, Jane. "Feminism." In *The Oxford Handbook of German Philosophy in the Nineteenth Century*, edited by Michael N. Forster and Kristin Gjesdal, 534–555. Oxford: Oxford University Press, 2015.

Kneller, Jane. *Kant and the Power of Imagination*. Cambridge: Cambridge University Press, 2007.

Kneller, Jane. "Sociability and the Conduct of Philosophy: What We Can Learn from Early German Romanticism." In *The Relevance of Romanticism: Essays on German Romantic Philosophy*, edited by Dalia Nassar, 110–124. New York: Oxford University Press, 2014.

Kollwitz, Käthe. *Die Tagebücher*. Berlin: Akademie Verlag, 1989.

Krätke, Michael R. "A Very Political Economist: Rosa Luxemburg's Theory of Wages." In *Rosa Luxemburg and the Critique of Political Economy*, edited by Riccardo Bellofiore, 159–174. London: Routledge, 2009.

Lange, Helene. *Lebenserinnerungen*. Munich: Herbig, 1921.

Licher, Maria Lucia. *Mein Leben in einer bleibenden Form aussprechen. Umrisse einer Ästhetik im Werk Karoline von Günderrodes (1780–1806)*. Heidelberg: Winter, 1996.

Luft, Sebastian. "Editor's Introduction." In *The Neo-Kantian Reader*, edited by Sebastian Luft, xx–xxxi. London: Routledge, 2015.

Lund, Hannah Lotte. "Emanzipation in Halböffentlichkeit? Geschlechterverhältnisse und politische Partizipation im literarischen Salon um 1800. Eine Annäherung." In *Revolution und Emanzipation. Geschlechterordnungen in Europa um 1800*, edited by Katharina Rennhak and Virginia Richter, 33–47. Cologne: Böhlau Verlag, 2004.

Luxemburg, Rosa. *The Rosa Luxemburg Reader*. Edited by Peter Hudis and Kevin B. Anderson. New York: Monthly Review Press, 2004.

MacIntyre, Alasdair. *Edith Stein: A Philosophical Prologue, 1913–1922*. Lanham, MD: Rowman & Littlefield, 2005.

Mackintosh, James. "*De l'Allemagne*, par Madame la Baronne de Staël-Holstein, 3 vols. London 1813." *Edinburgh Review* (October 1813): 198–239.

Marion, Jean-Luc. *Reduction and Givenness: Investigations of Husserl, Heidegger, and Phenomenology*. Translated by Thomas A. Carlson. Evanston, IL: Northwestern University Press, 1998.

Massardier-Kenney, Françoise. "Staël, Translation, and Race." In *Translating Slavery: Gender and Race in French Women's Writings, 1783-1823*, edited by Doris Y. Kadish and Françoise Massardier-Kenney, 135–145. Kent, OH: Kent State University Press, 1994.

Matherne, Samantha. "Edith Landmann-Kalischer on Aesthetic Demarcation and Normativity," *The British Journal of Aesthetics* 60, no. 3 (July 2020): 315–334, https://doi.org/10.1093/aesthj/ayaa007.

Matherne, Samantha. "Edith Landmann-Kalischer's Moderate Objectivism about Aesthetic Value." Forthcoming.

Matysik, Tracie. *Reforming the Moral Subject: Ethics and Sexuality in Central Europe, 1890-1930*. Ithaca, NY: Cornell University Press, 2008.

Mazón, Patricia M. *Gender and the Modern Research University: The Admission of Women to German Higher Education, 1865-1914*. Stanford, CA: Stanford University Press, 2003.

McAlister, Linda Lopez. "Gerda Walther." In *A History of Women Philosophers: Contemporary Women Philosophers*, Vol. 4, *Contemporary Women Philosophers, 1900-Today*, edited by Mary Ellen Waithe, 189–206. Dordrecht: Kluwer, 1995.

M. E. W. S. "A Curiosity of Literature." *Atlantic Monthly* 31 (1873): 210–217.

Mercer, Christia. "Descartes Is Not Our Father." *New York Times*, September 25, 2017. https://www.nytimes.com/2017/09/25/opinion/descartes-is-not-our-father.html.

Meysenbug, Malwida von. *Rebel in Bombazine: Memoirs of Malwida von Meysenbug*. Translated by Elsa von Meysenbug Lyons. New York: Norton, 1936.

Mikus, Birgit. *The Political Woman in Print: German Women's Writing 1845-1919*. Oxford: Peter Lang, 2014.

Mikus, Birgit, and Emily Spiers. "Split Infinities: German Feminisms and the Generational Project." *Oxford German Studies* 45, no.1 (2016): 5–30.

Millán-Zaibert, Elizabeth. *Friedrich Schlegel and the Emergence of Romantic Philosophy*. Albany: SUNY Press, 2007.

Moland, Lydia. "Is She Not an Unusual Woman? Say More: Germaine de Staël and Lydia Maria Child on Progress, Art, and Abolition." In *Women and Philosophy in Eighteenth-Century Germany*, edited by Corey Dyck. Oxford: Oxford University Press, 2021.

Moland, Lydia. "Lydia Maria Child on German philosophy and American slavery," *British Journal for the History of Philosophy* (2020), doi:10.1080/09608788.2020.1763911.

Moland, Lydia. *Never the Same Again: The Radical Conscience of Lydia Maria Child*. Chicago: University of Chicago Press, forthcoming.

Moland, Lydia, and Alison Stone, eds. *The Oxford Handbook of British and American Women Philosophers in the Nineteenth Century*. New York: Oxford University Press, forthcoming.

Moran, Dermot, and Rodney K. B. Parker. "Editor's Introduction." *Studia Phaenomenologica* 15 (2015): 11–27.

Morgenthaler, Walter, ed. *Karoline von Günderrode. Sämtliche Werke und ausgewählte Studien*. Frankfurt: Stroemfeld/Roter Stern, 1990–1991.

Mueller-Vollmer, Kurt. "Staël's *Germany* and the Beginnings of an American National Literature." In *Germaine de Staël: Crossing the Borders*, edited by Madelyn Gutwirth, Avriel Goldberger, and Karyna Szmurlo, 141–158. New Brunswick, NJ: Rutgers University Press, 1991.

Nassar, Dalia. "The Human Vocation and the Question of the Earth: Karoline von Günderrode's Philosophy of Nature," *Archiv für Geschichte der Philosophie*, 2021.

O'Neill, Eileen. "Disappearing Ink: Early Modern Women Philosophers and Their Fate in History." In *Philosophy in a Feminist Voice: Critiques and Reconstructions*, edited by Janet A. Kourany, 17–62. Princeton, NJ: Princeton University Press, 1997.

O'Neill, Eileen. "Early Modern Women Philosophers and the History of Philosophy." *Hypatia* 20, no. 3 (2005): 185–197.

Parker, Rodney. "Gerda Walther and the Phenomenological Community." *Acta Mexicana de Fenomenología* 2 (2017): 45–66.

Parker, Rodney, ed. and trans. "Gerda Walther, *Phenomenology of Mysticism*, Introduction and Chapter 1." In *Gerda Walther's Phenomenology of Sociality, Psychology, and Religion*, edited by Antonio Calcagno, 115–133. Berlin: Springer, 2018

Partington, John S. "Clara Zetkin on the Soviet Experiment, 1917–1934," in *1917: The Russian Revolution, Reactions and Impact*, edited by David Morgan, 56–82. London: Socialist History Society, 2017.

Paulin, Roger. *The Life of August Wilhelm Schlegel: Cosmopolitan of Art and Poetry*. London: Open Book, 2016.

Peters, H. F. *My Sister, My Spouse: A Biography of Lou Andreas-Salomé*. New York: Norton, 1962.

Porter, Roy, ed. *The Cambridge History of Science*, Vol. 4, *Eighteenth Century*. Cambridge: Cambridge University Press, 2003.

Project Vox. Duke University. http://projectvox.org/about-the-project/.

Quataert, Jean H. *Reluctant Feminists in German Social Democracy, 1885–1917*. Princeton, NJ: Princeton University Press, 1979. Reprint, 2015.

Rogers, Dorothy G. *America's First Women Philosophers: Transplanting Hegel, 1860–1925*. New York: Continuum, 2005.

Salice, Alessandro. "The Phenomenology of the Munich and Göttingen Circles." *Stanford Encyclopedia of Philosophy* (Winter 2019), edited by Edward N. Zalta. https://plato.stanford.edu/archives/win2019/entries/phenomenology-mg/>.

Salice, Alessandro, and Genki Uemura. "Social Acts and Communities: Walther between Husserl and Reinach." In *Gerda Walther's Phenomenology of Sociality, Psychology and Religion*, edited by Antonio Calcagno, 27–46. Dordrecht: Springer, 2018.

Salomé, Lou Andreas-. "The Dual Orientation of Narcissism." *Psychoanalytic Quarterly* 31 (1962): 1–30.

Salomé, Lou Andreas-. *Looking Back: Memoirs. The Intimate Story of her Friendships with Nietzsche, Rilke, and Freud*. Edited by Ernst Pfeiffer. Translated by Breon Mitchell. New York: Marlowe, 1995.

Salomé, Lou Andreas-. *Nietzsche*. Edited and translated by Siegfried Mandel. Urbana: University of Illinois Press, 2001.

Schlegel, Friedrich. "Über die Philosophie. An Dorothea [On Philosophy. To Dorothea]." In *Kritische Friedrich-Schlegel-Ausgabe*, Vol. 8. Edited by Ernst Behler, Jean Jacques Anstett, and Hans Eichner, 41–62. Munich: Schöningh, 1958–.

Schleiermacher, Friedrich. *Essay on a Theory of Sociable Behavior*. Edited and translated by Peter Foley. Lewiston, NY: Edwin Mellen, 2006.

Schultz, Hartwig, ed. *Salons der Romantik. Beiträge eines Wiepersdorfer Kolloquiums zu Theorie und Geschichte des Salons*. Berlin: De Gruyter, 1997.

Seidler, Miriam C. "Johann Wolfgang von Goethe." In *Bettina von Arnim Handbuch*, edited by Barbara Becker-Cantarino, 178–186. Berlin: De Gruyter, 2019.

Shapiro, Lisa. "Revisiting the Early Modern Philosophical Canon." *Journal of the American Philosophical Association* 2, no. 3 (2016): 365–383.

Shelley, Mary Wollstonecraft. *Lives of the Most Eminent French Writers*. Vol. 2. Philadelphia: Lea and Blanchard, 1840.

Simpson, Patricia A. "Letters in Sufferance and Deliverance: The Correspondence of Bettina Brentano-von Arnim and Karoline von Günderrode." In *Bettina Brentano-von Arnim: Gender and Politics*, ed. Elke Frederiksen and Katherine Goodman, 247–277. Detroit: Wayne State University Press, 1995.

Sluga, Glenda. "Madame de Staël and the Transformation of European Politics, 1812–17." *International History Review* 37, no. 1 (2015): 142–166.

Sotiropoulos, Carol Strauss. *Early Feminists and the Educational Debates: England, France, Germany 1760–1810*. Madison, NJ: Fairleigh Dickinson University Press, 2007.

Stackman, Valerie R. "Scottsboro Boys, 1931–1948," in *50 Events that Shaped African American History: An Encyclopedia of the American Mosaic*. Vols. 1 and 2, edited by Jamie J. Wilson, 282–299. Santa Barbara, CA: Greenwood: 2019.

Stadler-Labhart, Verena. *Rosa Luxemburg an der Universität Zürich, 1889–1897*. Zurich: Verlag Hans Rohr, 1978.

Staël, Germaine de. *Considerations on the Principal Events of the French Revolution*. Edited by Aurelian Craiutu. Indianapolis: Liberty Fund, 2008.

Staël, Germaine de. "Letter to Jefferson" (January 6, 1816). In *Madame de Staël: Selected Correspondence*. Edited by Georges Solovieff and Kathleen Jameson-Cemper. Translated by Kathleen Jameson-Cemper, 367–369. Dordrecht: Springer, 2000.

Stein, Edith. *Life in a Jewish Family: An Autobiography, 1891–1916*. Translated by Josephine Koeppel. Washington, DC: Institute of Carmelite Studies, 1986.

Stein, Edith. *On the Problem of Empathy*. Translated by Waltraut Stein. Washington, DC: Institute of Carmelite Studies, 1989.

Stein, Edith. *Philosophy of Psychology and the Humanities*. Edited by Marianne Sawicki. Translated by Mary Catharine Baseheart and Marianne Sawicki. Washington, DC: Institute of Carmelite Studies, 2000.

Stein, Edith. *Werke*. Vol. 6. Edited by Lucy Gelber and Romaeus. Leuven. Freiburg: Herder, 1962.

Stieda, W. "Frauenarbeit." *Jahrbücher für Nationalökonomie und Statistik/Journal of Economics and Statistics*, 3rd ed., Vol. 2, 57, no. 2 (1891): 189–208.

Stöcker, Helene. *Zur Kunstanschauung des XVIII Jahrhunderts*. Berlin: Mayer and Müller, 1902.

Stone, Alison. "Hegel on Law, Women and Contract." In *Feminist Encounters with Legal Philosophy*, edited by Maria Drakopolou, 104–122. London: Routledge, 2013.

Takeda, Chinatsu. *Mme de Staël and Political Liberalism in France*. Singapore: Palgrave Macmillan, 2018.

Trouille, Mary Seidman. *Sexual Politics in the Enlightenment: Women Writers Read Rousseau*. Albany: SUNY Press, 1997.

Voigtländer, Else. *Vom Selbstgefühl. Ein Beitrag zur Förderung psychologischen Denkens*. Leipzig: R. Voigtländer, 1910.

Waithe, Mary Ellen, ed. *A History of Women Philosophers*. 4 vols. Dordrecht: Kluwer, 1995.

Walther, Gerda. *Ein Beitrag zur Ontologie der sozialen Gemeinschaften*. Halle: Max Niemeyer, 1922.

Walther, Gerda. "Hitler's Black Magicians." *Tomorrow* 4, no. 2 (1956): 7–23.

Walther, Gerda. *Zum anderen Ufer. Vom Marxismus und Atheismus zum Christentum*. St. Goar: Reichl Verlag, 1960.

Wawrytko, Sandra A. "Lou Salomé (1861–1937)." In *A History of Women Philosophers*, Vol. 4, *Contemporary Women Philosophers: 1900-Today*, edited by Mary Ellen Waithe, 69–102. Dordrecht: Kluwer, 1995.

Weckel, Ulrike. "Gleichheit auf dem Prüfstand. Zur zeitgenössischen Rezeption der Streitschriften von Theodor Gottlieb von Hippel und Mary Wollstonecraft in Deutschland." In *Tugend, Vernunft und Gefühl. Geschlechterdiskurse der Aufklärung und weibliche Lebenswelten*, edited by Claudia Opiz, Ulrike Weckel, and Elke Kleinan, 209–249. Münster: Waxmann, 2000.

Weedon, Chris. "The Struggle for Women's Emancipation in the Work of Hedwig Dohm." *German Life and Letters* 47, no. 2 (1994): 182–192.

Weissberg, Liliane. "Schreiben als Selbstentwurf: Zu den Schriften Rahel Varnhagens und Dorothea Schlegels." *Zeitschrift für Religions- und Geistesgeschichte* 47 (1995): 231–253.

Weissberg, Liliane. "Turns of Emancipation: On Rahel Varnhagen's Letters." *Cultural Critique* 21 (1992): 219–238.

Westphal, Wolfgang. *Karoline von Günderrode und "Naturdenken um 1800."* Essen: Blaue Eule, 1993.

Wolf, Christa. *Karoline von Günderrode. Der Schatten eines Traumes.* Darmstadt: Luchterhand, 1979.

Wolf, Christa. *No Place on Earth*, trans. Jan van Huerck. New York: Farrar Straus Giroux, 1982.

Wolf, Christa. "Your Next Life Begins Today: A Letter about Bettine." In *Bettina Brentano-von Arnim: Gender and Politics*, edited by Elke P. Frederiksen and Katherine R. Goodman, 35–70. Detroit: Wayne State University Press, 1995.

Wolfe, Charles T. "On the Role of Newtonian Analogies in Eighteenth-Century Life Science: Vitalism and Provisionally Inexplicable Explicative Devices." In *Newton and Empiricism*, edited by Zvi Biener and Eric Schliesser, 223–261. Oxford: Oxford University Press, 2014.

Wollstonecraft, Mary. "Art. XLIX." *Analytical Review* 4 (August 1789).

Zahavi, Dan. "Editor's Introduction." In *The Oxford Handbook of Contemporary Phenomenology*, edited by Dan Zahavi, 1–4. Oxford: Oxford University Press, 2012.

Zahavi, Dan. "Empathy and Other-Directed Intentionality." *Topoi* 33, no. 1 (2014): 129–142.

Zahavi, Dan. *Self and Other: Exploring Subjectivity, Empathy, and Shame.* Oxford: Oxford University Press, 2014.

Cited in Translated Texts

Adler, Max. "Kausalität und Teleologie im Streite um die Wissenschaft." *Marx-Studien* 1 (1904): 195–433.

Aristotle. *Nikomachische Ethik*. Translated into German by Eugen Rolfes. 2nd edition. Leipzig: F. Meiner, 1911.

Burckhardt, Jacob. *Die Kultur der Renaissance in Italien*. Vienna: Phaidon, 1934 [1860].

Cohn, Jonas. *Allgemeine Ästhetik*. Leipzig: Engelmann, 1901.

Eckermann, Johann Peter, ed. *Gespräche mit Goethe in den letzten Jahren seines Lebens*. Vol. 1, *1823–1827*. Leipzig: Philip Reclam Jr., 1836.

Ferrand, W. Busfeild. Speech to the House of Commons. Ferrand, HC Deb, April 27, 1863, Vol. 170 cc 782–783.

Fichte, Johann Gottlieb. *Die Bestimmung des Menschen*. Berlin: Voss, 1800.

Fischer, Aloys. "Über Nachahmung und Nachfolge." *Archiv für Religionspsychologie* 1 (1914): 68–116.

Freud, Sigmund, and Lou Andreas-Salomé. *Letters*. Edited by Ernst Pfeiffer. Translated by William Robson-Scott and Elaine Robson-Scott. New York: Harcourt Brace Jovanovich, 1972.

Gebsattel, Viktor Emil Klemens Franz Freiherr von. *Zur Psychologie der Gefühlsirradiation*. Leipzig: Engelmann, 1907.

Giddings, Franklin Henry. *The Principles of Sociology*. London: Macmillan, 1896. Translated into German by Paul Seliger as *Prinzipien der Soziologie*. Leipzig: Klinghardt, 1911.

Heine, Heinrich. "Die Heimkehr 1823–1824 XX." In *Historisch-kritische Gesamtausgabe der Werke*, Vol. 1, *Buch der Lieder*. Edited by Manfred Windfuhr, with Pierre Grappin. Hamburg: Hoffmann und Campe, 1975.

Hilferding, Rudolf. "Böhm-Bawerks Marx-Kritik." *Marx-Studien* 1 (1904): 1–61.

Humboldt, Alexander von. *Versuch über den politischen Zustand des Königreiches Neu-Spanien*. Vol. 3. Tübingen: Cotta, 1812.

Husserl, Edmund. *Husserliana. Gesammelte Werke* (Hua.). Vol. 3. Edited by Marly Biemel, Walter Biemel, and Karl Schuhmann. The Hague: Martinus Nijhoff, 1950.

Husserl, Edmund. *Husserliana. Gesammelte Werke* (Hua.). Vol. 19. Edited by Ursula Panzer. The Hague: Martinus Nijhoff, 1984.

Husserl, Edmund. "Ideen zu einer reinen Phänomenologie und phänomenologischen Philosophie." *Jahrbuch für Philosophie und phänomenologische Forschung* 1, no. 1 (1913): 1–323.

Husserl, Edmund. *Logische Untersuchungen II*. Halle: Max Niemeyer, 1901.

Husserl, Edmund. "Natur und Geist. Vorlesungen Sommersemester." In *Husserliana: Gesammelte Werke* (Hua.), *Edmund Husserl Materialien*. Vol. 4. Edited by Michael Weiler. Leuven: Husserl Archives, 2002.

Klages, Ludwig. "Die Ausdrucksbewegung und ihre diagnostische Verwertung." *Zeitschrift für Pathopsychologie* (1914): 261–348.

Klages, Ludwig. *Sämtliche Werke* (SW). 2nd edition. Vol. 6. Edited by Ernst Frauchinger, Gerhard Funke, Karl J. Groffmann, Robert Heiss, and Hans Eggert Schröder. Bonn: Bouvier, 2000.

Lenin, Vladimir Ilyich. "Social-Democracy and the Provisional Revolutionary Government" [1905]. In *Collected Works*. Vol. 8, *January–July 1905*. Edited by J. Jerome. Translated by Bernard Isaacs and Isidor Lasker. Moscow: Progress Publishers, 1962.

Liebig, Justus von. *Die Organische Chemie in ihrer Anwendung auf Agricultur und Physiologie*. Teil 1. *Der chemische Proceß der Ernährung der Vegetabilien*. 7th edition. Braunschweig: Friedrich Vieweg und Sohn, 1862.

Lipps, Theodor. "Die soziologische Grundfrage." *Archiv für Rassen- und Gesellschaftsbiologie* 4, no. 5 (1907): 652–674.

Livingston, Angela. *Lou Andreas-Salomé: Her Life and Work*. London: Gordon Fraser, 1984.

Malthus, Thomas Robert. *Principles of Political Economy Considered with a View to Their Practical Application*. London: John Murray, 1820.

Marx, Karl. *Der achtzehnte Brumaire des Louis Bonaparte*. In Karl Marx and Friedrich Engels, *Werke* (MEW). Vol. 16. Berlin: Dietz, 1962.

Marx, Karl. *Das Kapital*. Bd. 1. *Kritik der politischen Ökonomie*. In MEW, Vol. 23. Translated by Ben Fowkes as *Capital: A Critique of Political Economy. Das Kapital*. Series 1. New York: Penguin, 1976.

Nietzsche, Friedrich. *Beyond Good and Evil: Prelude to a Philosophy of the Future*. Edited by Rolf-Peter Horstman and Judith Norman. Translated by Judith Norman. Cambridge and New York: Cambridge University Press, 2002. First published in German in 1886.

Nietzsche, Friedrich. *Daybreak: Thoughts on the Prejudices of Morality*. Edited by Maudemarie Clarke and Brian Leiter. Translated by R. J. Hollingdale. Cambridge: Cambridge University Press, 1997. First published in German in 1881.

Nietzsche, Friedrich. *The Gay Science*. Edited by Bernard Williams. Translated by Josefine Nauckhoff and Adrian Del Caro. Cambridge: Cambridge University Press, 2001. First published in German in 1882, 2nd edition 1886.

Nietzsche, Friedrich. *On the Genealogy of Morality*. Edited by Keith Ansell-Pearson. Translated by Carol Diethe. Revised student edition. Cambridge: Cambridge University Press, 2007. First published in German in 1887.

Nietzsche, Friedrich. *Thus Spoke Zarathustra: A Book for All and None*. Edited by Adrian Del Caro and Robert Pippin. Translated by Adrian Del Caro. Cambridge: Cambridge University Press, 2006. First published in German in 1883–1885.

Nietzsche, Friedrich. *Untimely Meditations*. Edited by Daniel Breazeale. Translated by R. J. Hollingdale. Cambridge: Cambridge University Press, 2006. First published in German in 1873–1876.

Oesterreich, Traugott Konstantin. *Die Phänomenologie des Ich in ihren Grundproblemen*. Vol. 1, *Das Ich und Selbstbewußtsei. Die scheinbare Spaltung des Ich*. Leipzig: Johann Ambrosius Barth, 1910.

Reinach, Adolf. "Die apriorischen Grundlagen des bürgerlichen Rechtes." *Jahrbuch für Philosophie und phänomenologische Forschung* 1, no. 2 (1913): 685–847.

Reuter, Gabriele. *Aus guter Familie. Leidensgeschichte eines Mädchens*. Berlin: Fischer, 1895.

Ricardo, David. *On the Principles of Political Economy and Taxation*. London: John Murray, 1817.

Royce, Josiah. "Self-consciousness, Social Consciousness and Nature." *Philosophical Review* 4, no. 5 (1895): 465–485; and 4, no. 6 (1895): 577–602.

Salomé, Lou Andreas-. *Friedrich Nietzsche in seinen Werken*. Hamburg: Severus, 2013.

Scheler, Max. "Der Formalismus in der Ethik und die materiale Wertethik. Neuer Versuch der Grundlegung eines ethischen Personalismus." *Jahrbuch für Philosophie und phänomenologische Forschung* 2 (1916): 21–478. Reprinted in Max Scheler, *Gesammelte Werke* (GW). Edited by Maria Scheler and M. S. Frings, Vol. 2, 61–100. Bern: Francke; Bonn: Bouvier, 1954-.

Scheler, Max. *Vom Ewigen im Menschen.* Leipzig: Neue Geist/Peter Reinhold, 1921. Reprinted in Max Scheler, *Gesammelte Werke* (GW). Edited by Maria Scheler and M. S. Frings, Vol. 5.

Scheler, Max. *Zur Phänomenologie und Theorie der Sympathiegefühle und von Liebe und Haß. Mit einem Anhang über den Grund zur Annahme der Existenz des fremden Ich.* Halle: Niemeyer, 1913. Revised (1923) edition reprinted as *Wesen und Formen der Sympathie* in Max Scheler, *Gesammelte Werke* (GW). Edited by M. S. Frings, Vol. 7, 150–208. Bern: Francke; Bonn: Bouvier, 1954–.

Schelling, Friedrich Wilhelm Joseph. "Allgemeine Deduction des dynamischen Processes oder der Categorieen der Physik vom Herausgeber." In *Zeitschrift für spekulative Physik*, edited by F. W. J. Schelling, Vol. 1, Issue 1, 100–136, and Vol. 1, Issue 2, 3–87. Jena: Christian Ernst Gabler, 1800.

Schelling, Friedrich Wilhelm Joseph. *Erster Entwurf eines Systems der Naturphilosophie.* Jena: Christian Ernst Gabler, 1799.

Schelling, Friedrich Wilhelm Joseph. *Ideen zu einer Philosophie der Natur.* Leipzig: Breitkopf und Härtel, 1797.

Schleiermacher, Friedrich. *Idee zu einem Katechismus der Vernunft für edle Frauen.* In *Kritische Gesamtausgabe.* Section. 1, Vol. 2. Edited by Hans-Joachim Birkner, 153–154. Berlin: De Gruyter, 1980–.

Simmel, Georg. *Soziologie. Untersuchungen über die Formen der Vergesellschaftung.* In *Georg Simmel Gesamtausgabe*, Vol. 11. Edited by Otthein Rammstedt. Frankfurt am Main: Suhrkamp, 1992.

Sismondi, Jean Charles Léonard de. *Études sur l'économie politique.* Vol. 1. Paris: Treuttel et Würtz, 1837.

Stein, Edith. *Zum Problem der Einfühlung.* Halle: Waisenhauses, 1917. Reprinted in *Edith Stein Gesamtausgabe.* Vol. 5. Edited by Maria Antonia Sondermann. Berlin: Herder, 2008.

Tönnies, Ferdinand. *Gemeinschaft und Gesellschaft.* Leipzig: Fues/R. Reisland, 1887.

Volkelt, Johannes. "Die Bedeutung der niederen Empfindungen für die ästhetische Einfühlung." *Zeitschrift für Psychologie und Physiologie der Sinnesorgane* 25 (1901): 1–37.

Wade, John. *History of the Middle and Working Classes; with a Popular Exposition of the Economical and Political Principles Which Have Influenced the Past and Present Condition of the Industrious Orders.* London: Effingham Wilson, 1833.

Weber, Max. "Über einige Kategorien der verstehenden Soziologie." *Logos* 4 (1913). Reprinted in *Max Weber Gesamtausgabe* (MGW), Section 1, Vol. 12, 389–440. Tübingen: Mohr & Siebeck, 1983–.

Wundt, Wilhelm. *Völkerpsychologie. Eine Untersuchung der Entwicklungsgesetze von Sprache, Mythos und Sitte*, Vol. 7, *Die Gesellschaft.* Leipzig: Alfred Kröner, 1917.

Index

aesthetics, 5n15, 25n4, 26, 46–48, 148, 182, 196–198
Arendt, Hannah, 3, 3n6, 206, 206n1
Arnim, Achim von, 86
Augustine, St., 48, 276

Baader, Franz von, 52, 52n24, 55, 55n36
Bacon, Francis, 51, 51n24
Beauvoir, Simone de, 17, 17n43, 122, 123, 125, 127, 157, 159
Bebel, August, 12, 160
  relationship with Zetkin, 12, 154
  works
    Woman and Socialism, 12
Beethoven, Ludwig van, 106–107
Bonaparte, Napoleon, 4, 23, 26, 130
Braun, Lily, 160–161, 161n9
Brentano, Clemens, 62n1, 64, 85, 101, 103
Brentano von Arnim, Bettina, 4, 6, 18, 63n4
  on Beethoven, 106–107
  correspondence with Goethe, 87, 87n5
  correspondence with Günderrode, 62, 81–91, 86–88, 88n9, 95–121
  on demonstration, 91, 115, 116
  on God, 103–104, 107–108, 109, 114
  on history, 98, 100
  on Hölderlin, 103, 111, 113, 114
  on language, 110–112, 115
  on music, 95, 99–100, 105–107
  on philosophy, 96–97, 117, 118
  on poetry, 103, 105, 112–114, 120
  on sociability, 87, 87n6
  sym-philosophy of, 85, 87
  works
    This Belongs to the King, 86
    The Book of the Poor, 86
    Günderode, 8, 86–91, 92–121

Child, Lydia Maria, 8, 8n19–20, 25n3, 29
Conrad-Martius, Hedwig, 5, 242, 247n14, 274, 275
Creuzer, Friedrich, 63, 63n4–5, 64

Davis, Angela, 156–157
Dilthey, Wilhelm, 180n12
Dohm, Hedwig, 4, 9, 16n40, 17, 179, 182–183
  on antifeminists, 123, 124, 124n6, 150–153
  critique of biological essentialism, 122, 125, 131–132
  on motherhood, 125–126, 139–144
  on the old woman, 123, 126–127, 145–149
  on Nietzsche, 123–125, 128–138
  on Salomé, 123, 124n6, 129–130, 134
  on self-transformation, 125, 133–134, 135–136, 152
  on women, 122, 126–127
  works
    Become who you are!, 124, 127
    "The New Mother," 123, 125, 138–144
    "Nietzsche and Women," 124, 128–138
    "The Old Woman," 123, 126, 127, 145–149
    "On the Agitators of Antifeminism," 123, 150–153
    "Sind Berufsthätigkeit und Mutterpflichten vereinbar?," 122n3, 122n4, 127n9

Emerson, Ralph Waldo, 8, 29, 89
Engels, Friedrich, 18, 86, 273
  and Luxemburg, 210–211, 234n25
  works
    The Origins of the Family, Private Property and the State, 12
  and Zetkin, 12, 155
epistemology, 40–45, 51, 52–54, 58–60, 67–68, 70–72, 76, 77–78, 91, 94, 115, 116, 118, 128–138, 184–185, 248–257, 262–267

Fichte, Johann Gottlieb, 14, 16, 55, 63, 64, 95
  and Günderrode, 65–67, 68, 70–74
  and Staël, 55
  works
    Foundations of Natural Right, 10, 65
    Vocation of Humankind, 65–67, 70–74

French Revolution, 1, 18, 26, 91, 227n19
Freud, Sigmund, 5, 177, 179, 182
Fuller, Margaret, 8, 26, 29, 89

Goethe, Johann Wolfgang von, 3, 14, 29,
    55, 60, 62, 62n1, 87, 87n5, 89,
    151, 153n76
Günderrode, Karoline von, 4, 7, 15, 18,
    52n26, 60n50, 93n12, 103n21
  on the absolute, 68, 76–80
  correspondence with Brentano von Arnim,
    62, 81–91, 86–88, 88n9, 95–121
  on Fichte, 65–67, 68, 70–74
  on force, 79–80, 80n33, 82
  on knowledge, 67–68, 71–72, 76, 77–78
  on life, 74, 79, 82–83
  on philosophy of nature, 65, 67–69, 75–84
  and Schelling, 65, 68, 75n23
  on self-determination, 65–67, 70–71, 72
  on the supersensible, 67
  syncretism of, 15, 64
  on virtue, 69, 83–84
  on the will, 67, 73–74works
    Hildgund, 65
    "Idea of the Earth," 63, 64–65, 82
    "Idea of Nature," 81
    Muhammad: Prophet of Mecca, 15
    "On Fichte's Vocation of
      Humankind," 65–66, 70–74
    "Philosophy of Nature," 67–68, 75–80

Hardenberg, Georg Philipp Friedrich von
    (Novalis), 14, 54n32, 60n50, 64,
    64n7, 65, 85n1
Hegel, Georg Wilhelm Friedrich, 10,
    10n28, 11, 11n32, 13, 16, 17, 273
Heidegger, Martin, 243–244, 274, 275,
    276n10, 287n23
Hemsterhuis, Franz, 60, 60n50, 104,
    104n23–24
Herz, Henriette, 3, 85n2, 86
Hippel, Theodor Gottlieb von, 9–10,
    10n23–25, 11–12
history of philosophy, 1–14, 24–26, 27–29,
    38–50, 123, 134, 150–152, 181,
    212–213
Hölderlin, Friedrich, 14, 64, 90n11, 103,
    111, 111n28, 113, 113n29, 114

Humboldt, Alexander von, 3, 14, 25, 51–52,
    52n25, 91, 218
Humboldt, Wilhelm von, 14
Hume, David, 24, 41
Husserl, Edmund, 241–242, 243n10, 244,
    244n12, 247, 251n16, 256, 260n26,
    269, 274, 274n3–4, 275, 276,
    276n9–10, 277, 279, 279n13, 283,
    283n19, 290n24

Jacobi, Friedrich Heinrich, 11n29,
    14, 28, 29

Kant, Immanuel, 2, 3, 10, 11, 16, 25–26, 28,
    29, 38–50, 64, 67, 68, 95, 178
  and Günderrode, 68
  and Staël (see Staël, Germaine de)
  works
    Critique of the Power of Judgment, 25,
      28, 39n16, 46
    Critique of Practical Reason, 38,
      39n16, 45
    Critique of Pure Reason, 38, 38n15,
      39, 41, 45, 49
Kepler, Johannes, 51, 51n23, 52, 60, 60n48
Kollwitz, Käthe, 5

Leibniz, Gottfried Wilhelm, 39, 39n17–18,
    40, 49, 51, 178
Lipps, Theodor, 244, 245, 265, 308
Locke, John, 39, 40–41, 54n31
logic, 115–116
Luxemburg, Rosa, 5, 7, 9
  on capitalism, 208, 213, 219–221,
    223–239
  on exploitation, 210–212, 219, 227–228,
    231–232
  on imperialism, 208, 213, 213n7
  and Lenin, 212
  on Marx, 209, 210, 212–213, 228–229,
    233, 234
  on money, 211, 214, 224, 229, 239
  on the necessary means of subsistence,
    214–216, 229–231, 235–237
  relationship with Zetkin, 158–159, 160,
    207–208
  on the reserve army of labor, 210, 232,
    233–234

on slavery, 210–211, 219–221, 223–224
on surplus value, 210, 226–227, 229, 236
on the workday, 224, 225–226, 226–228, 228n22,
works
  The Accumulation of Capital, 208
  Introduction to Political Economy, 208, 210
  "Wage Labor," 209–212, 214–240

Marx, Karl, 18, 86, 150, 155, 209, 210, 212, 220n16, 227n19, 228–229, 228n20, 233, 234, 234n25–26, 272, 278, 290n25
Marxism, 6, 169n10, 206, 208, 209–210, 212–213
metaphysics, 28, 39–43, 46, 49–50, 52–54, 70–84, 103–105, 188–190, 194–196, 198–200, 248–257, 267–271, 282–292, 295–309
Meysenbug, Malwida von, 129, 129n15, 134, 178, 182

Neo-Kantianism, 5, 5n15
Nietzsche, Friedrich, 5, 9, 13, 16, 16n40–41, 17, 123, 123n5, 124, 124n6, 125, 128–138, 177, 178, 179, 179n9, 182–183
  and Dohm (*see* Dohm, Hedwig)
  nineteenth-century discussions of, 123, 123n5, 124–125, 128–138, 178, 179, 182–183
  and Salomé (*see* Salomé, Lou)
  works
    Beyond Good and Evil, 124, 130, 130n22–23, 132n26
    Daybreak: Thoughts on the Prejudices of Morality, 128
    The Gay Science, 124, 125, 128, 128n11, 133, 137
    The Genealogy of Morality, 124, 131n25
    Thus Spoke Zarathustra, 130n23, 137n57, 138n58, 179

Pfänder, Alexander, 241, 273–274, 274n4, 277
phenomenology, 5, 5n15, 16n41, 241, 245, 246, 275–276, 276n10, 277n11, 280

philosophical canon, 9–11, 11n32, 12
  revision of the, 11, 12–17, 18–19
philosophy of art, 30–37, 95, 99–100, 103, 105–107, 111–114, 120, 182, 196–198
philosophy of language, 110–112, 114–116
philosophy of nature, 29, 51–61, 65, 67–69, 75–84
philosophy of science, 51–61, 257

Rée, Paul, 178
Rilke, Rainer Maria, 177, 180
romanticism, 2–4, 6, 18, 25, 64n7, 87, 87n6, 91, 152,
  in America, 89
  in Germany, 3, 86
Rousseau, Jean-Jacques, 2, 8, 17, 24, 27, 64, 123, 178

Salomé, Lou, 5, 9, 15, 123, 124n6, 129–130, 134
  on artistic creativity, 182, 196–198
  Dohm's critique of, 123, 124n6, 129–130, 134
  on the erotic, 5, 180–182, 184–205
    as love, 187, 189–190, 192–193, 194–196, 197–198, 201–202, 204–205
    as physical, 188–191
    as social, 203–205
  and psychoanalysis, 5, 179, 179n10, 182, 183
  relationship with Freud, 179, 182
  relationship with Nietzsche, 179, 182–183
  relationship with Rée, 178
  on religion, 182, 199–203
  on Schopenhauer, 181, 195
  on sex, 179, 186–187, 189, 194–195
  and the sexual process, 191–194
  works
    The Erotic, 180, 182, 184–205
    In the Struggle for God, 178
    Looking Back: Memoires. The Intimate Story of her Friendships with Nietzsche, Rilke, and Freud, 177, 177n3
salon, 3, 3n7–9, 11, 85n2, 86, 123
Scheler, Max, 247, 247, 271, 274, 302, 309n49
Schelling, Friedrich Wilhelm Joseph von, 14, 28, 52, 52n26, 55, 55n36, 64, 64n7, 65, 68, 75n23, 95

Schiller, Friedrich, 3, 28, 29, 89
Schlegel, August Wilhelm, 11, 24, 64n7
Schlegel, Dorothea von, 3, 11n30, 29,
    64n7, 85n2
Schlegel, Friedrich, 11, 11n30, 64, 64n7
Schlegel-Schelling, Caroline, 3, 64n7, 152
Schleiermacher, Friedrich, 14, 28, 29,
    64, 152
Schopenhauer, Arthur, 7, 123, 129, 130,
    131, 134, 178, 181, 195
Simmel, Georg, 179, 283, 283n16, 285
socialism, 9, 12, 155–156, 158–159,
    160–161, 161n9, 166, 169, 171, 207
Spinoza, Baruch, 91, 177, 178
Staël, Germaine de, 4, 7, 8, 8n20, 11,
    11n29, 14, 15, 16n40, 17, 18,
    85n2, 129n15
  on abolitionism, 18, 25, 24n4
  on beauty, 46–47
  on enlightenment, 27, 32, 34
  on enthusiasm, 47, 48
  on feeling, 41, 43, 45–46, 47
  on Fichte, 11
  on glory, 30–32, 34–37
  on idealism, 55, 57–58
  on Jacobi, 28, 29
  on Kant, 25–26, 28–29, 38–50
  on Kant's aesthetics, 46–47
  on Kant's moral philosophy, 45–46
  on Kant's theoretical philosophy, 41–43
  on Leibniz, 39, 39n17–18, 40, 49, 51
  on Locke, 39, 40–41
  on philosophy of nature, 29, 51–61
  on women's education, 32–37
  on women writers, 27, 30–37
  works
    Considerations on the Principal Events
        of the French Revolution, 26, 26n9
    Germany, 25, 26, 27–28, 29
    The Influence of Literature on
        Society, 26, 27
    "Letter to Jefferson" (January 6,
        1816), 25, 25n6
    Letters on the Works and the
        Character of J.J. Rousseau, 24, 27
Stein, Edith, 5, 7, 14, 18, 19
  on empathy, 240, 244–247
  on expression, 245, 246–247, 257–261, 265

  on Heidegger, 243–244
  on intersubjectivity, 246, 268–269
  on life, 271–272
  on Lipps, 244, 265
  on the living body, 245–247, 248–256,
      261–264, 266–268, 269–272
  on the problem of other minds,
      261–267
  on psychophysical causation, 256–257,
      258n23, 260, 261, 261n27, 268
  relationship with Husserl, 17n42, 242,
      244, 247
  relationship with Walther, 274, 274n4,
      277, 279–280, 280n14
  on sensation, 249–250, 251–252,
      255–257, 261–263, 264–266,
      269, 272
  works
    Essays on Women, 243
    Life in a Jewish Family 1891–1916, 242
    On the Problem of Empathy, 241,
        242, 244, 248–272
    Philosophy of Psychology and the
        Humanities, 243, 243n10
Stöcker, Helene, 180n12, 182

Varnhagen, Rahel, 3, 3n7, 86
Voigtländer, Else, 5n15, 16, 16n41, 246

Walther, Gerda, 5, 6, 7, 14, 17n42, 18, 19
  on empathy, 299, 303
  and Heidegger, 274, 275, 287n23
  on intentionality, 278, 282–283,
      284–290, 291–293, 296, 287–298
  on Max Weber, 273, 277, 278, 283,
      283n17, 291n28, 292, 293, 293n29,
      294, 294n30, 295, 297–298
  on ontology, 276, 276n9, 277
  on reduction, 276, 276n10, 277
  relationship with Husserl, 274,
      274n3–4, 277, 279–280
  relationship with Pfänder, 273–274,
      274n4, 277
  relationship with Stein, 274, 274n4, 277,
      279–280, 280n14
  on sympathy, 303–304
  on unity, 278–280, 295–298, 299, 304,
      306–309

works
"A Contribution to the Ontology of Social Communities," 275–276, 281–309
"Hitler's Black Magicians," 275n8
The Phenomenology of Mysticism, 275, 275n7
On the Other Bank: From Marxism and Atheism to Christianity, 275
Weber, Max, 273, 277, 278, 283, 283n17, 291n28, 292, 293, 293n29, 294, 294n30, 295, 297–298
Wolf, Christa, 62–63, 63n3, 87n4, 88n9
Wollstonecraft, Mary, 8, 9, 11, 25, 25n3

Zetkin, Clara, 4, 9, 12, 18
on capitalism, 164–165
on race, 156–157, 174–176
relationship with Luxemburg, 158–159, 160, 207–208
on socialism, 155–156, 162, 167–168
on women's emancipation, 157–158, 163
on women's labor, 158, 162–166
on women's suffrage, 158–161, 167–173
works
"For the Liberation of Women!," 157, 162–166
"Save the Scottsboro Boys!," 156, 174–176
"Women's Suffrage," 158–161, 167–173

CPSIA information can be obtained
at www.ICGtesting.com
Printed in the USA
BVHW032257290323
661433BV00002B/4